Continuity in Administrative Science

Ancestral Books in the Management of Organizations

A 31-volume facsimile series
reproducing classic works in the field.

Edited by
Arthur P. Brief
Graduate School of Business Administration
New York University

A Garland Series

Industrial Psychology

Joseph Tiffin

Garland Publishing, Inc.
New York • London
1987

For a complete list of the titles in this series
see the final pages of this volume

This facsimile has been made from a copy
in the Library of Congress.

Library of Congress Cataloging-in-Publication Data

Tiffin, Joseph, 1905.
Industrial psychology.

(Continuity in administrative science)
Reprint. Originally published: New York : Prentice Hall, 1942.
Includes index.
1. Psychology, Industrial. I. Title. II.Series.
HF5548.8.T5   1987   158.7   86-25803
ISBN 0-8240-8221-4   (alk. paper)

Printed in the United States of America

INDUSTRIAL PSYCHOLOGY

INDUSTRIAL PSYCHOLOGY

by
JOSEPH TIFFIN, Ph.D.

PROFESSOR OF INDUSTRIAL PSYCHOLOGY
PURDUE UNIVERSITY

New York
PRENTICE-HALL, INC.
1942

TO

F. B. K.

Preface

This book deals with applications of psychology that have been made in industry. These applications are not limited to employee selection and placement. Industrial psychology has also been applied to the improvement of merit rating, reduction of accidents, solution of visual problems, increasing the accuracy of inspection, improvements in training methods, and the measurement and improvement of employee morale.

The growth of interest in psychological methods during the past decade within such organizations as the American Management Association shows that psychology as a *technology* has been accepted as a tool of industrial management. This book covers the procedures and techniques that have been responsible for that acceptance. These techniques can be improved, of course. They will be improved as further industrial application of psychology points the way toward desirable modifications. But just as they are *now*, the industries that have given them a trial have not been disappointed in them.

A considerable amount of the content of this book is based on research that has not previously been published. This work has been in the nature of coöperative projects carried on by the Division of Education and Applied Psychology at Purdue University and a number of industries. Practically all of the material on industrial vision and accidents, and a considerable amount of the material on individual differences, merit rating, and employee placement tests is presented here for the first time.

The treatment of test application emphasizes the importance of the selection ratio—an emphasis first crystallized by H. C. Taylor and J. T. Russell of the Western Electric Company. Test programs conducted in terms of the principle have shown that a highly effective use of tests can be made even when *no* applicants are rejected for employment. The value of a testing program under such conditions has not always been recognized. To facilitate an understanding of the selection ratio among students and to make available to personnel men the use of this

vii

important procedure, the Taylor-Russell Tables have been reproduced in Appendix B, pages 363–367, with the permission of
Dr. Taylor.

The writer is indebted to a number of persons and organizations for assistance in this work. F. B. Knight, Director of the
Division of Education and Applied Psychology at Purdue University, has constantly encouraged and assisted the research in
industrial psychology. R. J. Greenly, Professor of Trades and
Industrial Education at Purdue University, has helped in numerous ways to apply psychology to industrial problems. The
Bausch and Lomb Optical Company has assisted and supported
research dealing with the construction and validation of a
battery of vision tests adapted to the needs of industry. Hedwig
S. Kuhn, M. D., furnished more than 9000 visual records from
an industrial survey. Most of the vision research is based upon
an analysis of these records. The joint committee on industrial
vision of the American Medical Association and the American
Academy of Ophthalmology and Otolaryngology has given valuable counsel in connection with the vision research. The industrial vision committee of the American Optometric Association
has also been enthusiastic in its interest and support.

Among the many men in industry who have given helpful and
sound counsel on the industrial applications of psychological
methods the writer is particularly indebted to Yandell Cline
and Paul Ortlieb, of Noblitt-Sparks Industries, Inc.; to I. P.
Egan, of the Real Silk Hosiery Mills; to William Pope, of the
Bear Brand Hosiery Mills; to E. D. Stoetzel, W. E. Strong, and
Ray Ganzer, of the Marathon Paper Company; and to F. J.
Martin, of the Belden Manufacturing Company.

Most of the research on industrial vision has been carried on
in collaboration with S. E. Wirt and Ray Reed, of the Bausch
and Lomb Optical Company. Chapter 6, which deals with this
subject, has been written in collaboration with Dr. Wirt. Collaboration with H. B. Rogers, Associate Professor of Industrial
Engineering at Purdue University, in research on the selection
and training of industrial inspectors, has resulted in a relationship between psychology and industrial engineering that has
broadened the horizon of applied psychology. The interest in
industrial psychology constantly expressed by Dr. Lillian Gilbreth, Professor of Management at Purdue University, has been

a source of inspiration. Mr. G. A. Satter read and suggested certain changes in the appendix dealing with elementary statistical procedures. Mr. Max Wastl, laboratory technician, constructed most of the apparatus used in instrumental research.

To all of the above, to the numerous workers whose published research has been drawn upon in writing this book, and to the other persons in industry who have helped with various phases of the research in industrial psychology, the writer is happy to acknowledge his sincere appreciation.

JOSEPH TIFFIN

Contents

APPENDICES

INDUSTRIAL
PSYCHOLOGY

1

The Significance of Individual
Differences in Industry

THE management of an expanding industry may obtain ten or a hundred or even a thousand new machines of a certain type with reasonable assurance that the new pieces of machinery will be identical in construction, equal in efficiency, and capable of uniform output. But to obtain an equal number of persons who are able to operate these machines with a satisfactory and uniform degree of competence is quite another matter. Every foreman knows that identical machines seldom deliver identical production when they are controlled by different operators. People are not alike by nature, training, education, or inclination. A job may be done well by one, fairly well by another, and very poorly by a third. The job may be a source of great personal satisfaction to one, a monotonous and boring task to another, and entirely beyond the capacity of a third. Modern industry is becoming increasingly aware of the importance of placing on every job an individual who is not only able to *do* the job well but who, in addition, is temperamentally adapted to the job in question. The success of personnel placement depends upon placing every individual on a job that matches the capacity of the individual. If the job is too difficult, the result is confusion, low production, and possible injury either to the operator or the machine. If the job is too easy, the result is boredom, mind wandering, and daydreaming with the dissatisfaction that so often accompanies these activities.

An individual is best adapted and is usually most satisfied—and this applies whether he is at work, at home, or on his vacation—when he has found an outlet for whatever energy, drive, and ability he may possess. If his job calls for abilities that he does not have and cannot develop, he continually experiences

1

the despair of failure. If, on the other hand, his job calls for only a fractional part of his ability, he is likely to develop other means of self-expression which, at their best, may be daydreaming or an unduly critical attitude and, at their worst, may become a definite and serious mental illness or disease. Energy not demanded by the job is usually released into some other channel. Too often the release of this "extra energy" is in a direction that not only fails to benefit either the employee or his employer but, on the contrary, is actually detrimental to the interests of one or both of these parties.

Many investigations, both experimental and statistical, furnish the basis for the above statements. In 1923, Bills [1] reported a significant correlation between intelligence and difficulty of work being done by clerical workers. She noted that after the workers had been two and a half years on the job, the correlation approximately doubled in amount. This she interpreted to mean that with seniority comes a definite shifting of employees toward levels of job difficulty that match their ability. In another investigation, Pond and Bills [2] found that labor turnover can be markedly reduced by a careful placement of employees in jobs of a difficulty commensurate with the ability of those employees. Low-ability employees—as revealed by mental tests at the time of employment—showed only half the turnover on certain simple jobs as did high-ability employees assigned to the same jobs. On jobs more difficult in nature, exactly the opposite situation prevailed: the low-ability employees showed the largest turnover and the high-ability employees the least. Standardized mental tests [3] reveal that on jobs of a repetitive, routine nature it is not uncommon to find negative correlations between productivity and mental ability. Such studies indicate the *practical* importance of placing employees on jobs that match their ability.

Industry has long recognized the existence and importance of

---

[1] M. A. Bills, "Relation of Mental Alertness Test Scores to Positions and Permanency in Company," *Journal of Applied Psychology*, VII (1923), pp. 154–156.

[2] Millicent Pond and Marion A. Bills, "Intelligence and Clerical Jobs. Two Studies of Relation of Test Score to Job Held," *Personnel Journal*, XII (1933), pp. 41–56.

[3] Joseph Tiffin and R. J. Greenly, "Employee Selection Tests for Electrical Fixture Assemblers and Radio Assemblers," *Journal of Applied Psychology*, XXIII (1939), pp. 240–263.

individual differences in training and skill. Personnel managers, in hiring tradesmen, make every effort to determine in advance the degree of skill that the applicant possesses. But often employers do not so clearly recognize the fact that differences in capacity for machine operation and other jobs that are ordinarily considered as unskilled or semiskilled are just as great and just as important as differences in skill among tradesmen. The significance to industry of individual differences among employees is far more important than that of differences in skill already developed or of differences that can be detected in an interview. The concept of individual differences is concerned with basic differences in capacity which are of importance in every phase of industrial personnel placement.

Recent social legislation makes the consideration of individual differences at the time of hiring more important than the placing of men and women on jobs that are neither above nor below their capacity to succeed. Ten years ago, any employee —new or old—could be dismissed whenever it became apparent to his supervisor that the employee's services were no longer advantageous to the company. Often employees were tried out on several jobs over a period of months and were then dismissed as unsuited for any of the jobs available. Recent legislation has made it costly—and in some instances impossible—for industry to continue this procedure. Unemployment insurance premiums are paid at least partly by the employer, and the schedule of premiums is so adjusted in many states that the amount which an employer pays is proportional to the labor turnover of the company. Union contracts often make it difficult to discharge an employee after he has been employed for a specified period of time. In addition to legislation and employee pressure, an increasing sense of social obligation on the part of employers themselves has tended to deter them from the arbitrary dismissal of their employees. For such reasons it has become more and more important for industry to evaluate the suitability of prospective employees *before hiring*. Differences in the suitability of applicants is a branch of the psychology of individual differences that, fortunately, has been quite thoroughly studied. To show the direct and practical application of these studies in the field of personnel administration will be a major purpose of this book.

Several questions concerning individual differences have probably already arisen in the mind of the reader. How great are individual differences? Are they large enough to be of practical importance? Do they indicate more or less permanent characteristics? How are they affected by experience and/or training on the job? If employees were given equal experience, would not their individual differences largely disappear? Questions of this type can be answered most satisfactorily by consideration and interpretation of statistical data and experiment.

The Magnitude of Individual Differences

Individual differences in productivity

Figure 1 is a frequency distribution showing differences in productivity among thirty-six electrical-fixture assemblers who

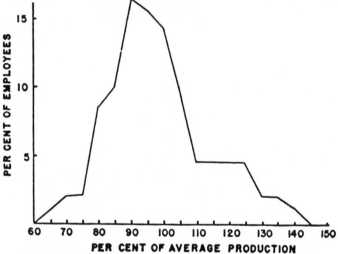

FIG. 1—Distribution of quantity of production among 36 electrical fixture assemblers.

were engaged in identical jobs. An incentive method of wage payment was in use and the best operator was earning slightly more than twice the average hourly wage of the poorest operator. The overhead to the company was identical for all the employees in this department, including the best and the poorest. Both used identical work layouts and assembling equipment. Both used identical amounts of space, heat, light, and other overhead expenses. But the best employee, in delivering more than twice the production of the poorest employee, was

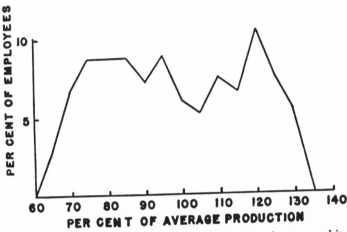

Fig. 2—Distribution of quantity of production among 33 employees engaged in an operation involving burning, twisting, and soldering the ends of insulated wire.

therefore using only half as much overhead and capital expense *per unit of production* as the poorest employee. This fact makes it clear that as new employees are added to the department it is profitable not alone to the employees or to the management but *both* to the employees and the management, to obtain persons who are capable of attaining the higher levels of production.

Figure 2 shows another distribution of the productivity of a group of operators on identical jobs (burning, twisting, and soldering) and utilizing identical investments in machinery and overhead. The distribution shows that the production obtained from the different identical sets of equipment varied in the ratio 65:135, *depending on the operator of the machine.*

Still more striking differences in productivity among a group of operators are shown in Figure 3. This distribution shows the production of 199 hosiery "loopers." The looping operation involves the gathering together of the loops of thread (each over a separate needle) at the bottom of a stocking after the garment is knit in order to close the opening left in the toe. Looping is a job calling for very careful and constant visual attention as well as a high degree of skill in placing the loops on the separate

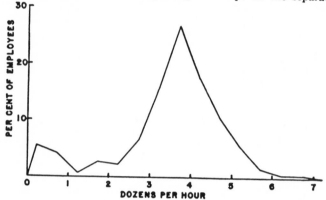

Fig. 3—Distribution of quantity of production in looping hosiery for 199 employees varying in experience from one month to five years.

needles. Production on this job is ordinarily computed in terms of dozens of pairs looped per hour. Payment is on an incentive basis.

Figure 3 shows a range of from .25 dozen pairs per hour (at the extreme left) to 7.00 dozen pairs per hour (at the extreme right). As might be expected, this great variation in production is due partly to differences in experience on the job. However, the fact that such differences do not account for all of the variability shown in Figure 3 is indicated by Figure 4, which shows a similar frequency distribution of production of 99 employees who had had one year or more of experience on the looping job. A careful analysis of the learning curve for looping shows that maximum production is reached after a year of experience. It therefore seems reasonable to assume that the differences in production shown in Figure 4 cannot be explained in terms of the experience factor. Yet the variation in production is still from three dozen pairs to more than seven dozen pairs per hour.

Differences in employee productivity of the type just discussed are usually consistent differences. The high-producing employee at any one time tends to remain in the high-production level, and the less efficient operator tends to remain at approximately the same low level from week to week. This fact is illustrated by the scattergram shown in Table I. This

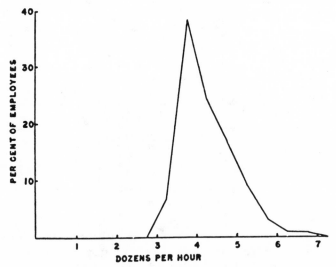

Fig. 4—Distribution of quantity of production in looping hosiery for 99 employees with one year or more of experience.

table shows the relation between productivity for two successive weeks among 203 hosiery loopers. No marked shifts in productivity from one week to the other occurred. It is therefore clear that, given the production of any operator for the first week, a fairly accurate prediction of the production of that operator for the following week can be made. The coefficient of correlation [4] between the production of the first and second week computed from the scattergram in Table I was .96.

These computations indicate that an employee's production level is not something that fluctuates willy-nilly or that he changes daily, as he does his necktie or his shirt, but that his production level is rather a relatively fixed and permanent characteristic.

Individual differences in productivity, then, are large enough

[4] The meaning of a coefficient of correlation is explained in Appendix A, p. 353.

TABLE I

SCATTERGRAM SHOWING CONSISTENCY OF PRODUCTION OF 203 HOSIERY LOOPERS

The correlation between production for the two weeks shown was .96

Average dozens per hour (second week)

	0–.4	.5–.9	1.0–1.4	1.5–1.9	2.0–2.4	2.5–2.9	3.0–3.4	3.5–3.9	4.0–4.4	4.5–4.9	5.0–5.4	5.5–5.9	6.0–6.4	6.5–6.9
6.5–6.9														1
6.0–6.4													1	
5.5–5.9											1	4		
5.0–5.4										1	11	1		
4.5–4.9								3	3	16	1			
4.0–4.4								11	16	3	1			
3.5–3.9							2	43	8	2				
3.0–3.4						1	25	3						
2.5–2.9					12	2								
2.0–2.4			1	3	1		1							
1.5–1.9				3	1									
1.0–1.4			2	1										
.5–.9		6	1											
0–.4	10	1												

Average dozens per hour (first week)

to warrant careful attention. This truth may be more easily understood if the fact, often lost sight of in the rush of industrial production, is kept in mind that differences in productivity of employees are basically and from a cost angle *differences in overhead expenses and capital investment.*

Individual differences in job qualifications

Before employees have had an opportunity to reveal their differences in productivity on the job (that is, before they are hired) they will often, if given an opportunity, exhibit very great differences in qualifications for the job. A large manufacturing industry recently examined 112 applicants for the job of machine-shop apprentice. Several tests were given to the applicants, among which was the Technical Information in Machine Shop Test of the Purdue Vocational Series.[5] Figure 5 shows that the scores on this test varied from five items correct

---

[5] C. C. Stevason, H. G. McComb, and Joseph Tiffin, "Purdue Vocational Tests, Technical Information in Machine Shop," Purdue University, 1940. This test is described briefly on p. 104.

to 125 items correct. All of the applicants either had taken high-school vocational courses, which presumably had prepared them in the technical aspects of machine-shop practice, or had had industrial experience as machinists' helpers. In spite of

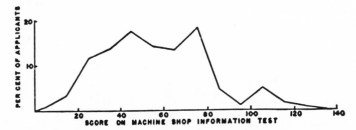

FIG. 5—Distribution of scores of 112 applicants on 130-item multiple-choice test covering technical information in machine shop practice.

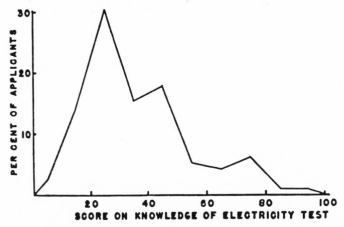

FIG. 6—Distribution of scores of 104 applicants on 100-item multiple-choice test covering knowledge of practical electricity.

these opportunities to learn the technical details of their craft, the test revealed enormous differences among the applicants in actual qualifications for the apprenticeship openings.

A similar situation among applicants for electrical apprenticeships is revealed in Figure 6. In this instance, the test covering Technical Information Related to Electricity of the Purdue Vocational Series * was used. Here again marked individual differences in qualification for the apprenticeships were revealed.

After finding the wide range in scores on the qualification tests described above, it was decided to administer the Otis Self Ad-

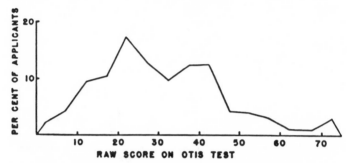

FIG. 7—Distribution of scores on Otis Self Administering Test of Mental Ability (Highor Exam, Form A) of 112 applicants for machine shop apprenticeships.

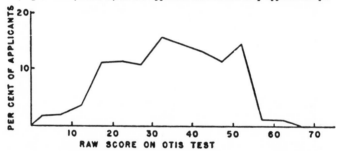

FIG. 8—Distribution of scores on Otis Self Administering Test of Mental Ability (Higher Exam, Form A) of 117 applicants for electrical apprenticeships.

ministering Test of Mental Ability,[7] a standard intelligence test described briefly on page 49, as a means of obtaining additional information about the applicants in these two groups before a selection was finally made. The distributions of the intelligence-test scores for the two groups are shown in Figures 7 and 8. Many psychologists will find it hard to believe that high-school

* H. R. Goppert, Joseph Tiffin, and H. G. McComb, "Purdue Vocational Tests, Technical Information in Electricity," Purdue University, 1940. This test is described briefly on p. 105.

[7] Arthur S. Otis, Otis Self-Administering Tests of Mental Ability (World Book Company, 1922).

graduates of vocational courses tested as low as did those individuals at the left end of the scale in Figures 7 and 8. However, the distributions represent the scores exactly as they were obtained. It is very doubtful whether a boy with a raw score of 15 or less on the Otis test would be able to profit from an apprenticeship in machine shop or electricity to a sufficient extent to make the venture worthwhile either to the boy or to the company.

Job qualification tests are not limited to tests of technical information or intelligence. Many, if not most, jobs of a routine nature demand capacity for dextrous and co-ordinated activity more specifically than they demand technical information and mental ability. Just as one hundred persons selected at random would hardly be likely to possess equal capacities to become 100-yard-dash men, so one hundred persons selected by interview or otherwise would not be likely to possess equal capacity for a given production job *unless capacity for the production job is measured before they are hired.*

The above fact is illustrated in Figure 9, which shows frequency distributions of four different groups [8] on the O'Connor test of finger dexterity.[9] This test consists of a 100-hole pegboard which is filled as rapidly as possible (three pins to a hole) from the pins located in a shallow tray. The greater one's finger dexterity, the more rapidly he will be able to fill the board and the smaller will be his score, which is simply the time in minutes required to fill the board. The original method of scoring this test, as described by Hines and O'Connor,[10] was somewhat more complicated than the simple determination of time in minutes required to fill the board. However, since Tiffin and Greenly [11] found a correlation of .99 between the simple time score and the scores obtained by the original formula, it was not necessary to compute the scores by the original formula. In Figure 9, the left side of the scale represents the small-time values or good scores, and the right side the long-time or poor scores. The upper curve, or A, in Figure 9 shows the distribution of finger

[8] Tiffin and Greenly, *op. cit.*
[9] M. Hines and J. O'Connor, "A Measure of Finger Dexterity," *Personnel Journal*, IV (1926), pp. 379–382.
[10] Hines and O'Connor, *op. cit.*
[11] Tiffin and Greenly, *op. cit.*

dexterity—as measured by this test—among a very large number of randomly selected persons. The remaining distributions in this figure (B, C, and D) show how finger dexterity is distributed among three groups of employees engaged in work for

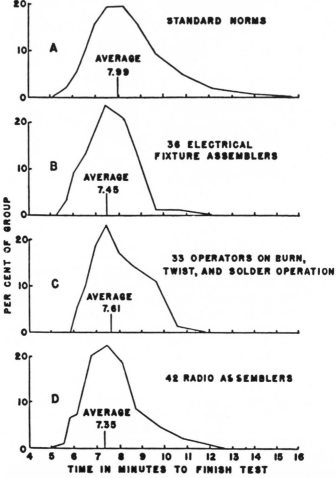

Fig. 9—Frequency distributions of scores on O'Connor Finger Dexterity Test of random group of subjects (top) and three groups of industrial employees engaged in rapid finger work.

which finger dexterity is presumably an important qualification. A marked similarity among the four distributions is revealed. Operators on the three industrial jobs are little better in finger dexterity than are randomly selected persons, which

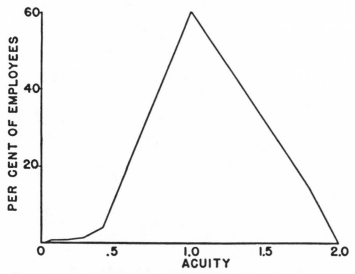

FIG. 10—Distribution of binocular visual acuity among 8,694 employees in a steel mill. The acuity scale is described on page 129.

means that persons equally qualified for this job would have been obtained if the employees had been selected by lot from a telephone directory.

The questions will naturally be raised: What of it? How do we know that the finger-dexterity pegboard is a job qualification test for these jobs? Are the persons who test high in finger dexterity better employees than those who test low?

Detailed answers to these questions must be postponed at this point (they will be given in Chapter 4); but we may definitely say here that the test in question does measure something that is necessary for efficient production on the jobs under consideration, and we may add that the employees testing high on the finger-dexterity test are, in general, the same employees who are also most productive at their work.

Differences in vision furnish a further example of individual differences in job qualification. Figure 10 shows a distribution of binocular visual acuity of 8694 employees in a steel mill. Al· though this curve reveals that the large majority of employees have an acuity of 80 per cent or higher, it also shows a small, but definite, percentage well below this point. The curve also reveals a scattering of employees with acuity so low that they are, on certain types of jobs, severely handicapped at their work. This statement is based upon investigations showing the relationship between vision and efficiency (see page 136). Visual acuity is not the only aspect of vision in which individual differences among employees exist. Numerous tests dealing with other aspects of visual performance and efficiency reveal equally marked variations. A detailed treatment of vision as it relates to employee efficiency on different kinds of work will be covered in Chapter 6.

Merit ratings furnish another indication of individual differences in employee qualifications for certain jobs. A merit rating is a periodic judgment of an employee by his supervisor. It consists, usually, of a blank which permits separate ratings of the employee in terms of such factors as safety, productivity, industriousness, initiative, and so on. A recent survey indicates that approximately one-third of American industries were making use of merit ratings in some form in 1939.[12] Merit-rating systems, which will be discussed in detail in Chapter 9, usually result in a single over-all rating for each employee. This over-all rating may be taken, with certain qualifications, to indicate the employee's suitability on the job.

A distribution of the over-all ratings of 710 men from one department of a steel mill is shown in Figure 11. Many cautions should be observed in interpreting the significance of these merit ratings, but it is safe to conclude that the spread of over-all ratings from 240 to 450 points suggests definite differences in the quantity and quality of service rendered by the different employees.

Many additional instances of individual differences which affect industrial production could be cited, and all of them would point toward the conclusion that on many jobs a good employee is at least twice as valuable to the company for which

[12] R. B. Starr and R. J. Greenly, "Merit Rating Survey Findings," *Personnel Journal*, XVII (1939), pp. 378–384.

he works as a poor employee. We may answer the question about the magnitude of individual differences, then, by saying that the differences are not only real but they are large enough to be of vital practical importance to industry.

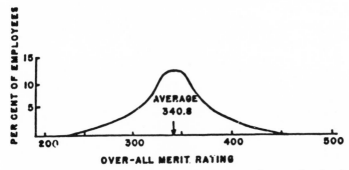

Fig. 11—Distribution of over-all merit ratings of 710 men from one department of a steel mill.

The Effect of Training Upon Individual Differences

Many psychologists have attempted to reach a general conclusion from experimental investigations of the effect of training upon individual differences. Three possible conclusions might be considered: training may increase the differences, it may decrease them, or it may leave them unaffected.

Examination of experimental studies in this field reveals what seems to be a good deal of contradictory evidence. In certain kinds of situations it seems clear that training tends to increase whatever differences in ability may exist at the beginning of the training. A group of persons placed upon an entirely new task of a complicated nature are not likely to differ much among themselves in their ability to handle that task at the beginning. Their skill is likely to be quite uniform and, it might be added, uniformly low until appropriate training has given those with capacity to do the task an opportunity to forge ahead. The operation of any complicated industrial production machine will furnish an example of this principle.

In Figure 12 the heavy black line shows the average production of hosiery loopers in dozens of pairs per hour plotted against the amount of experience on the job. This curve is really the learning curve for this operation, even though it was obtained by taking the average production of loopers of varying amounts of experience rather than by following the improvement in skill of a given group of loopers as experience increased.

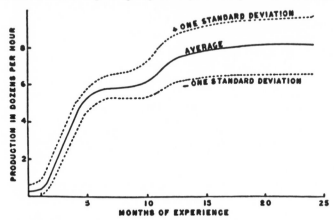

FIG. 12—Relation between experience and production in looping hosiery, and the effect of experience on individual differences in productivity. Results based on 199 loopers of varying experience.

The dotted lines in Figure 12 indicate a standard deviation[13] above and below average production for the varying amounts of experience. It is clear that the variability is greater among the loopers with considerable experience on the job than among those who have been recently hired or who are in the early stages of learning the operation. Here, then, is a specific case in which training *increases* the magnitude of individual differences with performance upon a given job. The operators are much more nearly like one another in the early stages of their training than in the intermediate or later stages.

One should not infer from the foregoing illustration, however, that the effect of training is always to increase the magnitude of individual differences. For example, Hartmann,[14] using four tests of manual ability, found that three months of training re-

---

[13] The standard deviation, a measure of variability or spread of scores, is explained in Appendix A, p. 344.

[14] G. W. Hartmann, "Initial Performance as a Basis for Predicting Ultimate Achievement," *School and Society*, XXIX (1929), pp. 495–496.

sulted in definitely more improvement among those who initially tested low than among those who initially tested high. The ability of everyone was improved as a result of the training, but, in this experiment, the training also tended to decrease the difference between the good and the poor scores.

It would be possible to cite numerous other experiments that support the apparently contradictory conclusions of one or the other of the investigations cited above. A study of the experiments in question, however, suggests a possible explanation for the seeming discrepancy in results. Wherever the effect of training has been to increase the magnitude of individual differences, a study of the task involved usually reveals it to be fairly complicated. By complicated we mean that it is one in which the average individual does not reach his maximum level of performance without a fairly long learning period. Wherever training results in a decrease in individual differences, the task is usually found to be a rather simple one, that is, one upon which the average individual shows little improvement after a relatively short practice period. In the light of these facts we may venture the tentative generalization that training tends to increase individual differences in proportion to the complexity of the task in question. Although a few minor exceptions to this principle may come to mind, it seems to be at least provisionally acceptable as a working hypothesis.

Whatever may be the effect of training on the magnitude of individual differences, it seems clear that training seldom changes the relative standing of individuals in their ability to perform any given task. This conclusion is in accord with the findings of Bishop,[15] Peterson,[16] Hartmann,[17] Viteles,[18] and others. No industry, therefore, should expect its training program to bring all employees up to the same high level of efficient performance unless the employees have initially been selected in terms of their capacity to reach that high level.

---

[15] M. K. Bishop, "A Study of Individual Differences in Learning," *Psychological Review*, XXXII (1925), pp. 34–53.

[16] J. Peterson, "The Effects of Practice on Individual Differences," *27th Year Book* (National Society for the Study of Education, Bloomington, Ill., 1928), Part II, p. 212.

[17] Hartmann, *op. cit.*

[18] Morris S. Viteles, *Industrial Psychology* (W. W. Norton & Company, Inc. 1932), p. 107.

The Bases of Individual Differences

Psychologists have long been interested in determining the ultimate cause of individual differences among people. Usually they have divided the major causes into the two general categories of heredity and environment. Those upholding one point of view have often minimized or even completely ignored the possible influence of the other factor. It seems probable that both factors are usually operative but that their relative importance differs markedly in the determination of different personal characteristics. Heredity would seem to be of most importance in determining such traits as height, weight, and strength, although it is clear that environment also has some effect upon these factors. The environmental factors of training or education are of basic importance in determining trade skills, or any other type of skill that is reached only after experience on a particular job. But to conclude that differences in skill are dependent upon differences in training does not mean that other factors have no significant effect upon the level of skill which the training produces. Whenever different levels of final performance are achieved by a group of individuals who were apparently equal when the training began, it may safely be assumed that individual differences were present at the beginning of the training which, although they may have completely escaped notice, nevertheless were instrumental in setting the level of attainment which the several individuals later reached.

An example will make this clear. It has long been standard practice in the hosiery industry to hire girls to be trained as loopers only after rigid scrutiny and interview, careful study of school records and previous employment, general physical and visual examination, and a thorough consideration of all other factors that standard employment procedure has indicated to be of importance. Obviously the girls could not be selected on the basis of their looping ability because, never having seen a looping machine, they have no skill whatever on this job at the time of employment. Only those girls are hired who, in the judgment of the personnel manager, are likely to become good loopers with training. But in spite of this extensive examination and investigation at the time of employment, and in spite of the elimination of all those who for obvious reasons are clearly unlikely to become efficient on this particular job, the girls hired do not by any means become equally efficient on the operation. In fact, as Figure 4 shows, after a year of experience some of the girls are more than twice as productive as others. This fact would indicate that, though the girls might have *seemed* to be potentially equal at the time of employment, and indeed probably *were* equal in terms of all factors considered, they were not really equal at all. They differed significantly at the time of employment in one or more of the factors that determine capacity for success upon this job, but—and this is the important point—*the differentiating basic individual differences were not detected by the standard employment procedure.* It should be added that a dexterity test (described on page 83) and certain vision tests (described on page 131) were successful in detecting at the time of employment an appreciable number of girls who were quite satisfactory from the point of view of standard employment procedure but who did not have the basic capacities necessary for developing a high level of skill in the muscular and visual co-ordination involved in close work.

One should not infer from the foregoing illustration that the industrial psychologist recommends the elimination of standard employment procedure. He fully recognizes that a good personnel man will detect all of the obvious, and many of the subtle, reasons why some applicants should, and others should not be placed upon a specific job. But experiments clearly show that even the best personnel men cannot determine the muscular co-ordination or dexterity of an applicant from a general interview or from an examination of his or her hands. Many if not most industrial jobs call for a combination of certain basic capacities that cannot be detected at the time of employment without special technique and often standardized test procedures. These basic capacities, which are measurable (even if not often measured) at the time of employment, are related to future productivity, accuracy, accident proneness, promotion, versatility, tenure with the company, and many other factors that differentiate between a profitable and a nonprofitable employee. One of the major functions of this book will be to show how these basic factors affect the development of an employee and to cite a number of illustrations of the use of selection and placement tests in industry.

2

General Principles of Employee Testing

THE preceding chapter has given an indication of the nature and significance of individual differences among industrial employees. Since every personnel man recognizes the existence of such differences, it is quite unnecessary for the industrial psychologist to re-emphasize the importance of proper employee placement. The personnel procedures in use in the modern employment office have been installed primarily for the purpose of making a careful and adequate selection and placement of employees. The psychologist's function, rather, is to bring to the attention of the personnel manager those aspects of the theory and application of modern psychology that have been found helpful in the performance of this difficult task.

General Concepts

Testing-supplemental to present employment procedures

Many industrialists are skeptical about the use of psychological tests in employment because they do not wish to risk a change from present methods which are known to be reasonably satisfactory to new methods that have not been thoroughly tried in actual practice. Their skepticism is clearly justified. When psychological methods are used in an employment office they should always be looked upon as supplementing—not replacing —other methods that are in use. No psychologist who has thought at all about the problems of modern industry would seriously suggest that present employment procedures should be eliminated. Indeed, many of the advances that modern industry has made during the past quarter of a century can be traced directly or indirectly to the procedures now in use in every modern industrial employment office. But the fact that these methods, though excellent in many respects, are still not perfect is proved by the marked individual differences among employees which any study of differential production will reveal. A considerable amount of research, both in industry and in the laboratory, has shown that still further improvements in employment methods can be attained when psychological tests and methods are used as supplements to other employment procedures. Let us keep in mind this word "supplement." Psychological tests are among the tools that are necessary for the most effective selection and placement of employees.

Selection or placement as the function of tests

Employee tests have often been considered primarily as devices to aid in the selection of employees. This viewpoint is followed by the assumptions that (1) when tests are used systematically, many applicants will be rejected—that is, not employed at all—and that (2) unless there are significantly more applicants than there are jobs to be filled, the testing program loses its effectiveness.

It is unfortunate that the selective rather than the placement features of employee tests have been given the greater emphasis in most discussions of this subject. Perhaps this is due to the fact that many industrial testing programs were inaugurated during the depression years of 1930 to 1935, at which time there was an unusual abundance of applicants for nearly every job. But in a period of emergency production there is usually not an abundance of applicants. Indeed, many industries find it necessary to relax all employment standards, including not only psychological test results (in industries where these have been established) but also standards dealing with medical and physical requirements, age, and marital status. When a testing program has been installed around the basic philosophy that it is a *selection* program, the fact that it is also an excellent *placement* program is often forgotten. Yet the value of a testing program in placing employees during a period of rapid plant expansion is fully as great as its value in selecting employees during more static periods. One of the most effective uses of a testing program that the writer has observed was in a war industrial plant that was hiring, as the medical director stated, "anyone healthy enough to walk into the plant." In this plant the sole purpose of the tests was *placement* of the many new employees on the specific jobs to which each was best adapted. The value of tests is by no means limited to situations in which there is an abundance of job applicants.

Psychological methods are not infallible

A further point which the advocate of testing procedures should make clear is his recognition of the fact that psychological tests are not infallible; that they will, occasionally, be wrong. Any new procedure, whether in employment, production, advertising, or the like, should be evaluated not in terms of whether it achieves perfection, but whether it results in some improvement over methods that have preceded it. Thus, if the labor turnover in a given department has been 25 per cent per year among employees placed by previous methods; if it is found that new employees placed by psychological tests show a turnover of only 20 per cent per year (all other factors which indicate a desirable employee remaining constant); and if the expense of administering the testing program is less than the amount saved by the reduction in labor turnover, the testing program would ordinarily be considered a sound investment even though it did not achieve perfection in reducing labor turnover to zero. Evaluation of a testing program should be made in terms of a statistical comparison between the employment situation with the tests and without the tests. This statistical comparison should include such factors as the productivity of employees, labor turnover, accuracy and safety, ease of shifting employees to different types of work, ease of learning the job, and any other factors that may be indicative of a desirable employee. It seems only fair to evaluate a testing program in terms of averages rather than in terms of specific cases. This point is emphasized because unless one is careful he is likely to allow one serious failure in a testing program to outweigh the less spectacular though much sounder averages that really indicate the value of the method.

Types of tests

Tests that have been and are being used for employee placement may be classified in several different ways. They may be *group* or *individual* tests. The group variety may be given to almost any number of persons simultaneously, the only limitation on the number usually being seating and writing facilities and provision for adequate hearing of the instructions given by the group examiner before the test is begun. Examples of group tests are the Purdue Achievement Tests (see page 104), the Otis Self Administering Tests of Mental Ability (see page 49), the Wonderlic Personnel Test (see page 51), and the Bennett Test of Mechanical Comprehension (see page 61). Individual tests, on the other hand, are given to one person at a time and usually call for the undivided, or nearly undivided, attention of the examiner while the test is being administered. The phrase "nearly undivided attention" is used because in certain cases, as with the Purdue Pegboard Test of Manual Dexterity (see page 81), it is possible for an attentive examiner to test several persons simultaneously if the necessary sets of equipment are available.

Another classification of tests may be made according to whether they are *instrumental* or *paper and pencil*. The former, as the name implies, make use of instruments and ordinarily are individual in nature. The latter make use of written responses and ordinarily are group tests.

A very important division of tests may be made according to whether they measure *aptitude* or *achievement*. Aptitude tests measure whether an individual has the capacity or latent ability to learn a given job if he is given adequate training. Such tests are most useful when the majority of applicants for a certain job have had no experience on the job and when a relatively long period of training is required before their aptitude or lack of aptitude for the job will be apparent on the job itself. A good example of a job for which aptitude tests are particularly adapted is looping in a hosiery mill. This is a job which requires a year of experience, on the average, for complete mastery. New employees are usually hired directly out of high school with no previous experience on the operation of a looping machine or anything even remotely resembling it. Aptitude tests that have been found to be effective for this job deal with such factors as finger dexterity (see page 83) and certain visual characteristics (see page 131). Interestingly enough, the tests that "came through" [1] (see page 46) in no way resemble the actual looping

---

[1] The phrase "come through" means that the test scores are found significantly related to success on the job.

operation; rather they measure certain basic capacities that are necessary for an efficient performance on that job.

Achievement tests, on the other hand, measure how well the individual can do the job or what he knows about it at the time he is tested. Achievement tests are of greatest value when many of the applicants for a job have had, or claim to have had, experience on the same or a similar job in some other organization. For example, a standardized test of knowledge pertaining to a machine shop will quickly reveal how much the applicant really knows about the machinery and operations in use in a standard shop. It is true that he may evidence considerable knowledge on such a test and still be a poor machinist because, for example, he lacks manual skill. But experience shows that if he reveals little or no knowledge on such a test he is exceedingly unlikely to be a good machinist. This type of achievement test, therefore, is of definite value in eliminating from consideration those who lack the basic information necessary for satisfactory performance on the job. Achievement tests, such as the punch press test described on page 100, may also be instrumental in nature.

Definition of terms

The term *capacity* refers to potential or latent ability. One might have high capacity for a certain skill although he may have none of the skill at the time of testing. Thus, one might have exactly the combination of keen vision at close distances, finger dexterity, and mechanical ability necessary to become a watchmaker or repairer, but, if he has had no training in watchmaking, he might know nothing about the mechanism of a watch. It is always advisable to know how much capacity one has for a certain job before training is given on that job. Ordinarily those with capacity for the job will learn quickly and efficiently; those without capacity for it will not.

The term *ability* refers to developed capacity, or actual knowledge or skill already developed. One with little capacity might, if he has been given a great deal of training, show more ability at the time of testing than one with high capacity who has not been trained; but if the latter is trained he will soon excel the former. Therefore, from a long-time viewpoint, it is more important to know the capacity of applicants before they are placed than to know their ability. For purposes of immediate addition of personnel who will get out some production, the opposite situation is of course true.

A relationship may be inferred between types of tests and the above definitions of capacity and ability. Aptitude tests ordinarily measure capacity; achievement tests measure ability.

Testing the Tests—the Experimental Approach

It is of utmost importance in any testing program to use only tests that have themselves been tested, or to make provision for testing the tests before finally accepting them as valid devices for employee placement. Two general methods may be followed in testing the tests. One of these methods consists of measuring present employees and correlating the test results against whatever criteria of desirability in the employees may be available. The other method consists of testing new employees at the time of hiring, filing the test results, and later determining the relationships between the test results obtained at the time of hiring and the success of the employees on the job after they have been on the pay roll for a period of time. Each of these methods of testing the tests has advantages and disadvantages. A long-time testing program should make use of both methods. Only by so doing can an employment manager hope to obtain the maximum benefits from a testing program.

Testing the tests on present employees

This method involves testing a group of employees and determining the relationship between test results and employee efficiency. When a plant begins, for the first time, a project of test validation that involves testing a large group of present employees, the question of the reaction of the employees naturally arises. Will they become anxious or unduly excited? Is there a possibility of the testing program causing worker unrest? In this book will be summarized research work and test results that have been obtained by testing hundreds of employees in numerous plants. Some of these plants have been open shop, some closed. In the union plants, several labor organizations have been represented. In no case has any trouble arisen either with employees or union representatives. Wherever the management has signed a union contract, representatives of the union are contacted and the project explained to them before actual testing is begun. Usually a mimeographed slip reading somewhat as follows is given to each employee:

The Personnel Department is co-operating with Purdue University in a series of experiments. If you are called to help with this work, we want you to know that this will in no way affect your present standing with the Company.

One result of the experiments may be that they will uncover abilities in some people that have not been known. If this should happen, every effort will be made to give you the benefit of these results in your own work.

PERSONNEL DIRECTOR

After the test results have been obtained, the results may be analyzed in several different ways. One method is to divide the employees into two groups according to whether they score above or below average on the test in question, and compute the average efficiency (according to wage earned, merit ratings, or some other criterion) of the "high-testing" group and the "low-testing" group. If a significant difference between the efficiency of these two groups is shown, it may safely be assumed that the test is measuring something of importance on the job. Under these conditions it is usually desirable for the employment manager to know whether an applicant is in the high- or the low-testing group before the applicant is placed.

Another, and even more effective, method of determining the relationship between the test results and employee efficiency is to determine the coefficient of correlation between the test scores and the efficiency of the employees. This method has numerous advantages over simply dividing the employees into a high-testing and a low-testing group. In the first place, it gives a more accurate indication of the *amount* of the relationship between test scores and efficiency. In the second place, it enables the employment manager more effectively to take advantage of the all-important selection ratio (see page 34) in using the test. In the third place, it makes possible the computation of the relative importance of several tests in an employment battery so that the tests may be "weighted" according to their importance. Finally, the use of the correlational method makes possible the use of partial and multiple correlation to eliminate statistically whatever effect such factors as experience on the job or age may have had in determining the correlation between test scores and job performance.

From the logical viewpoint, one objection to the "present employee" method of "testing the test" is that the test may be measuring something that is improved significantly by experience on the job. In other words, the test may be an achievement test rather than an aptitude test. Consider again the operation of looping in a hosiery mill. If a test is proposed which imitates the operation of a looping machine, it is almost certain that present employees will divide themselves in their ability to score well on this test in much the same way that they have already divided themselves in their ability to do the actual job. This simply means that the test, being in itself a miniature of the job, will divide the employees in much the same way that they have already been divided on the basis of the job itself. Such a test would have little value for placement of new employees unless the surplus labor supply included a large number of employees who claimed to have had looping experience in some other hosiery mill. Under ordinary circumstances, however, persons employed for this job are freshly out of school. They have had no experience in looping, and their capacity for the job would not be measured effectively by a test of this type. Since none of them can loop at the time of employment, all of them, even those who would potentially be the best employees if given the training, would score zero or close to zero on any test that calls for ability to loop at the time of employment.

In testing tests according to this principle it is therefore necessary to be sure that the tests, in addition to dividing the employees according to their ability on the job, do not show a significant correlation with experience on the job. In other words, it is necessary to be sure that the employees who score high on the test are not scoring high simply because they have had an opportunity to learn the skill being tested. Whether this is the case may be determined by correlating the test scores against experience on the job. If the test is to be used later for employment and/or placement it must satisfy two requirements. First, it must show a correlation with ability on the job. Second, the scores on it must not be appreciably related to experience on the job. When these two conditions are satisfied, it may be assumed that the test is *not* measuring something that is improved markedly by experience on the job, but that it *is* measuring something that is necessary for adequate performance on the job. This reasoning applies only to *aptitude* tests, not to *achievement* tests. When tests of the latter type are used, a significant correlation between test scores and experience is to be expected and in no way reduces the value of the tests.

If the test scores show *some* correlation with experience, the net relationship between test scores and job performance, after the effect of experience has been eliminated, can be determined by partial correlation. The procedure for computing partial correlations may be found in any standard textbook of statistics.[2]

The above discussion applies only in cases where the applicants have not had experience on the job for which they are being hired. If they have had experience, then an achievement test that is similar to the job or even a *miniature* (that is, the job itself in standardized test form) of the job may identify the best employees even more satisfactorily than an aptitude test.

Testing the test on new employees—the "follow-up" method

A second and, in general, a more effective method of determining the value of a test, is to test the test on new employees. This method consists of giving the test, at the time of employment, to a large number of employees whose placement has already been decided upon by ordinary methods of selection and placement. These employees are hired just as they have always been hired, but before they have been put upon the job or, in fact, before they have been told that they have been selected for employment, they are required to take a battery of tests. These tests at this time have no effect whatever upon whether the employees will be hired. As already mentioned, it has been decided to hire the employees who are to be tested before the tests are given, but the employees are not informed of this decision. When this method of testing the test is followed, the test results are filed and, for all practical purposes, forgotten until the employees have had an opportunity to show whether or not they are successful on the job. When sufficient time has elapsed so that it is known which of the employees have been successful, which average, and which unsuccessful on the job, the test re-

sults are taken from the file and the statistician goes to work.
His job is to determine the relationship between the test results
obtained at the time of employment and the later success or
failure of the employees on the job. Numerous indications of
the success or failure of the employees are usually available
when the statistician begins his work of correlation. He may
consider the wage earned by the employees, the amount of production, the proportion of working days the employee has been
on the job, freedom from accidents, rapidity of learning the new
job, ratings by supervisors on quantity and quality of work,
tenure of the employee before layoff or resignation, or any other
of several indications of success in an employee that a given
company may feel to be important in its particular situation.

This method requires more time than testing the tests with
present employees. Frequently, it does not result in any proved
tests until the program has been under way for several months
or, in some cases, several years. Should the first battery of tests
selected for tryout prove entirely unsatisfactory, it is necessary
to start the whole procedure over again. This involves the loss
of a great deal of time.

Fortunately, in practice the employment manager need not
decide upon one or the other of the methods discussed and then
limit himself exclusively to that particular method. He may
proceed with both methods simultaneously. When this is done
it is possible to produce a working battery of tests almost at
once (by using the present employee method of testing the tests)
and to obtain still more evidence of the value of these tests as
new employees are tested at the time of placement. This may
seem to be contradictory because it may be argued that if a test
is used for placement there will be no variation in the scores on
this test among the new employees placed on any given job and,
therefore, it will be impossible to correlate the scores with later
success on the job. Actually, even though a test is used at the
time of placement, there will ordinarily be a sufficient spread of
scores on the test, even among employees who are hired for a
specific job, to make possible the subsequent statistical evaluation of the test in terms of the follow-up method. Though the
variability of the group of employees placed on any given job
will be smaller than that of all the applicants, nevertheless the
variability of all the applicants and the variability of the appli-

cants who are placed on the job will be known and it will therefore be possible to determine on the basis of the follow-up method just how much the test in question increases the efficiency of the placement procedure for the particular job.

The point to be emphasized throughout this discussion is that no one—whether he is an employment manager, a psychologist, or anyone else—can predict with certainty which tests will be desirable tests for placement on any particular job. Often a rather accurate estimate can be made; but it is always necessary to check this estimate against correlations between the efficiency of the employees and the scores which they made on the tests at the time of placement.

Factors Determining the Functional Value of Selection Tests

Several factors of both a practical and theoretical nature determine the functional value of a testing program in an industrial plant.

1. When many applicants are being hired for a variety of jobs

Tests furnish a highly effective means of placing employees in the particular jobs for which each is best adapted. Thus, in the case of an assembly line, some jobs may require keen eyesight, others manual strength, and still others good color vision. Sometimes still different factors or a combination of factors are involved. Even when there is no thought of using tests to "pick and choose" from among applicants, the placement value of tests during a period of rapid plant expansion is very great. Indeed, it is during such a period, when it is necessary to hire and place a large number of employees about whom relatively little is known, that tests are of greatest value to the personnel manager.

2. Validity and reliability

Further factors determining the value of tests are their *validity* and their *reliability*. A test is valid if it measures what it is supposed to measure. It is reliable if it measures something accurately and consistently. Much of the preceding discussion under the heading "testing the tests" will be recognized as a means of determining the validity of industrial placement tests. The industrial psychologist is in a favorable position with respect to determining the validity of his measuring instruments.

Almost always he has available, in the plant records, various means of determining in objective terms the degree of success an employee has attained upon the job. He thus has a *criterion* —an indication of the success or failure of the employee— against which to validate the test that he is studying. Much as the industrial psychologist may strive to improve these criteria of validity, he usually has at the outset criteria that are more satisfactory than those available in many other fields of psychological testing. These readily available criteria, which almost any modern industrial plant can supply, greatly facilitate the validation studies that are so important a part of any testing program.

The validity of a psychological test is usually expressed as the coefficient of correlation between the scores on the test in question and some outside criterion—that is, an indication or measurement of what the test is supposed to measure. It has already been mentioned that these criteria include wages earned, quality of work, freedom from accidents, merit ratings, or other factors that the company accepts as indicative of a desirable employee. In using any test it is necessary not only to know the validity of the test, but also just what criterion has been used in determining that validity.

Tests used in industrial placement must also be reliable; that is, they must measure consistently whatever they measure. A test is reliable if it consistently gives the same score to an employee when he is retested. The retesting may be done with the same test used originally, if practice or memory does not markedly affect the test score. If practice or memory factors significantly affect the score, however, retesting should make use of a duplicate form of the test containing items similar in nature but different in actual content.

Since no test, no matter how perfect, will give *exactly* the same score on a first and second repetition to all persons tested, a method of measuring reliability is used which expresses the degree of reliability or the *extent* to which the test gives the same score to an employee on repeated testing. The reliability of a test is expressed as a coefficient of correlation, which may be interpreted as the correlation between scores obtained from repeated testing with the same or duplicate forms of the test. When duplicate forms are not available but there is reason to believe that the memory factor will influence the scores, a method known as "chance-halves" or "odds vs. evens" is often used in determining the reliability of a test. This method involves correlating certain parts of a test against the remainder. Technical descriptions of the research work involved in standardizing a test state not only the reliability of the test but what method of determining the reliability was used.

A test may have high reliability and yet be quite worthless for any given employment situation. A test might measure height, weight, or even general intelligence with high reliability and yet show little or no correlation between test scores obtained and the efficiency of the employees on the job. In other words, the test might have high *reliability* but low *validity*, or even no validity at all. But if a test has a *low* reliability, it is not likely to have a satisfactory validity. This is simply another way of saying that no test is likely to correlate with anything higher than that test will correlate with itself. Thus a test which on repeated testing gives scores that correlate with the first testing only .45 is not likely, except by chance, to correlate higher than .45 with production or any other criterion of employee desirability. It is primarily for this reason that the psychologist using tests in industry insists that they be reasonably reliable before he makes any attempt to determine their validity for particular situations.

A question that is often raised when the validity or reliability of tests is under discussion is: How reliable and valid must a test be in order to be worthwhile? This is both a reasonable and a natural question when one considers that our measurements of both reliability and validity are usually expressed in the form of a coefficient of correlation which makes possible a variation in the degree of reliability or validity all the way from zero (or even a minus quantity, if we wish to be theoretically exact) to 1.00. If we remember that reliability in a test is necessary because it determines the ceiling of validity, we may phrase the question more simply by asking: How high must the validity coefficient of a test be for the test to be worthwhile?

The answer to this question depends upon the use that is being made of the test. The user of tests is nearly always interested in one of two objectives, but is seldom interested in both at the same time. Either he is interested in making a careful and accurate aptitude analysis *of each person tested,* which is to be used for individual prediction or vocational guidance, or he is interested in selecting from a large group of individuals a smaller group which, *on the average,* will excel the larger group in some particular respect. In individual consulting work, which deals with vocational aptitude and guidance, the psychologist is interested in the first-named objective. His work will stand or fall on the accuracy of his predictions for individual clients. He therefore has little use for aptitude tests that do not have a validity sufficiently high to justify their use in individual prediction. The exact value which the validity of a test should have to meet this requirement is not completely agreed upon by all students of the subject. It is uniformly agreed, however, that the higher the validity of the test, the better; that unless the test is used as a member of a battery (the battery as a whole having a higher validity coefficient than the individual tests) the validity should be in the neighborhood of .90; and *that there is no substitute for high validity for individual prediction.*

On the other hand, one may be interested in segregating from a large group of persons tested a smaller group which, on the average, will excel the larger group in whatever trait is being tested. This is, in fact, the situation that confronts the employment manager. He is willing to allow the tests to induce him to place upon a job a few individuals who will fail on the job and to reject (or place upon some other job) a few who, if placed upon that job, would have succeeded, *if on the whole his percentage of successful placements is higher with the tests than it is without them.* In other words, the employment manager is not so much interested in every strike resulting in a home run as he is in improving his batting average. Under these circumstances the validity of the tests can be much lower. But one may still ask: How low can it be? A categorical answer to this question can be given, but the full significance of the answer will be clear only after a thorough study of the next section, which deals with the *selection ratio.* The answer is that a test will be valuable, no matter how low the coefficient of validity, if it indicates *some* relationship between test scores and the criterion; or, in statistical terms, if the coefficient of validity is at least four times its probable error. Often this rule will admit tests whose validity is as low as .30, or even lower. The use of tests with such low validity is sufficiently contradictory to much current thought among psychologists to warrant a fairly detailed justification for the above conclusions.

3. The selection ratio

Given a selection test that has a validity coefficient indicating *some* relationship with the criterion, and given more employees to be placed than can be placed on the job in question, the functional value of the test to an employment manager depends upon the ratio of those placed to those tested who are available for placement. This has been referred to as the selection ratio.[3] An example will clarify the operation of this principle.

If a certain test is given to a large number of employees for whom a criterion of successfulness as employees is available, and if the scattergram of test scores against the criterion is plotted, the points will ordinarily fall into an oval-shaped area somewhat similar to the oval in Figure 13. The higher the coefficient of validity, the narrower will be the oval; and the lower the validity, the more the oval will approach a circle. A validity coefficient of approximately .60 will result in a scattering of scores approximately covering the oval area shown in Figure 13. Now, if employees are placed without regard to test scores, their criterion scores will be the average of all individuals falling within the oval. If only those are placed upon this job who have test scores as high as or higher than T_1, those not placed on the job will clearly have, on the average, lower criterion scores than the group as a whole, and those placed will accordingly be higher in their criterion scores, on the average, than the group as a whole. A still higher average criterion score for the group placed can be achieved by setting the critical test score at T_2. By moving the critical score to T_3, T_4, or even higher, still more favorable placements, according to average criterion score, can be made.

If a given number of persons, say 60, are to be placed, any one of the above conditions may exist; which one exists will depend upon the selection ratio that is utilized, that is, the ratio of the number placed to the number tested. Suppose we work with a

[3] H. C. Taylor and J. T. Russell, "The Relationship of Validity Coefficients to the Practical Effectiveness of Tests in Selection: Discussion and Tables," *Journal of Applied Psychology*, XXIII (1939), pp. 565–578.

ratio of 1.00; that is, all those tested are placed. In this case, the distribution of test scores will be over the whole range of possible test scores, the criterion scores will be over the whole range of possible criterion scores, and the test will contribute nothing whatever to the efficiency of the placement procedure. Now suppose that we test 80 individuals and place the 60 who

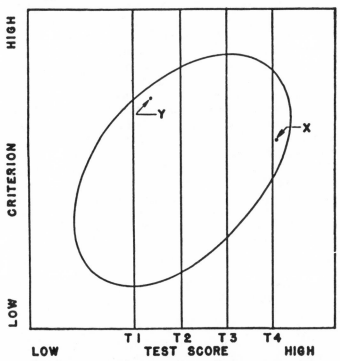

Fig. 13—Effect of shifting the critical score required of applicants on average criterion score of employees hired.

score highest on the test, either not hiring the 20 who score lowest or placing them on some other job. We thus reduce those placed to 75 per cent of those tested, or reduce the selection ratio to .75. Under these conditions, we will place on this job only individuals who test at least as high as T_1, and the average criterion scores of those so placed will clearly be higher than the average of the group as a whole. By testing 120 and placing the

60 who score highest on the test, the selection ratio will be reduced to .50 and only individuals to the right of T_3 will be placed. The average criterion score of this group will not only be higher than that of the whole group, but will also be higher than that of the group placed when the critical test score was at T_1. Thus, by increasing the number tested before the 60 to be placed are identified, the selection ratio will be decreased with a continuous increase in the average criterion score for the group of 60 finally placed. If, for example, the plant is expanding so greatly that 600 new employees could be tested before 60 are selected for location upon this particular job (or if the labor market were such that 600 applicants were tested before 60 were hired for this job), the selection ratio would be decreased to .10, only those testing at least as high as T_4 would be placed upon the job, and the average criterion score of the group of 60 placed under these circumstances would be much higher than the score of 60 placed under any larger selection ratio.

The above discussion is of course based on the assumption that the placement of employees is successful in proportion to the average success of the employees placed. Anyone can readily see that even working with a selection ratio of .1, some individuals (like X in Figure 13) will be placed who will be poorer according to the criterion than a few other individuals (like Y in Figure 13) who have not been allocated to this job. But if one is willing to measure the success of the testing program by average results rather than by individual cases, the results will be more and more favorable as the selection ratio is decreased.

We have already stated that psychologists dealing with vocational guidance and individual consultation are usually more interested in making accurate individual predictions than in making group predictions. Most of these psychologists have tended, therefore, to evaluate a test almost entirely in terms of its validity coefficient. They have stressed the fact (which is unquestionably true for individual prediction) that there is no substitute for high validity: that if two tests have been validated against the same criterion, and one has a higher validity coefficient than the other, there is no way to make the one having the lower validity serve as well as the other. The main point of the above discussion is that in group testing, where one is interested in average rather than individual results, one can make the test with the lower validity perform as well as the other *by sufficiently reducing the selection ratio.*[4] In other words, in group testing, *a reduction of the selection ratio is a substitute for high validity.* This statement does not mean that this substitute will work if the test has no validity at all, but it does mean that if the test has any significant validity, however small, it is possible for the employer to get the same functional value from it that he could get from a test of any validity, however high, if he is able sufficiently to reduce the selection ratio.

A practical objection to the principle of increasing the efficiency of a test by decreasing the selection ratio may be raised, namely, that there is a limit to the number of applicants who can be tested before the desired number are placed. It is true that, for numerous reasons, an employment manager is seldom able to test 600 or even 200 men before 60 are placed. But it should be remembered that a ratio of 10:1 can be achieved by placing one person out of ten tested just as well as by placing 60 out of 600 tested. One does not need to wait for a great expansion in hiring before advantage can be taken of a reduced selection ratio. *A reduction in the selection ratio can be utilized whenever two or more employees are being placed on two or more different jobs, and if tests of some validity are available for each of the jobs.*

The objection may also be raised that advantage cannot be taken of a reduced selection ratio unless there are more applicants than there are jobs to be filled. This is true if all persons employed are to be placed upon the same job. But almost always an expansion of plant personnel involves hiring for several jobs, not just for a single job. Therefore, the advantage of a reduced selection ratio usually can be achieved even when, as in a period of emergency production, there is difficulty in getting *enough* applicants to fill the jobs. Even when all applicants are hired, placements can be made on various jobs in such a way as to take advantage of individual differences by means of reduced selection ratios.

[4] *Ibid.,* also Clark L. Hull, *Aptitude Testing* (World Book Company, 1928). See *footnote* on page 276.

4. Percentage of present employees considered satisfactory

A further factor which affects the efficiency of a selection test in a given employment situation is the percentage of present employees who are considered satisfactory. This factor may be made clear by reference to Figure 14. Suppose we are working with a test having a validity coefficient such that the employees

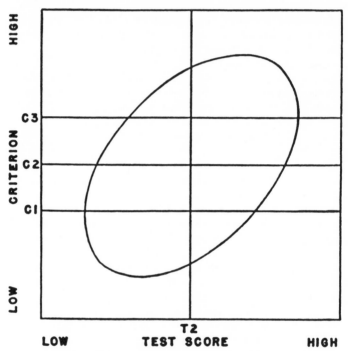

Fig. 14—Variation of efficiency of an employment test with differences in percentage of present employees who are considered satisfactory.

tested fall into the oval-shaped area. Suppose, further, that we are working with a selection ratio of .5—that is, only persons falling in the oval-shaped area to the right of T_2 will be placed on the job. If 50 per cent of the present employees are satisfactory, any increase over this amount in the percentage of satisfactory employees placed that can be achieved by using the test is a gain. Under these conditions, the ratio of satisfactory employees among those placed to the total of those placed would be the ratio of the number of individuals falling to the right of line T_2 and above C_2 to all persons falling to the right of line T_2. This ratio would clearly be higher than .50, and the amount by which it exceeds .50 would be indicative of the functional value of the test under the conditions discussed.

If all conditions named above remain the same except that previous employment methods have resulted in 75 per cent satisfactory employees, then the criterion separation line of the successful and unsuccessful employees would be C_1 and the percentage of satisfactory employees placed by means of the test would be the ratio of the individuals to the right of line T_2 and above C_1 to all persons to the right of line T_2. In the latter case, a larger percentage of employees hired will be satisfactory than in the former case, even though the test, selection ratio, and other controlling factors remain the same. In other words, if everything else is equal, the smaller the percentage of present employees who have been placed satisfactorily without tests, the larger will be the percentage increase of satisfactory employees when employees are placed by means of test results. This may be illustrated by an example. Suppose we have available a test with a validity coefficient of .50 and are working with a selection ratio of .50. Table II shows the increase due to test in percentage of satisfactory employees which might exist prior to the use of the test. The values in Table II were obtained from the Taylor-Russell tables reproduced in Appendix B. If only 5 per cent of employees placed by traditional means are successful, then the expected increase to 9 per cent represents an 80 per cent increase in the number of satisfactory employees placed by the test, under the specified conditions of test validity and selection ratio. For larger percentages of satisfactory employees that have been achieved without the test the percentage of increase achieved by using the test becomes increasingly smaller. If 90 per cent of employees placed by traditional means have been successful, the increase of this percentage to 97 per cent by the test, used under the specified conditions, results in an improvement of only 8 per cent in the number of employees satisfactorily placed.

The general conclusion is that, other things being equal, the more difficult it has been to find and place satisfactory employees without using test procedures, the greater the gain one may expect from a testing program.

TABLE II

INCREASES IN PERCENTAGE OF SATISFACTORY EMPLOYEES PLACED ON A JOB OVER VARIOUS ORIGINAL PERCENTAGES OF SATISFACTORY EMPLOYEES WHEN A TEST WITH VALIDITY COEFFICIENT OF .50 IS USED WITH A SELECTION RATIO OF .50

A Percentage of Satisfactory Employees Placed on the Job *without* the Test	B Percentage of Satisfactory Employees Placed on the Job *with* the Test	Difference in Percentage Between Columns A and B	Percentage of Increase of Values (B) over Values in (A)
5	9	4	80
10	17	7	70
20	31	11	55
30	44	14	47
40	56	16	40
50	67	17	34
60	76	16	27
70	84	14	20
80	91	11	14
90	97	7	8

The purpose of the above discussion is to make clear the fact that several factors, each relatively independent of the others, operate to determine the functional value of a selection test to an employment manager. If the employment man knows these factors—that is, if he knows the validity of his tests, the selection ratio with which he is working, and the percentage of present employees considered satisfactory—he can predict definitely just how much he will improve the placement process by using the test. And if this amount of improvement is not satisfactory, he can improve his placement by almost any reasonable amount if the selection ratio can be decreased.

Figure 15 reproduces a chart that shows how the percentage of employees selected who will be successful is determined by the validity of the test and the selection ratio. This chart deals with an employment situation in which 50 per cent of present employees are considered satisfactory. The base line in this figure gives the selection ratio, and each of the curves plotted indicates a different test validity. It will be seen that by using a test with a validity of .90, and by reducing the selection ratio to .60, the percentage of satisfactory employees placed will be raised from 50 per cent to 77 per cent. It will also be noted that

a corresponding increase to 77 per cent in the number of satisfactory employees will be achieved by a test with a validity of
only .50 if the selection ratio is decreased to .20.

The Taylor-Russell tables,[s] reproduced in Appendix B, make
it possible to determine what percentage of employees hired will
be satisfactory under different combinations of test validity, selection ratio, and percentage of present employees considered
satisfactory.

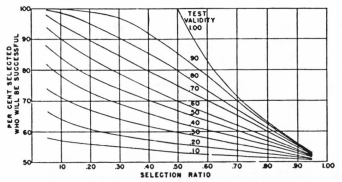

FIG. 15—Effect of test validity and the selection rates upon the working efficiency
of an employee selection test.

The use of these tables may be made clear by an example.
Suppose an employment manager has a test with a validity coefficient of .40, has twice as many applicants or employees available as there are jobs to be filled, and is placing in a department
where 30 per cent of the present employees are considered satisfactory. Looking in the lower half of the table on page 364 (en-
titled "proportion of present employees considered satisfactory
= .30"), we find in the row representing a validity coefficient of
.40 and in the column representing a selection ratio of .50, the
value .41 where the indicated row and column cross. This means
that under the conditions specified 41 per cent of the employees
placed will be satisfactory instead of the 30 per cent attained
without the test. If conditions are such that the selection ratio
may be still further reduced, the same test will place a still
higher percentage of successful employees. For example, if only

[s] Taylor and Russell, *op. cit.*

the highest 10 per cent of the persons tested are placed on the job, the percentage of satisfactory employees will be raised to 58 per cent, or nearly double the percentage of satisfactory employees placed without the test.

5. Combining tests into a battery

No single test will measure all of the capacities or abilities required on any job. Even the simplest of jobs is complex if one considers the combination of capacities or abilities required of a person who is to remain on the job and to do it well. Johnson [*] has pointed out that aptitude for any job consists of a syndrome of abilities and that one needs all of these to be successful. This fact makes it desirable, and in some cases necessary, to use a battery of tests rather than a single test. By means of statistical methods, the results of several tests can be combined into a composite score so that each is weighted to give the maximum correlation between the battery test score and the criterion. An example of the use of such combinations and weighting may be found in a set of tests worked out for placing menders in a hosiery mill. A number of tests were given to one hundred employees on this job. For each employee, data were obtained on age and experience as well as average hourly earnings for the twelve-week period preceding the administration of the tests. The correlations between several of the tests and the earnings criterion are given in Table III.

TABLE III

CORRELATIONS BETWEEN SEVERAL DEXTERITY TESTS AND
EARNINGS OF MENDERS IN A HOSIERY MILL

(Effect of age and experience statistically eliminated)

	Correlation with Earnings
Purdue Hand Precision Test [*]	.27
Finger Dexterity Test (Error Score)[*]	.18
Hayes Pegboard [*]	.16
Composite Score of Three Above Tests	.35

[*] Details of construction and administration of these tests are given in Chapter 4.

It will be noted in Table III that the maximum correlation of any individual test with earnings was .27, but that a battery made up of all three correlated .35 with the same criterion. In

[*] H. M. Johnson, "Some Neglected Principles of Aptitude Testing," *American Journal of Psychology*, XLVII (1935), pp. 159–165.

obtaining the composite score the following formula was used:
Composite Test Score = 12 (Hayes Pegboard) – 4 (Purdue
Hand Precision Test) – 2 (Finger Dexterity Error Score). The
constants by which the raw test scores are multiplied in this
formula result in the best combination of the tests to make a
prediction of job success from a combination of test scores. The
usefulness of a test battery that correlates to the extent of .35
with a criterion may be inferred from Figure 16, which shows

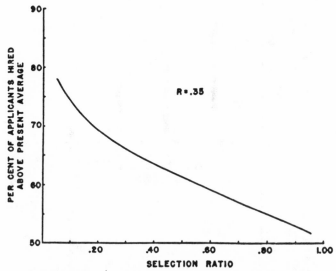

Fɪɢ. 16—Variation in per cent of employees who will be above the present average of employees when different selection ratios are used with a test having a
validity coefficient of .35.

the percentage of employees placed by this battery who will be
above the average of present employees when different selection
ratios are used in hiring or placement. For example, if the selection ratio could be reduced to .10, approximately 70 per cent
of the employees placed would be above the present average.
The value of the testing procedure in this case is definitely en-
hanced by the use of several tests in combination, since no single
test, of those tried, gave as high a validity coefficient as the battery as a whole.

The way in which a battery of tests may be expected to function in selecting the highest earners on a manipulative job is illustrated in Figure 17. To obtain this figure, another group of 150 hosiery workers (seamers) were first divided into four quar-

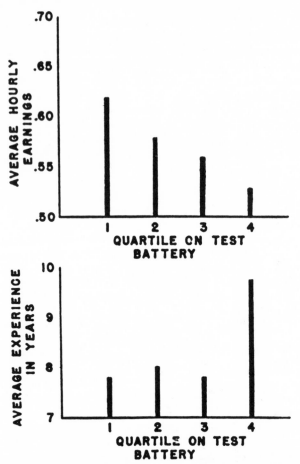

FIG. 17—Average earnings and average experience of four quartiles of "seamers" divided according to composite score on a battery of dexterity tests.

tiles according to their composite score on two tests (Purdue Hand Precision and error score of the O'Connor Finger Dexterity) which had been found related to production on this job. For each quartile of employees, the average earnings and average experience were computed and plotted in Figure 17. It will be noted that there is a progressive decrease in average earnings from the best to the poorest quartile, in spite of the fact that the poorest quartile of employees on the test had a greater amount of experience, on the average, than any of the other quartile groups. Graphic representation of this type is possible, of course, only to the extent that no marked differences in experience exist among the groups compared. For example, if the low-testing group had two or three times as much average experience as the high-testing group (which actually occurred in the case of the menders previously mentioned), one could not make a direct comparison of the earnings of the different groups.

Further need for using a battery of tests, rather than an individual test, in many cases arises from the fact that since any single test will at best cover only one of several qualifications that are necessary on the job, a battery is required in order to obtain a more complete picture. The general appearance of the scattergram obtained by plotting test scores against a criterion often, in itself, indicates that a test, even a good test, covers only one phase of the job requirements. The scattergram often shows that persons testing high on the test may either be high or low on the criterion, whereas those testing low on the test are almost always low on the criterion.

An example of this tendency is shown in Table IV. The scattergram in this table shows the relation between the learning cost of 35 loopers in a hosiery mill and their scores on the Purdue Grooved Pegboard Dexterity Test (see page 83). The minimum wage law now in effect requires that every employee be paid a certain minimum wage regardless of whether his piece-rate earnings reach this amount. A slow learner will thus have to be paid a large amount of "minimum make up" before she is earning her wage, whereas a fast learner will reach the legal minimum more quickly. Thus one indication, and a rather important one, of the desirability of an employee is the total amount of money that the company must contribute in minimum make-up wages while the employee is learning the job. It will be noted in Table II that this amount varies from $15.00, in the case of very rapid learners, to more than $60.00 in the case of slow learners. The grooved pegboard is scored in time required to fill the board (best two trials out of four). The shorter the time, the better the score.

Table IV makes several points clear. Employees with a favorable test score definitely tend to show a lower *average* learning cost to the company than do employees with a poor test score. In this case the correlation between test score (speed of filling the grooved pegboard) and economy in learning cost was

TABLE IV

Scattergram Showing Relation between Learning Cost to Company of 35 Loopers in a Hosiery Mill and Scores at Time of Employment of the Purdue Grooved Pegboard Dexterity Test

LEARNING COST TO COMPANY	SCORE ON GROOVED PEGBOARD DEXTERITY TEST				
	60 seconds or over	55–59	50–54	45–49	40–44
$15–$24			2	2	5
$25–$34		1	3	3	
$35–$44			2		3
$45–$59	1			3	
$60 or over	2	3	3	1	1

.48. This figure may therefore be taken as the validity coefficient of the test for the job in question according to the learning-cost criterion.

But another characteristic of the scattergram shown in Table IV that is commonly found in data of this sort is the *triangular* rather than the *oval*-shaped area into which the employees fall. Several employees who tested high actually turned out to be slow learners. However, no individuals with poor test scores turned out to be rapid learners. The significance of this finding is that the test in question apparently is measuring one essential requirement of a rapid learner, but only one requirement. An employee who lacks this requirement is practically certain to be a slow learner. But an employee who tests high, that is, who has an abundance of this requirement, may still be a slow learner if she lacks certain other basic requirements for the job. The triangular shape of the scattergram thus indicates the existence of a hierarchy or syndrome of capacities required for this job.

A question may be raised as to whether the reasoning on pages 34–37, in which the significance of the selection ratio concept was discussed, is valid when the scattergram is triangular rather than oval in shape. This reasoning applies equally well regardless of the shape of the scattergram as long as a vertical line drawn through the distribution at any point will divide the individuals plotted so as to give a higher average score to those on the right of the line than to those on the left. This situation is certain to occur when a positive correlation between test scores and criterion exists. Thus, the rather common existence of a triangular scattergram does not invalidate the importance of the selection ratio; but it does quite definitely add to the evidence that a hierarchy of traits is basically necessary for satisfactory performance on most jobs.

6. Adequate training of testers

The impression that the tester makes upon applicants or employees is of vital importance to the success of a testing program. This fact, obvious to the experienced employment manager, has often been underemphasized or even completely overlooked by psychologists themselves. "Everyone has shoes but the shoemaker's wife," says an old proverb. The professional psychologist often becomes so absorbed in the statistical phases of a test program that he forgets the importance of personal and industrial relations in actual test administration. Often the test administrator spends more time with an applicant than anyone else in the employment office. First impressions are lasting ones, and applicants who are employed may long remember the impressions of the company formed the first day at the plant. And the rejected applicants—upon whose reactions the industrial relations of the company within the community are also dependent—have no further opportunity to reach a different opinion of the company. The man who administers the tests should be understanding, sympathetic, and courteous. He should give the applicant a feeling of importance. If the test results do not justify employment, the applicant should be made to understand that, although he is not properly adapted or trained for the job now open, he may be quite qualified for some other job at a later time or for some job now open in another plant. The applicant should be given an understanding of the fact that he himself would not profit from employment on a job on which he would be likely to fail.

To explain such matters to rejected applicants is neither easy nor routine. It must be done individually, thoroughly, and sincerely. Many of the qualities of a successful salesman are of real value to the test administrator in industry. Testing human beings is not the same as testing materials or processes. People *react*, either favorably or unfavorably, to a test situation. It is one job of the tester—indeed, one of his most important jobs— to be sure that they react favorably. Others may have prepared adequate tests; light, roomy, and attractive rooms may be available in which to give the tests; but unless the test administrator creates a favorable reaction to the testing program, the full advantage of this tool for employee selection and placement is not likely to be realized.

3

Mental Ability and Mechanical Comprehension Tests

FOR several reasons, we shall consider tests of mental ability before we consider tests in such areas as mechanical aptitude, dexterity, or trade ability. It is hoped, however, that such prior consideration of the field of mental ability will not give a wrong impression of the relative importance of mental ability tests. We do not consider intelligence tests first because they are more important than other tests, nor because most jobs demand persons of high intelligence. We consider this field first because probably no other area of psychological testing has been so thoroughly explored. As a result of this exploration we know the fields in which mental ability tests are of definite value and also the fields in which they offer little or no promise. Given a job description, therefore, we can predict with reasonable assurance whether a mental ability test will be of value in allocating employees to that job and what test or type of test is most likely to "come through" for the job. But it should be kept in mind throughout this discussion that for many jobs in modern business and industry intelligence or mental ability tests now available give no correlation whatever, either positive or negative, with job success. Later we shall discuss a number of jobs of this type and summarize certain studies that suggest other types of tests that have been found more satisfactory than mental ability tests in those particular areas.

Typical Mental Ability Tests

Otis Tests [1]

The Otis Self-Administering Tests of Mental Ability are typical of the more widely used and thoroughly standardized tests in this field. This series is called "tests" rather than "test" be-

---

[1] Arthur S. Otis, Otis Self-Administering Tests of Mental Ability (World Book Co., 1922).

cause it consists of four equivalent forms of a higher examination, designed for high-school students and college freshmen, and an additional four equivalent forms of an intermediate examination, designed for grades four to nine. These examinations are modeled after a group test of mental ability designed by Otis for use in a large commercial establishment. They are made up of logical and arithmetical problems, beginning at a very easy level, such as:

Which one of the five words below means the opposite of north?
1. pole,   2. equator,   3. south,   4. east,   5. west. ( )

The number of the correct answer is placed in the parentheses at the right. Among the special features which the series embodies are: the principle of self-administration which eliminates the need for a trained examiner, a simplified scoring system, a variety of test material, separate norms for a twenty- or thirty-minute time limit, and a simplified chart for computing percentile scores from raw scores on the test.

A person's percentile score indicates that percentage of persons in the group on whom the test was standardized who are at or below the score of the person tested. Thus if one does better on a certain test than 20 per cent of the standardizing group, he is said to have a percentile score of 20 or to be at the twentieth percentile. If he excels 90 per cent of the standardizing group he is said to have a percentile score of 90.[2]

The Otis tests also provide for conversion of raw scores into equivalent I. Q. (intelligence quotient) values. The I. Q. is a concept that is used widely in school testing of young children, and has become a somewhat common term in popular writing. However, since it is used very little in industrial testing programs (because it is not a particularly serviceable concept when used with scores of adults, and because of a certain feeling of resentment that it arouses in many applicants and employees), we shall not explain its technical derivation in this discussion.[3]

---

[2] A detailed treatment of the meaning and computation of percentiles is given by H. E. Garrett, *Statistics in Psychology and Education*, second edition (Longmans, Green and Company, 1937).

[3] The interested student will find a description of the meaning and derivation of the I. Q. in any elementary textbook of psychology such as, J. Tiffin, F. B. Knight, and C. C. Josey, *The Psychology of Normal People* (D. C. Heath and Company, 1940).

The Otis tests are in common use in numerous industrial and business employment offices, and a number of investigations that have made use of these tests will be summarized. (See page 53.)

Wonderlic Personnel Test [4]

This test is an adaptation of the higher form of the Otis Self-Administering Test and is particularly adapted to the needs of business and industry. The word *personnel* rather than *mental ability* or *intelligence* is used in the title to avoid the negative reaction that many applicants and employees have to a test that obviously deals with mental ability. The adaptation consisted in selecting from the original Otis Test those items that were found to differentiate most markedly between superior and inferior employees on various types of industrial and business jobs. The result of this careful selection of items is that for many industrial jobs the revision differentiates more satisfactorily than does the original form, and that the test may be given in twelve minutes instead of the twenty or thirty required for the original test. The general form of the questions on the Wonderlic test is similar to that of the Otis test. The test is begun with such items as:

Of the five things below, four are alike in a certain way. Which is the one not like these four?
1. smuggle, 2. steal, 3. bribe, 4. cheat, 5. sell.   (   )

The correct answer of course is *sell*, the other four choices all being alike in the fact that each involves an element of dishonesty.

The Revised Beta Examination [5]

This is a group test of mental ability that is strictly non-verbal; that is, it does not call for ability to read. It is particularly useful in measuring persons who have a foreign language background or whose previous work or training has been such as to penalize them on a test that involves reading and language.

[4] E. F. Wonderlic, Personnel Test, Form D (E. F. Wonderlic, 919 N. Michigan Ave., Chicago).
[5] C. E. Kellogg and N. W. Morton, Revised Beta Examination (The Psychological Corporation, 522 Fifth Ave., New York, N. Y.).

The Psychological Examination of the American Council on Education [*]

This is another group test of mental ability which, because of its longer time limit of fifty minutes, has not been used so extensively in business and industry as has either of the foregoing tests. For some purposes, however, particularly college placement and vocational guidance, it has proved to be an excellent instrument. Several studies [7] indicate that it has also definite value for business and industry.

The preceding tests have been mentioned only as illustrative of the kinds of mental ability tests that are available. It is not our purpose here to attempt even a partial listing, to say nothing of an evaluation, of the many excellent measuring devices available in this field. *The Mental Measurements Yearbook* [8] gives a fairly complete listing of intelligence tests. For most of the tests listed, the *Yearbook* gives the title, a description of the group for which the test was constructed, the date of copyright or publication, whether the test is individual or group, the number of forms, the cost, the time required for administration, the author and the publisher, references to studies dealing with validity and reliability, and a brief evaluation of the test by one or more competent authorities. The industrial personnel man looking for a test that will serve some particular purpose can usually decide from the information given which test will be most likely to serve his purpose.

Another list of mental ability tests that have been used successfully in business and industry is reproduced in Appendix C on page 369.

What tests to use

Once an employment manager has decided to use intelligence

---

[*] L. L. Thurstone and Thelma Gwinn Thurstone, Psychological Examination of the American Council on Education (Science Research Associates, 1700 Prairie Ave., Chicago, Ill.).

[7] S. R. Laycock and N. B. Hutcheon, "A Preliminary Investigation into the Problem of Measuring Engineering Aptitude," *Journal of Educational Psychology*, XXX (1939), pp. 280–289.

J. B. Rhinehart, "An Attempt to Predict the Success of Student Nurses by the Use of a Battery of Tests," *Journal of Applied Psychology*, XVII (1933), pp. 277–293.

[8] Oscar K. Buros, *The 1938 Mental Measurements Yearbook* (Rutgers University Press, 1938).

tests, it is not uncommon for him to ask a psychologist, "What intelligence test do you recommend?" It is difficult, if not impossible, to give a categorical answer to this question. The test to use is the test that works, and all tests do not work equally well in all situations. Asking a psychologist what intelligence test he recommends is not unlike asking a physician what drug he recommends. The physician's recommendation depends upon a number of factors which include what is wrong with the patient, what the drug is intended to accomplish, and the present physiological condition of the patient. The psychologist cannot answer the question "What test do you recommend?" by mentioning any specific test. The question can only be answered by summarizing the results of studies that have been obtained by using various tests and types of tests in industrial and business situations. The test to be used in any new situation should then depend upon the extent to which the new situation is parallel or equivalent to those situations that have been studied.

Mental Ability Tests in Clerical Selection

Although a number of studies indicate that it is often advisable to use a standardized intelligence test in the selection of persons for clerical jobs, it should be kept in mind that the term clerical is very broad. Under this category might be included regular clerks, comptometer operators, stenographers, secretaries, and persons on other related jobs. Even in any one subcategory—as stenographer—the importance of mental ability might vary all the way from being an essential requisite on the job to being of no importance at all. For example, a secretary who is expected to answer mail during the employer's absence should have a high degree of what we ordinarily refer to as tact, judgment, and discretion—the things that constitute mental ability. On the other hand, a secretary whose main function is to greet customers or guests in the outer office and to keep them happy and contented until the employer has time to see them does not need a high level of mental ability so much as she needs personal attractiveness, social intelligence, and the ability to carry on a light conversation. A standard mental ability test might be a very desirable instrument to use in selecting a secretary for the former type of work, though there would be little to recommend such a test for the selection of the receptionist. Each test, therefore, must be evaluated in terms of whether it is measuring something that the employee must possess if he is to do the job well. If this point is kept in mind, we can readily understand why some investigators have found appreciable correlations between intelligence and clerical ability while others have reported little or no correlation. The choice of a test to be used, then, should depend upon the type of clerical ability under consideration.

Typical of studies in this field is one made by McMurry [9] who found correlations varying from .34 to .57 between Otis Intelligence Test scores and job efficiency among bank employees. The employees considered were for the most part engaged at least partially in a type of clerical work that involved careful and accurate computation and machine operation. Pond and Bills [10] have reported a study which further shows the importance of intelligence tests in selecting individuals for certain types of clerical jobs. Their investigation shows that on the easiest jobs the greatest turnover is among the employees with highest test scores, whereas on the more difficult jobs the greatest turnover is among the employees testing lowest in mental ability. In other words, the more difficult clerical jobs call for employees with the type of ability that a mental ability test measures. If all the employees possessing such ability are placed upon such jobs, whereas those not possessing such ability are placed on the easier jobs, the total turnover of the employees on both types of jobs will be definitely reduced.

Shellow [11] reports some interesting correlations between intelligence test results and the ratings of ability of a group of stenographers. The employees studied were given two tests—an intelligence test and a test measuring proficiency in stenographic skills. The intelligence test contained proverbs, items of the completion type, the analogy type, and so on—all items of the type included in most standardized tests of intelligence. It may safely be assumed that the particular test used measured

[9] R. N. McMurry, "Efficiency, Work-Satisfaction and Neurotic Tendency. A Study of Bank Employees," *Personnel Journal*, XI (1932), pp. 201–210.

[10] M. Pond and M. A. Bills, "Intelligence and Clerical Jobs. Two Studies of Relation of Test Score to Job Held," *Personnel Journal*, XII (1933), pp. 41–43.

[11] S. M. Shellow, "An Intelligence Test for Stenographers," *Journal of Personnel Research*, V (1926), pp. 306–308.

much the same aspect of mental ability that is measured by a standard intelligence test. The stenographic test was an ordinary test of proficiency in stenography of the type discussed on page 103. The correlations reported by Shellow are as follows:

Intelligence Test versus Ranking .... .73
Proficiency Test versus Ranking .... .48
Combined Tests versus Ranking .... .59 (multiple $r = .83$)
Intelligence Test versus Proficiency Test...... .12

These correlations show that, for the group of stenographers studied, intelligence as measured was even more important than stenographic proficiency in determining rated ability on the job. The results also show, as might be expected, that the combination of intelligence and proficiency in stenography makes for a higher ability on the job than either of the two taken alone. It is interesting to note that the rough combination of the intelligence and the proficiency tests gave a correlation with ranking of only .59, which was lower than the .73 between intelligence alone and the ranking. This simply means that when two tests are to be combined for prediction the tests cannot be optimally weighted except in the light of the multiple correlations involved. As the table shows, when the optimal weighting had been obtained, the correlation was .83 between the combined score on the two tests and the ranking on the job.

In the selection of cashiers, Clarke[12] has reported correlations as high as .57 between productive efficiency as measured by transactions handled per day and scores on the Otis Test, a Sales Checking Test, a Change Making Test (speed and accuracy), manual dexterity, and the Bernreuter Scale. The Bernreuter Scale, which will be discussed later (see page 113), could hardly account for all of the relationship found. It seems clear, therefore, that the abilities tapped by the mental ability test are of primary importance in determining the job efficiency of the cashiers studied. A study by Stevens and Wonderlic[13] reports the relationship between scores on the Otis Mental Test

---

[12] W. V. Clarke, "The Evaluation of Employment Tests," *Personnel,* XIII (1937), pp. 133–136.

[13] S. N. Stevens and E. F. Wonderlic, "The Relationship of the Number of Questions Missed on the Otis Mental Tests and Ability to Handle Office Detail," *Journal of Applied Psychology,* XVIII (1934), pp. 364–368.

and ability to handle office detail. Their study indicates that the employees who missed most items on the Otis Scale are the ones most criticized by company supervisors.

It would seem safe to conclude, on the basis of numerous studies such as those here summarized, that an employment manager can safely use some sort of mental ability test in selecting employees for most types of clerical jobs.

Mental Ability Tests in Selecting for Other Jobs

A number of other investigations suggest the usefulness of mental ability tests for selecting individuals for various types of jobs. Harrell [14] reports a correlation of .37 between Otis scores and the ability of cotton mill supervisors. Copeland [15] reports a low but positive correlation between a test battery made up of the Otis Test and the Minnesota Clerical Test and the ratings of supervisors, clerks, and enumerators in the census department. Wadsworth [16] reports that among the entire force of a utility plant intelligence correlated .68 with "man-to-man" estimates by supervisors. He also reports that after testing was adopted as a part of the employment procedure, the percentage of unsatisfactory employees hired dropped from 29 per cent to 5.5 per cent. Sheddan and Witmer [17] report that a battery of tests consisting of the Ohio State Psychological Test (an intelligence test), the Moss Social Intelligence Test, the Thurstone Personality Test, and a Relief Attitude Scale was found to have a correlation of .72 with job efficiency of 61 relief visitors as measured by their scores on a test of technical information about their duties and by merit rating of their performance by superiors. Holliday [18] reports that an investigation of the selection of apprentices for the engineering industry revealed that standard intelligence tests definitely improved selection. Monro

[14] W. Harrell, "Testing Cotton Mill Supervisors," *Journal of Applied Psychology*, XXIV (1940), pp. 31–35.

[15] H. A. Copeland, "Validating Two Tests for Census Enumeration," *Journal of Applied Psychology*, XXI (1937), pp. 230–232.

[16] G. W. Wadsworth, "Tests Prove Worth to a Utility," *Personnel Journal*, XIV (1935), pp. 183–187.

[17] B. R. Sheddan and L. R. Witmer, "Employment Tests for Relief Visitors," *Journal of Applied Psychology*, XXIII (1939), pp. 270–279.

[18] F. Holliday, "An Investigation into the Selection of Apprentices for the Engineering Industry," *Occupational Psychology*, XIV (London, 1940), pp. 69–81.

and Raphael[19] found that a ten-minute test designed to measure intelligence, arithmetical accuracy, attention to instructions, and tact significantly differentiated "good" from "fairly good" salesgirls. Laycock and Hutcheon[20] found that a test battery consisting of high-school grades, the American Council Psychological Examination, Cox Mechanical Aptitude Test (see page 67), Minnesota Paper Form Board (see page 66), and interest in physical science gave a multiple correlation of .66 with success in engineering.

Jobs in Which Success Is Not Related to Mental Ability

The preceding discussion of mental ability tests has involved a deliberate selection of investigations in which the tests have "come through." It should be pointed out and emphasized that in a good many investigations the mental ability tests did not come through. One example of a failure of a mental ability test to contribute anything of value with regard to predicting probable success of employees is an extensive study by the follow-up method of 749 employees hired for bench work in the Hawthorne Plant of the Western Electric Company.[21] After these employees had been on the job long enough to give a variety of indications of their success or failure on the job, including such things as promotion, average wage increase since hiring, merit ratings by supervisors, average tenure with the company, and freedom from accidents, the correlations were computed between the several criteria of successful job performance and the original test scores obtained at the time of hiring. Of four tests given at the time of employment, one was the Otis higher form of the mental ability test. The Otis scores showed practically no relation with later success or failure of the employees on their shop assignments, though it is of interest to note that this test indicated ability to progress to higher level shop occupations or office jobs. In other words, the intelligence test was definitely an indication of "promotability." However, two tests dealing with dexterity, also given at the time of hiring, did show a defi-

---

[19] M. S. Monro and W. S. Raphael, "The Value of a Short Test for the Selection of Workers," *Human Factor*, VI (1932), pp. 244–246.

[20] Laycock and Hutcheon, *op. cit.*

[21] "Analysis of 1935–37 Experience in Selecting New Men for Shop Occupations." Privately Printed Monograph (Western Electric Company, Hawthorne Plant, 1939).

nite relationship with later success of the employees. These will be discussed on page 91.

Still other investigations have shown that mental ability tests sometimes show a negative relationship with success on the job. For example, Tiffin and Greenly,[22] in studying routine manipulative assembly, found a negative correlation between the Otis scores and both actual amount of production and supervisors' ratings of productivity. This is in accord with studies already referred to by Bills[23] and by Pond and Bills[24] showing that individuals who test high on mental ability usually should not be placed on routine, easy jobs.

General Recommendations Concerning Mental Ability Tests

After studying the preceding and similar investigations, one feels a strong temptation to generalize concerning the role of mental ability tests in business and in industrial employment offices. Such a generalization might be that mental ability tests are of value in selection and placement to the extent that the employees being hired are to be placed on jobs calling for adaptability, accuracy, carefulness, and the exercise of judgment in situations that are not likely to be exactly the same from day to day. At the other extreme, individuals testing average or below on mental ability tests would seem to be most suitable for jobs involving a completely repetitive or mechanical type of manipulation of a not-too-difficult nature. A question that will naturally be raised by the last statement is "how low can an individual be in mental ability and still be able to do satisfactory work on a routine manipulative job?" It would seem that for many simple and routine jobs, individuals testing at the very bottom on standardized tests of mental ability are as well or even better adapted than persons testing at average or above. Figure 18 shows the test profile of an individual who, for the two months period preceding the administration of the test, had consistently been the highest-producing operator among 42 operators on this job. The job was one that involved routine

[22] Joseph Tiffin and R. J. Greenly, "Employee Selection Tests for Electrical Fixture Assemblers and Radio Assemblers," *Journal of Applied Psychology*, XXIII (1939), pp. 240–263.

[23] M. A. Bills, "Relation of Mental Alertness Test Scores to Positions and Permanency in Company," *Journal of Applied Psychology*, VII (1923), pp. 154–156.

[24] Pond and Bills, *op. cit.*

manipulative assembly. It will be noticed that while this employee is above average in dexterity, she is far below average in her Otis Test score. Indeed, one would conclude from a literal interpretation of this test score, in the light of the published

	Decile	Finger Dexterity Minutes to fill board		Hand Precision Error score		Otis Test Raw score	
Highest 10 percent	1	5.85 or less		0-56	✓	58 or above	
	2	5.86-6.42		57-79		53-57	
	3	6.43-6.82		80-104		49-52	
	4	6.83-7.17	✓	105-144		45-48	
Average	5	7.18-7.49		145-170		43-44	
	6	7.50-7.81		171-232		39-42	
	7	7.82-8.16		233-273		37-38	
	8	8.17-8.56		274-279		33-36	
	9	8.57-9.13		380-719		27-32	
Lowest 10 percent	10	9.14 or longer		720 or over		26 or below	✓

Fig. 18—Psychograph of an operator 32 per cent above average production on manipulative work.

norms for this test, that this employee is feeble-minded. However, it should be kept in mind that these norms were derived from the point of view of an individual's ability to succeed in adjusting himself to new and novel situations. The individuals who are lowest on this test might be most likely to succeed in jobs that do not call for such adaptation to new and novel situations. Figure 19 shows a psychological profile for another individual who was very low on the Otis Test and yet who was close to the top in productivity on the job in question.

Conclusions cannot, of course, be reached from such single cases. Yet when one considers that for the group as a whole negative correlations were found between mental ability test scores and productivity, and that a few individuals who tested at the very bottom on the Otis Test consistently led the group in productivity on the job, one is forced to conclude that it may be a serious mistake to place persons scoring high in mental ability tests on jobs of this type, unless they are being given job experience in preparation for supervisory positions.

The management of many industries has often made the mis-

Decile		Finger Dexterity Minutes to fill board		Hand Precision Error score		Otis Test Raw score	
Highest 10 percent	1	5.85 or less		0-56		58 or above	
	2	5.86-6.42		57-79		53-57	
	3	6.43-6.82		80-104	✓	49-52	
	4	6.83-7.17		105-144		45-48	
Average	5	7.18-7.49	✓	145-170		43-44	
	6	7.50-7.81		171-232		39-42	
	7	7.82-8.16		233-273		37-38	
	8	8.17-8.56		274-279		33-36	
	9	8.57-9.13		380-719		27-32	✓
Lowest 10 percent	10	9.14 or longer		720 or over		26 or below	

FIG. 19—Psychograph of an operator 27 per cent above average production on manipulative work.

take, during times of depression when applicants are available in large numbers, of hiring only individuals who offer a certain minimum of education—for example, high-school graduates. When an employment manager hires only high-school graduates he is, in effect, hiring only individuals who are above a certain level of mental ability. The content of courses taught in high school has no relationship to an industrial plant assembly job. But we know that only individuals who on the average possess a certain minimum level of mental ability are able to pass these courses and be graduated from high school. Thus the selection of high-school graduates is equivalent to selecting only those individuals who make a certain minimum score on a mental ability test. In one department of a large industry which employed approximately 400 operators for a routine job, the policy for several years during the depression of 1930 to 1935 was to employ only high-school graduates. This hiring policy resulted in an unusually high turnover, since individuals with high mental ability left the job as quickly as they could find something better. The policy was accompanied by, and may actually have caused, a condition of unrest and dissatisfaction among the employees. It has been said that nearly every individual finds some sort of outlet for whatever ability he may possess. It is not unreasonable to suppose that a large part of the unrest and dissatisfaction arising among the 400 employees in this department was due in no small measure to the fact that the high-school graduation requirement resulted in placing individuals on this job who in terms of ability were "above the job."

It should be re-emphasized at this point that the primary function of mental ability tests in industry is to help the employment manager in his placement of employees. Adequate placement means that some jobs should be filled by high-scoring individuals and that other jobs should be filled by low-scoring individuals. A mental ability test is simply another tool that the employment manager may use in placing every individual on a job that is equal to and not above or below his natural level of accomplishment.

Typical Group Mechanical Ability Tests

Bennett Test of Mechanical Comprehension [25]

This test was developed to aid in selecting employees for jobs that require a mechanical "knack," such as the operation of conversion machinery in a paper mill. The principle of the test is illustrated in Figure 20. The person tested is required to make a judgment from an examination of a drawing or schematic diagram. No mathematical or arithmetical computations are required, and the verbal or reading element is reduced to a minimum. As modern industry hires vast numbers of persons with practical mechanical experience but without formal education, the test fills a definite need in enabling an employment manager to measure mechanical ability among such persons. An illustration of the use of this test in a practical situation is given on page 74.

[25] George K. Bennett, Test of Mechanical Comprehension, Form AA (Psychological Corporation, 522 Fifth Avenue, New York, N. Y., 1940).

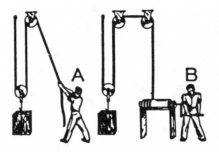

Which man can lift more weight?

FIG. 20 — Two items from Form AA of the Bennett Test of Mechanical Comprehension.

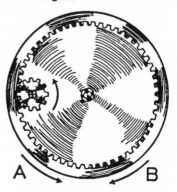

If the small wheel goes in the direction shown, in which direction will the large wheel go?

Detroit Mechanical Aptitudes Examination[26]

This test consists of several parts, some of which deal with the understanding of certain mechanical principles on a non-verbal level—such as the belt-pulley arrangement shown in

Figure 21—and others with familiarity with tools and power machinery used in a wood shop or a machine shop. Figure 22

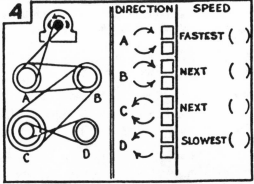

FIG. 21—An item from Part I of the Detroit Mechanical Aptitudes Test for Boys. The subject checks in the indicated blanks to show the direction and speed of the several pulleys.

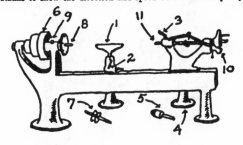

CARRIES BELT – – – – – – – – – ( )
ADJUSTS HEIGHT OF REST– – –( )
SUPPORTS TOOL– – – – – – – –( )
OILS BEARING– – – – – – – – –( )
FASTENS TAIL STOCK CENTER–( )
REVOLVES WORK– – – – – – – –( )
ADJUSTS TAIL STOCK CENTER–( )
HOLDS WORK– – – – – – – – – ( )
FASTENS TAIL STOCK– – – – –( )
HOLDS DRILL– – – – – – – – –( )
HOLDS EMERY WHEEL– – – – ( )

FIG. 22—An item from another part of the Detroit Mechanical Aptitudes Examination for Boys. The parentheses are to be filled in with the correct numbers.

illustrates one item from a part of the test that deals with power machinery. Perhaps the major differences between the Bennett Test of mechanical comprehension and the Detroit Mechanical Aptitudes Test is that the latter is based to a much greater extent upon familiarity with actual tools and machines. This statement is not intended as a criticism of either test. It means simply that the tests are likely to find their greatest degree of usefulness with different groups of applicants.

Stenquist Mechanical Aptitude Test [27]

This test is one of the oldest and perhaps one of the best known of all tests in this general field. It was first published in 1921 and at that time represented a real achievement in the application of group testing methods to the measurement of mechanical ability. An item from this test is illustrated in Figure 23. The Stenquist test, like the Detroit test, is based to a large extent upon familiarity with actual shop machinery. This char-

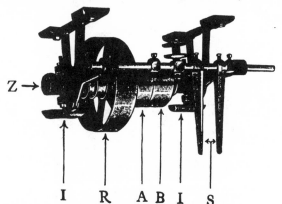

1 Oil is kept from dripping on the floor by........ .... 1 _____
2 The belt is pushed back and forth by part.................... 2 _____
3 If pulley R is loose on the shaft, write L. If it is fastened to the
    shaft and turns with it, write F......................... 3 _____
4 Does the belt which drives this machine run on pulley marked R?
    Write Y if yes; N if no.................................... 4 _____
5 Look at the two pulleys A and B. If both turn with the shaft Z,
    write B. If neither does, write N. If only one does, write O... 5 _____

FIG. 23—An item from the Stenquist Mechanical Aptitude Test. The questions are to be answered by filling in the blanks at the right.

[27] J. L. Stenquist, Mechanical Aptitude Test (World Book Company, 1921).

SAMPLES

Each of the three pictures marked with a number is used with a picture at the right marked with a letter. Look at the picture marked 1. Then look at the pictures marked A, B, and C and decide which is used with 1. Write the letter of the picture which goes with 1, on the line marked 1 at the right of the pictures. Then find the picture that is used with picture 2, and write the letter of that picture after 2 on the line at the right. The first sample is done correctly. Picture C is used with picture 1, so "C" is written after 1 on the line at the right. B is used with 2, so WRITE "B" ON THE LINE AT THE RIGHT AFTER 2. "Nail," marked A, is used with "hammer" marked 3, so WRITE "A" AFTER 3 ON THE LINE AT THE RIGHT.

NUMBERED   LETTERED

Fig. 1.

(Write answers here)

1. C
2. —
3. —

Under each set of pictures you will find some questions. In each square at the right of the questions, write a number or a letter to show which tools you would use to do what is asked. Where there are two squares, be sure to write a number or a letter in each square. Pictures 3 and A show what is used to fasten a board to a box, so 3 and "A" are written in the squares at the right after question 1. Picture 2 is the correct answer for question 2. Pictures 1 and C are the correct answers for question 3, so WRITE 1 IN THE FIRST SQUARE AND "C" IN THE SECOND SQUARE AFTER QUESTION 3.

In each square at the right of the questions below, write a number or a letter to show which tool in Figure 1 you would use:

1. To fasten a board to a box.
2. To tighten a nut.
3. To fasten a door so as to use a padlock.

(Write an answer in EACH square)

FIG. 24—An illustrative section from the O'Rourke Mechanical Aptitude Test. These items illustrate the principle but not the difficulty of the test.

acteristic is illustrated in Figure 23, which shows an overhead pulley assembly.

O'Rourke Mechanical Aptitude Test [28]

This test, like the Stenquist test described above, measures knowledge of and familiarity with tools and operations involved in shop work. It is, therefore, basically an *achievement* test rather than an *aptitude* test. However, experience has shown that applicants who have the aptitude for mechanical achievement ordinarily create for themselves opportunities for familiarizing themselves with shop equipment, and that such applicants are able, because of this experiential background, to obtain favorable scores on this and similar tests. This fact justifies the use of this type of test as an aptitude test for selecting applicants who are to receive additional training, such as apprentices. An illustrative item from the O'Rourke Mechanical Aptitude Test is shown in Figure 24 on page 65.

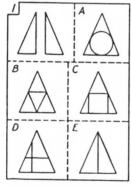

Fig. 25—An item from the Minnesota Paper Form Board Test. The person tested is asked to select the set of lettered parts (*A, B, C, D,* or *E*) which may be formed by the parts shown in the upper-left square.

Revised Minnesota Paper Form Board Test [29]

This is a unique test that deals with ability to visualize and assemble a set of blocks mentally. It largely eliminates the element of familiarity with actual tools or machines. The test consists of a series of items, such as the one illustrated in Figure 25. These items vary from simple problems, which are successfully solved by nearly 100 per cent of industrial applicants, to problems so difficult that an extremely high degree of visualization is required for their solution. An illustration of the use of an early form of this test in a practical situation is given on page 74.

[28] L. J. O'Rourke, O'Rourke Mechanical Aptitude Test (The Psychological Institute, 1937).

[29] Minnesota Paper Form Board Test (Science Research Associates, 1700 Prairie Ave., Chicago).

MacQuarrie Test for Mechanical Ability [20]

Although this scale is called a mechanical ability test, it deals more with dexterity than with an understanding of mechanical principles or familiarity with tools and instruments. A description and discussion of it therefore will be given in the section on dexterity tests rather than in the present treatment of mechanical ability tests.

Typical Individual Tests of Mechanical Ability

All of the preceding tests are of the group variety; that is, they are accomplished with paper and pencil and may be given to a large number of applicants or employees at the same time. Several individual tests of mechanical ability in this field are also available. These make use of apparatus and can usually be given to only one or two persons simultaneously.

Cox Mechanical Models Test [21]

This test consists of a series of mechanical models such as the one illustrated in Figure 26. The person tested is shown the view of the model illustrated on the left of this figure and is

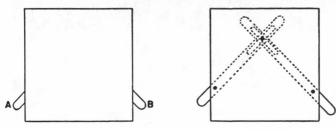

PROBLEM   **SOLUTION**

Fig. 26—One of the problems from the Cox Mechanical Models Test.

shown further, by the operation of the model, that as Lever A is moved up and down, Lever B follows this vertical movement. The task of the person being tested is to show, by simple sketch or design, what mechanism must be involved in the model in order to accomplish this result. The correct mechanism is shown in the sketch at the right, and the sketching of the

---

[20] See page 83.

[21] J. R. Cox, *Mechanical Aptitude* (Methuen and Company, Ltd., London, 1928).

mechanism is considered the correct solution of the problem. The test in all contains eight such models varying in complexity from the rather simple type of problem illustrated in Figure 26 to problems considerably more complex.

It should be mentioned that the Cox tests also include a number of printed problems, involving somewhat similar models, which may be given to groups. The Cox tests in their entirety, therefore, embrace both the individual and group forms of testing.

Minnesota Mechanical Assembly Test [32]

This is another individual test of mechanical ability which has been found useful in a number of industrial situations. One form of the test is illustrated in Figure 27. It consists essentially of a number of commonplace mechanical devices such as a

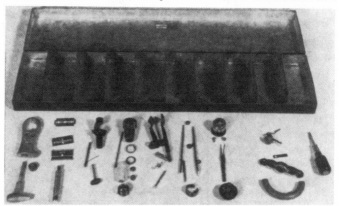

FIG. 27. One Form of the Minnesota Assembly Test.

safety razor, a mousetrap, and an electrical plug fixture, all of which may be easily taken apart and re-assembled. The person tested is required to assemble the parts of each article into the finished product. One criticism that has been leveled against this type of test is that the persons tested are likely to vary in their familiarity with the various items, and hence the test is likely to measure this familiarity rather than mechanical ability. In spite of the validity of this criticism from a theoretical view-

[32] D. G. Paterson, R. M. Elliott, L. D. Anderson, H. A. Toops, and E. Heidbreder, *Minnesota Mechanical Ability Tests* (University of Minnesota Press, 1930).

point, the fact remains that, in practical situations, the test has shown itself to be a serviceable measuring scale. This fact, rather than a theoretical criticism, is the basis upon which it should be evaluated.

O'Connor Wiggly Block Test [23]

Another test that has become well known within the past few years, particularly among industrial men, is the O'Connor Wiggly Block Test. This test consists of nine pieces of wood cut after the fashion of a three-dimension jig-saw puzzle so that the parts may be assembled into a single rectangular block. Experimental investigations of this test, such as the one reported by Remmers and Schell,[24] indicate that its validity is high within the limit of its reliability, but that the coefficient of reliability of the test is only .35. This low reliability is no doubt due, at least in part, to the fact that the entire test consists of assembling a single block; that is, the test really consists of only a single item or task. Experience has shown that the reliability of a test is nearly always increased by increasing the length or content of the test. This is due to the simple fact that, with a large sampling of behavior responses of the person tested, a chance success or failure on one or two items will not appreciably affect the total score. But if a whole test consists of only one item or task, the chance element becomes very important in determining the final test score. Thus with only a single test item, such as the Wiggly Block, high reliability could hardly be expected. It is quite possible that the reliability of this test would be much higher if it consisted of a series of such blocks similar in principle but differing slightly in design.

Since such a set of test blocks is not at present available, it is suggested that users of the Wiggly Block Test use it in conjunction with other tests of mechanical comprehension and interpret the Wiggly Block score only as a part of a more complete test profile. This procedure will avoid the mistakes in measurement that are likely to result when complete confidence is placed in a one-item test.

---

[23] Johnson O'Connor, *Born That Way* (The Williams and Wilkins Co., 1928).
[24] H. H. Remmers and J. W. Schell, "Testing the O'Connor Wiggly Block Test," *Personnel Journal*, XII (1933), pp. 155–159.

Purdue Mechanical Assembly Test [35]

This test, illustrated in Figure 28, consists of a series of eight boxes of uniform floor area. In each box a mechanism may be assembled so that a certain type of mechanical action takes place. The person tested is first shown the nature of the task by means of a simple illustrative box, and then is allowed a certain predetermined time for assembling the mechanism in each box.

The test involves several changes over previous mechanical

FIG. 28—Purdue Mechanical Assembly Test.

assembly tests. The mechanisms involved are entirely new to all testees. They do not consist of familiar objects such as have been utilized in many mechanical assembly tests. The series of boxes encompasses every principle of mechanical operation, that is, various types of levers, gears, rack, pinion, worm, and so on. A sufficient number of assembly tasks are included so that a satisfactory reliability has been achieved ($r = .88$). Studies on the validity of this test are discussed on page 74.

General Versus Specific Factors in Mechanical Ability

In considering the preceding tests of mechanical ability or

---

[35] M. R. Graney, "The Construction and Validation of a New Type of Mechanical Assembly Test," *Ph.D. Thesis*, Purdue University (1942).

comprehension, several questions are likely to arise in the mind of the reader. Why is it necessary to have several tests of mechanical ability rather than just one? Is mechanical ability a single, unitary characteristic, like height or weight, or is it a series of partially unrelated abilities, like musical talent? Are there different types of mechanical ability that are needed in different amounts for success in different mechanical jobs?

Although these questions have not been finally answered by psychological experiments, sufficient data are available to justify certain general statements upon which the answers depend. Evidence from several studies shows that some degree of general or common element is involved in the skills or abilities that we ordinarily think of as mechanical abilities. In Stenquist's [36] early work, it was found that a series of mechanical tests showed average correlations with each other in the neighborhood of .65. Such high intercorrelations can be explained only in terms of a general factor operating in all of the tests. The work of Cox [37] also supports the concept of a general factor in operations in which the subject is called upon to deal mentally with mechanical movements.

In support of the contrary idea—that most mechanical tasks are essentially different from each other and consequently call for a specific type of mechanical ability—Viteles [38] mentions specifically the work of Perrin, [39] Muscio, [40] and Seashore. [41] However, a comparison of the kinds of tests used by Stenquist and Cox, on the one hand, and Perrin, Muscio, and Seashore, on the other, reveals that the tests employed by the former men deal primarily with mental comprehension or understanding of mechanical principles, whereas those used by the latter group are primarily tests of muscular co-ordination or dexterity. In view of this marked difference in the nature of the tests them-

[36] J. L. Stenquist, "Measurements of Mechanical Ability," *Columbia University Contributions to Education* (1923), No. 130.

[37] Cox, *op. cit.*

[38] M. S. Viteles, *Industrial Psychology* (W. W. Norton & Co., 1932).

[39] P. A. C. Perrin, "An Experimental Study of Motor Ability," *Journal of Experimental Psychology*, IV (1921), pp. 24–56.

[40] B. Muscio, "Motor Capacity with Special Reference to Vocational Guidance," *British Journal of Psychology*, XIII (1922), pp. 157–184.

[41] R. H. Seashore, "Stanford Motor Skills Unit," *Psychological Monographs*, XXXIX (1928), pp. 51–66, and "Individual Differences in Motor Skills," *Journal of General Psychology*, III (1930), pp. 38–66.

selves, it is not surprising that different conclusions concerning the existence of a general factor were reached. In the mental aspects of mechanical ability, that is, in the understanding of mechanical principles, there seems to be considerable evidence for the existence of a general factor, which, when present, will enable the applicant to perform well on most or all tests of mechanical comprehension. But in the manipulative aspects of muscular performance, we most certainly agree with Seashore's conclusion that "the independence of skills measured by these [motor] tests argues against any theory of general motor ability."

A consideration of the skills demanded of the industrial tradesman or skilled machine operator indicates that this employee usually succeeds or fails in proportion to his training and general mechanical comprehension, not in proportion to his basic dexterity. This does not mean that successful tradesmen do not need skilled movements, but it does mean that such muscular co-ordination as may be needed can be developed by the majority of tradesmen in training and that it is a lack of mechanical comprehension, rather than inability to develop the muscular aspects of the job, that may prevent them from becoming really proficient in this line of work. For this reason, tests such as the Bennett, Stenquist, O'Rourke, and Revised Minnesota Paper Form Board are more serviceable in selecting apprentices for the several trades than are tests of muscular co-ordination or dexterity. It is unlikely, however, that any one of the above tests can be used as a substitute for the others. As mentioned in their respective descriptions, these tests differ markedly in content, and these differences often result in one or another of the tests being adapted to specific industrial jobs. In evaluating these tests for any specific purpose it is necessary to determine experimentally which type of test correlates with known ability on the job in question. Any company contemplating the use of mechanical comprehension tests should carry on sufficient experimentation in its own plant to be sure that the tests used are actually measuring what is desired in the employee. The following sampling of studies of this type illustrates what may be expected of these tests if care is used in their selection and validation.

Uses of Mechanical Ability Tests

Selection of pressmen and machine operators

Hall [42] has reported a study in which the relationship was determined between scores on the Minnesota Paper Form Board Test and ratings of skill of 89 job and cylinder pressman apprentices. A correlation of .58 was found between test scores

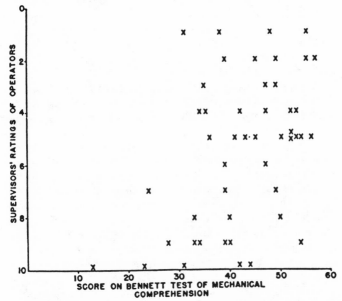

Fig. 29—Relation between score on Bennett Test of Mechanical Comprehension and rated ability of paper machine operators.

and rated job ability. It was also found that 70 per cent of the inferior workers obtained test scores below 45, whereas only 6 per cent of the workers of average skill and 5 per cent of those of superior skill received scores below 45. Hall concludes from this investigation that this test may profitably be used as one tool in the selection of pressman apprentices.

---

[42] O. M. Hall, "An Aid to the Selection of Pressman Apprentices," *Personnel Journal*, IX (1930), pp. 77–85.

Shartle [43] has reported similarly favorable results from a battery of tests designed to select electrical troublemen. Shartle's final battery consisted of six tests, several of which were similar in general content to the mechanical ability tests described in the preceding section. His results show that the scores on this test battery correlated .67 with foremen's ratings of ability on the job.

In an unpublished study by the author, a correlation of .47 was found between scores on the Bennett Test of Mechanical Comprehension and foremen's ratings of job performance for a group of forty-seven paper machine operators. A scattergram showing the relationship between rated job performance and test scores for this group is shown in Figure 29. Although the relationship as revealed in this scattergram is far from perfect, it will be noted that a critical score set anywhere between thirty and fifty items correct will divide the employees so that those scoring above the critical score will include a definitely higher percentage of high-ability employees than will be found among those scoring below the critical score. For example, ten of the eleven employees testing above fifty-one on this test are in the top half of the distribution according to rated performance on the job. Harrell [44] reports a similar study of the relationship between mechanical ability test scores and the job performance of cotton mill machine fixers. In this investigation it was found that a fifteen-item adaptation of the Stenquist test showed a correlation of .42 with foremen's ratings of the job performance of the employees.

In a study of power sewing machine operators conducted by Otis, [45] it was found that a battery of tests which included the Minnesota Paper Form Board Test yielded a multiple correlation of .57 against the quality of work of these operators.

An investigation with the Purdue Mechanical Assembly Test [46] showed that this test correlated .55 with supervisors' rat-

[43] C. L. Shartle, "A Selection Test for Electrical Troublemen," *Personnel Journal*, XI (1932), pp. 177–183.

[44] W. Harrell, "The Validity of Certain Mechanical Ability Tests for Selecting Cotton Mill Machine Fixers," *Journal of Social Psychology*, VIII (1937), pp. 279–282.

[45] J. L. Otis, "The Prediction of Success in Power Sewing Machine Operating," *Journal of Applied Psychology*, XXII (1938), pp. 350–366.

[46] Graney, *op. cit*.

ings of machinists and machinists' helpers in one plant. In another plant, a correlation of .35 was found between the test scores and ratings of machinist apprentices by their instructors.

Selection of students for vocational training

Tests of mechanical ability or comprehension are not limited in their application to the machine operating and maintenance jobs of modern industry. A number of investigations have shown that such tests are ideally suited as a part of an aptitude test battery for the prediction of success in several types of vocational training. For example, Laycock and Hutcheon [47] have reported that a test battery consisting of high-school grades, the American Council Psychological Examination, the Cox Mechanical Aptitude Test, the Minnesota Paper Form Board Test, and a questionnaire covering interest in physical science gave a multiple correlation of .66 with later achievement in engineering courses.

From such investigations as these we may safely conclude that mechanical aptitude or comprehension tests furnish a real aid to the employment manager in the selection of employees for a wide variety of industrial jobs. In general, these tests do not measure the same capacities or abilities that are measured by general mental ability tests, as evidenced by the fact that a study from the Hawthorne works of the Western Electric Plant [48] shows a correlation for 749 employees of only .39 between the Otis Self-Administering Test of Mental Ability and the Minnesota Paper Form Board Test. This does not mean that one should adopt the either-or philosophy of using a mental ability test *or* a mechanical comprehension test. Rather it means that one should use in proper combination whatever tests have been found individually to relate to success on the job in question.

What Mechanical Aptitude Tests Should Be Used

The remarks made on page 52 relative to the choice of a suitable intelligence test for any given job apply also to the choice of a mechanical aptitude test.

The several available mechanical aptitude tests differ in con-

[47] Laycock and Hutcheon, *op. cit.*
[48] Western Electric Company, *op. cit.*

tent, emphasis, extent to which they measure aptitude or immediate knowledge, and in several other respects. These differences result in the several tests being of quite different value for different jobs of placement. No one can say with certainty which test will be of greatest value in selecting employees for a specific job without carefully studying the relationship between test scores of employees on that job and their actual job success. The fact that several tests of mechanical aptitude are available increases the chances that at least one of these will be suitable for any specified purpose if a sufficient study of the job is made to locate the proper test. With experience, one can make a reasonably judicious choice from a careful study of the job and an analysis of the content of the various tests available. But such a choice should always be checked by correlating the test scores against actual success on the job; and the final decision as to whether or not the test is to be used should be based upon the size of this correlation rather than upon a subjective judgment as to the suitability of the test.

4

Dexterity, Manipulative, and Achievement Tests

A PREVIOUSLY discussed principle of testing is that usually no single test is sufficient for prediction of job success. Just as most jobs call for a combination of aptitudes, so adequate placement calls for a combination of psychological tests. In addition to determining the mental ability or mechanical aptitude requirements of a job, it is often necessary to determine the amount of muscular co-ordination, bodily dexterity, and aptitude for manipulative work that the job requires.

Dexterity Not Related to Mental Ability or Bodily Measurements

Dexterity and mental ability

The measurement of dexterity and of mental ability requires entirely different kinds of tests. The layman often assumes that the person who is "clever with his head" is also "clever with his hands," and that the individual who is high in mental ability is likely to be equally high in bodily dexterity, muscular co-ordination, and aptitude for learning skilled movements. Such is not the case. Numerous investigations have shown that the correlation between muscular skills and mental skills is very close to zero. This, of course, does not mean that the individual who is above average in one is likely to be below average in the other; but it does mean that it is impossible to predict whether an individual who is high in one will be high, average, or low in the other. In an investigation of the Western Electric Company,[1] the correlation between the O'Connor Finger Dexterity Test (described on page 78) and the Otis Mental Ability Test was

[1] Analysis of 1935–37 Experience in Selecting New Men for Shop Occupations. Privately Printed Monograph. (Western Electric Company, Hawthorne Plant, 1939.)

found to be .07. The correlation between the Hayes Pegboard (another dexterity test described on page 80) and the Otis Test was found to be zero. Each of these correlations was based on test scores of 749 employees. These results are typical of the results of many similar investigations. They prove that one cannot measure finger or hand dexterity by means of a mental test, nor mental ability by means of a dexterity test. If one wishes to determine how much dexterity an applicant possesses, he must measure that dexterity by means of a dexterity test designed for a particular purpose.

Dexterity and bodily measurements

Neither is there any relation between anthropometric measurements and dexterity. Some employment managers judge the dexterity of an applicant by examining his hands and fingers; but when careful anthropometric measurements are made and the results correlated against the measured dexterity of the applicants, no significant relationships have been found. This conclusion was reached by Griffitts [2] and has been corroborated by other investigators. Perhaps in extreme cases, where an applicant has fingers that are stiff or very stubby, one could predict from an examination of his hands that he would probably be low in finger dexterity; but in the great majority of cases such a judgment would be no more than a guess. What an applicant can do with his hands, not the appearance of the hands, determines his qualifications for a manual dexterity job.

Typical Dexterity Tests

The O'Connor Finger Dexterity Test [3]

This test, illustrated in Figure 30, is a widely used manipulative test. The equipment for giving the Finger Dexterity Test consists of 310 cylindrical brass pins one inch in length and .072 inch in diameter placed in a shallow tray, about 5 by 6 inches, with gently sloping sides, and a metal plate in which 100 holes have been sunk to a depth of ¾ inch with a number 9 drill. The diameter of the holes is .196 inch; they are spaced ½ inch apart, thus forming ten rows of ten holes each.

---

[2] C. H. Griffitts, "The Relation Between Anthropometric Measures and Manual Dexterity," *Journal of Applied Psychology*, XX (1936), pp. 227–235.

[3] For reference and source of this test, see Table VI on page 86.

After a brief period of preliminary instruction the applicant is asked to fill the board—three pins to a hole—as quickly as possible. The frequency distributions shown in Figure 9, page 12, were obtained by means of the O'Connor Finger Dexterity

Fig. 30—O'Connor Finger Dexterity Test.

Test. These distributions show that the time required to fill the board varies from around five to around fifteen minutes depending upon the amount of finger dexterity possessed by the applicant. The reliability of the test, obtained by correlating the first half against the second half, is .98. A number of investigations showing the practical applications of this test in industrial situations are discussed on pages 85–92.

The Hayes Pegboard [4]

This test, illustrated in Figure 31, also measures finger dexterity but involves, in addition, an element of hand and arm coordination. The board contains two rows of 26 holes. The rows are one inch apart and the holes in each row are spaced one-half inch apart. Each hole is .125 inch in diameter. The two boxes containing the pins each have inside measurements of 2⅜ inches

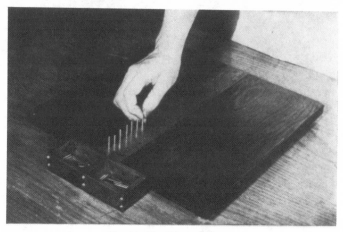

FIG. 31—The Hayes Pegboard.

by 1½ inches by 1 inch. The pins are 1½ inches long and .115 inch in diameter. The center of the top hole in each row is ⅞ of an inch from the closest inside edge of the pin box.

The administration of the test calls for a brief (ten or fifteen second) practice period after which the applicant is given nine trials of one-half minute each. These nine trials are arranged as shown in Table V.

The score on this test is the total number of pins placed during the 4½ minutes of actual testing time distributed in the nine trials summarized in Table V. Specific studies in which this test has been found of value in placement are discussed on page 88.

---

[4] Elinor G. Hayes, "Selecting Women for Shop Work," *Personnel Journal*, XI (1932), pp. 69–85.

TABLE V

SEQUENCE OF TRIALS IN ADMINISTERING THE HAYES PEGBOARD

Trial	Time	Description
1	½ minute	Placing pins from right box in right row with right hand.
2	½ minute	Placing pins from left box in left row with left hand.
3	½ minute	Simultaneously placing pins from right box in right row with right hand and from left box in left row with left hand.
4	½ minute	Placing pins from right box in right row with right hand.
5	½ minute	Placing pins from left box in left row with left hand.
6	½ minute	Simultaneously placing pins from right box in right row with right hand and from left box in left row with left hand.
7	½ minute	Placing pins from right box in right row with right hand.
8	½ minute	Placing pins from left box in left row with left hand.
9	½ minute	Simultaneously placing pins from right box in right row with right hand and from left box in left row with left hand.

Purdue Dexterity Test [5]

This test, which is illustrated in Figure 32, measures separately two basic aspects of manipulative dexterity. The assembly of a series of pin-collar washer arrangements measures fine finger dexterity of the type measured by the O'Connor Finger Dexterity Test. The placing of pins into a series of holes measures manual dexterity of the type involved in the Hayes Pegboard. These two measurements may be obtained with the same board and require only 2½ minutes of testing time. The Purdue Dexterity Test results in separate measurements for right hand, left hand, and both hands.

A further advantage of the Purdue Dexterity Test is that it can be given to ten or more persons simultaneously. All that is required for such group testing is a test board for each person and the careful attention of the test administrator. In one industrial employment office this test has been successfully given by a single examiner at the rate of fifty applicants per hour. Ten test boards were used simultaneously in this office.

Purdue Hand Precision Test

This test, which deals particularly with precision of hand movement, is illustrated in Figure 32. The applicant punches a

[5] Distributed by Science Research Associates, 1700 Prairie Ave., Chicago, Ill. For reference, see Table VI, on page 86.

stylus successively into holes that are uncovered by a rotating shutter at the rate of 126 holes per minute. The holes uncovered are .5 inch in diameter and are located on the corners of an equilateral triangle measuring 3.5 inches on a side.

FIG. 32A—Purdue Hand Precision Test.

The applicant is shown that his task is to punch the stylus into each hole as it is uncovered without allowing the stylus to touch the side of a hole or be caught by the rotating shutter. The shutter is driven by a friction clutch so that in case the stylus is caught the apparatus is not damaged. After a thirty-second practice period, a switch is thrown that connects a cumulative timer which operates whenever the stylus is in contact with the side of a hole or the shutter. The test consists of a two-minute period of punching which follows immediately and without interruption after the practice period. The score is the number of seconds of contact time (contact of stylus with side of hole or shutter) occurring during the two-minute testing period. The score measures *inaccuracy;* thus the larger the figure, the *poorer* the score. Studies in which this test has "come through" are summarized on page 272.

MacQuarrie Test for Mechanical Ability

The dexterity tests described above are instrumental and all but the Purdue Dexterity Test must be given individually. This is true of most dexterity tests. A few are of the paper-and-pencil

Fig. 32B—Purdue Dexterity Test.

type and are therefore adapted to group testing. Of these, one of the most serviceable is the MacQuarrie Test for Mechanical Ability.[*] Several parts of this test are illustrated in Figure 33. The test measures speed and accuracy of tracing, tapping, dotting, copying, letter location, block identification, and visual pursuit. The first three of the parts deal primarily with manual dexterity. The several parts may be scored separately. This makes it possible to correlate each part against a criterion and determine the optimal weighting of the parts for any specific type of predictive use.

Other dexterity tests

A dexterity test that worked well in placing operators on the job of looping in the hosiery industry is made with a grooved

[*] T. W. MacQuarrie, *MacQuarrie Test for Mechanical Ability* (California Test Bureau, 1925).

pegboard. This test calls for a board containing five rows of five holes each. The holes are .125 inch in diameter and are spaced ½ inch apart. On one side of each hole a groove has been cut. The location of these grooves is varied randomly from one

Tracing: Applicant draws a line from "start" to X without crossing a vertical line.

Dotting: Applicant places three dots in each circle as quickly as possible.

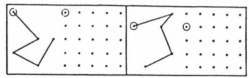

Copying: Applicant reproduces the drawings by connecting the appropriate dots in the area to the right of each drawing.

FIG. 33—Several parts of the MacQuarrie Test for Mechanical Ability. This test is essentially a group test of muscular co-ordination and control.

hole to another. Each of the pins to go in the holes has a key along one edge so that the pin may be inserted in the hole only when the key and groove are located correctly with respect to each other. This test is referred to as the Purdue Grooved Pegboard. The test is scored by determining the average time required to fill the board for the third and fourth trials of four that are allowed.

Many other tests of dexterity, muscular co-ordination, or manipulative ability are available. Some of these are specifically adapted to certain jobs and are of little value for other types of placement. Others have been found suitable as placement tests for several different kinds of jobs. Before accepting any one of these tests as suitable for any given job, one should be sure the test actually "comes through" in an evaluation of the type described on pages 25–30. The names and sources of some of the more commonly used tests of this type are summarized in Table VI.

The Uses of Dexterity Tests

It has been amply proved both by experiment and experience that the finger and manual dexterity of applicants, as well as their muscular co-ordination, is revealed much more accurately by dexterity tests than by any other procedure that may be used at the time of placement. As Hurt [7] has said, "Remarkable differences among individuals have been revealed by these tests, differences which a simple interview would never have brought to light." The magnitude of these differences in the case of finger dexterity has already been indicated by Figure 9 on page 12. It remains now to discuss the relation between dexterity, as measured by such tests, and efficiency on the job after the employees have been placed.

Finger dexterity in watch making

Candee and Blum [8] have reported a study of the relation between finger and tweezer dexterity and the efficiency of workers in a watch factory. They found a statistically significant difference between average scores on the O'Connor Finger Dexterity Test of the superior and mediocre workers. This relationship is represented by a correlation of .26 between foremen's ratings and test scores. The fact that the obtained correlation was no higher was due, in all probability, to the unreliability of the foremen's ratings. However, even with a validity coefficient of .26, the test will have real value as a placement device if a sufficiently small selection ratio is utilized. A tweezer dexterity test [9] (a similar test in which a pair of tweezers instead of the fingers is used in placing the pins), on the other hand, showed practically no relationship with foremen's ratings. One might conclude, a priori, that since much of the work in a watch factory is done with a pair of tweezers, a test involving tweezer dexterity would be a more desirable test for this type of work than one involving finger dexterity. The experimental facts, however,

[7] J. Hurt, "Evaluating Applicants by Dexterity Testing," *Employment Service News*, VI (1939), pp. 7–8.

[8] B. Candee and M. Blum, "Report of a Study Done in a Watch Factory," *Journal of Applied Psychology*, XXI (1937), pp. 572–582.

[9] For reference and source of this test, see Table VI on page 86.

TABLE VI

DEXTERITY AND MUSCULAR CO-ORDINATION TESTS

Name of test	What is measured	Source	Reference
Zeigler's Rate of Manipulations.	Finger and Hand Dexterity	Psychological Corporation, 522 Fifth Ave., New York City	H. J. Green, R. I. Berman, D. G. Paterson and M. R. Trabue, *A Manual of Selected Occupational Tests*, Bulletin of the Employment Stabilization Research Institute II (1933), pp. 59–85.
O'Connor Finger Dexterity....	Finger Dexterity (fine movements)	Human Engineering Laboratory, Stevens Institute of Technology, Hoboken, N. J.	Mildred Hines and Johnson O'Connor, "A Measure of Finger Dexterity," *Personnel Jr.* IV (1926), pp. 379–382.
Purdue Dexterity..........	Finger Dexterity (fine movements) and Finger dexterity (gross movements)	Science Research Associates, 1700 Prairie Ave., Chicago, Ill.	Manual of Instructions for the Purdue Dexterity Test, Science Research Associates, 1700 Prairie Ave., Chicago, Ill.
Purdue Hand Precision........	Precision of Hand Movements	Div. of Educ. and Appl. Psych., Purdue Univ., Lafayette, Indiana	Joseph Tiffin and H. B. Rogers, "The Selection and Training of Inspectors," *Personnel*, XVIII (1941), pp. 14–31.
O'Connor Tweezer Dexterity...	Dexterity in Using Tweezers	Human Engineering Laboratory, Stevens Institute of Technology, Hoboken, N. J.	Johnson O'Connor, "Born That Way," Williams and Wilkins Co. (1928).
Stanford Motor Skills Unit.....	A Variety of Motor Skills	C. H. Stoelting & Co., 424 N. Homan Ave., Chicago, Ill.	R. H. Seashore, "Stanford Motor Skills Unit," *Psychol. Monog.*, XXXIX, No. 2 (1928), pp. 51–66.

support the opposite conclusion. This case will serve to illustrate again that tests should not be accepted merely because of logical considerations in the absence of experiments which clearly show whether they will or will not work for the job in question.

Finger dexterity in small assembly work

A study of the O'Connor Finger Dexterity Test in selecting electrical fixture assemblers and radio assemblers has been reported by Tiffin and Greenly.[10] In the case of electrical fixture assemblers, after experience on the job had been ruled out by partial correlation, the test scores were found to correlate with productivity, as indicated by earnings, to the extent of .22, and to correlate with general efficiency as indicated by merit ratings to the extent of .33. Although these validity coefficients are not as high as might be desired, the statistical chances are ninety-eight out of one hundred that even the lower one represents a real relationship between the test scores and production. If the selection ratio is kept small, say in the neighborhood of .10, one may reasonably expect the test to be a definite value in placing employees on this job.

In the case of radio assemblers, no objective criterion of employee success was available because the wiring of a radio is a line assembly job and the operators are paid on a straight hourly basis. In the absence of differential earnings, pooled ratings of the employees by four raters (the department foreman, line foreman, former line foreman, and personnel manager) were used as the criterion of employee efficiency. These pooled ratings had a reliability of .77. With experience on the job held constant by partial correlation, the correlation between these pooled ratings and finger dexterity test scores was .27. It might be added that a composite test score obtained by combining the finger dexterity scores with scores on the hand precision test (see Figure 32), visual acuity, and color perception gave a multiple correlation of .60 with rated efficiency on the job.

Dexterity on other jobs

An experiment showing the value of dexterity tests in select-

---

[10] Joseph Tiffin and R. J. Greenly, "Employee Selection Tests for Electrical Fixture Assemblers and Radio Assemblers," *Journal of Applied Psychology*, XXIII 1939), pp. 240–263.

ing coil winders, operators of punch presses (and similar machines), operators of insulation machines, and bench hands has been reported by Hayes.[11] Hayes used two dexterity tests—the Hayes Pegboard and the O'Connor Finger Dexterity Test. A scoring system which combined the two test scores, with weights determined by their respective relations to job success, was worked out for each of the jobs studied. The criterion of success in the case of machine operators was output during the first eight weeks on the job. The reliability coefficients for this criterion for the three types of machine operators were as follows:

	Reliability of the Criterion
Coil Winders	.78
Operators of Punch Presses and Similar Machines	.81
Operators of Insulation Machines	.87

The criterion for bench hands was the supervisors' estimates of whether the employees were quick, fair, or slow learners based on the percentage of standard tasks, which had been set up for the bench-work jobs, attained during the first month. The reliability of this criterion for the four-week period was .89.

The results of Hayes' experiments are summarized in four charts, Figures 34–37. In each of these figures, the key identifies the proportion of employees who were quick, slow, or fair learners, or who did not complete the training. In each case the employees were divided into six groups according to the composite score on the pegboard dexterity tests at the time of hiring. Throughout these results, for all four types of jobs studied, there were, among employees scoring high on the tests, a relatively large proportion of quick learners and a relatively small proportion of learners who were average or slow, or who did not finish the training period. These results are sufficiently clear-cut to justify the use of the dexterity tests as an aid in selecting employees for the jobs studied.

A thorough "follow-up" study of the value of dexterity tests (as well as certain other tests) in the selection of male employees for a variety of occupations has been carried on in the Hawthorne

---

[11] *Op. cit.*

Works of the Western Electric Company.[12] In this study, 749 of the men hired between October 1, 1935, and April 30, 1937, were given a battery of four tests, two of which were the O'Connor Finger Dexterity Test and the Hayes Pegboard.   The essen-

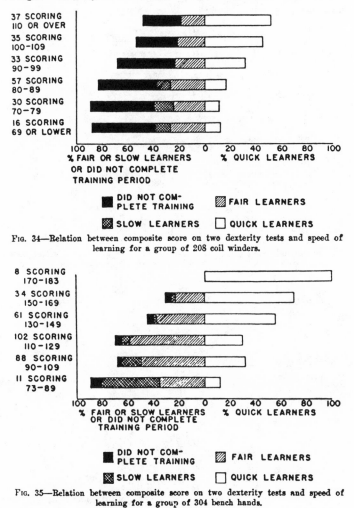

FIG. 34—Relation between composite score on two dexterity tests and speed of learning for a group of 208 coil winders.

FIG. 35—Relation between composite score on two dexterity tests and speed of learning for a group of 304 bench hands.

[12] Western Electric Company, *op. cit.*

tial procedure of the study consisted in "follow-up" analyses of the work history of these employees to determine what facts about this work history could have been predicted in a better-than-chance manner from a knowledge of the test scores at the time of hiring.

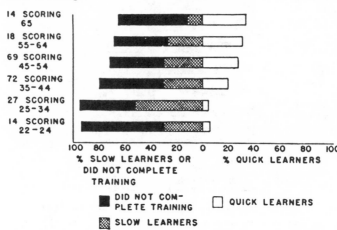

Fig. 36—Relation between composite score on two dexterity tests and speed of learning for a group of 214 insulation machine operators.

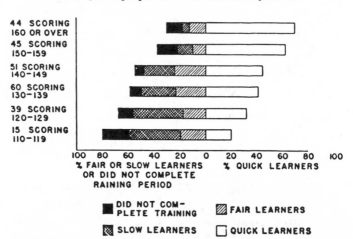

Fig. 37—Relation between composite score on two dexterity tests and speed of learning for a group of 254 operators of punch presses and similar machines.

As there was some variation in the average score on certain tests from one three-month period, or quarter, to another during the six quarters in which the study was conducted, it was necessary to exclude the effect of this time factor in analyzing the results. This was done by separating the records into six quarter-year periods according to the quarter in which the man entered the company. The analyses were made separately for the men in each quarter and the final result obtained by later combining these results.

Table VII shows the difference in several criteria of job performance between employees testing above and below average on the dexterity tests. In evaluating the results summarized in this table, it should be kept in mind that the test scores were filed shortly after the employees were hired. The scores could in no way have influenced the judgment of supervisors in determining those criteria of job performance in which judgment is a factor.

In Table VII the column labeled "high" refers to the employees testing above average on the test. The column labeled "low" refers to employees testing below average. While it will be noted that the high-testing employees are not greatly superior, on the average, to the low-testing employees in the several criteria of job success, it is probably not a matter of chance that the high-testing employees on the Hayes Pegboard excel the employees testing below average on this test in six out of the seven criteria.

The results with the O'Connor Finger Dexterity Test are in general not quite so favorable, but this test seems to be even better than the Hayes Pegboard in selecting employees who are not likely to leave the company for "reasons other than resignation," that is, not likely to be laid off. The difference between the 43.6 per cent of low-testing employees and 32.8 per cent of high-testing employees who left the employ of the company for reasons other than resignation is significant from a statistical viewpoint. One may safely conclude that by using these simple dexterity tests as an aid in placing employees, persons will be placed who will tend to stay longer on the job, who will be considered the best employees by their superiors, who will show more rapid increases in piece-rate or daily earnings, who will progress more rapidly in labor grade, and who will be at least no

TABLE VII

DEXTERITY TEST SCORES RELATED TO VARIOUS MEASURES OF JOB PERFORMANCE

CRITERION	O'CONNOR FINGER DEXTERITY TEST			HAYES PEGBOARD		
	High	Low	Diff.*	High	Low	Diff.*
Per cent of persons who have left the company for reasons other than resignation......................	32.8	43.6	+10.8	34.2	41.6	+7.4
Personnel Rating (1937).............	75.9	72.8	+ 3.1	76.1	72.6	+3.5
Increase in weekly earnings since employment (Piece rate employees)....	$9.91	$9.54	+ $.37	$10.10	$9.36	+$.74
Increase in weekly earnings since employment (Day rate employees).....	$5.24	$5.43	− $.19	$5.54	$5.14	+$.40
Progress in Labor Grade since employment...........................	.76	.78	− .02	.82	.72	+ .10
Per cent of persons without accidents since employment.................	47.3	45.4	+ 1.9	45.8	47.4	−1.6
Per cent of persons without an illness since employment.................	88.2	88.3	− 0.1	88.8	87.7	+1.1

* A plus value is given to the difference if it indicates that the high-testing employees are more favorable on the criterion.

more likely to experience accidents or sickness than persons placed without the tests.

A number of other organizations have found tests of dexterity and muscular co-ordination helpful in the placing of employees on certain types of jobs. Typical of such investigations is a series of studies by Drake [13] in the selection of inspectors for the Eagle Pencil Company. Most of the tests that Drake describes are of the manipulative type, though some deal with other aspects of employee aptitude, such as visual perception and acuity. One new pegboard test described by Drake has a reliability of .92 and a validity of .59. A test having a validity coefficient as high as .59 is of considerable value even when it is not possible to work with a low-selection ratio.

Another illustration of the practical effectiveness of a dexterity test in selecting employees is the case discussed in an earlier chapter (page 45) of loopers in a hosiery mill. It will be remembered that a dexterity test alone provided the means of markedly reducing the learning cost of employees on this job.

[13] C. A. Drake, "Aptitude Tests Help You Hire," *Factory Management and Maintenance*, XCV (1937), pp. 55–57.

Selection of apprentices

Trade apprentices need much more than capacity for developing the manipulative aspects of their trade. They need, first of all, capacity for learning the fund of knowledge that is required of an expert tradesman. This capacity is better measured by tests of mental ability and mechanical comprehension than by tests of dexterity and muscular co-ordination. Yet, in spite of the fundamental importance of these mental capacities, the element of dexterity is also of some importance in achieving success as a trade apprentice. Allen,[14] for example, reports that a battery of seven tests covering intelligence, mechanical aptitude, mechanical ability, and dexterity was found of value in selecting boys who are able to make satisfactory progress in learning the various skilled trades. While three of the four elements measured in this study deal with the mental aspects of the trainees, it is significant to note that dexterity also was of some importance. In a later study, Allen and Smith[15] report that the same battery of tests showed a correlation of .82 between scores obtained before training and after training. The significance of this finding is that such tests may be used with confidence *before* training is given; that is, the ranking of applicants at the time of hiring will not be significantly modified by training on the job.

The preceding discussion has been largely concerned with dexterity tests alone. In actual practice, the most effective use of any program of tests usually involves a combination of several types of tests, as in the work of Allen and Smith just described. Typical of such combinations or batteries is the group of tests proposed by Otis[16] for the selection of power sewing machine operators. Otis followed the customary procedure of correlating a large number of tests, each individually against a criterion of job success, and then determining which combination of the original tests best predicted the criterion. He used separate criteria for quality of work and quantity of work, and found that a somewhat different battery should be used in predicting these

---

[14] E. P. Allen, "The Selection of Engineering Apprentices," *Journal of the National Institute of Industrial Psychology*, V (1931), pp. 379–384.

[15] E. P. Allen and P. Smith, "The Selection of Engineering Apprentices II," *Human Factor* (London), IX (1935), pp. 63–67.

[16] J. L. Otis, "The Prediction of Success in Power Sewing Machine Operating," *Journal of Applied Psychology*, XXII (1938), pp. 350–366.

two phases of job performance. A battery consisting of the Minnesota Vocational Test for Clerical Workers (name comparison),[17] Poppelreuter Tracing Test[18] (time score), the Poppelreuter Weaving Test[19] (paper folding test), the Minnesota Spatial Relations[20] (time score), and Minnesota Paper Form Board Test,[21] Forms A and B, gave a multiple correlation of .57 with the quality of work of the sewing machine operators. In predicting the quantity of work produced by these operators, he found that the O'Connor Tweezer Dexterity Test, the Poppelreuter Tracing Test (time score), the O'Connor Finger Dexterity Test, the Minnesota Rate of Manipulations Test, and the Minnesota Vocational Test for Clerical Workers (number comparison) gave a multiple correlation of .64 with the actual amount of work produced by the employees. It is interesting to note that the Tweezer and Finger Dexterity Tests are both of value in selecting the most rapid sewing machine operators but are of no help in selecting the individuals who will do the highest quality of work. The use of separate criteria for speed and quality of work, or even a still larger number of criteria, such as listed in Table VII on page 92, in the validation of tests and batteries of tests, is often of exceptional importance to management. For some kinds of work or some orders, quantity is of greater importance than quality; and for other types of work an opposite situation may prevail. By knowing specifically whether the employees placed by means of any test program will excel in quantity or quality, safety, or other factors, management can decide more easily whether the battery of tests will select employees who will be able to achieve the objectives that have been set up as desirable by company policy. Thus, one company which specializes in an exceptionally high-quality product might use a certain battery of tests in selecting and placing employees, while another company which makes the same product in quantity at a very low price might use quite a different test battery.

[17] Minnesota Vocational Test for Clerical Workers (Psychological Corporation, 522 Fifth Ave., New York, N. Y., 1933).

[18] W. Poppelreuter, "Die Arbeitskurve in der Eignungsprüfung," *Industrielle Psychotechnik*, III (1926), pp. 161–167.

[19] *Ibid.*

[20] D. G. Paterson, R. M. Elliott, L. D. Anderson, H. A. Toops, and E. Heidbreder, *Minnesota Mechanical Ability Tests* (University of Minnesota Press, 1930).

[21] See page 66.

This example should serve to emphasize again the fact that a test battery should be adopted not only in accordance with the particular job which the employees are doing, but also in accordance with the major policies and objectives of the company. Loopers in a hosiery mill that produces thirty-nine cent hose might be selected by quite a different battery of tests than loopers in a mill that produces nothing but $1.39 hose. The first organization wants operators who are skillful and rapid even though the quality of their work may at times be somewhat imperfect. The second organization wants employees who produce a perfect product even though their output may fall far below that of employees on a similar job in the first-mentioned mill.

Achievement Tests

The tests discussed in the preceding chapter and in the first part of this chapter are essentially tests of aptitude, not of achievement.[22] They are, therefore, of value primarily in the selection of individuals to be trained for various types of work. However, when applicants are being hired who have had or who claim to have had a certain type of work experience, the most serviceable type of selection device is usually an achievement test. For example: suppose that an industry is hiring a number of employees to operate a certain type of machine. The correct operation of the machine requires a certain amount of experience and training. Among the applicants are a few who claim to have had the necessary experience with some other company. Perhaps the best way to determine whether such applicants really are expert machine operators would be to put them on the machine in question for a trial period, give them little or no specific instruction, and determine by try-out on the job how well they can operate the machine. Since often the operation of such a machine is a definite hazard to an individual who is not actually proficient, it would be unwise, and might even be dangerous, to allow an uninstructed applicant to operate an actual machine. It is possible, and in times of depression even probable, that some applicants may profess to have had certain experience that they have not had or may claim a degree of proficiency that they do not possess. It is, therefore, highly de-

---

[22] The distinction between these two types of tests is made on page 23.

sirable to make use of appropriate achievement tests in the selection of such employees. Such tests are simply means of determining in a convenient, simple, and economical manner whether applicants actually possess the job proficiency that they claim to have.

Job achievement tests may be of several forms. They may consist of standardized oral questions, objective written questions of the true-false or multiple choice variety, or, in some cases, of a miniature (and safe) replica of the job itself. Some job achievement tests must be given individually while others may be readily administered to large groups of applicants simultaneously. The essential characteristic of the achievement test as such, in contrast with the aptitude test, is that the achievement test measures how much actual job proficiency the applicant is able to demonstrate at the time he seeks employment. Achievement tests are therefore of greatest value in the selection of employees for jobs that are reasonably consistent from one industrial plant to another.

Oral Trade Questions

Oral trade questions are among the most widely used types of achievement test. Such questions are convenient to administer and simple to interpret. The most extensive research with this type of test has been carried on by Stead, Shartle, and associates.[22] The general procedure followed by this group has been described in detail in their book, *Occupational Counseling Techniques*. Since the many trade questions developed are in constant use by the various state employment offices, and since the publication of the actual questions used would cause them to lose much of their value, Stead and Shartle publish only a few sample questions to illustrate the method by which the validity of the questions has been determined. This procedure is sufficiently important to the general subject of test validation to warrant a somewhat detailed discussion.

Validation of oral trade questions

The general procedure in validating these questions consists in finding for each trade a few questions, usually fifteen, that can

---

[22] W. H. Stead, C. L. Shartle, and Associates, *Occupational Counseling Techniques* (American Book Company, 1940).

be answered correctly by a large proportion of successful jour-
neymen in that trade, but that are answered correctly by a definitely smaller percentage of apprentices in this trade, and are

FORM I

Score	Expert Asbestos Workers (50 Subjects)	Apprentices and Helpers (25 Subjects)	Related Workers (25 Subjects)
15	xxxxxxxx		
14	xxxxxxxxxxxxxxxxxxx*		
13	xxxxxxxxxxxxx		
12	xxxxxx	xx	
11	xx		
10	x	x	
9	x		
8	xx	xx	
7	x	x	
6		xxxxxxxx*	
5		xxx	xxxx
4		xxxx	xx
3		xxx	xxx
2		x	xx
1		x	xxxx*
0			xxxxxxxxxx

FORM II

Score	Expert Asbestos Workers (50 Subjects)	Apprentices and Helpers (25 Subjects)	Related Workers (25 Subjects)
15	x		
14	xx		
13	xxxxxxxx		
12	xxxxxxxxx	x	
11	xxxxxxxx*		
10	xxxxxxxx		x
9	xxxxx	x	x
8	xxx	x	
7		xxxx	xxx
6	xxx	xxxx	
5		xx*	x
4		xx	xxx
3		xxxx	xxx
2		xx	xxxx*
1		xxxx	xxx
0			xxxxxx

* Median Score

FIG. 38—Distributions of scores for expert asbestos workers, apprentices and helpers, and related workers on a 15-question oral trade test.

answered correctly by a still smaller, or negligible, percentage of employees in related trades. Each question to be retained must show a significant dropping off in the percentage of correct answers from the journeyman group to the apprentice group to the related trades group. When a set of questions for a given trade has been obtained in this manner, it is a simple matter to determine whether an applicant who claims to possess journeyman abilities for that trade actually is able to answer these questions as well as known tradesmen have answered them. The differentiation obtained by such a set of oral trade questions for asbestos workers is shown in Figure 38. The expert asbestos workers vary from seven to fifteen correct answers, apprentices and helpers from zero to twelve, and related workers from zero to five. Thus, an applicant who is able to answer correctly only six or fewer of the fifteen questions is very unlikely to be an expert asbestos worker, regardless of what he may say or feel about his own skill. Even if he answers up to twelve items correctly, he is probably not highly proficient in his trade, because the majority of men known to be experts were able to answer thirteen or more of the questions correctly.

Factors affecting the validity of trade questions

The success with which such a set of trade questions will differentiate among applicants possessing different degrees of skill is dependent upon the very careful selection of questions comprising the test. This selection can only be made by starting with many more questions than will finally be retained and by eliminating every question that does not actually show a differentiation among the several groups tested. Likewise, if the test is to be used on a country-wide basis, the preliminary validation work must be carried on in the several geographical areas where the test is later expected to function. The following question for a roofer illustrates the necessity for considering geographical factors in the validation of the question.

Q.   What type of asphalt is glued on a flat roof?
A.   Flat (F) (low melt).[24]

Experts west of the Mississippi River answered this question

---
[24] *Ibid.*, p. 38.

with unusual consistency, but there tended to be a reduction of consistent answers by experts when the validation took place eastward. Therefore this question could not be used in a test that was intended for country-wide use. In general, questions that could be answered simply, preferably by one or two words, were found to be better than those that called for more extensive answers. Often the best questions were those that could be correctly answered only by terms peculiar to the trade in question, even though such terms might not be found in a dictionary.

Trade questions of this general type have been prepared for most of the standard trades and are in use in many state employment offices. The procedure followed has given such excellent results that a number of industries are now adopting this method in the formulation of questions for the use of the employment manager. A number of industrial plants now make up their own questions for their own particular jobs. This procedure enables the test constructor to make up a test that is of much greater value to the industry in question than a test that has been constructed for more general application. Examples of such questions in true-false form covering the job of heater in a steel mill are given in Table VIII.

TABLE VIII

TRADE QUESTION IN TRUE-FALSE
FORM COVERING THE JOB OF HEATER IN A STEEL MILL

1. The furnace checkers are always located directly below the car bottom.   T F
2. The gas flow and air flow must always come from opposite sides of the furnace...   T F
3. The only way to tell if the stock gas is burning is to look at the top of the stock...   T F
4. The purpose of the stock gas is to help the furnace draw...............   T F
5. In lighting a cold furnace, the rear parts are always the first ones to be opened..   T F

The Miniature or Job Sample

The miniature or job sample method of constructing an achievement test consists in trying out the applicant in a test situation that reproduces all, or an important sampling, of the actual operations that the job itself requires. The miniature test usually consists of apparatus, but the apparatus is constructed to eliminate whatever hazard might be involved in operating a production machine. The applicant is asked to operate the miniature under conditions that simulate the operation of the real machine. Norms of performance of experienced and inexperienced operators are obtained in the test situation so that the status of an applicant can quickly be determined by a comparison of his score with the norms.

A miniature punch press

An example of this approach is the miniature punch press de-

Fig. 39—Applicant being given the Miniature Punch Press Test.

scribed by Tiffin and Greenly.[25] This test is used in the selection of punch press operators. This apparatus, which is illustrated in Figure 39, is a replica in all essential features of a small industrial punch press. It differs from a real press in that the punch

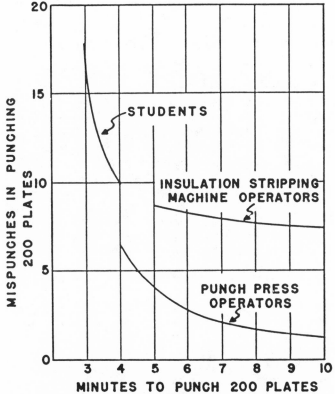

Fig. 40—Relation between speed and accuracy for three groups of subjects in operating a small punch press.

is located in a vertical bearing and is held down only by a spring. This feature prevents the punch itself from descending when an obstacle is encountered. When this occurs, the punch remains stationary while a mechanical counter records an error or mis-

[25] Joseph Tiffin and R. J. Greenly, "Experiments in the Operation of a Punch Press," *Journal of Applied Psychology*, XXIII (1939), pp. 450–460.

punch. The test is administered by having an applicant put through the press two hundred pre-punched pieces of galvanized sheet iron. The time required to feed these pieces is recorded by means of a stop watch. During the test period, the mechanical counter records the number of errors or mispunches. The test thus results in a simultaneous time and error score.

Studies of the validity of this test have been made in several ways. One method consisted of comparing the average performance of different groups of persons to whom the test had been given. The curves in Figure 40 summarize the results obtained for three specific groups. These curves show the relation between mispunches or errors in punching two hundred plates and the time in minutes required to punch the two hundred plates. As might be expected, the errors decrease as the time increases for all three groups of persons upon whom these results are based. It is interesting to note, however, that the curve for the students and the one for the insulation stripping machine operators are almost identical mathematically and simply represent different segments of the same curve. This suggests that the students, though punching much more rapidly and hence making many more errors, are not significantly different from the insulation stripping machine operators in genuine ability. The employees in this latter group, though offering no experience in the operation of a punch press, were industrial employees and, as such, were more accustomed to the need for careful, slow operation of any machine. The curve for the industrial punch press operators, however, is markedly different from that of either the students or insulation stripping machine operators. For any given speed of operation the punch press operators were more accurate than either of the other groups, and for any given level of accuracy, punch press operators were more rapid.

From a knowledge of the speed and accuracy of a given applicant and a comparison of this information with the data graphed in Figure 40, it is possible to determine the status of the applicant in comparison with the corresponding test performance of persons who are known to be experts on this job.

The method illustrated by the miniature punch press has been utilized in selecting employees for numerous other jobs. For example, in hiring persons for such jobs as packaging, inspecting, and certain types of machine operation it is often extremely helpful for the personnel manager to obtain a sample of the quality and speed of work that the applicant is able to perform. The miniature or job replica furnishes such a sample of job performance with a minimum of effort and with no danger to the applicant while the test is being administered.

The job sample in clerical work

Another area in which the job sample method of testing has resulted in very satisfactory results is the selection of employees for stenographic, clerical, and secretarial positions. One of the most widely used tests of this type is the series known as the Blackstone Stenographic Proficiency Tests.[26] This series includes a stenography test and a typewriting test. The stenography test is made up of seven parts, namely, knowledge of English grammar (which includes punctuation, capitalization, and spelling); syllabication; office practice; alphabetizing; abbreviations; knowledge of business organization; and ability to take dictation and shorthand and to make the correct transcription. Separate norms are available for each of these seven parts so that in hiring an applicant for a given job it is possible to match the test results with a job analysis of the work to be performed. The second part of the Blackstone series consists of a typewriting test. This part requires the applicant to copy a standard page of typewritten material. The result may be scored separately for speed and accuracy and the norms available permit a rapid determination of the exact level of proficiency possessed by an applicant.

Another standard test used in measuring proficiency in the use of a typewriter is the Thurstone Examination in Typing.[27] A part of this test consists of a page of corrected copy that the applicant is asked to type, making the indicated corrections. A sample of the material to be copied is shown in Figure 41. The ability to copy corrected material of this kind, though frequently called for in many stenographic positions, seems to be quite different from the ability to make an exact copy of material requiring no corrections. For example, in one employment office a girl who had recently won a state contest for speed in typing was

---

[26] Blackstone Stenographic Proficiency Tests (World Book Company, 1932).
[27] Thurstone Employment Tests, Examination in Typing (World Book Company, 1922).

unable, when tested with the Thurstone test, to obtain even an average score in typing this corrected copy. Apparently her ability consisted of a strictly mechanical and automatic method of "copying the copy." While such ability might be very useful

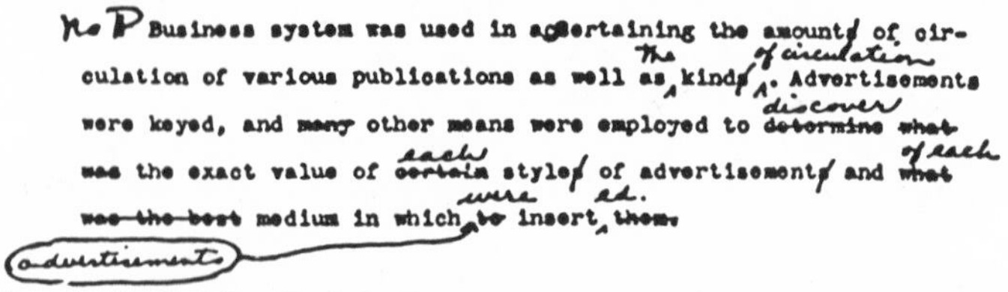

No P Business system was used in ascertaining the amount of circulation of various publications as well as kinds. Advertisements were keyed, and many other means were employed to determine what was the exact value of certain style of advertisement and what was the best medium in which to insert them.

FIG. 41—Part of Test I of the Thurstone Typing Test. The person tested is required to copy this material, making the indicated corrections.

in winning state contests, it is of little use in a business situation because one is seldom asked to copy material that is perfect at the outset. A test of the Thurstone type, therefore, is a much better measure of the kind of ability called for in a business or industrial job than is a test that requires only straight copying of material.

Many other standardized tests in the general field of clerical aptitude and achievement are available commercially. A list of some of those in most common use is given in Appendix C.

Written Achievement Tests

The Purdue Vocational Tests [28] comprise a series of paper-and-pencil tests that measure achievement in technical information related to various areas of trade training. These tests, although developed primarily for the use of vocational teachers in public-school systems, are being used also by industrial personnel men for the purpose of determining the qualifications of applicants for jobs connected with the various trades. Three standardized tests are now available in this series.

Technical information in machine shop [29]

This test consists of 149 questions (partly multiple choice and partly matching) that cover material well known to any qualified machinist and that should be reasonably familiar to any

[28] Joseph Tiffin, *Purdue Vocational Achievement Tests: Manual of Directions, Keys, and Tentative Norms* (Purdue University, 1940).

[29] C. C. Stevason, H. G. McComb, and Joseph Tiffin, *Technical Information in Machine Shop* (Purdue University, 1940).

boy who has received adequate vocational instruction in this field. Four examples of the multiple-choice items follows:

In each of the multiple choice statements listed below there are four possible answers, but only one is correct. Read each statement carefully before making your choice of answers. Place the number indicating your choice in the parentheses at the right.

The hammer most commonly used by the machinist is a (1) set, (2) ballpeen, (3) claw, (4) sledge......................... (   )

The most important purpose of the lathe back gears is to (1) decrease the power, (2) decrease the speed, (3) lock the spindle, (4) remove tight chucks.............................. (   )

Each revolution of the thimble of a micrometer makes a difference in measurement of (1) 10 thousandths, (2) 25 thousandths, (3) 50 thousandths, (4) 100 thousandths of an inch.. (   )

In laying out an unfinished casting for drilling, the common coating material is (1) red lead, (2) blue vitriol, (3) Prussian Bluing, (4) chalk... (   )

The test covers such topics as hand tools, bench tools, bench work, lathe, milling machine, shaper, planer, and drill press. The test has a reliability coefficient of .97, computed by the chance-halves method. The published norms were obtained on the basis of a fifty-minute time limit. The scoring is simple and rapid. Separate norms are available for students or applicants offering different amounts of vocational training or practical experience.

Technical information in electricity [20]

A second test in the Purdue Vocational Series deals with industrial electricity. This test consists of 150 questions (multiple choice and matching) covering material of a practical nature in the field of electricity. Four sample questions from this test follow:

In the following section of this test select the numbered word or phrase after each incomplete sentence which makes the most nearly true statement and place its number in the parentheses at the right of the question.

[20] H. R. Goppert, Joseph Tiffin, and H. G. McComb, *Technical Information in Electricity* (Purdue University, 1940).

Connecting battery cells in series (1) increases current capacity, (2) decreases total resistance, (3) increases the voltage, (4) decreases the efficiency.................................. ( )

Thickness of insulation for any circuit is determined by (1) the current to be carried, (2) the voltage of the line, (3) the load on the circuit, (4) the price of electricity................... ( )

The voltage on a 40 ohm circuit which draws 2.5 amperes is (1) 220 volts, (2) 110 volts, (3) 100 volts, (4) 16 volts....... ( )

What is the total resistance between A and B in the above line? (1) 12 ohms, (2) 18 ohms, (3) 2 ohms, (4) 1.67 ohms........ ( )

This test covers such topics as common electrical circuits, measuring units, conductors, and common electrical devices. Its reliability, computed by the method of chance halves, is .95. The time limit is fifty minutes. Separate norms are available as an aid in interpreting the scores of applicants offering various amounts of training or experience.

Technical information in industrial mathematics [31]

In its construction, scoring, and administration this test is similar to the tests just described. It deals primarily with operations of an arithmetical, or simple mathematical, type that a tradesman in industry is likely to encounter. The reliability of the test, computed by the chance-halves method, is .89. A sample of the test follows:

In each of the multiple choice statements listed below there are four possible answers, but only one is correct. Place the number indicating your choice in the parentheses at the right. Do all figuring on the back of the opposite page.

A short cut for dividing by 25 is to multiply by:
(1) $\frac{200}{6}$ (2) $\frac{50}{2}$ (3) $\frac{4}{100}$ (4) $\frac{75}{3}$ ( )

$\frac{2}{3} \div \frac{1}{2} =$ ( )

A discount of 5 per cent on $12.00 is:
(1) 80¢   (2) 60¢   (3) 40¢   (4) 20¢   ( )

If 3a + 7 = 22, then "a" equals:
(1) 3   (2) 4   (3) 5   (4) 6   ( )

[31] D. H. Price and Joseph Tiffin, *Technical Information in Industrial Mathematics* (Purdue University, 1940).

These group achievement tests in the different trade areas enable an employment manager to obtain a thorough picture of the strong and weak areas of information possessed by applicants. Because the tests may be given to many applicants simultaneously, they can be made much longer than oral trade tests and therefore are much more exhaustive than the latter in covering the technical field.

Uses of Written Achievement Tests

Selection of apprentices

Because of the increasing availability of public-school vocational courses, applicants for industrial apprenticeships often have had a certain amount, and sometimes a substantial amount, of instruction in the trade area they wish to enter. It is important for the industrial personnel manager to know how much of this instruction has been retained by the applicant, because the boy who has profited most by the instruction he has received in his chosen area is most likely to progress with further industrial training toward becoming a skilled tradesman. Although school grades and recommendations of former teachers furnish some indication of progress already made by an applicant, it is frequently desirable to supplement these sources of information with a well-standardized test covering the area in question. The necessity for using a test of this type is illustrated in Figures 5 and 6 reproduced in Chapter 1 on page 9. The first illustration shows that among 112 applicants for the job of machine shop apprentice a considerable number made a score of less than 40 (number of items correct) and a scattered few made a score of less than 20 on the machine shop achievement test. Although most of these applicants had had at least one semester of machine shop instruction, and many had had much more than this amount of training, 25 per cent of them did so poorly on the machine shop achievement test that they were below the lowest 10 per cent of students in vocational classes. It was clear, therefore, that among these applicants were a considerable number who would be very unlikely, even with prolonged training, to become expert machinists. The company concerned set 90 items correct as the critical score for hiring for this job and was able, by this process, to select for apprenticeships boys who made very rapid strides in developing the necessary skill to become expert machinists.

A similar situation was found in the selection of boys for apprenticeships as electricians. Here again a considerable number of the applicants made scores on the Test of Technical Information in Electricity considerably below what would be considered a poor score even among first semester vocational students of this subject. By adopting a critical score for employment that eliminated these unqualified applicants, the apprentices selected constituted a homogeneous group of well-qualified boys who were able to advance rapidly under the systematic apprentice training offered by the industry.

Transfer of employees

The problem of transfer is one that continually confronts every employment manager. Persons hired in one capacity often wish to be changed to a job that offers, or is believed to offer, greater opportunity for advancement. Every personnel manager is not only willing but anxious to transfer employees wherever possible to jobs where they will have a greater opportunity for development. It often happens, however, that an employee wishes to be transferred to a job that he not only cannot perform satisfactorily at the time of transfer but on which, because of lack of aptitude or capacity, he is never likely to be successful. An example in point is the case of tradesmen's helpers. Quite often an employee after working for a period of years as a tradesman's helper feels that he has acquired the necessary information and skill to assume the responsibilities of the tradesman's job. Often such a helper is able to talk quite glibly in terms common to the trade; and this verbal skill, together with a certain familiarity with a few elementary principles of the trade, may convince the employment manager that the employee seeking transfer is now ready for the promotion. In such cases the use of a standardized achievement test furnishes a highly satisfactory means of determining whether or not the employee is really eligible for the transfer desired. If his score is well below that which is characteristic of apprentices in this trade, the employment manager not only is justified in refusing to make the transfer but, in explaining the reason for his refusal to the employee, he is supplied with the necessary objective information so that his refusal cannot be attributed to

prejudice or lack of understanding. Not long ago one employment manager made the comment that the most difficult part of
his job was in saying "no" to an applicant seeking employment
or an employee seeking transfer. This employment man felt
that although he was usually right in his judgment, it was very
difficult for him to explain the reasons for his decision to the
employee or applicant. It is interesting to note that the judicious use of test results solved his problem. Whenever a request
is refused because an employee or applicant has a very low score
on an objective test that measures his capacity for the job he is
seeking, the person concerned is much less likely to feel that he
has been discriminated against.

The use of tests in connection with promotion and transfer
supplements rather than replaces such factors as seniority, being
"in line" for the job, and the needs of the business.

Discovery of areas needing training

Many industries are devoting more and more time to the systematic training of both new and old employees. The need for
such training is a natural result of the continuous technological
changes occurring in modern industry. No matter how well
qualified an employee may be today, technological change in
methods or processes may require that he be completely re-
trained tomorrow. The systematic use of technical information
tests among present employees furnishes a convenient means of
determining those areas in which training is needed. An example of this use of information tests is shown in Table IX. This
is a set of matching items to determine whether the employees
are familiar with the color code used in the plant in which they
work. Several other important areas were covered in the test.
The content of the training program that followed the administration of this test was based largely upon the results obtained.

TABLE IX

PART OF AN ACHIEVEMENT TEST COVERING INFORMATION THAT SHOULD BE
KNOWN TO EMPLOYEES SEEKING TRANSFER OF PROMOTION

Instructions: On the right is a list of colors. On the left is a list of the materials carried in pipes in this mill. You are to show how well you know the color
code by matching each color with the figure or figures which you find before the
appropriate materials. Mark your choice in the parentheses at the extreme right.
The first one is correctly marked to show you how it should be done. There will
be some colors unused. Some others will be used twice.

Materials	*Colors*		
1. Stabilized Gas	Aluminum	(6)	( )
2. Steam	Black	( )	( )
3. Hot Water	Brown	( )	( )
4. Cold Water	Bright Red	( )	( )
5. Coke Oven Gas	Ceiling Blue	( )	( )
6. De-oxidized Gas	Dark Purple	( )	( )
7. Compressed Air	Dark Red	( )	( )
8. Natural Gas	Gray	( )	( )
9. Fuel Oil	Green	( )	( )
10. Sulphuric Acid	Blue	( )	( )
11. Farval Grease	Pink	( )	( )
12. Bowser Oil	Olive Green	( )	( )
13. Gasoline	Orange	( )	( )
14. Kemp Lines	Lavender	( )	( )
15. Water Fire Lines	White	( )	( )
16. Foamite	Yellow	( )	( )
17. Hydraulic Lines			

Measurement of vocational achievement

Every vocational teacher expects to place his students in industrial jobs. The success of these students in such jobs, however, depends largely upon the adequacy of training they have received while students. Teachers in the field of general education have long made use of standardized achievement tests to determine student achievement in the several school subjects and to compare the achievement of students in various school systems, under different types of instruction, and in different geographical localities. Administrators and teachers of vocational subjects are now beginning to make similar use of objective achievement tests, and there is every reason to believe that the judicious use of such tests in this area will be fully as valuable as in the field of general education. The tests of machine shop, electricity, and industrial mathematics discussed in the preceding section are ideally suited for this purpose, and achievement tests in other vocational areas are now in the process of construction. Since vocational demands differ from one industry to another and from one industrial center to another, it is often wise to build tests that are "tailor made" for the particular situation. Such tests, when constructed through the joint efforts of vocational teachers, school administrators, vocational co-ordinators, and representatives of the industries concerned, furnish an ideal means of facilitating the co-ordination between industries and schools that every community desires to encourage.

5

Tests of Personality and Interest

EMPLOYMENT managers universally recognize the importance of personality traits in employees whom they hire. Indeed, one of their reasons for sometimes being hesitant in adopting psychological tests is that they often think of tests only in terms of intelligence or dexterity, and these tests do not, of course, take into account the more general personality traits of the applicant. An applicant might be very high in mental ability or in manipulative dexterity and yet have a personality that would not only make him unfitted for the job for which he is applying but would also make him a definitely undesirable individual to employ in any capacity.

The foregoing sections, which have dealt with aptitude and achievement tests without regard to the applicant's general personality, do not imply that the more general personality traits are unimportant. Psychologists are the first to recognize the importance of personality traits in helping an employee adapt himself to any job or to any organization. Psychological tests have emphasized tests of specific aptitude because psychologists recognize the importance of job aptitude, as such, aside from personality characteristics, and because, up to the present time, it has proved possible to develop adequate tests of such aptitudes as finger dexterity or intelligence to a greater extent than it has been possible to develop adequate tests in the complicated field of personality.

Within recent years, however, both employment managers and consulting psychologists have increasingly demanded some reasonably satisfactory and accurate method of determining certain personality traits of an applicant at the time he applies for employment. It is now recognized not only that an applicant who does not have the aptitude to learn the job will fail, no matter how desirable his personality traits may be, but also that if he does have the aptitude for the job he will probably still fail if his other personality characteristics make it difficult for him to fit into the organization and to work co-operatively with other persons. Although this conclusion is sound common sense, we do not need to rely entirely upon sub-jective judgment to reach it. Such investigations as those of Hunt [1] and Brewer,[2] which have been carried on with thousands of employees in a variety of industries, show that personality factors, rather than lack of ability on the job, are responsible for a large number of layoffs and failures to be promoted. These studies deal with layoffs due to factors other than failure to pro-duce. The rising voice of labor in determining managerial poli-cies, particularly with respect to hiring and firing, and the growing importance of seniority as a determining factor in lay-off, have made it increasingly important to determine, at the time of hiring, whether an applicant has any incipient personality maladjustments that might prevent him from fitting properly into the organization. It is with the hope of developing some sort of test or tests to accomplish this purpose that a number of psychologists have developed scales for the measurement of per-sonality or temperament traits.

Tests of Personality

Probably the first attempt to develop a scale of this type was made by Downey [3] and resulted in the Downey Will-Tempera-ment Scale. This test was based on a number of assumptions that were later found to be untenable, and for that reason the scale was never very widely used. It is noteworthy, however, in that it served the purpose of directing the attention of psycholo-gists toward the need for a measuring instrument in this area. Some time later the Thurstone Personality Schedule [4] was pub-lished. This scale gives a single gross score indicating the pres-ence or absence of neurotic tendencies. With this scale, Thur-stone was able to show that neurotic tendencies are relatively

---

[1] H. C. Hunt, "Why People Lose Their Jobs or Aren't Promoted," *Personnel Journal*, XIV (1935–1936), p. 227.

[2] J. M. Brewer, "Religion and Vocational Success," *Religious Education*, XXV (1930), pp. 29–41.

[3] J. E. Downey, "The Will-Temperament and Its Testing" (World Book Com-pany, New York, 1923).

[4] L. L. Thurstone and T. G. Thurstone, "Personality Schedule" (University of Chicago Press, 1929).

independent of mental ability, but are related to accomplishment in certain areas, particularly college and university work. An abbreviated form of Thurstone's scale has been published by Willoughby.[5]

Another widely used scale of this type has been constructed by Bernreuter.[6] Bernreuter's scale differs from those that preceded it in that an ingenious selection of items and system of scoring make it possible to score the scale separately for four different personality traits. These are: emotional instability, extroversion-introversion, self-sufficiency (absence of need for companionship, encouragement, and sympathy), and dominance-submission. This four-way method of scoring results in a test that is at least partially diagnostic, and this diagnostic feature is helpful in pointing toward specific characteristics of the person's emotional and temperamental make-up.

As the above scales and others in the general field have appeared, each has found a place for itself in personality measurement and each has usually incorporated one or more improvements over those published previously.

The Humm-Wadsworth Temperament Scale [7]

This scale has been produced by two men whose work has been in the field of industrial personnel. It is the first personality scale intended primarily for industrial use and has been used more extensively in industry than has any other personality test.

The scale consists of 318 questions which the person tested answers by checking *yes* or *no*. From the answers to these questions it is possible, by differential scoring, to obtain separate scores for seven aspects of temperament. These aspects are as follows:

1. **The Normal Component.** This is primarily a control mechanism providing rational balance and temperamental equilibrium. It underlies the conservatism, toleration, and conformity to socially acceptable

---

[5] R. R. Willoughby, "Thurstone Personality Schedule, Clark Revision" (Author, Worcester, Mass., 1932).

[6] R. G. Bernreuter, "The Personality Inventory and Manual" (Stanford University Press, 1931).

[7] D. G. Humm and G. W. Wadsworth, "The Humm-Wadsworth Temperament Scale, Test Booklet and Manual," second 1940 revision (Doncaster G. Humm Personnel Service, Los Angeles, California).

behavior observed in the well-adjusted person. Essentially a "control mechanism" or "balance wheel," the normal component presents mainly characteristics associated with restraint, and persons in whom it is over-accentuated may be given to undiscriminating conservatism. In diagnosis the term "normal" is rarely used alone except for such ultra-conservatism. It is usually used in combinations such as "normal-cycloid," "normal-schizoid," and so on, where it refers to individuals whose temperament is under control, and who are essentially well-adjusted, but who also show a large degree of cycloid or schizoid temperament.

2. The Hysteroid Component. An individual with an excess of the hysteroid component possesses a character defect with ethically inferior motivation manifested by stealing, lying, cheating, and similar antisocial behavior. A moderate degree of hysteroid tendency underlies much of our prudence, shrewdness, diplomacy, and may even contribute to social adjustment, as the ends of self-interest are often best served by conformity to socially acceptable conduct.

3. The Manic Cycloid Component. This is characterized by emotionality, fluctuation in activities, and interferences with voluntary attention, some degree of elation, pressure of activity, and distractibility together with such manifestations of excitement as jests, pranks, enthusiasms, impatience, and so forth.

4. The Depressive Cycloid Component. This is manifested by some degree of sadness, lessened activity, and associated characteristics such as worry, timidity, and feeling of malaise. The manifestations of a general cycloid nature are fluctuations from emotional equilibrium, hot-headedness, difficulty in sleeping, and so forth. Cycloid subjects are enterprising, sensitive to social situations, wistful, and sympathetic. They are handicapped by such tendencies as emotional thinking, lack of perception, and changeability of moods.

5. The Autistic Schizoid Component. This is characterized by heightened imagination, leading to a tendency toward a day-dream life concerning which the subject is sensitive. The autistic manifestations are seclusiveness, shyness, and suggestibility, accompanied by an ability to visualize and concentrate upon special tasks, excluding diverting interests.

6. The Paranoid Schizoid Component. This includes stubborn adherence to fixed ideas, suspicion, and contempt for the opinion of others, with behavior fitting these traits. In the presence of sufficient normal component the paranoid phase is of value in pushing through programs that meet with resistance.

7. The Epileptoid Component. This is characterized by inspirations to achievement that are meticulously developed and pushed through to completion. It causes the subject to spend endless time in working out projects, and yet, at times, to appear inconsistent because of some contradictory inspiration. The inspirational tendency is often of a belligerent nature. The temper manifestations are explosive, often appearing on slight provocation after long periods of endurance. Some physiological symptoms associated with epileptics as well as epilepsy itself are likely to be present or to appear in the history.

In Table X are listed the components covered by the Humm-Wadsworth Temperament Scale, together with the symbols used to identify each and a brief statement of the constitutional, mental, or nervous disorder in which an extreme degree of each component is typically observed.

TABLE X

THE COMPONENTS OF TEMPERAMENT MEASURED BY THE HUMM-WADSWORTH TEMPERAMENT SCALE

Component	Symbol	Constituted of Traits Associated with
"Normal"	N	Self-control, self-improvement, inhibition.
Hysteroid	H	Self-preservation, selfishness, crime.
Manic Cycloid	M	Elation, excitement, sociability.
Depressive Cycloid	D	Sadness, retardation, caution, worry.
Autistic Schizoid	A	Day-dreams, shyness, sensitiveness.
Paranoid Schizoid	P	Fixed ideas, restiveness, conceit.
Epileptoid	E	Ecstasy, meticulousness, inspiration.

Everyone who studies the above list of components with their brief descriptions will recognize certain persons of his acquaintance who, from long observation, are clearly known to possess an excessive amount of one or another or of some combination of these characteristics. One does not need the Humm-Wadsworth Scale, or perhaps even training in psychology, to identify the Hysteroid or the Cycloid if he is constantly thrown into contact with an individual of this type. Indeed, one thrown into contact with such a person is more likely to recognize that something is wrong than is the afflicted individual himself. The mentally ill or "near ill" often feel that they are quite normal but that everybody else is wrong. It is, however, one thing to recognize the presence of such personality characteristics in a person with whom one is thrown into constant contact, and it is quite another thing to recognize them in an applicant whom one is interviewing for the first time. It is claimed by users of the Humm-Wadsworth Temperament Scale that it will accomplish this result.

It is, however, expecting a good deal of any scale to identify such personality traits in persons who are "after" jobs and who can therefore be expected to answer the questions in whatever way they feel the questions should be answered in order to be sure they get the jobs. It has been, therefore, particularly important to study the validity of the scale in industrial situations. This has been done by a number of follow-up studies in which the scale has been administered to employees at the time of hiring. One of these investigations has involved the extensive testing of applicants at the Lockheed Aircraft Corporation, Burbank, California.[*] In this organization the policy has been to reject applicants for employment whose scales reveal "weak Normal"; Hysteroid or Paranoid scores higher than "Normal"; Manic scores, Depressive scores, and Autistic scores that were either extremely high or higher than "Normal"; and high Epileptoid scores accompanied by physiological evidences of epilepsy. The results of this hiring policy in terms of employee turnover has been quite satisfactory. Out of 185 engineering employees, 184 met these standards and one was accepted as doubtful. Of these employees, the doubtful case and one other were discharged later for reasons arising out of temperamental maladjustments. The other 183 employees were found to be entirely satisfactory from the personality viewpoint. Of 1500 other employees engaged for work in tool designing, welding, sheet metal assembly, machine shop, wood shop, and precision assembling, at the time of the report only 18 had been discharged for reasons arising out of temperamental maladjustments. Transferred into percentages, this would mean that 98.8 per cent of the employees selected according to this policy were satisfactory from the temperamental point of view. Recently the entire plant was surveyed by the Federal Bureau of Investigation. Of 1500 employees tested only two were found who had criminal records whose scales had not revealed a high Hysteroid component. Evidence of this type indicates that this scale at least partially reveals at the time of employment whether an applicant has a temperamental make-up that is likely to make him unsuitable as an employee.

On the other hand, there is reason to believe that many enthusiastic users of the Humm-Wadsworth Scale are expecting

---

[*] D. G. Humm and G. W. Wadsworth, Jr., "The Humm-Wadsworth Temperament Scale," Manual of Directions, 1940 Revision (Wadsworth-Humm Personnel Service).

more from it than it is likely to yield. We have already mentioned that the questions are of a type that can be answered either *yes* or *no*, and that an applicant for a job may not be too honest if he feels that honest answers will decrease the chances of his being employed. The extent to which the scores on the seven components may shift when a person is changed from a frank or clinical situation to a job-application situation is revealed in a recent study conducted with 65 college students.[*] Each student was given the scale twice: first, with instructions to be as frank as possible, and second, to assume that he was in an employment office after a job and had been asked to take the test as a part of the employment procedure. Table XI shows the mean scores for the seven components obtained under these two conditions.

TABLE XI

Mean Scores on Humm-Wadsworth Temperament Scale Obtained in a Clinical and an Employment Situation by 65 College Students [*]

Component	Clinical Mean	Employment Mean	Shift from Clinical to Employment
"Normal"	981	1023	+ 42
Hysteroid	1023	980	− 63
Manic	1035	937	− 98
Depressive	1061	913	− 148
Autistic	1024	938	− 86
Paranoid	970	955	− 15
Epileptoid	983	1002	+ 19

[*] All scores were computed by the log method, with correction for no-count, as described in the second 1940 revision of the manual of directions.

It is apparent from Table XI that the employment situation, when compared with the clinical, shows a higher average value for the normal component and lower values for all except epileptoid of the remaining six components. In other words, the students were able, by assuming an attitude of "applying for a job," to change their test profiles toward more of the normal and less of the undesirable traits. All differences shown in Table XI are significant from a statistical viewpoint, and only scores were used in the computation that fell within the no-count limits, for both the clinical and employment situations, within which the manual of instructions states that the scale should be "accepted as probably valid."

[*] This study was conducted by W. J. Giese and F. C. Christy at Purdue University.

Even with the shift in means from one situation to the other, it would still be possible to infer one's score in one situation from a knowledge of his score in the other situation if scores in the two situations were highly correlated. The correlations were computed and are shown in Table XII.

TABLE XII

CORRELATIONS BETWEEN CLINICAL AND EMPLOYMENT SITUATIONS ON THE HUMM-WADSWORTH TEMPERAMENT SCALE FOR 65 COLLEGE STUDENTS

Component	Correlation
"Normal"	− .03
Hysteroid	+ .42
Manic	+ .09
Depressive	− .10
Autistic	+ .11
Paranoid	+ .61
Epileptoid	+ .23

The only correlation in Table XII that is large enough to be significant is the one for the Paranoid Component.

We are thus forced to conclude that, although the Humm-Wadsworth Temperament Scale is probably superior to any other instrument of this type that has been proposed for industrial use, it will not give a completely invariable picture of a person under any and all conditions of testing or point of view of the applicant. In spite of these criticisms, many industrial personnel men have reported excellent success with this scale, and we should not dismiss lightly the experiences of practical men. While a shift in one's profile may, and does, occur from one situation to another, it is possible that a truly psychotic or mentally ill person produces an undesirable profile under all conditions of testing and will therefore be detected even when applying for a job. Even the borderline case may be detected in the job application situation if an excess amount of the Paranoid Component is present. Tables XI and XII show that this component shifted least from one situation to the other and is correlated to the greatest extent between the two situations. While final judgment on this scale cannot be given at present, it is quite possible that with continued revision and improvement, and with the establishment of further norms upon persons tested at the time of employment, the scale will become of real value to the employment manager.

Entirely aside from the use of the Humm-Wadsworth Scale as a device for selecting employees, the possibility exists of using this test as a means of helping present employees overcome possible weaknesses that may exist in their temperaments. A number of industrial men have reported the successful use of the test for this purpose. The procedure consists in having the test taken by those employees or supervisors who are having some sort of trouble in adjusting their personalities to the demands of the situation. Very often it is possible to awaken among employees an interest in self-improvement that will inspire them to take the Humm-Wadsworth Scale as an experimental venture. Under such circumstances, they often give rather frank and honest answers to the questions. The resultant profiles bring into sharp relief any personality deviations that may be present. With the profile before him, a skillful counselor can often bring the person tested to realize that the picture presented by the test is fairly accurate. When this much has been accomplished; when the employee has been given an insight into his weaknesses as well as his strength, he is much more able to do something about himself than if he goes about from day to day without realizing that certain aspects of his behavior may be "rubbing people's hair the wrong way."

For such a purpose, it is not necessary that the test give a completely accurate representation of an individual's personality. If it brings into relief even partially those aspects of his personality which most need attention, and if a skillful counselor can bring about an insight into this condition without upsetting the employee's general emotional balance, a very real step in the direction of self-improvement has been made. Industries have found the Humm-Wadsworth Scale a real help in connection with such counseling procedures within their plant.

The Measurement of Interest

Everyone realizes that an individual's interests direct his activities. The student who is interested in engineering will study long hours, apply himself with diligence, and achieve a mastery of the engineering subjects that is limited only by his capacity to master those subjects. A student who lacks this interest, even though he may have the same or even greater capacity, will find excuses for not studying his calculus, will go to the movies or to a dance when he should be writing up laboratory reports, and will in other ways avoid those hours of prolonged study without which successful accomplishment cannot be attained.

Vocational Guidance counselors have long recognized that it is just as important to be sure a boy is studying for a vocation in which he has a real and driving interest as to be sure that he has the capacity to achieve success in that field. Without an interest, no amount of capacity will be sufficient; just as without the capacity, no amount of interest will be sufficient.

Up to the present time, very little has been done in the industrial placement of employees by way of ascertaining their interests and placing them upon jobs for which they not only have the necessary capacity but in which they also are definitely interested.

The accurate measurement of the true interests of persons applying for jobs is subject to the same difficulties as the measurement of their personalities. If one is very anxious to obtain a certain job (for monetary or other considerations) it is not likely that he will reveal his true interest if that interest happens to be in some direction that is not related to the job. The industrial application of interest-measuring techniques is therefore limited largely to situations in which the person tested is not to be selected or rejected for employment as a result of the test but rather is to be hired anyway and will be placed or later transferred in accordance with his basic interests.

Several investigations have indicated that the interest questionnaire, when used in this manner, is of value in industry. Shartle [10] made a study of two groups of foremen, one consisting of highly successful supervisors and the other made up of foremen approximately equal in job skill but less able than the first group in handling the personal aspects of their supervisory jobs. In Shartle's investigation the Strong Vocational Interest Blank [11] was given to all the supervisors and this was followed by a detailed clinical interview. The results showed that the less successful foremen were characterized by more interest

---

[10] C. L. Shartle, "A Clinical Approach to Foremanship," *Personnel Journal*, XIII (1934), pp. 135–139.

[11] E. K. Strong, Jr., "Vocational Interest Test," *Educational Record*, VIII (1927), pp. 107–121.

in withdrawing from others, by more indifference to the actions of others, and by more antagonistic reactions toward others. The study suggests that interest in dealing with others is one of the prime requisites of the successful supervisor. Laycock and Hutcheon [12] have reported a study in which a battery of tests containing, among other things, a measure of interest in physical science gave a correlation of .66 with success in engineering courses.

Although the Strong Vocational Interest Blank measures interests for a large number of vocations, it is possible that a much smaller number of basic interests is involved. Thurstone [13] reports a multiple factor study of vocational interests that shows by an analysis of Strong Blank results that interests may be basically divided into four general fields: science, language, people, and business. It would seem to be important for the personnel manager to consider these interests as well as abilities, particularly in the case of college graduates or others who are expected to show considerable development over a period of years. It is probably unwise to place in the scientific development department young college men whose basic interests are in people and business; and it would seem to be equally unwise to put into the sales department those whose basic interests are scientific. Fortunately, it is often possible to obtain a fairly accurate picture of an applicant's or employee's interests by means of an interview in which a number of questions are asked about such topics as present and past activities, hobbies, and how vacations are spent.

Within recent years two new techniques for the measurement of interest have been published. One of these, the Kuder Preference Record, [14] furnishes a measure of the relative amount of an individual's interest in seven fields: scientific, computational, musical, artistic, literary, social service, and persuasive. The test is easy to give, self-scoring, and has been found to be very serviceable in the general field of vocational guidance.

---

12 S. R. Laycock and N. B. Hutcheon, "A Preliminary Investigation into the Problem of Measuring Engineering Aptitude," *Journal of Educational Psychology*, XXV (1939), pp. 280–289.

13 L. L. Thurstone, "A Multiple Factor Study of Vocational Interests," *Personnel Journal*, X (1931), pp. 198–205.

14 Kuder Preference Record, Test and Manual (Science Research Associates, Chicago, 1939).

The other test, the Cardall Primary Business Interests Test,[15] is of even more immediate practical importance in business and industrial situations. This test is designed to measure an individual's preferences for the specific job activities that characterize beginning business jobs. These immediate and specific preferences point to the initial job, determine the individual's interest or boredom in his first activities, and often determine to a considerable extent his progress in his work. The five business fields in which this blank measures interest are: accounting, collecting and adjusting, sales office work, sales store work, and stenographer-filing.

While it is not always possible for an employment manager to place employees according to their interests, it is perhaps possible for him to do so more frequently than is often realized. In the shifting and transfer that continually occur in any large business or industrial plant, it is good business as well as good industrial relations to consider whenever possible the basic interests and desires of employees who are being shifted. Adequate consideration of these interests goes deeper than basing transfers upon mere statements of preference. It is entirely possible that in many cases the employee himself does not know what type of work he would be most interested in because he is not sufficiently familiar with various types of work. Business interest tests, such as the Cardall Scale, measure an individual's basic interests by sampling a number of activities that represent different kinds of jobs. Such a test gives a reasonably accurate indication of the individual's basic interest in various jobs even though he is not familiar with the details of the job in question.

Much remains to be done in the fields of personality and interest tests. A serious obstacle in the way of both of these tests is the employee who does not want to be measured, or who wants to be falsely measured, and who may not, therefore, give useful test results. Certainly this difficulty is a much greater obstacle to personality and interest measurement than to the measurement of intelligence, dexterity, or trade achievement. An employee whose mental ability is such that he is able to answer correctly only ten problem questions out of fifty questions asked is utterly unable to answer twenty or thirty of the questions in

[15] A. J. Cardall, Primary Business Interests Test (Science Research Associates, Chicago, 1941).

order to give the false impression that he has more mental ability than he really has. The test itself sets the limit of his performance; and while he may have more ability than is shown on the test (because of being ill or otherwise indisposed when the test was taken), we can safely assume that he does not have less ability. But in the measurement of both personality and interest it is necessary to be sure, before the test is administered, that the employee himself has been convinced that sincerity and truthfulness in answering the questions will operate to his own eventual advantage in helping the employment manager place him where he is most likely to achieve success. Unless the situation is such that the employee can be so convinced, it is seldom wise to place too much confidence in the results of the personality and interest tests that are now available.

6

Visual Problems of Industry

PRACTICALLY every industrial job requires some degree of vision, and many jobs require a high degree of skill in some particular visual function. The inspector of small parts for "appearance" must have keen vision at close distances. The operator of certain knitting and other textile machines must not only have keen vision at close distances but also must be able to maintain such vision for long periods of time with only occasional interruption. The truck driver, crane operator, and signal man must have keen vision for greater distances and good perception of space relationships. Color discrimination is of importance to an employee wiring a radio (because he must discriminate between wires of different color), to the operator of a color-printing press, to the pipefitter tracing a color code through the plumbing system of a plant, and to the operator of mobile equipment who must depend upon colored signals to determine whether roads are open or pathways clear. Various measurable visual characteristics have been found to be related to successful performance on certain jobs—even on jobs in which these visual factors could not be inferred from ordinary job analysis procedures.

Measurement of Vision

Management in productive industries has long recognized the importance of vision in employees. Some form of vision test, administered either in the employment office or as a part of the medical examination, is perhaps more common in industry than is any other form of employee test. It is important for the industrial psychologist to know the various purposes and points of view that are represented in existing visual programs in industry so that he may relate his own work to the activities already under way.

Measurement for compensation purposes

Certain minimum visual requirements have seemed desirable if employees are to move safely around a plant or simply to and from their work stations. Underwriters of industrial accident and compensation insurance have recommended, and industries have widely adopted, certain minimum standards of vision *for new employees* on the basis of the best professional opinion available, expecting that the adoption of such standards would result in a reduction of accidents and insurance costs. Visual tests given at the time of employment for purposes relating to compensation insurance serve not only as an aid in classification of employees on the basis of suspected accident liability but also are useful in compensation cases when it is important to know whether a condition of visual deficiency was caused by injury or disaster on the job during an employee's period of service, or whether that condition was present when he was first employed. Several different aspects of visual function have been proposed [1] for appraisal in determining relative loss of competence for earning a living due to visual disaster; but in common practice, such consideration is frequently limited to a single visual factor. Usually this factor is the ability, measured separately for each eye, to discriminate detail at a standard distance.

Purposes relating to accident compensation are often accomplished satisfactorily by simple standardized methods of testing. A widely used test for these purposes is the Snellen letter chart, which consists of several rows of block letters of decreasing size, usually placed at a distance of twenty feet from the subject. A typical Snellen chart is shown in Figure 42. The test is administered by determining, separately for each eye, the smallest letters that the subject can read.

Letters with a uniform size of parts and details, so that at the testing distance these details subtend angles of one minute of arc, are accepted as the minimum readable size of letters for a "standard eye." The values attached to the different sizes on a chart represent the distances at which the "standard eye" can read these letters of various sizes. The larger the letters at twenty feet that are necessary for readability, the poorer the

[1] "Report of the Committee on Compensation for Eye Injuries: Appraisal of Loss of Visual Efficiency" (*American Medical Association*, Atlantic City, N. J., May 26, 1925).

visual acuity. The Snellen notation of acuity scores is in the form of a fraction—the smaller the fraction, the poorer the vision. In this fraction the numerator is constant and represents the distance of the test, and the denominator represents the pro-

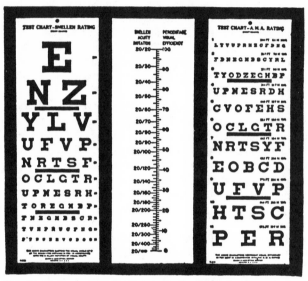

Fig. 42—Snellen and "A.M.A." test charts with scale for converting Snellen scores to per cent of visual efficiency.

portionate size (or "standard" distance) of the smallest letter that an individual subject can read with one eye at the testing distance. Thus visual acuity scored 20/20 is standard. A score of 20/40 means that the subject, with one eye, can read at twenty feet what the "standard eye" can read at forty feet. Scores are usually obtained separately for right eye, left eye, and both eyes together. Scores below 20/20 (smaller fractions) represent substandard visual acuity at a distance of twenty feet, and may range even lower than 20/200, which is usually considered the equivalent of blindness from the standpoint of industrial opportunity. Similarly, scores above 20/20 represent above-standard visual acuity and may range as high as 20/10. Average acuity for different groups of employees frequently will be above the standard 20/20, although too few test levels are provided on the chart for adequate classification in the range of standard and superior acuity.

The Snellen acuity designations are not intended to represent fractions of useful vision. It might appear that the employee who scores 20/40 at a distance of twenty feet can see only half as well as an employee who scores 20/20 at the same distance. As a matter of fact, he may see equally well *if he is only half as far away,* and at other test distances he may be able to score just as high. He is certainly not handicapped 50 per cent in opportunity to earn a living. In order to simplify interpretation of visual acuity scores and to set up an equitable scale for awarding compensation in proportion to actual incapacity due to eye injury, the American Medical Association has adopted [2] and recommended for use in industry a percentage system of acuity notation, with the distinguishing title of "Visual Efficiency." [3] Where the Snellen test measures acuity in terms of an actual minimum visual angle, the American Medical Association notation interprets this angle in terms of percentage of visual efficiency. The difference between this percentage and 100 per cent is the percentage "loss of vision." A conversion scale for translating acuity scores into the percentage notation is shown in Figure 42. A letter test chart that measures visual angles in steps directly equivalent to intervals of 5 per cent on the American Medical Association scale is also shown in Figure 42.

The American Medical Association per cent notation is ordinarily not carried above 100 per cent or below 20 per cent, and for compensation purposes in industry no extension of this range is necessary. Acuity above standard is usually considered as only 100 per cent in computing compensation awards; and in the absence of records, 100 per cent acuity is assumed prior to the time of an eye injury. Twenty per cent acuity or less is frequently considered as complete lack of acuity or industrial blindness, and is therefore not measured or classified more precisely. These practices vary in different states, and the industrial relations officer should be familiar with the legal practices in his state regarding compensation for injury in industry.[4] In the upper

---

[2] *Ibid.*

[3] Albert C. Snell and Scott Sterling, "The Percentage Evaluation of Macular Vision," *Archives of Ophthalmology,* LIV (1925), pp. 443–461.

[4] See A. C. Snell, *Medicolegal Ophthalmology* (C. V. Mosby Company, St. Louis, 1940).

range of acuity scores (standard or above) adequate segregation of differences in acuity is not possible with these letter charts, since the common Snellen chart provides only two or three test levels above standard and the percentage chart provides none. It is in this range that the great bulk of acuity scores fall. Other limitations of the Snellen letter test have been pointed out,[5] and nonliterate test charts have been developed. These charts eliminate letters and require the subject to identify a spatial pattern, such as a broken ring that may have its open area at the top, bottom, right, or left. In spite of the limitations of both the Snellen and American Medical Association charts, these tests have furnished industry with a convenient and satisfactory basis for segregating and classifying cases of substandard acuity.

In using either a Snellen or an American Medical Association letter test chart, or in accepting the results of such a test, the following points should be kept in mind:

1. It is a legally acceptable means for determining keenness of vision.

2. It is subject to external influences such as illumination, glare, distance, and opportunity to memorize the chart. These influences should be standardized as much as possible.

3. It represents only one aspect of visual performance, namely, keenness of vision at a distance.

4. It measures "readability of letters." This gives the more highly literate employees some advantage. For illiterate employees, a substitute for letters is necessary. Even for literate employees other types of acuity test objects correlate better with successful performance on some jobs.

5. It measures acuity at a standard distance. For many jobs requiring close vision, acuity must be measured at close distances. In large unselected groups the correlation between acuity scores at different distances may be very low if not actually zero (see page 150).

6. Standard acuity of 20/20 is not an average or a norm in the statistical sense; it represents satisfactory acuity in the legal and in the clinical sense.

7. It adequately differentiates only substandard levels of acuity; at standard and superior levels it differentiates only grossly.

[5] C. E. Ferree and G. Rand, "A New Method of Rating Visual Acuity," *Journal of General Psychology,* XXV (1941), pp. 143–176.

8. Its reliability and validity have not been established statistically. The average difference in readability of different letters of the same size has been shown by item analysis, but since these differences vary among individuals, no standard correction for them has been made.

9. In order to get valid measures of means and standard deviations of acuity scores on these scales, it is necessary to convert all scores to their equivalents on an acuity scale that yields an approximately normal distribution. The reciprocals of minimum visual angles in minutes of arc, converted to decimals, comprise such a scale and are used for acuity studies summarized in this chapter. Values on this scale do not represent fractional parts of useful vision any more than do Snellen values. The acuity levels of a typical letter chart are spaced unequally on such a scale.

Measurement for employment

Minimum visual requirements for employment have been increasing in prevalence and comprehensiveness, along with more stringent government standards for license to operate public or private automobiles and airplanes. Often these standards vary from job to job. In the commercial aviation industry, vision standards are comprehensive, severe, and selective for pilots and employees on certain other jobs. The standards are enforced rigorously not only at the time of initial employment but also throughout the entire period of service of these employees. Rigorous enforcement of visual standards has long been a practice among railroads for their trainmen and is rapidly being adopted for drivers of commercial transport trucks and busses. In these industries, the "common carriers," minimum visual and other physical standards are set and enforced by government regulation.

Measurement of vision for this purpose is usually satisfactory with simple "screening tests," which measure performance at the lower levels of ability and "screen out" those who score below some set level. The Snellen test is used widely for this purpose. The Keystone Visual Safety Tests* are a battery of such screening tests adapted from a battery for visual screening among school children. The limitations of screening tests in industry,

---

* The Keystone View Company, Meadville, Pennsylvania.

which will be pointed out later, prevent them from being very useful for other industrial purposes, such as job analysis studies and careful placement of employees.

A reaction has been voiced [7] against visual screening tests and enforcement of minimum visual standards for employment in productive industry. Some workers with substandard vision, especially experienced workers, may be valuable employees on certain jobs if proper precautions are taken for their safety and transportation. Successful attempts to fit seriously handicapped workers into some types of productive jobs in industry have been reported through the Society for the Prevention of Blindness.[8] During periods of emergency production it is necessary to find some job for every possible worker, and even during periods of normal production it is not advisable to segregate a large group to whom employment is denied because of their uncorrectable visual deficiencies. This is especially true if the standards have been set arbitrarily without adequate evidence of the importance of such visual characteristics in industry.

Instances have been found in which arbitrary minimum standards of vision have not only failed to select the better potential employees but actually selected the poorer ones (see page 140). Such standards also deprive an industry of some of the skillful and experienced workmen who apply for jobs. Even when a correlation exists between visual performance and efficiency on a certain job, it should not be assumed that all applicants who have just barely more than a standard amount of that characteristic will be more successful on the job than all applicants who have barely less than the standard amount. The principle of employee placement in such circumstances is that, other factors being equal or unknown, employees with relatively greater amounts of a certain characteristic are more likely to succeed than others. However, since an employment office often has a limited number of applicants, the standards for employment on any job must be flexible. Moreover, those who are not hired for some specific job may be entirely satisfactory if hired for some other job that has different visual requirements.

[7] A. C. Snell, "Subnormal Vision and Occupational Aptitude," *New York State Journal of Medicine*, XLI (1941), pp. 1165–1171.

[8] E. B. Merrill, *Occupational Adjustment of the Visually Handicapped*. Publication No. 212 (National Society for the Prevention of Blindness, 1936).

Measurement for placement

For purposes *of allocating employees to specific jobs* after they have passed all minimum requirements, and of selecting employees to whom costly training will be offered, it has been found most important to differentiate carefully among levels of visual performance higher than any minimum standard. This differentiation should consider not only visual acuity but also several other measurable visual functions and aspects of visual performance or visual aptitude that have been found related to safety, successful job performance, tenure, or other criteria of employee desirability. Such placement procedures must be based on the principle of the "selection ratio" (discussed in Chapter 2) in terms of the number of employees available for placement, rather than on invariable standards. And in order to take advantage of this principle, it is necessary to use visual measures that differentiate adequately among levels of performance at both ends of the range. It must be possible, with reasonable precision, to segregate any desired percentage of employees at either end of an acuity scale or any other measure of vision. This necessitates a type of test different from simple screening tests and yet also different from highly technical and diagnostic clinical tests.

The investigations reported in this chapter have clearly indicated the need for adequate visual classification and placement tests *specifically adapted to industrial purposes and conditions.* These investigations in many types of industry have indicated certain aspects of visual performance as being of most general importance for classifying and placing employees according to differences in visual characteristics.

1. *Keenness of vision (visual acuity) at appropriate distances* —usually tested at twenty feet and thirteen or sixteen inches. This visual function is the ability to discriminate black and white detail, measured in terms of the minimum separable areas that can be distinguished. For industrial placement such a test should be equally valid for illiterate and literate subjects and should avoid the complications introduced by a factor involving discrimination and recognition of different shapes, such as letters. The scale should make it possible to classify acuity scores adequately at either end of the range. Separate scores should be

recorded at least for both eyes together and the worse eye alone. Since acuity is modified by brightness, glare, and other external conditions, the acuity test must be given under controlled and standard conditions.

2. *Discrimination of differences in distance (depth perception, or stereopsis).* This function is an important phase of correct perception of spatial relationships. Of several cues for judging relative distances of objects, the most important for normal two-eyed persons, and the one that can be controlled and measured most reliably, depends on the slight difference in the position of the two eyes. The two eyes perform a geometric triangulation upon a distant object, and the distance of that object is perceived through an integration of the minute differences in appearance of the object to the two eyes. Other cues for perceiving distance in the third dimension may augment but cannot adequately substitute for this cue from two-eye functioning. Stereopsis is measurable quantitatively like any other human function and should be so measured for employee placement.

3. *Discrimination of differences in color.* Accurate color discrimination is important on some jobs, and it may also reflect certain aspects of health that are important for adequate performance on many jobs. The particular colors to be differentiated should include as many combinations as there are factors in color sensitivity. The most important combinations are those that represent common colors in signal lights. In order to read such signals correctly, it is important not only that an employee should be able to differentiate between them but also that he should be able to identify and interpret correctly the meaning of each color. Any test of color vision can and should be scaled for quantitative measurement and classification of employees.

4. *Postural characteristics of the eyes (phorias) at appropriate distances*—usually twenty feet and thirteen or sixteen inches. Under certain testing conditions, which eliminate the necessity for the eyes to converge on a single point, the eyes assume a posture that may converge or diverge from that required in normal seeing at the test distance. Such postures (called "phorias" in clinical terminology) are measured in terms of angular deviation from the posture normally required for that distance. The deviation may be lateral or vertical and is measured separately in each direction. The explanation of this phenomenon has not

been determined finally; nevertheless such characteristics should
be measured because they are related to performance on certain
industrial jobs. Such measurement must be done with adequate
control and standardization of the several factors that may mod-

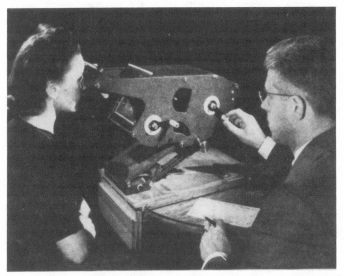

Fig. 43—The Ortho-Rater: a device for the visual classification and placement of
industrial employees.

ify the measurement, such as the distance and focus requirement
of the test.

These are not, of course, the only visual functions that are of
importance in all industries, but they comprise a reasonable
minimum for a program of testing applicants and employees.
These tests have been adapted satisfactorily for simple and rapid
use in industry, and they are the ones most widely recommended
by leaders in industrial ophthalmology [9] for use in industry.

The Bausch and Lomb Visual Classification and Placement
Tests for Industry [10] are the first battery of vision tests to be
constructed on the basis of specifications derived from extensive

[9] Hedwig S. Kuhn, *A New Concept of Visual Performance in Industry.* Publication No. 340 (National Society for the Prevention of Blindness, 1940).

A. C. Snell, "The Field of Industrial Ophthalmology," American Medical Association, Section of Industrial Health (Chicago, Jan. 13, 1942).

[10] The Bausch and Lomb Optical Company, Rochester, N. Y.

investigations among industrial employees in industrial situations. These tests cover the visual functions described above and, for maximum speed and convenience in testing, are incorporated in a single instrument, shown in Figure 43. This instrument, called the Ortho-Rater, is a precision stereoscope of relatively long focal length that permits adequate and separate control of test stimuli for each eye. Tests are given at optical equivalents of twenty feet and thirteen inches. Stereoscopic methods of vision testing have been used since the late nineteenth century and were early described by Wells.[11] The statistical data upon which these tests are based, together with the results of validating studies, will be published in monograph form.

Individual differences in vision

Employees and applicants differ just as markedly in visual characteristics when they are adequately measured as in any

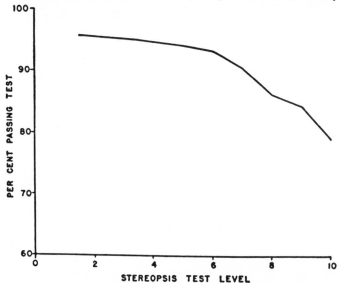

Fig. 44—Per cents of employees passing a test of depth perception at different levels of difficulty. Curve based on 6964 employees.

[11] David Wells, *The Stereoscope in Ophthalmology*, second edition (Globe Optical Company, 1918).

other characteristics, and these differences correlate in many respects with differences in job performance. Differences in visual acuity have already been mentioned (page 13). Figure 44 shows differences in the percentage of 6964 employees in a steel mill who were able to pass various levels of a simple screening test of depth perception. Passing percentages range from 96 per cent on the easiest level to 79 per cent on the most difficult. It is impossible with such a test to discriminate among the best 79 per cent of these employees with respect to depth perception. Figure 45 shows differences in percentage of 7153 employees who

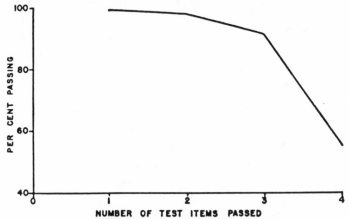

Fig. 45—Per cents of employees passing a test of red-green discrimination at different levels of difficulty. Curve based on 7153 employees.

passed different levels of a screening test of red-green color discrimination. The passing percentage ranges from 99 per cent at the easiest level to 55 per cent at the most difficult level. The two easiest levels are of practically the same difficulty and the most difficult level did not differentiate among the best 55 per cent of employees. Each of these functions varies in degree among different employees and can be measured on a continuum with the proper steps or intervals.

All of the visual functions proposed above for use in industry can be measured quantitatively, and should be so measured to give the most satisfactory results in employee placement. Screening tests indicate relationships between vision and job performance, but are not adequate for placement of employees according to the *amount* of any visual skill that they possess.

Vision and Job Proficiency

The importance of vision in industry can be satisfactorily demonstrated only in relation to acceptable industrial criteria, such as hourly production, proportion of work rejected for defective workmanship, supervisors' ratings of employees, employee absences, rate of labor turnover, or some other measurable aspect of employee value to the company. The visual characteristics that correlate with these industrial criteria differ from job to job and cannot consistently be predicted without correlational evidence.

Vision on fine assembly work

Different visual characteristics will vary in their relative importance on different small assembly operations; and on any one

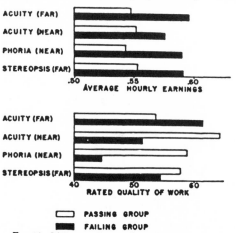

Fig. 46—Differences in quantity and quality of work among 33 employees, of equal experience on a job of electrical assembly, who passed or failed four vision tests.

operation visual characteristics will vary in importance with respect to different industrial criteria, such as quantity and quality of work. Such a situation is illustrated in a job in assembly of small electrical parts. Figure 46 shows the differences in quantity and quality of work for employees of equal experience who passed or failed at certain levels on each of a battery of visual tests. Each white bar represents the passing and the adjacent black bar the failing group on each visual test. The length of bar in the upper part of the figure shows the average production of the employees in the "passing" and "failing" groups on each vision test. Those who failed on the vision tests produced more, as shown by the relatively longer black bars, than those who passed these tests. Supervisors' ratings on quality of work showed a different relation with visual performance on most of these tests. In the lower part of the figure the length of each bar represents the supervisors' ratings on quality of work of these same groups of employees: a white bar for the group who passed each test and a black bar for the group who failed. Those who passed, except on distance acuity, did better work.

A reasonable conclusion from this contrast in evidence of the two criteria is that employees with more critical near vision had a more critical concept of standards for this job. They observed and corrected their own mistakes more frequently, and therefore slowed down their production more than those with less critical vision. Whether speed or accuracy of work is to be the primary criterion for placing employees on such jobs is a matter of company policy, as discussed on page 95.

Vision for inspection

Visual operations in inspection for size and other physical standards can often be reduced to problems of reading gauges and meters; but inspection for appearance is primarily a matter of vision and training. For a study of the relation between vision and accuracy of inspection, 150 tin plate inspectors were tested on a battery of visual screening tests and classified in three groups according to the number of tests they passed. A complete summary of this work will be given in Chapter 10, but it should be mentioned here that a definite relation between the vision of these employees and the accuracy of their inspection was revealed. Figure 47 shows the percentage of accuracy of inspection for three groups of employees (A, B, and C) on four types of defective tin plate. Employees in Group A passed most vision tests; those in Group B passed some; and those in Group C passed fewest. It will be observed that as we go from the group with good vision to the group with poor vision, the accuracy for the various types of defect usually tends to become progressively poorer. The one marked exception to this rule occurred in the detection of weight defects. Among the inspectors studied,

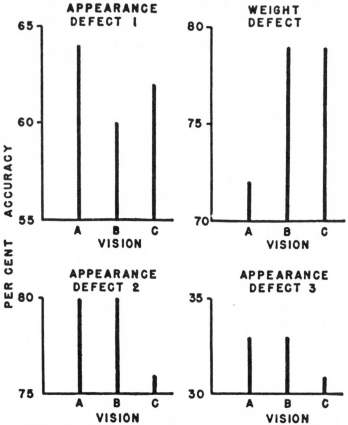

Fig. 47—Accuracy of inspectors with good vision (A), average vision (B), and poor vision (C) in spotting four types of defective tin plate. Results based on 150 inspectors.

those with poor vision were more accurate in spotting this particular defect than were those with good vision. Perhaps this may be explained by the fact that this group has compensated for a handicap in one respect (visual) by developing greater than average skill for another aspect of the job where vision is not essential.

Vision in clerical work

The relationship between vision and one type of clerical work is indicated in Table XIII, which gives average hourly production and average hourly errors for 23 clerks classified as "passing" or "failing" on each of a series of visual screening tests. No consistent relation was apparent from these tests between vision and quantity of production, but those who failed made more errors on the average than those who passed. On the two tests (phoria, far and near) that showed a negative relationship with production, the standards for passing were not appropriate for selecting clerks with respect to production on this job.

TABLE XIII

AVERAGE PRODUCTION AND AVERAGE ERRORS OF CLERKS WHO PASSED AND FAILED FOUR VISION TESTS

TEST	AVERAGE HOURLY PRODUCTION		AVERAGE HOURLY ERRORS	
	Passing test	Failing test	Passing test	Failing test
Acuity, far..............................	69.8	64.8	.27	.40
Depth perception......................	68.7	68.0	.30	.33
Phoria, far............................	63.3	74.9*	.26	.37
Phoria, near..........................	65.8	74.6*	.22	.51

* Reversals in the data.

Vision for looping hosiery

The looping operation, which accounts for about 20 per cent of the total labor cost in the manufacture of cheaper types of hosiery, requires continuous critical vision at an average working distance of eight inches from the eyes. The relationship between visual discrimination at a distance of twenty feet and production for 199 operators on this job is shown in Figure 48. Keener vision is plotted to the right on this chart and higher production at the top. Operators with poorer vision were quite consistently better producers. This discrepancy can be explained by the extreme difference between testing distance (twenty feet) and working distance (eight inches). Those operators who were visually best adapted to the job were not adaptable to demands for distance discrimination. At a distance of thirteen inches all of these operators had such keen

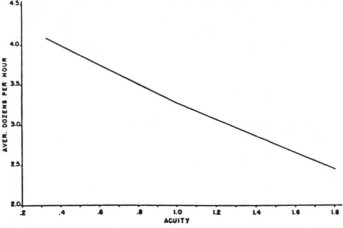

Fig. 48—Relation between distance acuity test scores and production of 199 hosiery loopers.

vision that a simple test failed to differentiate among them. In selecting operators for this job (and also on some other jobs requiring very close vision) a distance acuity test selects poorer operators and rejects many of the better ones. It would not be wise, however, to allocate to such jobs only those who failed the distance test, because keen discrimination and other visual characteristics *for nearer distances* are important qualifications. The relationship between one such characteristic, focus posture tendency, and production in looping is graphed in Figure 49. The focus posture test [12] measured the tendency of these operators to focus closer or farther away than a test stimulus at sixteen inches. Tendencies to focus closer are plotted to the left and tendencies to focus farther away are plotted to the right. Operators who tended to focus closer showed higher average production.

---

[12] The test used was adapted from the fused cross cylinder test described by S. K. Lesser, *An Introduction to Modern Analytical Optometry*, revised edition (Optometric Extension Program, Duncan, Okla., 1937).

These results indicate that the selection and placement of employees on close vision jobs of this type can best be made by means of vision tests that measure how well the employees' vision is adapted *to the job.* Adequate placement cannot be ac-

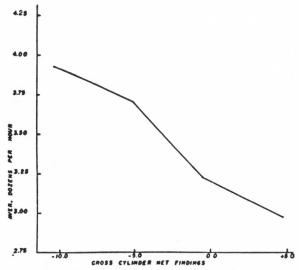

Fig. 49—Relation between fused cross cylinder test scores and production of 103 experienced hosiery loopers.

complished by means of a single acuity test given at 20 feet. Indeed, the use of such a test for employees on this type of work may result more often than not in placing the *least* adapted employees on the job.

Vision in miscellaneous jobs

On one group of over 6000 steel workers, unclassified as to job, vision tests were related to supervisors' ratings of the employees. The employees, who had been rated on a uniform rating scale, were classified according to these ratings into high, low, and middle thirds. The percentages of employees in the high and low thirds—according to the ratings—who passed different tests of vision are given in Table XIV. Such a gross classification does not show all of the relationships that exist between certain visual characteristics and success on particular jobs; but the fact that some relationships can be demonstrated in such a miscellaneous group of employees with such crude criteria indicates the general importance of visual factors in determining employee efficiency.

TABLE XIV

PERCENTAGES OF MISCELLANEOUS EMPLOYEES IN HIGH AND LOW RATED GROUPS WHO PASSED TESTS OF VISION

The high rated group included 2045 employees; the low rated group included 2096 employees

| TEST | PERCENTAGE PASSING VISION TESTS | | |
	High Rated Group	Low Rated Group	Ratio
Acuity, far	94.2	93.3	1.010
Acuity, near	64.6	56.8	1.137
Color vision	59.3	48.0	1.235
Depth perception	81.8	77.6	1.054

Vision and accidents

An area in industrial problems of vision that has frequently dominated all other considerations is protection for the eyes of workmen. Injuries to the eyes of workmen are one of the most common types of injury in industry. In one large steel mill, minor eye injuries accounted for 18.8 per cent of all minor injuries. A proportion of eye injuries as large as this is not uncommon in other industries, and the total economic loss from such accidents is tremendous. Extensive programs of visual safety have been developed in many large industries. Eye injuries, besides being costly, impair the visual proficiency of plant personnel; and therefore visual safety has merited the vigorous attention it is now receiving.[13]

A more subtle problem of accident prevention is the preventing of injuries caused by faulty vision. The relation between vision and accidents has been established by statistical research on automobile drivers.[14] In industry these relations are often ob-

[13] L. Resnick, Eye Hazards in Industry, Extent, Cause, and Means of Prevention (National Society for the Prevention of Blindness, 1941).

[14] E. D. Fletcher, "Capacity of Special Tests to Measure Driving Ability," Preliminary Report on Special Tests, Part I (State of California, Department of Motor Vehicles, Division of Drivers Licenses, 1939).

scured by lack of adequate data from accident reports.[15]   Such reports are concerned primarily with the employee or employees who were injured, whereas the defective vision of someone else may have been responsible for the accident.   In spite of this possible uncontrolled factor, a recent investigation indicates a relationship between poor vision and accident experience. Table XV shows the percentage of employees who sustained lost-time accidents over a two-year period in a group of several thousand steel mill employees unclassified as to job but segregated according to whether they passed or failed several vision tests.   Those who failed had more accidents on the average than those who passed, except on the test of color vision.   Such figures, however, need to be determined separately for each job in order to eliminate differences in factors of job hazard and job standards of vision that affect the total result.

TABLE XV

PERCENTAGE OF EMPLOYEES PASSING AND FAILING ON TESTS OF VISION WHO HAD SUSTAINED LOST-TIME ACCIDENTS

TEST	PERCENTAGE OF LOST-TIME ACCIDENTS		
	Passing Test	Failing Test	Ratio
Acuity, far..........................	1.09	1.37	1.26
Depth perception...................	1.23	1.57	1.28
Color vision	1.21	1.14	.94 *
Phoria............................	1.26	1.82	1.44

* Inversion in the data.

For this same unclassified group of employees the relationship between scores on a distance phoria test (in units of deviation from the mean) and serious accidents (home cases and lost-time cases) is graphed in Figure 50.   Employees showing a tendency to *converge* their eyes more than normal had experienced significantly more than the average number of serious accidents, while employees with a tendency to *diverge* their eyes more than normal had experienced fewer than the average number of serious accidents.   While it is possible that these relationships are due to a third common factor such as age (since both con-

15 P. W. Cobb, "The Limit of Usefulness of Accident Rate as a Measure of Accident Proneness," *Journal of Applied Psychology*, XXIV (1940), pp. 154–159.

vergence tendency and accident frequency decrease with age),
these results suggest that it may be possible to identify some
of the most accident-prone employees by means of vision tests.
For proper evaluation of the relation between vision and

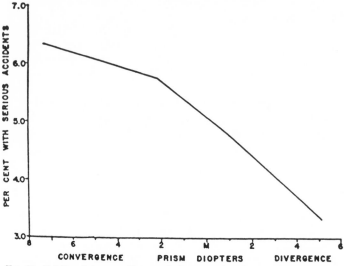

Fig. 50—Relation between a distance phoria test and serious accidents, based on
440 accident cases covering two years.

accidents, however, it will be necessary to have visual data not
only on the employee who was injured but also on all other
employees who were in any way associated with the accident.

Ocular service and job performance

Some visual requirements on some jobs may be such that
only a small proportion of employees can ever perform the jobs
satisfactorily; but on most jobs the visual characteristics that
correlate with successful job performance are those of normal,
healthy, and active eyes. (This, however, is not true for jobs
like looping hosiery.) Individual shortcomings and anomalies
of vision, rather than some of the universal limitations of human
vision, account for much of the lack of visual aptitude among
employees. Many of these anomalies can be compensated or
corrected by means of adequate professional eye care, and

employees who have received such care are more likely to have satisfactory vision for ordinary jobs. The most convenient criterion, though by no means a perfect one, for classifying employees according to whether they have received ocular services is whether they use eyeglasses. Figure 51 shows, for

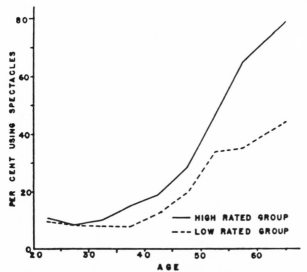

Fig. 51—A comparison of the use of spectacles for general wear by employees who had been rated by their supervisors as high and low in job performance. Curve based on 7171 employees.

over 6000 employees in a steel mill, the differences in percentage among employees using spectacles for general wear who had been rated high and low in job performance by their supervisors. Figure 52 shows similar differences in percentage of employees in high- and low-rated groups who wore spectacles or had "reading glasses" in their pockets for near vision. The percentages are plotted separately for various ages. Glasses, either for general use or for close vision only, are more common among employees rated high than among those rated low. Glasses of both types are used by more employees in the older age groups, particularly over the age of fifty.

Figure 53 shows differences in acuity between employees who do and do not use spectacles for distance or general vision.

Below the age of fifty those wearing spectacles have lower average acuity than those who do not use spectacles. Probably those in this age range who are using glasses are the ones who most need them to bring acuity up to average, and those who do with-

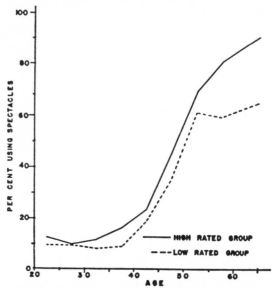

Fig. 52—A comparison of the use of spectacles for near vision by employees who had been rated by their supervisors as high and low in job performance. Curve based on 7171 employees.

out glasses most frequently have average or superior acuity. After the age of fifty, however, those who are already accustomed to spectacles maintain their vision by occasional change of glasses, but those who have done without spectacles suffer considerable loss before they obtain help.

A test of near vision on employees over thirty-five years of age shows striking differences in average performance for groups of employees who do and do not use spectacles. Among those wearing glasses for general use (including bifocals), 77 per cent passed the near-vision test. Among those who did not use glasses on the job, 60 per cent passed; and among those who carried "reading glasses," only 25 per cent passed *with the aid of their glasses*. Many of these reading glasses were ready-made

spectacles bought "over a counter" without adequate professional services and others were obsolete. About a third of the
employees in this group volunteered the information that they
had "good glasses" at home but did not bring them to work for

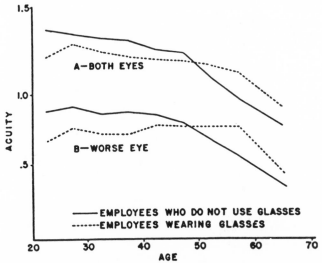

FIG. 53—Differences in acuity between employees who do and do not use spectacles.

fear of breaking them. It is highly significant that these "reading glasses," bought for the specific purpose of obtaining clear
vision at near distances and worn "in the pocket" for such occasions, were actually inadequate for this purpose in 75 per cent
of the cases. This is evidence that professional eye care, not
simply the purchase of spectacles, is important for better performance of industrial employees.

Changes in Vision With Age and Job Experience

Visual standards applied in the initial placement of employees
do not guarantee continued high levels of visual performance.
At least one change in vision with age is common knowledge—
the change that makes it necessary for older persons to use extra
lens power to see clearly at close distances. Recent research has
increased our knowledge of the significance of this change in maturity and has revealed several other changes that occur with

increasing age and that often affect an employee's job performance. Indirect evidence of these changes appeared in Figures
51 and 52, which showed the increase with age in percentage of
employees who used spectacles not only for near seeing but also
for distance or general use.

Distance acuity and age

The distribution of distance visual acuity scores shown in
Figure 10 on page 13 was constructed from data obtained in a

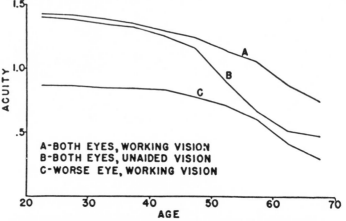

FIG. 54—Changes in distance acuity with age. Curves based on 7332 employees.

survey of a plant that had been using a minimum standard of
acuity for employment. After a few years on the job, this retest
of employees showed very nearly the same distribution of acuity
scores as would be found in an unselected group of applicants.
Probably at least one cause of this is the decrease of distance
acuity that occurs with increasing age.

Changes in distance acuity with age among more than 7000
employees in a steel mill are shown in Figure 54. This graph
shows the change in average acuity with age in each of three
measures of acuity: (1) both eyes, with glasses if customarily
worn; (2) both eyes, unaided vision; and (3) worse eye, with
glasses if customarily worn. The average loss of acuity with age
in each of these measures is consistent and significant, especially
after the age of forty. Figure 55 shows for one of these measures

("1" above) the changes in the spread or variability of acuity scores with age. The upper and lower lines in Figure 55 embrace 25 per cent of the acuity scores above and 25 per cent below the median for each age group. The distance between the upper and lower lines includes the middle 50 per cent of all scores.

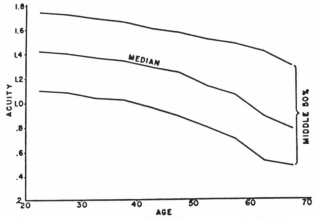

FIG. 55—Changes in range of acuity with age. Curves based on 7332 employees.

The spread of acuity scores changes very little with age. This means that loss of acuity with age is practically universal.

Near acuity and age

Changes in near acuity, at an optical distance of sixteen inches, are a more complex function of age, as shown in Figure 56. The curve in this graph represents the percentage of employees in this same group at different age levels above the age of thirty-five who passed a simple visual discrimination test at this distance with the aid of any glasses they wore or carried with them. Figure 56 shows that this loss is already affecting a significant proportion of employees at the age of thirty-five and that for the group as a whole this loss is not arrested (by means of spectacles) until the age of fifty, is not well compensated until the age of sixty, and not fully compensated at any age. The group of employees between the ages of forty and fifty-five, where the loss is greatest, includes the majority of specialists and tradesmen, supervisors, and other key men in industry whose functions involve reading blueprints, instructions, and reports, and directing others. The seriousness of this situation among building tradesmen and an estimate of its annual cost have been reported for one community by Carroll.[16]

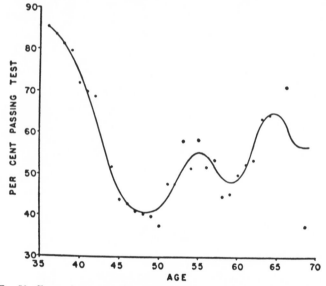

Fig. 56—Changes in per cent of employees passing a near acuity test with increasing age. Curve based on 3351 employees.

A comparison of the curves in Figures 54 and 56 raises the question as to whether acuity scores for different distances show any correlation. From the data gathered in a survey, the correlation between acuity at 20 feet and at 16 inches was computed for 2653 employees above the age of forty and was found to be zero. The corresponding correlation for 859 employees between the ages of thirty-five and thirty-nine was also found to be zero. The general conclusion in the light of these correlations is that one cannot select the best-adapted employees for a sixteen-inch work distance by using an acuity test given at 20

---

[16] Francis E. Carroll, "Defective Eyesight in the Building Industry," *The Bausch and Lomb Magazine*, XVI, No. 3 (1940), pp. 19–23.

feet. Acuity must be measured at a distance comparable to the expected working distance.

Color discrimination and age

Color vision also diminishes with age, as shown in Figure 57. This graph shows the percentage of employees at different ages who passed a simple test of red-green discrimination. This per-

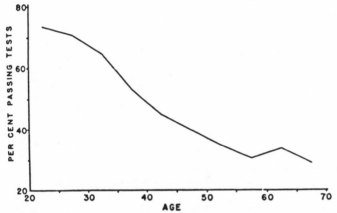

FIG. 57—Changes in per cent of employees passing a red-green discrimination test with increasing age. Curve based on 7141 employees.

centage varies in the ratio of approximately two to one from the age of twenty to the age of sixty. Since poor color vision is ordinarily believed not to be amenable to correction or compensation, it is important that employees selected for training and service on jobs requiring color discrimination should have a very high initial amount of color discrimination ability. It was shown on page 135 that color vision is a matter of degree and can be classified on a continuous scale from best to poorest.

Depth perception and age

Figure 58 shows changes in the percentage of employees at different ages who passed the most difficult level of a very simple test of depth perception. The early rise in this curve reflects an increase in average ability to discriminate distances up to the age of thirty to thirty-five. A possible explanation of this increase [17] is that the experience of workers in certain activities requiring a perception of depth, or the third dimension, may improve this function. This explanation implies that increased ability to perceive depth may be accelerated by specific training.

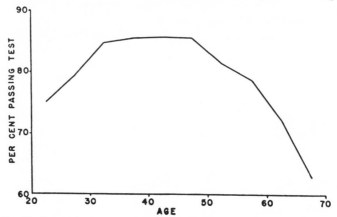

Fig. 58—Changes in per cent of employees passing a test of stereopsis (depth perception) with increasing age. Curve based on 8412 employees.

Changes in vision with job experience

Experience on a particular job often tends to develop in employees some of the visual characteristics that are desirable on the job and some that may not be desirable. These changes may be in the same direction as the changes with age or in the opposite direction. Loopers in hosiery mills tend to develop exceptional amplitude in focus range for very near objects and to maintain this facility in spite of the general tendency to lose it with increasing age. Exceptional visual performance that characterizes experienced employees on a particular job is in part the result of practice and incidental training on the job and in part the result of a selection process, entirely apart from any formal selection with respect to vision. Those employees who have or can easily develop the desirable qualifications for the job tend to remain on the job and accumulate experience. Those who do not have or cannot easily develop these qualifications tend to

[17] This explanation was proposed independently by Dr. A. C. Snell of Rochester, New York, and Dr. Hedwig S. Kuhn of Hammond, Indiana.

drop out or to be transferred to other jobs before they acquire much experience. Consequently, the relationship between visual characteristics and experience is augmented by this selection process that operates in the same general direction as experience. The results of such selective and adaptive processes have been investigated for jobs requiring close vision.[18]

Experience in looping hosiery

The first year of looping hosiery is a period during which marked changes in visual characteristics occur. Figure 59 shows

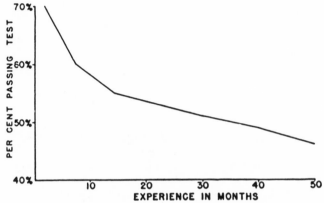

FIG. 59—Changes in distance acuity with increasing experience on the job of looping hosiery. Curve based on 206 hosiery loopers.

the relation between experience and distance acuity for 206 loopers. Distance acuity tends to decrease with experience, and this relation holds whether employees wear corrective spectacles or not. Figure 60 shows the relation between experience and focus posture tendency[19] at sixteen inches for these loopers. Focus tendencies are closer with increasing experience; but with experience greater than that found in this particular group, the age influence may reverse this trend. Experiments in producing these visual characteristics through special occupational eye-

---

[18] W. S. Duke-Elder, "An Investigation Into the Effect Upon the Eyes of Occupations Involving Close Work," *British Journal of Ophthalmology*, XIV (1930), pp. 610–620. Also see M. Luckiesh and F. K. Moss, "Functional Adaptation to Near-Vision," *Journal of Experimental Psychology*, XXVI (1940), pp. 352–356.

[19] See footnote 12, page 140.

glasses, so that the eyes themselves do not have to make an adjustment to the close requirements of this job, will be discussed later.

Determining Job Requirements of Vision

Even when adequate tests are available and are systematically used both with new and old employees, the effective placement

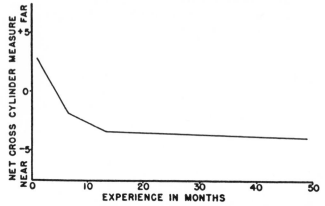

FIG. 60—Changes in near focus posture with increasing experience on the job of looping hosiery. Curve based on 166 hosiery loopers.

of new employees or proper rehabilitation of old employees cannot be accomplished without a thorough knowledge of the visual requirements of different jobs within the plant. Specific visual characteristics desirable for any job cannot always be inferred from traditional job analysis, nor can they always be adequately determined on the basis of opinion, even if the opinion is given by someone thoroughly familiar with the job. Few employment managers, supervisors, industrial engineers, or psychologists, for example, suspected that proficiency in very close work, such as is involved in looping hosiery, would be *inversely related* to scores on a distance acuity test.

Job differences in vision

Visual conditions that characterize employees on several jobs in a sheet and tin mill indicate the effects of experience and informal selection. Formal selection standards for initial employment on these jobs included only acuity and, for some jobs, color vision. But, as shown in discussing age trends, even these differences in vision due to differential selection for initial employment on different jobs are rapidly eliminated by age trends and also by transfer from one job to another. Certain job factors, however, result in training and further selection on the job. Table XVI gives the percentages of employees on different payroll jobs who passed several visual screening tests. This table also shows, for comparison, the percentage of all employees in the plant who passed these tests. Small differences between groups are of no significance, but large differences indicate real variations from the plant average and indicate real job differences. Those figures in Table XVI that differ by a statistically significant amount from the plant average are marked. Every job row and every vision column shows one or more significant differences.

TABLE XVI

PERCENTAGE OF EMPLOYEES ON DIFFERENT JOBS WHO PASSED VARIOUS TESTS OF VISION

Employees	Approximate N	Acuity, Far, Both Eyes	Acuity, Far, Worse Eye	Depth Perception	Color Vision	Phoria, Far	Phoria, Near	Acuity Near
1. Foremen....	320	95.9	77.8	85.1*	66.5*	57.0	63.7	81.4*
2. Clerks......	590	94.1	73.7	79.5	79.2*	63.1	69.4*	88.9*
3. Electricians.	430	94.5	68.4†	86.4*	59.6	57.9	59.6	61.7
4. Machinists..	380	93.7	73.3	92.4*	60.0	60.9	66.2	65.6*
5. Cranemen...	250	97.6*	82.1*	81.9	57.0	61.3	66.2	52.2
6. Hookers....	250	94.7	75.0	81.0	59.1	71.1*	67.9	59.8
7. Laborers....	710	92.3	72.2	74.5†	52.7	62.9	66.0	52.4†
Plant Total....	7000	94.0	73.1	79.2	55.3	61.1	63.6	61.0

* Significantly high. † Significantly low.
Note: These figures are corrected for differences in age on the different job groups.

The specific visual requirements of different jobs can only be determined by careful studies of the relationship existing between vision test results and the employee's actual efficiency on the job. Examples of the determination of visual requirements of different jobs have been discussed in the preceding pages. The data presented are limited to a few typical jobs from a selected group of industries. It would be quite unwise to use the data presented in Table XVI for the determination of visual job requirements in other industries or under different conditions. But the principle that has been followed in the industries studied has given specific evidence that job differences in visual requirements do exist and that it is clearly advantageous both to management and employees to place individuals upon jobs in the light of these job requirements. By applying the same method to other jobs in other industries it is a relatively simple task for an employment manager to determine for his particular plant some of the critical visual skills that are required on various jobs.

If employees on different jobs are drawn from different populations, differences from job to job may be due to differences in the source of the employees. Table XVII shows separately for white men, Negro men, and white women in a large plant the percentages passing a test of distance acuity and a test of red-green color discrimination. The women were best on color vision, the Negro men best on acuity. Since Negroes and women in this plant were only on certain types of jobs, these differences between races and sexes might be mistaken for characteristic job differences. Also differences in age have not been ruled out in this comparison.

TABLE XVII

PERCENTAGE OF NEGRO MEN, WHITE MEN, AND WHITE WOMEN EMPLOYEES PASSING TWO VISION TESTS

EMPLOYEES	PERCENTAGE PASSING TESTS	
	Color Vision	Distance Acuity
White Women............................	74.5	76.0
White Men................................	60.4	76.1
Negro Men................................	40.7	80.7

In this same plant, watchmen and police in the plant protection department showed surprisingly poor scores on many of the vision tests, especially distance acuity. One reason was their average age, which was considerably more than the plant average. Another possible reason was that in the past veteran employees who could no longer be kept on productive jobs were transferred to the plant protection department. These extraneous selective factors will often obscure job differences in vision or create spurious differences unless they are carefully controlled in statistical studies of job differences.

Establishing visual criteria

Some characteristics desirable for operators on certain jobs may be inferred from job analysis or from experienced observation of many operators. Visual characteristics, however, are not ordinarily apparent by observation; they must be measured with adequate instrumentation. Opinion regarding visual requirements and standards for different jobs may be correct, partly correct, or entirely incorrect. The only sound basis for evaluating visual factors is adequate testing. As specific visual characteristics that are demonstrably related to job performance are catalogued for a wide variety of jobs, it becomes more and more feasible to predict the desirable characteristics for some job not yet analyzed. But the problem still remains of testing this prediction and demonstrating the relationship of at least some characteristics to performance on the new job. On many jobs certain desirable visual characteristics have not been correctly inferred from observation by visual experts, and often suspected similarities in visual requirements for different jobs have not been verified by evidence of test results and correlation studies.

The various tests used in determining desirable characteristics may be more elaborate than the battery of tests finally evolved for classification and placement of employees; but ultimately the relation between these characteristics and job performance must be validated and stated *in terms of the same tests that are to be used for classification.*

Any exceptional visual characteristics of all experienced employees on a certain job, in comparison with inexperienced employees on that job or with experienced employees of equal age on other jobs, may be due to job requirements and a natural selection process among employees on that job, as explained on page 152. Such characteristics might, therefore, give at least a clue as to what is desirable for employees on the job. At best, however, they give an incomplete and unreliable picture. The two satisfactory bases for validating any tests for employee placement are discussed in detail on pages 25–30. Criteria for visual classification and placement of employees, determined by these methods on the job itself, are not only valid in terms of actual job conditions but also are appropriate to the type and quality of employees who are available in the industrial community. These standards may vary not only from job to job but from community to community.

The initial battery of vision tests should include all the items that are most likely to be of significance, on the basis of previous investigation rather than of opinion. In a battery like the one already described (page 133), the tests included have been selected by statistical research in industry for most probable significance in the largest number of jobs.

Job simplification

An important part of an industrial program of vision is the recognition and simplification of visual operations in the plant and the improvement of visual working conditions. Visual factors in job operations can often be eliminated. Where they cannot be eliminated altogether, sometimes simpler visual functions can be substituted for more complex ones. Jigs and fixtures for positioning tools and materials help to reduce visual operations to a minimum. Another factor in the simplicity of visual operations is the area over which they are performed. Ordinarily eye movements should be substituted for head movement and small eye movements for large ones. Some visual cues can be simplified so that they can be observed with peripheral or "side vision" without turning the eyes. Figure 61 shows the spread of visual operations on two repetitive jobs. In general, the visual operations on any job should be organized into a restricted area at a convenient and fairly uniform distance from the eyes. The visual working distances can best be measured from the plane in front of the eyes where spectacles are usually worn (the lower forehead or base of the nose approximates this position) to the various points of visual attention on the job. The angular deviation of these "lines of vision" from horizontal is also important in connection with the use of spectacles, especially bifocals or special occupational glasses. Such information may be useful in determining job requirements of vision and should be incorporated in job analyses and descriptions for use of the personnel department in finding employees to fill these jobs.

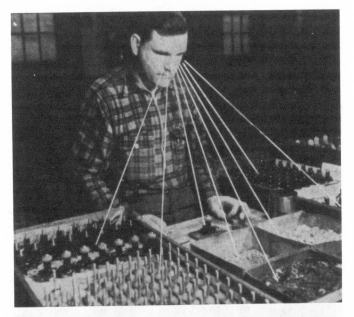

Fig. 61—Visual work areas and working distances on two assembly jobs.

Optical aids and occupational eyewear

While job simplification and adequate lighting may reduce the visual requirements on some jobs, other visual requirements can be modified by the use of optical devices that permit a larger proportion of available employees to perform a job satisfactorily. Special types of microscopes, magnifiers, and micro-photographic apparatus permit visual inspection and scaling of very small surfaces and pieces and analysis of material structure. Small machined parts can be magnified in profile for direct comparison with original large-scale drawings by means of the contour projector, shown in Figure 62. Polariscopes reveal stresses and strains in transparent models of castings. These are only a few of the many types of optical instruments, developed for specialized work in industry, that, like gauges, meters, and dials, bring important manufacturing operations within the range of visual observation of average employees.

Without colored glass (optical filters) some operations, such as welding and melting, would be practically impossible. The use of clear, hardened protective glass enables employees on other jobs, such as chipping, sanding, planing, drilling, and grinding, to face their work without flinching or averting their eyes, thus making full use of their visual capacity. The importance of spectacles for the compensation of individual anomalies of vision is shown on page 145. Because of the differences in visual performance for different distances, mentioned on page 150, such spectacles would seem to be most appropriate for industrial purposes when they are designed to meet not only the individual, personal needs but also the specific visual requirements of a particular job at some particular work distance or range of distances.

Experiments in the use of special types of occupational lens correction for jobs requiring very close vision have been carried out in England.[20] These prescriptions include a component, over and above what would be indicated for ordinary lens corrections for these persons, that has the same optical effect as though the work were removed farther from the eyes but without loss of

---

[20] H. C. Weston and S. Adams, *On the Relief of Eyestrain Among Persons Performing Very Fine Work* (London, H. M. Stationery Office, 1928), and *Further Experiments on the Use of Special Spectacles in Very Fine Processes* (London, H. M. Stationery Office, 1929).

visibility.   In psychological terms these lenses modify the visual requirements of the job so that they come within the range of adaptability of a larger number of potential operators. These spectacles are worn *only on the job;* they are part of the

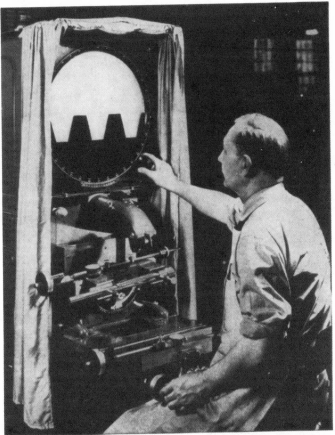

FIG. 62—The Contour Measuring Projector. The view before the operator is an enlargement of the teeth on a machine tool.

job equipment or tools.   At other times each operator wears whatever spectacles may be desirable for general use, or, if none are needed, no spectacles at all.

These early experiments have recently been duplicated under the medical supervision of Dr. H. S. Kuhn on one job in hosiery manufacture—the operation of looping. This job requires an average visual working distance of eight inches. Figure 63

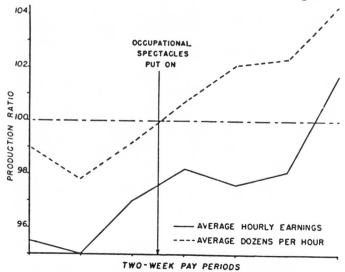

Fig. 63—Increase in production of fine-gauge hosiery loopers with the use of special occupational spectacles.

shows the production of experienced loopers on fine-gauge hosiery who wore such spectacles, in proportion to the production of a comparable group of employees who did not wear such spectacles. Figure 64 shows the production of learning loopers on coarse-gauge hosiery who wore such spectacles, in proportion to the production of a comparable group who did not wear such spectacles. In each instance the production of the non-spectacle group, which fluctuated from week to week, is plotted for each two-week period as 100, with the production of the experimental group plotted in proportion. Loopers who wore these spectacles showed an average increase in production of about 5 per cent in a relatively short time, in comparison with the control group, and learning loopers more rapidly reached their peak of production when the occupational spectacles were worn. Since this one operation accounts for about 20 per cent of the labor cost in the manufacture of circular-knit hosiery, more economical operation through the use of such spectacles would seem to be possible.

The spectacle prescriptions for these experiments varied from

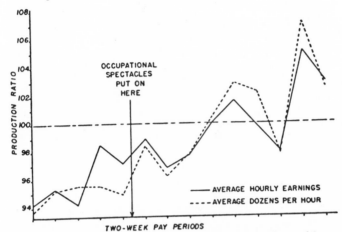

Fig. 64—Increase in production of learning hosiery loopers wearing special occupational spectacles.

one operator to another because of individual differences in visual characteristics, although the job requirements were uniform.[21] Not all of the operators would or could wear such spectacles successfully, but the advantages might become available to a larger proportion of such operators with improved bases for predicting individual lens prescriptions for occupational use. Thirty operators who wore these spectacles successfully showed on a visual retest six months later a pronounced and uniform shift of visual characteristics away from the peculiar conditions that characterize most operators on this job and toward what is generally considered normal; and their subjective reports indicated in most cases less fatigue during work and greater pleasure from activities involving the use of their eyes after work.

Such specialized occupational eyewear cannot be introduced

---

[21] The optical addition was varied by Dr. Kuhn for different employees according to the results of an examination. The average optical addition was an amount that changed the focus requirement from 8 inches to 11.5 inches and the convergence requirement from 8 inches to 9.5 inches.

in any industrial situation except by a competent and ingenious ophthalmologist or optometrist who is not only qualified as an eye expert but also is familiar with the visual problems of specific jobs and with typical management attitudes and methods of approach to such problems. Ideally such a project should be carried on in collaboration with an industrial psychologist who can set up adequate criteria as a goal. The first step is to demonstrate a relationship between certain visual characteristics and service or success on the job. For example, preliminary studies on other jobs in the manufacture of full-fashioned hosiery indicate that occupational glasses like those for loopers might be generally beneficial for menders but not so beneficial for seamers, for whom, possibly, some other type of special occupational eyewear would be of benefit. The second step in carrying on such a project is to determine how certain visual characteristics may be induced safely and beneficially by lenses. The final step is to evaluate the success of the project.

Visual classification and placement of new employees

A program for taking advantage of individual differences of vision in placement of employees on different jobs must make provision for the visual testing of applicants for employment before they are hired. Such testing does not imply that inflexible standards for employment will be adhered to in the employment office. Indeed, the discussion in the preceding sections has shown that desirable characteristics of vision may and frequently do vary from one job to another. It is a part of the responsibility of those in charge of administering employment policies to determine the best visual qualifications for groups of employees on different jobs and to utilize this information in the selection of new employees. Visual standards for employee placement by this method are not matters to be fixed by policy. The policy governing placement is to get the best employees available for certain jobs. The selection ratio, with a system for testing and classifying applicants, is a flexible instrument for enforcing that policy. The same principle holds both in placement of new employees and in transfer, promotion, and replacement of veteran employees. This principle of employee placement for certain jobs where vision is important often can be enforced regardless of the proportion of applicants who are hired.

If all applicants are being hired, the visual classification standards are applied to all of them in order to allocate the best of those hired to visual jobs and other critical posts. Many jobs exist in a large industry for which visual skills of high degree are not necessary; and such testing procedures, if properly administered in the light of job requirements, usually result in satisfactory placement of a larger rather than a smaller proportion of applicants.

Visual qualifications of applicants as well as employees frequently can be improved; therefore it is not necessary always to be satisfied with the visual characteristics of available applicants. Marked individual differences may exist even among applicants who are suited to certain jobs, and those who can improve their visual qualifications should be urged to do so.

Adequate testing of new employees, so that they may be placed on jobs in accordance with the plan just outlined, presupposes a battery of visual placement tests that covers a number of aspects of visual performance. It is shown in the preceding section, upon the basis of experimental evidence, that a person may be definitely deficient in one aspect of vision—as, for example, distance acuity—and be quite satisfactory in certain other aspects of vision that may be of prime importance for certain jobs in the plant. Regardless of what single test is used or how well that test measures any single aspect of vision, it is unlikely that employees who score low on this test will be unsuited for all jobs. A battery of tests, interpreted in the light of the plant requirements, has been found a considerably more effective device for the selection and placement of employees than any single test.

If the individual tests are constructed with adequate scales, the direct scores for each applicant can be weighted according to their significance on a particular job and combined into a composite score representing his probable success on the job. Scores in certain parts of the possible range on some of the tests may be more directly related to job performance than scores in other parts of the range. In fact, there may be zones within the total range where individual differences are relatively unimportant. Such a situation was illustrated in Figure 60, which showed for hosiery loopers the relation between a focus posture test and production. In the middle range of scores on this test, differences in production are more pronounced than they are at either end of the range. In establishing guide posts for employee placement on the basis of such tests, it is often convenient to designate zones on the test scale that are related to excellent, good, fair, poor, or unacceptable job performance. After some experience with tests in a particular industrial population, a personnel officer can classify applicants according to any predetermined selection ratio. With flexible methods of classifying visual test scores, the selection ratio can be shifted to meet changing conditions.

A means of facilitating employee classification by this method is the "visual profile" score illustrated on the lower part of the visual record form shown in Figure 65. This particular record form, called a Selectograph, has been designed to accompany the tests described on page 133. All possible scores on all of the tests are presented in a convenient table, and a continuous line drawn through an applicant's score on each test makes the profile. This profile can then quickly be compared with master profiles that show, for each job separately, the zones in which desirable, undesirable, and indifferent vision scores fall.

Another type of classification problem arises when it is necessary to select quickly, from the visual test records of a number of employees or applicants, those that represent the most desirable visual characteristics for a particular job. Some type of mechanical sorting facilitates such a search. Record forms like that in Figure 65 can be sorted and classified quickly by means of the system of holes and slots around the edge.[22] The visual test scores are slot-punched on the card and a needle separates those that are slotted from those that are not slotted at any point on the periphery of the card.

Visual Maintenance of Personnel

Wherever visual characteristics are important for placement of employees on particular jobs, maintenance of those characteristics is a factor in continued good performance on the job. Among employees of equal experience and initial qualities, those who maintain their original vision or improve it will do better on the average than those who lose their visual qualifications.

---

[22] This is an adaptation of the McBee Keysort system, the McBee Company, Athens, Ohio.

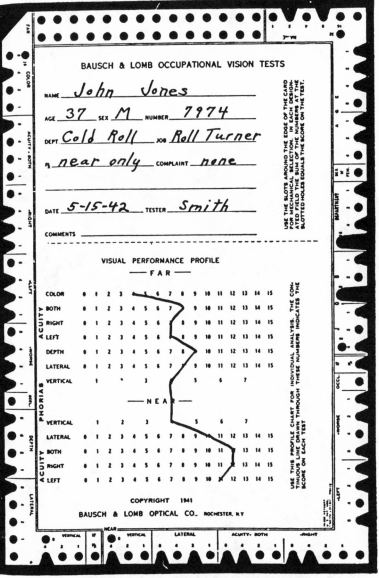

Fig. 65—The chart for recording the visual test scores yielded by the Ortho-Rater.

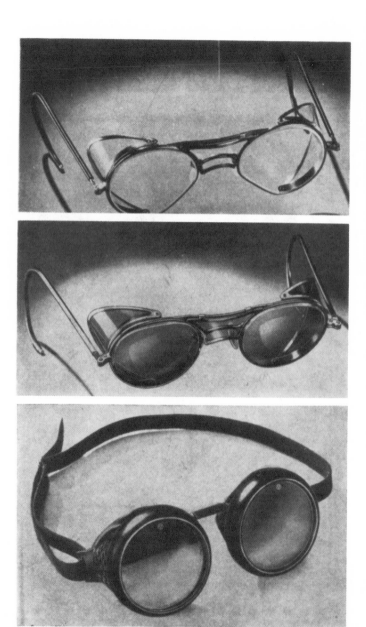

FIG. 66—Some common types of eye-safety devices (on this and facing page).

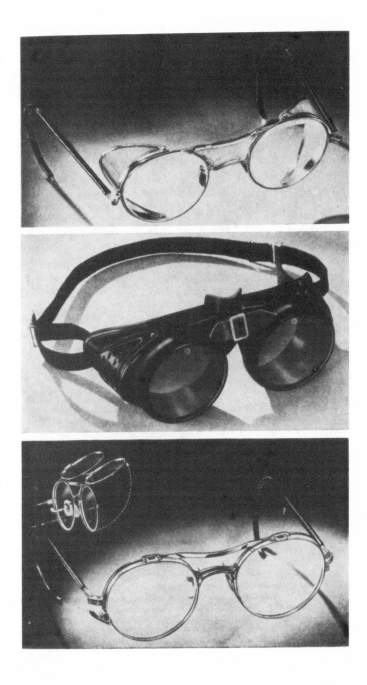

Proper placement of employees is only one part of a program for taking advantage of visual differences among employees. The other part is proper maintenance of these skills.

Good practices in simplification of jobs, adequate lighting, and use of various types of occupational aids will help in the maintenance of adequate visual performance among employees. Proper job lighting should give attention not only to general illumination but also to specific job requirements for illumination. Standard general practices for lighting have been codified by illuminating engineers.[23]

Adequate physical protection of the eyes of workmen also helps in maintaining standards of visual performance on the job. Visual hazards in industry that threaten visual competence of employees include the possibilities of sudden injury (trauma) or of cumulative ill effects like industrial diseases, such as ultra-violet "burns" among welders. Some visual hazards in industry, against which protection is possible, are:

1. Ultra-violet radiations (arc and acetylene welders, welders' helpers).

2. Infra-red radiations (melters, furnacemen, and others working around furnaces and molten metal).

3. Air-borne dust and noxious fumes (sand blasters, colliers, millers, trainmen, truckers, aviators, workers in some chemical operations).

4. Splash and spatter (welders, grinders, handlers of acid and other caustic chemicals, solderers, foundrymen).

5. Severe impact and explosion (riveters, chippers, chemists, drillers, powder men).

Each of these hazards requires a different type of eye protection, including masks, optical filters, and lenses highly resistant to breakage and shattering. Minimum standards for such protective devices have been formulated by government agencies.[24] Manufacturers have made progress toward adapting the design of such devices to specific job requirements of vision and visibility, to individual differences in facial size and contour, and to

[23] Committee on Lighting Practice, Illuminating Engineering Society, *Recommended Practice of Industrial Lighting*, The Society, New York City.
[24] U. S. Department of Commerce, National Bureau of Standards, *American Standard Safety Code for the Protection of Heads, Eyes, and Respiratory Organs*, National Bureau of Standards Handbook H24 (U. S. Government Printing Office, 1938).

various combinations of hazards. Figure 66 shows some of the more common types of eye-protective devices. The economic value of such devices has been demonstrated repeatedly.[25]

Although such measures for the maintenance of visual proficiency are taken, it is still certain that changes in vision will take place in a majority of employees with increasing age and job experience. Some of these changes, such as the loss of near vision with age, have long been accepted as inevitable. Yet even this change, universal and serious as it is for individuals who must do any reading or close scrutiny on their jobs, is often not recognized and corrected until the efficiency of the employee has been definitely reduced. Perhaps one reason for this is that the loss of near vision with age does not occur suddenly like a broken arm or a sprained ankle, but develops so gradually that an employee is often unaware of his increasing handicap until long after his work has been seriously affected. Indeed, paradoxical as it may sound, no one can tell from the way things look to him whether his vision is normal or below normal. Just as many persons go through life without knowing that they are color-blind—unless they have been tested and told the result—so also many persons with seriously deficient visual performance in other respects are unaware of their real condition unless it is demonstrated to them in terms of objective test results. These facts make it necessary to check periodically the vision of present employees.

Periodic retests of vision

Employees in certain critical positions in industry can usually be required to maintain good vision. Operators of mobile equipment have responsibilities for the safety of other employees. Supervisors have responsibilities for correctly interpreting instructions to workmen and maintaining both quality and quantity of production. Maintenance and repair men have responsibilities for keeping other men from becoming idle on account of breakdown. Inspectors have far-reaching responsibilities for quality of product. These and other employees

[25] H. P. Davidson, "Two Years of Industrial Ophthalmology at the Pullman Car Works," *Journal of Industrial Hygiene*, VIII (1925), pp. 247–253.

L. Resnick, *Fifteen Years Progress in Eyesight Conservation*, Publication No. 297 (National Society for the Prevention of Blindness, 1939).

whose functions directly affect other groups of workmen or the general welfare of the plant can and should be made to feel their responsibilities with respect to maintaining their own physical functions at a high level of efficiency. Employees in some industries, such as the common carriers and other public utilities, whose operations are subject to public observation, frequently show great pride in the physical qualifications that they maintain and demonstrate in repeated examinations.[26] Visual requirements for license to drive a car in many states have given a great impetus to such attitudes.

Periodic retests are usually administered in the same place and follow the same routine as the pre-employment examination. At designated periods, and upon due notification, an employee presents himself for re-examination. At that time he is usually interested and ready to discuss his personal health and efficiency and to take any steps that are advisable to maintain them. This feature of a visual program can well be inaugurated with supervisors (to set the precedent), extended to cranemen, truckers, and others in the field of transport within or outside a plant, to inspectors, to gang leaders, to men on hazardous jobs, and to any other group that has an easily recognizable visual responsibility. The interval between tests need not be uniform for all groups. Indeed, it should be determined separately for each group in proportion to the importance of vision in that group.

These retests cannot be done all at once, but they can be distributed over a long period and thus made a small part of routine, rather than special, activities. This usually involves a separate file for each group of employees arranged in calendar order of their next examinations. Sometimes, however, greater economy in such testing operations can be achieved by consolidating them into a limited period at a specific time.

The visual survey

More general vision testing among employees in a plant or a department may be advisable from time to time in an attempt to combat the losses that occur with age and to raise average levels of visual proficiency in the plant. Such gains are effected

[26] Hart E. Fisher, "What Periodical Examinations Can Accomplish," *National Safety News*, XXXII (Dec., 1935), pp. 33–34.

in proportion to the number of employees whose vision can be improved somewhat rather than to the amount of improvement that can be achieved in the vision of a few employees. It is important and economical to retain employees with experience on the job, to "salvage" as many as possible of the employees whose visual proficiency has deteriorated, and to find other jobs for those who have become visually incapacitated for their present jobs.

A visual survey is a major undertaking. Testing in such a survey usually has to be done during working hours, taking each man from his job for the briefest possible time. In a large plant the testing has to be scheduled on different shifts and in different parts of the plant in order to reduce traveling distance for employees and time away from the job. In a survey of nearly 10,000 employees in a steel mill, the testing schedule for a crew of testers required 24 different testing stations, some of them for three shifts. In order that the major operations of the plant can be carried on at high efficiency, the visual survey (like stand-by services in the plant) must be operated at relatively low efficiency.

A complete survey that is rushed through a plant may easily result in a definite disinclination on the part of management and workers ever to repeat it. Surveys by outside professional survey organizations, which may do the work for a fee or for the privilege of selling glasses to the employees, also are likely to result in general dissatisfaction among employees. A survey is best operated as a normal repetitive process by the industrial staff. It can be completed "once over" a little at a time and then started again.

The immediate objective of a visual survey is to identify employees whose visual performance is low and to stimulate them to obtain professional attention. Since such professional treatment requires both time and money, it becomes necessary to select those employees who are most in need or who would be most likely to be benefited by such services. Some of these employees can be selected on the basis of their own complaints or their progressive loss of proficiency on a job requiring visual ability; but too often a serious visual deficiency will long be undetected by these means.

In cases of promotion or transfer, or of visual selection and allocation tests that are given at the time of initial employment, it is often necessary to classify or segregate applicants at relatively high levels of visual proficiency. But in the use of visual "screening" tests for the purpose of detecting extreme cases of substandard visual performance, selection is always in the low levels of performance. The primary purpose of such tests is to "screen out" those who are to be classified as most in need of visual attention or least acceptable with their present vision for tenure on their present jobs. However, there is no reason why employees with acceptable visual proficiency should not also try to, or be urged to, improve that proficiency. The concern of management is primarily with the poorest of those who are to be retained on the job. Because of limitations of necessary professional services available to workers in a plant or in a community, and because of the sheer size of a survey program, it is necessary to promote visual maintenance first among those with the lowest levels of proficiency, and gradually to extend the campaign to higher but still substandard levels. For this reason, even "screening" tests must be constructed on continuous scales rather than as simple pass-or-fail tests, so that levels for segregation of substandard visual performance can be set conveniently and can be progressively modified.

Adequate tests for employee classification can always be used as screening tests by defining certain minimum levels of performance as "passing." However, these standards should be set in terms of the prevailing quality of visual performance rather than arbitrarily on the basis of opinion. This means that the standards will be set *after at least a portion of the testing has been completed.* Scores on all the vision tests can be recorded carefully and then sorted by a convenient means to pick out the employees with poorest vision—say the poorest 5 per cent on any test or the poorest 10 per cent or 15 per cent on the total battery. These are the employees at whom the survey is primarily aimed.

In one survey [27] of nearly 10,000 steel workers, a division of employees into five groups resulted in the following percentage in each group:

[27] H. S. Kuhn, "An Appraisal of Visual Defects in Industry," American Academy of Ophthalmology and Otolaryngology, Cleveland, Oct., 1940.

1. Satisfactory 62.8%
2. Satisfactory with
   present glasses..................... 5.4
3. Minor problems................... 18.5
4. Serious problems................. 7.5
5. Very serious problems with greatest
   likelihood of pathology............ 5.8
   _____
   100.0%

Employees in the last group were summoned before the plant physician for general examination. The others were given a standardized report as to their classification with appropriate instructions for each group. Those in Group 4 were urged to get professional eye care, and the same recommendation, with less urgency, was made to employees in Group 3.

Survey testing in no way takes the place of professional eye examination and service; it merely reveals cases of deficient vision that should receive such help. Some means of putting employees in touch with the professional help that they need should be an integral part of an industrial vision program. Indeed, the most thorough and adequate program of visual testing will be of little benefit unless professional services are received by those employees who are in need of such attention. Problems of industrial relations involved in notifying employees of visual disabilities and in getting professional help for them will be discussed later in this chapter.

Maintenance of occupational eyewear

Any glass before an employee's eyes should not only be the best glass for his needs but should be maintained in the correct position for maximum value. In a survey of employees in a steel mill only one-half of one per cent of employees showed a serious tendency for one eye to point slightly higher than the other; but when this condition occurs it is often the forerunner to double vision during periods of fatigue. Among the employees who were not wearing glasses .42 per cent showed this tendency, but among those wearing glasses .78 per cent showed it. This condition can be induced by glasses that are not maintained level and in the correct position. Apparently this fact accounts for the greater percentage of this tendency among employees wearing glasses.

Employees who have obtained their glasses on prescription from a reputable eye man have in most instances thereby established contact with adequate services in adjusting and maintaining their glasses. But many employees do not have such contacts or do not make use of them frequently enough. A few industries have hired men permanently to supervise employee eyewear. Such a supervisor selects the right kinds of safety eyewear and fits them to an employee's face, makes adjustments and repairs on all types of eyewear, makes up special devices for special purposes, cleans and sterilizes safety eyewear, and instructs employees in the use and maintenance of their eyewear. He does not make professional examinations or fill prescriptions. Such a man can pay his own way in a plant by the savings he effects from salvage of damaged goggles. The total economic saving from his work is likely to be many times the cost.

Industrial Relations in a Vision Program

Unless visual testing programs in industry are backed by a sound and consistent policy, they frequently result in a mass of recorded and unused data. Mere testing of employees accomplishes little except perhaps to stimulate employee interest (or resentment) in their vision. A sound visual program must take into consideration existing industrial relations within the plant and in the community, and it must be adapted to the particular type of organization in a plant.

The scope of a visual program and the policies governing it must be determined primarily with reference to specific purposes or objectives. Some of the objectives that are commonly set up for a visual program are:

1. To obtain visual records for compensation cases.
2. To aid in the selection and placement of new employees.
3. To reduce accidents, especially eye injuries.
4. To improve employee job satisfaction.
5. To reduce labor turnover.
6. To increase production.
7. To improve quality of product.
8. To improve the bases for transfer, promotion, and, when necessary, layoffs.
9. To impress upon employees the need for proper visual hygiene.

Evidences of the relation between vision and job performance indicate that these objectives are not unreasonable, and several reports from industries which have a vision program in operation indicate that these objectives have been achieved. Typical of such studies is a report of the Metropolitan Life Insurance Company [28] summarizing the experience of several industries that operate industrial eye clinics. What form a program should take to achieve these results depends largely on the organization of a company and its policies with respect to industrial relations, both within the plant and in the community.

Departmental relations

The several approaches to industrial vision have developed from almost as many branches of management. The industrial psychologist and employment manager are interested in placing employees according to their visual aptitude; the industrial engineer is interested in illumination; the safety engineer in employee safety; and the plant physician in the maintenance of employee health. As a result of these varied interests, the problems arising in connection with a visual program for industry must be considered from the viewpoint of the whole of management. An industrial vision program must be satisfactory to all branches of management, and therefore must ordinarily be conceived on a much broader basis than is likely to develop from the interests of any single department. A vision program naturally incorporates functions of several departments or divisions of industrial organization. Most frequently it is associated with the health bureau or employment bureau. The safety bureau is usually responsible for providing eye protection and enforcing policies governing the use of such devices. The training bureau should be concerned in vision programs, not only with respect to selection of personnel for training, but also in training personnel in the use of various types of optical aids that can be brought to bear on the solution of some problems. The engineering and personnel divisions have reciprocal responsibilities in working out the visual requirements on various jobs and finding adequate personnel for the jobs. A program must include a plan and system for gathering factual data, classifying and

---

[28] *Functions of an Industrial Eye Clinic* (Metropolitan Life Insurance Company, New York, N. Y.).

evaluating it, and making it available to the various departments that can make use of it advantageously.

Professional relations

Correction or improvement of visual characteristics of employees in service by means of spectacles or other eye treatment

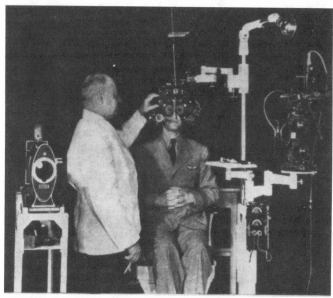

Fig. 67—A view of the United Air Lines Eye Clinic. Part of an eye examination being conducted in the Medical Department of United Air Lines at Chicago,
Illinois, by Colonel A. D. Tuttle, M. D., Medical Director. In recognition of the
importance of visual efficiency in industry and of "Eyes for the Job," not only
pilots, but all other employees of United Air Lines as well, are given a complete
and searching eye examination as part of their preemployment and periodic physical examinations.

involves specialized professional services. Qualified and licensed
ophthalmologists and optometrists are able to evaluate the
causes and history of any individual condition of visual deficiency and to determine what specific steps must be taken to
change that condition. Such services cannot be rendered except
in well-equipped professional offices or clinics. Some large industries provide the necessary equipment and professional staff

on their own premises for service to their own employees. Such an industrial eye clinic is shown in Figure 67. Others retain professional eye men as consultants. A major point of policy, involving professional and industrial relations, is to determine whether such facilities and services shall be provided at company expense and whether management or employees shall assume the responsibility for seeking or soliciting such services in individual instances. Small industries must usually depend upon the facilities and services that are available among private practitioners in the community.

Since the local ophthalmologists and optometrists will inevitably share the responsibility for visual efficiency of employees, management should make an effort to acquaint them with the visual requirements for employees on various jobs and the specifications for safety lenses and assemblies that will be acceptable on certain jobs. And the local eye men should certainly familiarize themselves with the jobs and job requirements of workers who are their patients.

Occasionally physical factors or health conditions of an employee make it impossible for the professional man to bring vision up to normal. Management should not be hasty in deciding that inadequate professional service has been given if an employee's vision has not improved after receiving professional attention. In many communities the local eye men are encouraged to report such conditions directly to the employer.

Employee relations

The personal aspects of such a program are so great that the employee relations involved in the work often assume major importance. Some employees will not want to have their "eyes tested." They feel that they can "see all right" and that, in any event, it is no more the business of management to tell them whether they need professional attention for their eyes than it is to tell them when to trade in their old car on a new one. It is therefore important for the success of visual testing programs that these personal relations should always be handled with tact and discretion. Few industrial relations are more personal and intimate than in a testing situation of this kind. What bureau or department a tester works in, or what qualifications he has as a tester, are not as important as whether he is satisfactory to all departments of management as a representative of management in these very personal relations with labor.

Vision tests of applicants and new employees, for purposes of selection or placement, do not involve the same problems of industrial relations as do vision tests of employees in service. The management is not committed to an agreement with applicants with respect to tenure, seniority, or compensation. In some industries, such as railroads and aviation, tenure on a particular job is contingent on continuance of an employee's ability to pass certain vision tests at stated intervals. A continuance of certain physical qualifications is implicit in such agreements in many industries.

Testing of employees already on the job is necessary to establish visual qualifications for jobs, to arrange appropriate tests for new employees on those jobs, to determine what losses of vision have occurred among employees since they were hired, and to provide an improved basis for transfer and promotion.

Problems of professional and employee relations are most likely to become acute during a survey. It is not advisable in a survey to attempt to make judgment on each case at the time of the test. Many cases cannot be properly classified except in comparison with others. Standards for identifying employees who need professional services can be determined with respect to average levels of visual performance among employees in the plant rather than upon the basis of arbitrary *a priori* opinion. Further, if a survey is to be operated with reasonable efficiency, the available time must be allocated to best advantage. An employee wants to satisfy himself that he has had time and opportunity to demonstrate the best he can do on the tests. He wants also to know something of the purpose of the tests. Time spent in discussing results of the tests is best reserved for those who are to be urged to get help for their eyes.

Another point of policy concerning both professional and industrial relations is the matter of who is to be the authority in notifying employees of their visual shortcomings and of how he is to inform them. Any official statement to an employee comes best not from the person who makes the test but from the person under whose authority the survey is conducted. The form of notification to employees can be standardized, and the person who signs such communications should be a responsible officer in the organization.

The professional eye men should rightfully insist that such notification to an employee should not prejudice him with respect to what type of service he will solicit or what type of aid he should receive. For example, a recommendation to "get glasses" is indefensible because it implies a diagnosis and a decision that glasses are the only proper form of therapy. The right recommendation is to "get professional attention." The aspects of visual performance in which an employee is deficient can be stated in his notification for transmittal to his eye doctor. The professional eye men also insist that employee vision that is satisfactory to management in all respects should not be interpreted to an employee as being "perfect" or entirely satisfactory in a clinical sense. An employee should not be permitted to infer that "passing" industrial tests of vision is as good as a "clean bill of health" from a professional eye man, nor that he has had the equivalent of a professional examination when he has only been tested on simple performance tests.

In a visual survey of engineering students at Purdue University, students were told, "Your test scores will be compared with others and you will receive a report on your standing." Each student received the following report with a check mark at one of the four categories of visual performance:

Notice to _____ Date _____

According to visual performance tests your visual efficiency is:

I—Satisfactory at present.

II—Satisfactory with present glasses.

III—Somewhat below average. If you have any discomfort with your eyes, especially during visual activities, have your eyes examined by a competent specialist. If not, have your visual performance checked again next semester.

IV—Apparently in need of immediate attention. Consult an eye doctor to find out how your visual efficiency can be improved to the benefit of your school work, your safety, and your enjoyment.

WEAR SAFETY GLASSES IN THE SHOP

Department of General Engineering
by_____

Employee education in vision

It should be evident from the preceding discussion that a visual program for employees now in service is a phase of personnel maintenance and therefore involves problems of employee training or education. Employees must be motivated to develop habits of personal maintenance, to expect to meet certain standards of visual proficiency, and to discover for themselves a source of professional eye care that can keep their visual proficiency at a maximum. The visual testing itself and the experience that it involves are important elements in this training. The effect of survey tests as a frankly educational device in improvement of job performance, apart from any other corrective measure, has been demonstrated,[29] and many reports of improvement in production, safety, and employee morale as a result of visual surveys can well be attributed in part at least to this factor. It is reasonable to expect that any real improvement in job performance due to improvement in visual proficiency will be reflected in improved performance on vision tests.

A special problem in vision education is employees' attitudes toward vision tests and visual standards. Employees often have only a few vague notions and many misconceptions as to the scope of visual functions, the nature of visual deficiencies, and the significance of optical aids. A concept widely in use at a former time, but still heard among older persons, is "weak eyes." Glasses were for "weak eyes," and those who wore glasses had "weak eyes." This term no longer has any true or specific reference among the concepts of professional men and has been replaced largely in popular thinking by other terms. A current term, under which are included most problems of vision, is "visual defect"—professional ocular services and optical aids "correct" visual defects. This seems an unfortunate concept because of the universal resistance to admission of personal defect. A person who solicits ocular services and accepts optical aid for his eyes must go through the mental operation of admitting and accepting a personal defect—unless he can find some other rationalization for his conduct. This attitude has been further promoted by visual surveys and visual standards in em-

[29] E. D. Fletcher, "Effect of Special Tests on Driving Ability," *Preliminary Report on Special Tests* (State of California, Department of Motor Vehicles, Division of Drivers Licenses, 1939).

ployment, automobile driving, and other areas of activity, since those who are selected for ocular attention by these methods show substandard performance, and the corollary implication is that ocular attention is primarily if not exclusively for those with substandard or "defective" vision. The result of this attitude is that many workmen deny themselves ocular advantages because of pride. In an attempt to overcome this psychological handicap to visual improvement, concepts of "visual efficiency" and "visual skills" have been popularized in recent years.

An industrialist responsible for employee education should be able to help an employee understand his visual problems and to appreciate the purposes of industrial vision testing so as to elicit maximum co-operation toward improving his employability. From an industrial standpoint, visual conditions are considered functionally as elements of aptitude or adaptability. Whether the limits in visual adaptability are functional, structural, or pathological is not the concern of the industrialist—nor, for that matter, of anyone except the professional eye man. The industrial problem is to discover such limitations *insofar as they are related to industrial performance and insofar as they can be determined reliably by simple, non-professional tests,* such as those mentioned on page 133. These tests may be thought of as sampling different aspects of visual adaptability. Limitations in such functions are to the professional eye man symptoms of some basic dislocation of visual responses. To the industrialist they represent individual differences in visual aptitude or adaptability for specific job requirements. Visual aptitude, in the sense of adaptability, is different from aptitude as ordinarily defined, for visual adaptability can often be modified in many respects by means of spectacles, magnifiers, microscopes, and other optical aids. Eyeglasses mediate between the visual demands of the job and the visual capacity of the worker. The end result should be better efficiency in activities of major importance.

The employee can be encouraged to anticipate functional improvement in his visual characteristics and to look upon glasses or other methods of eye care as a means to this end. If he wishes to verify the result, after a period of readaptation, in terms of the same industrial tests that he originally failed to pass, he should have an opportunity to do so.

Another problem of education in visual hygiene is the attitude of the employee toward using occupational eyewear of various types. In some instances, protective or corrective spectacles may be actually uncomfortable or otherwise not adapted to an employee's individual needs and conditions. But a more general unreadiness to accept optical aids of this sort can be traced in part to the popular misconceptions previously mentioned and in part to employment policies that have sometimes been followed. In many industries, an applicant wearing glasses has been considered ineligible to undertake a physically active job. Surreptitious use of spectacles has been reported [30] among workers in the building trades. On jobs where ordinary spectacles are liable to breakage their use is certainly unsafe, not only because of the hazard to the wearer's eyes but also because an employee who has broken his customary glasses is visually unadapted to his job and may therefore endanger himself and others. With the development of combination corrective and protective lenses, or "prescription goggles," the hazard of glasses is not only eliminated but eyes are actually safer behind such lenses than they are without them. Corrective spectacles, whether they have safety lenses or not, play an important part in progressive industry today. This is indicated by the relation between use of such eyewear and supervisors' ratings of employees, shown in Figures 51 and 52.

"Getting glasses" is not necessarily the answer to the visual needs of employees. Neither is it the right recommendation to make to employees who show substandard performance on industrial tests. Some basic causes of visual deficiency must be attacked by other means than eyeglasses, and many functional deficiencies cannot be remedied by spectacles alone. The right recommendation is to get professional eye care: a competent examination, treatment, properly fitted glasses if and as prescribed, and any necessary aftercare.

---

[30] Francis E. Carroll, "Defective Eyesight in the Building Trades," *The Bausch and Lomb Magazine*, XVI, No. 3 (1940).

7

Training of Industrial Employees

EMPLOYEES must be systematically trained if they are to do their jobs well. No matter how carefully men have been selected, or how much aptitude they may have for their jobs, systematic training is essential if they are to reach a satisfactory level of job performance. Formerly it was standard practice to have training done by the foreman or supervisor in charge of the work. Inexperienced men were sent to the supervisor (or hired by him) and it was his job to see that the new men were given the necessary training. But just as modern scientific management has found that experts should supplement the work of the foreman in making job analyses and setting rates, so also management is finding that the use of experts in training is advantageous as a supplement to the work of the foreman. This does not mean that outside experts need necessarily *do* the training. Their function, rather, is to set up the machinery for the training to be done by properly qualified persons, to supervise the construction or writing of necessary manuals or other materials, and to keep in close touch with the accomplishment of the trainees during the instructional period. Through this procedure training costs of various departments and various jobs may be compared, and the relative efficiency of different training methods may be evaluated in an objective (and often financial) manner.

A comparison of training methods, or the evaluation of any single method, requires some means of measurement. The value of precise means of measurement of a type thoroughly accepted in other branches of management is now being recognized as of equal value in industrial training. Training is teaching, and where there is teaching there should be learning. Therefore, the effectiveness of training may be measured in terms of the amount that the trainees learn. The evaluation of training may proceed by measuring how much has been learned at various stages of training.

The Measurement of Training

Machine operation

In many industrial jobs the work has been time-studied, rates based on these studies have been set, and output or production of employees is indicated by production or earnings. A comparison of production from one time to another reveals immediately how effective the intervening training has been and whether new or different methods should be tried out. A typical example of this method has been reported by Blankenship and Taylor [1] for the operations of trimming, covering, and hemming among textiie workers. The learning curves for these three operations, as published by Blankenship and Taylor, are reproduced in Figure 68. In order that these curves may be comparable from one operation to another, the production in each case has been plotted in terms of Bedaux units. These units consider the actual motions involved in each operation and equate these so that a given number of Bedaux units means a given amount of production, regardless of the operation involved. Thus, thirty Bedaux units of production in trimming may be considered equal to thirty Bedaux units in covering or hemming.

It will be noted that for each operation employees with less than five weeks of experience produced from thirty-one to forty-one Bedaux units. With increasing experience, the output in each case rose until, for trimming and hemming, it reached sixty-nine units at the end of thirty-five weeks; while in the case of covering, only sixty-two units were reached in this length of time. It is apparent that no serious discrepancy in speed of learning exists among the three operations studied. It will also be apparent, however, that if a serious discrepancy did exist, that is, if employees on any one of these jobs tended to lag consistently behind employees on the other jobs in speed of learning, an exact quantitative measurement of the amount of the lag would be indicated immediately by learning curves of this type. Such curves, therefore, serve the very useful purpose of providing a means of evaluating the successfulness of an operator-training program and spotting decisively those oper-

[1] A. B. Blankenship and H. R. Taylor, "Production of Vocational Proficiency in Three Machine Operations," *Journal of Applied Psychology*, XXII (1938), pp. 518–526.

ations in which training is inadequate, either in quantity or quality.

The question may be raised as to whether such curves as those in Figure 68 indicate the effect of *training* or the effect of *experience* on the job. The answer depends on the type of activity

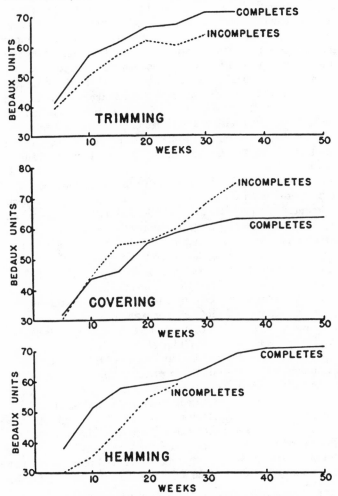

Fig. 68—Learning curves for three operations in a textile mill.

that has taken place during the period studied. Obviously, if no formal training has been given and each operator has been left free to pick up the "tricks of the trade" in whatever way he or she can, the curves would indicate only the improvement due to experience. On the other hand, if formal training has been given systematically over a period of weeks, the curves will indicate the amount of improvement in job performance occurring as a result of the training and experience. The curves simply show the change in job performance that takes place. Whether this change is due to training or experience or to a combination of these factors can be decided only in the light of a complete knowledge of the conditions under which the operators have been working. But when the curves for a given operation are available, together with a knowledge of the working conditions, it is possible to evaluate in objective and accurate terms the effectiveness of the method that has been used in training new operators.

A similar curve showing the relationship between production and experience on the job of looping in a hosiery mill has been reproduced on page 16 in connection with the discussion on individual differences among operators at different stages of the learning process. Although this curve has not been graphed in terms of Bedaux units, the general principles involved in its construction are the same as those just discussed.

The use of some method that embodies the general principle of measurement should be considered an essential feature of any training program. Without such measurement, there is no way of knowing whether the training is worth what it costs or, indeed, whether it is worth anything at all.

An excellent example of the application of this method to the evaluation of a job-training program has been published by Greenly.[2] Figure 69, reproduced from Greenly's article, shows the reduction in time required to change the knives on a flying shears following a program of job training dealing with this operation. The graph shows that the average time required for the operation for the year preceding the installation of the training program was twenty-nine minutes. Immediately after the training was undertaken a drop in the time required for the

---

[2] R. J. Greenly, "Job Training," National Association of Manufacturers Labor Relations Bulletin, No. 35 (1941), pp. 5–8.

operation is apparent. This drop continued for three successive months, at the end of which time the operation required an average time of only eighteen minutes. From a graph of this type it is a simple matter to compute the dollars-and-cents savings

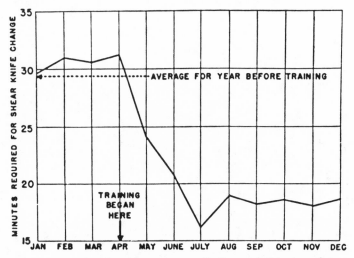

Fig. 69—Effect of a job training program on the time required to change knives in a flying shears.

effected by such a job-training program. In this instance the twelve minutes saved times the minutes labor cost times the average number of changes resulted in a saving of $1740 per month or $20,880 per year.

The results of a similar job-training program for rollers in a sheet and tin mill are also presented by Greenly.[1] The effectiveness of this training is shown in Figure 70. In this figure the solid line shows the average production of all rollers by weekly periods over a four-months interval. The dotted line shows the corresponding production of rollers who at the outset were below average in production and who were selected to receive training because of their previous poor production record. The graph shows that after the four-months period the men who received training had increased their production by an amount

---
[1] *Ibid.*

that brought them up approximately to the average of all rollers in the plant.

One should not expect such striking results to follow the installation of a job-training program in every instance. The

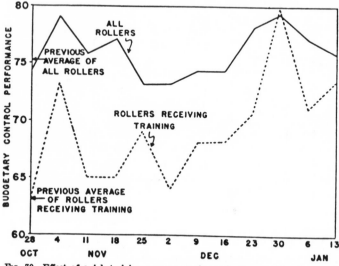

Fɪɢ. 70—Effect of a job training program on the production of rollers in a steel mill.

point to be emphasized here is not that job training will always and invariably produce a marked increase in production or a marked monetary saving, but that only by the use of some quantitative comparison of job performance after the training is given is it possible to know the effect of the program. It is even more important to have such information in the case of job training that does not result in a marked improvement, for otherwise there would be no way of knowing that the money spent for the training program is not a good investment.

Company policy and technical information

To measure the effect of training in terms of immediate monetary savings is not always possible. This does not mean, however, that such measurement is impossible. On the contrary, measurement may often be made of the effectiveness of training in such matters as company policy, knowledge of job, technical information, and so on, by means of specially constructed tests. For example, many industries devote a considerable amount of attention to supervisory training conferences. Such conferences frequently emphasize the importance of company policy and devote a considerable amount of time to instructing supervisors in ways of handling numerous kinds of problems, the solution of which requires a knowledge of company policy. It is not necessary to *assume* that such conferences implant the necessary or desired information in the mind of the supervisor, nor is it necessary to rely upon the supervisors' answers to such questions as, "Have these conferences improved your ability to handle situations?" in order to find out whether the conferences have actually had the desired effect. A more satisfactory method of evaluating such conferences is to resort to the general principle of measurement. Such measurement can readily be made by means of specially constructed true-false or multiple-choice questions that cover thoroughly the subject matter of the conferences and that determine in quantitative terms just what the supervisors know and do not know about the subject matter before and after the conferences have been held. Typical examples of the kind of questions that may be used for this purpose have been published by Mapel.[4]

If an employee is called out for work at 8:00 P.M. because of a vacancy in a position regularly filled by another employee, and he works until 12:00 P.M., he should be paid for:

1. 4 hours work.
2. 5 hours work.
3. 6 hours work.
4. 8 hours work.

In department "A" there are three shears; John Jones is first helper on No. 1 shear, who, due to sickness of the shearman, has acquired two weeks experience as a shearman. Several months later a vacancy exists in the shearman's position. First chance at the vacancy should be given to:

1. John Jones.
2. The first helper with the longest departmental service.
3. First helper with the greatest plant service.

[4] E. B. Mapel, "Stimulating Employee Self-Improvement," *Personnel Journal*, 19 (1941), pp. 316–324.

4. The first helper with the longest service where combined factors are relatively equal.

Questions such as these result in a *measurement*—not an estimate or a guess—that reveals whether the men who have been trained actually have achieved an increased understanding of company policy.

Questions of this general form may be used in still other areas of training to determine the effectiveness of instruction. Many industries have in-service training that covers technical information or content peculiar to their individual industries. The trade of pipe fitting, for example, though many of its details are common in various industries, often involves certain particular information of a technical nature that is required of the pipe fitters in a given industrial plant. If training covering this specific technical information has been given, it is only reasonable for management to ask whether the training has been effective. This can be determined by such questions as the following, taken from a typical test used in a large steel mill:

The correct pressure to use when unloading an acid tank car is
(1) 27   (2) 36   (3) 64   (4) 90 pounds.   ( )

The correct pressure to use when unloading an oil tank car is
(1) 27   (2) 36   (3) 64   (4) 90 pounds.   ( )

Oil and grease must be kept out of a pipe used for explosive materials because (1) contaminated gases do not burn so well, (2) an explosion will result, (3) it will cause clogging of the burners, (4) it makes repair work more difficult.   ( )

City water lines should not be connected to mill water lines because (1) this would contaminate the city water, (2) city water is more expensive and should be used for drinking only, (3) the chlorine in the city water would damage machinery and steel product, (4) mill water is under high pressure and this would burst the city water lines.   ( )

The above illustrations will suffice to show that whatever may be the subject matter of industrial in-service training it is possible to devise some sort of quantitative method to measure its effect. The measurement may involve production records before and after the training, scores on tests designed specifically to cover the subject matter of the training, or reduction in the time required to perform a certain typical operation in which the employees have been trained. It is possible, indeed, in some instances, to utilize several of these methods to measure the effectiveness of training. Management need no longer accept a training program on faith or because of someone's flowery statements about the presumed value of the program. The application of psychological measurement makes it possible to evaluate training objectively.

Types of Training

Job training of present employees

Modern industry is in a process of continuous technological change. No matter how well an employee may be able to do his work today, tomorrow he may find his job so changed that additional training is needed if he is to remain efficient. Continuous job training is a necessary corollary of continuous technological change. Job training to keep present employees efficient on their job was formerly conducted by supervisors. The ever-increasing complexity of industrial machines has caused the supervisor to become less and less able to cope with the technical phases of this training. In 1916, nearly any handy man with a few tools could do a reasonably satisfactory job of repairing his own automobile, even to the point of overhauling the motor. But the modern automobile has become so complex that a mechanic without specific training in the particular adjustments and tolerances recommended by the factory is quite unlikely to accomplish anything like a satisfactory job of overhauling. This problem has been met by supplying factory-trained mechanics, specially prepared manuals, and the offering of refresher courses to cover new developments.

Modern industry finds itself in a position similar to that of the automobile service station. No longer can any mechanically minded man be expected to perform satisfactorily in the operation of producing units. And no longer is the foreman able to analyze for himself the intricacies of the machines and to train new operators without outside help. This situation has resulted in the development of training as a new branch of management. The job trainer is essentially a man who has been "factory trained" in the maintenance or operation, or both, of certain producing units. His job is to relay this information by specific training to the employees who are to operate these units. Ordinarily the job trainer is not responsible for production and often he is responsible only indirectly to the foreman or supervisor who is in direct charge of production. In one sense, he is an "outsider," just as the industrial engineer, the safety expert, and the personnel manager are "outsiders." But this does not mean that he should have little contact with the supervisor. He should, indeed, make every effort to develop a co-operative working arrangement with the supervisors of those departments in which he is doing training. He is not ordinarily allocated for any long period of time to a single department. His job is to work as frequently and for as long periods as are necessary in various departments as an expert who brings technical information and skill to the trainees.

The effectiveness of a well-organized program of job training may be inferred from an inspection of Figures 69 and 70. In both of these instances the improvement in job performance was directly traceable to the activities of job trainers who had been assigned to these specific jobs.

The sources of information for the job trainer himself are varied. In some instances it may be desirable for him to spend a period of time in the factory in which the machine itself is manufactured. By so doing he often learns many things about the operation of the machine that could be learned only with great difficulty, if at all, without this factory experience. It is often desirable for the job trainer to work in close co-operation with the industrial engineering department. By analysis of motion study it is often possible to change the work pattern so that the actual number of motions or complexity of motions in performing the job is considerably reduced. In nearly every instance it is advisable to have the trainer work as a *trainer* while he is on this job and not partly as a trainer and partly as a producer. The illustration cited in Chapter 10 on the training of inspectors typifies the difficulties often experienced when training is offered by an employee who also is responsible for certain production. Of course it is often impossible to allocate any man or men permanently to the job of training. When the training has been completed, the job trainer often returns to his former activities, either as a producer or a supervisor. But usually it is advisable for him to function as a trainer when he is doing training and as an operator or supervisor when he is not doing training and not attempt to do both jobs at the same time.

The value of job training is so great that one division of the Office of Production Management has been created specifically to assist industry in setting up and administering such training. This organization is known as the Training Within Industry (TWI) Division of the Advisory Commission to the Council on National Defense. It has arranged for the publication and distribution of numerous materials, typical of which is the Manual on Job Instruction [5] of the Western Electric Company.

Job training of new employees

A great deal has been said in the early part of this book concerning the magnitude and significance of individual differences in employee productivity. It was emphasized that these differences are often due to individual differences in employee capacity for the job, which is measurable by appropriate tests at the time of hiring or placement. But it should also be recognized that individual differences in employee productivity are due often in large part to differences in the training that employees have been given. Seashore [6] has pointed out that at least three basic factors may cause individual differences in human abilities. These factors are: differences in biological bases of performance, differences in the amount of previous training, and differences in the particular work methods that are adopted by each individual during the learning period. If several new employees are started simultaneously upon a new job that is somewhat complex in nature, and if these employees are not given identical and standardized instruction in the operations of that job, it is quite unlikely that all will be equally skillful in adopting the most satisfactory work methods. It is exactly as if a number of persons start simultaneously, without instruction, to learn the operation of a typewriter. Some, if not most, persons in this situation will adopt the so-called "hunt

---

[5] *Job Instruction: A Manual for Shop Supervisors and Instructors* (Western Electric Company, 1940).

[6] R. H. Seashore, "Work Methods: An Often Neglected Factor Underlying Individual Differences," *Psychological Review*, XLVI (1939), pp. 123–141.

and peck" system, because this system is easily understood even without instruction and because it results almost at once in some evidence of accomplishment. A few, perhaps, who take the trouble to study the nature of the problem and thus become familiar with the fact that the touch system exists, and who are willing to sacrifice immediate evidence of accomplishment in favor of a learning procedure that eventually will result in considerably greater accomplishment, will not attempt the hunt-and-peck system at all but will start immediately to learn the touch system. After a period of time, say three months, those who learn the touch system will be many times more able to operate a typewriter in terms of both speed and accuracy than those who followed the more immediately apparent method of "hunting and pecking." With full recognition of the greater efficiency of the touch system, every commercial school supervises the training of students in typing so that all are taught the more desirable method. To facilitate the instruction, use is made of such devices as the blank keyboard to insure adherence to the preferred method and to avoid any relapse, even temporarily, to an undesirable method.

In many ways, performance on an industrial job is similar to typing. If employees are placed upon a new job without formal instruction in the operation of the job, each will adopt a method of work that is determined by (1) his insight into what is right and what is wrong, (2) his willingness to forego immediate accomplishment for greater later accomplishment, and (3) what he is able to observe of the activities of other employees on the same job. Management should not expect a new employee to have very much of the first factor mentioned above, that is, insight into improved work methods. Such insight comes only as a result of extended study in the field of motion analysis, the use of special equipment for performing motion analyses, and a considerable amount of specific study of each job. Neither should management expect employees to have very much of the second factor mentioned above. Each employee when placed on a new job assumes, if he is not instructed otherwise, that he is expected to obtain some production immediately upon that job. It would often be unwise, if not fatal, for him to attempt to teach himself a method that would result in no production for a period of four or five weeks, even if it were possible for him to do so. Management, on the other hand, should certainly not expect employees to have the time, training, or inclination to carry on a prolonged study of the job before attempting to achieve some production. For these reasons new employees will, in the vast majority of cases, adopt an inferior method of job performance if they are not subjected to a formal program of instruction. They will use work methods, to use Seashore's terminology, that will become fixed in the form of work habits that result in generally low production and that later must be unlearned before proper methods can be instituted.

This situation can largely be offset by a program of job training organized so that every new employee is taught from the outset the proper way to do his job. The job trainer must be a man who is thoroughly acquainted with motion study and who either has conducted motion studies of the job or has available such motion studies from the industrial engineering department. He must be a man who is able to teach the proper method to the new employees. The ability to teach presupposes something more than personal skill which he himself may possess. He must be both able and willing to explain the approved methods, be patient while these methods are being understood and followed, and be willing to devote considerable energy to the encouragement of employees during those periods in the learning process when little or no improvement or accomplishment seems apparent to the learners themselves. For example, reference to Figure 12 on page 16 will show that the average looper in the hosiery industry reaches what is called a *plateau* in learning from the seventh to the twelfth month on the job. During this plateau period little if any improvement in production is attained and as a result many employees, feeling that they have attained the limit of their production and being unsatisfied with their earnings, are likely to quit the job. A considerable investment is required by the company to bring an employee up to this level of performance. If an employee decides to quit at this point, the investment is largely wasted. One of the functions of the job trainer, then, is to keep the employees on the job until this plateau is passed. To do this requires a knowledge of the existence of the plateau and ability to explain it to the employees.

The job trainer has many responsibilities in addition to

instruction in the specific routine of job performance. Often he is the only man with whom the new employees are in daily contact. The impressions of the company which they form in the early stages of their employment, and which often remain with them as long as they remain employees, are often largely dependent upon their reactions to the job trainer. He must be able to explain company policy to the employees and to give them convincing reasons for the existence of these policies. He must be able to explain the wage-payment plan in operation and to show why this plan has been adopted by the company rather than some other plan which the employees might think is more fair. If he finds that certain phases of company policy are not in general understood or are not accepted by new employees, it is his job to relay this information to the department of industrial relations or to the other management men who are responsible for the adoption of the policies in question.

Employee training, as a branch of management, is becoming so important that many industries have set up as a part of their industrial relations department a specific training division.

Supervisory training

Perhaps no job in industry has undergone such great changes during the past twenty years as that of the supervisor or foreman. Two decades ago, when a supervisory position was to be filled, the best producer in the department was usually given the job without regard to his ability (or lack of it) in the industrial-relations phases of the supervisory position. As a result of this policy the foreman was often a "bull of the woods." He hired and fired, set the rates for his men, dealt with problems of discipline as he saw fit, was responsible for his own quality control, determined methods of work, did his own training, and took care of his own maintenance. The emergence and development of scientific management gradually took many of these responsibilities away from the foreman. Problems of hiring have largely been taken over by the personnel department. Responsibility for layoff has been assumed by the department of industrial relations. Wage rates have been established on a scientific basis by industrial engineers. Problems of discipline have largely been delegated to the supervisor of industrial relations. Quality control has often become so dependent upon the use of technical equipment that the creation of an inspection department has been necessary. Methods of determining the most efficient layout of work have been taken over by motion study specialists from the department of industrial engineering. Because of the increasing complexity of machinery, a specialized department dealing with the maintenance of equipment has been established. And now the training of new employees is becoming specialized with job trainers assigned to do work that was formerly conducted by supervisors alone.

Many foremen feel that these changes have gradually removed from the supervisor so many of his former duties and responsibilities that the very need for the foreman has almost disappeared. But with the removal of many of his former responsibilities and duties has come the assignment of many new duties with which the foreman was not concerned twenty years ago. The foreman of today must know the law. Daily, almost hourly, problems arise and decisions must be made in which the voice of the foreman is the voice of management. Recent social legislation has made it imperative that decisions made by management with respect to such matters as layoff, transfer, seniority, hours of work, wages, and a host of other matters must conform to certain legal requirements. Decisions on such matters must be made by the foreman. Often these decisions must be made at once, with no time for conferences or for consultation of statements of the law. Decisions may involve such problems as hours of work, settlement of a grievance, or interpretation of a union contract for determining the seniority of one man over another. Such decisions cannot be made by rule of thumb. They must be made, always, in the light of written laws, policies, and union contracts. The foreman must know these documents and their interpretation. He must be able quickly and accurately to size up a situation and outline a course of action that will not be in conflict with laws or agreements. A good producer might have made a good supervisor twenty years ago, but today the foreman must in addition be something of a lawyer and, incidentally, a pretty good one.

The foreman today must be a statesman who has both wisdom and power to act. Disputes were settled easily twenty years ago. The rule was simple and easy to learn—in any dispute the foreman was right and the employee wrong. Today both may be right or both may be wrong, or each may be partly right and partly wrong. A decision reached by management today must be made after consideration of all angles and the viewpoints of all parties. It is a commonplace observation that when authoritarian judgments give way to discussion as a means of settling grievances, a degree of mutual understanding must be developed by both parties. The foreman of today must not boss his men so much as he must understand them. He must know why this one becomes disgruntled upon slight pretext, why that one is often late to work. His job is to help the men help themselves. This is particularly true in periods of emergency production when, as one foreman put it, "You don't dare bawl a man out. If you do, he might quit." The foreman of today must know how to handle men without making use of a "big stick." Though the foreman has seldom studied the subject of psychology, it is very important for him to know, if he is to do his job well, that the desires and wishes of his men must be both understood and considered. Without such understanding he cannot hope to be a satisfactory supervisor.

The foreman must look upon the experts in personnel, motion study, rate setting, and so on, not as rivals and substitutes but as specially trained men who have been assigned to help him with his job. He must understand the services performed by these experts and be able to explain these services to the men. The wage incentive plan may be installed by an industrial engineer, but it is the foreman, not the industrial engineer, who must be able to explain the plan to the employees. When an employee cannot figure out why his pay check came to only $28.60 instead of $28.70, the foreman must be able to explain how the figure of $28.60 was reached. If he cannot do so, the worker may be disturbed out of all proportion to his imagined loss of ten cents.

Changes in the job of the supervisor such as those described above have made it necessary for management to devote considerable time and effort to the training of supervisors. Many industries have set up a complete program of supervisory training conferences, the purpose of which is to train the present supervisors in the newer aspects of their job that are developing almost daily and to prepare younger men who are to become supervisors. One plan in common use is to have every supervisor, or potential supervisor, attend a conference or class on company time for a period of from one and a half to two hours at approximately two-week intervals. The subject matter covered in such conferences varies considerably from plant to plant, and in each case is decided upon by management in the light of the needs of the industry. A typical list of the subjects covered in one series of supervisory conferences is shown in Table XVIII.

TABLE XVIII

TOPICS COVERED IN A SERIES OF SUPERVISORY TRAINING CONFERENCES [7]

1. Accident Prevention
2. Waste Prevention
3. Training for the New Employee
4. Re-training of the Present Employees
5. Cost of Maintenance
6. Cost of Materials Used in Ingot Production
7. Incentives (Financial and Non-financial)
8. Job Training
9. Stability of Employment
10. Co-operation
11. The Cost of a Ton of Steel
12. Direct Application of a Cost System
13. Inspection
14. Recognition of Ideas (old and new)
15. Transportation (inter and intra)
16. Methods of Handling Complaints
17. Plant Protection
18. Why Condition—Semi-finished Material
19. Discipline
20. Proper Methods of Dealing with Men
21. Product and Machine Innovations
22. Publication of Management's Policies (uniformity)
23. The Application of Conference Conclusions
24. Job Analysis versus Man Analysis
25. Service—What is it?
26. Quality versus Quantity
27. Seniority
28. "What's on the Worker's Mind?"
29. Collective Bargaining
30. Unemployment Insurance

While many of the topics listed in Table XVIII deal with matters of production, it will be noted that several are devoted to such matters as company policy, industrial relations, union

[7] R. J. Greenly, "Conference Leadership: Report on First Conference Leaders' Conference, Carnegie-Illinois Steel Corporation, Gary Works." (Indiana State Board for Vocational Education in Co-operation with the Training Division of the Industrial Relations Department, Carnegie-Illinois Steel Corporation, Gary, Indiana, 1937.)

TABLE XIX

A TEST USED IN MEASURING WHAT SUPERVISORS KNOW ABOUT COMPANY POLICY *

CASE NUMBER 1
SUPERVISORY PROBLEMS

Joe Blake is a tractor operator in No. 8 shipping department. He has worked for the company six months and had a clean record until a week ago. Before coming to this job he worked for a neighboring company and was highly recommended by them. A week ago his tractor became overheated because of a dry radiator and had to be sent to the shop for repairs. Both shipping and repair departments were behind schedule and the resulting delay due to the absence of this tractor caused considerable confusion and loss.

One of the tractor rules states that each operator shall inspect his machine thoroughly before work is begun, and also before turning the machine over to the next operator. Joe Blake, like all other operators in the department, does not make the first inspection but, according to agreement among the tractor operators,

makes a careful inspection at the end of the turn so the following man finds the machine ready to go.

After investigating, the foreman reported the incident as an act of carelessness and a clear violation of the plant rules, and consequently penalized Joe by giving him a one-week layoff. Joe reminded the foreman that it was a well-known and tolerated practice to omit the first inspection and brought in the previous operator who insisted that he had filled the radiator just before the breakdown. Being a new man, Joe did not feel it wise to argue further and accepted the penalty with good grace.

During the following week the rumor arose and was substantiated that the tractor breakdown was caused by a group of six Packagers who, as a joke, drained the radiator of Joe's tractor while he was away in the lavatory. These details and the names of the men involved were known to nearly everyone in the department.

INDUSTRIAL RELATIONS—CARNEGIE-ILLINOIS STEEL CORPORATION

The following statements apply to this situation. Study each one carefully. If you agree, put a circle around the "T" following the statement. If you do NOT agree, encircle the "F." If you are in doubt, encircle the double "??." Be sure to show your response clearly.

1. The six Packagers should be given penalties equal to Joe Blake's.	T	??	F	
2. The foreman should apologize to Joe and void the rule violation report.	T	??	F	
3. The foreman should let the report stand as it is, since responsibility for the continuous operation of the tractor is Joe's, regardless of the action of others.	T	??	F	
4. Joe should be given enough overtime work to make up for his week's loss.	T	??	F	
5. The foreman should be fired for allowing the inspection rule to be violated openly.	T	??	F	
6. The foreman should not change his action unless Joe takes the matter up with his grievance committee and threatens to demand redress.	T	??	F	

202

	T	??	F
8. Joe should be transferred to another department and other steps should be taken to "hush up" the foreman's action.	T	??	F
9. The company should refuse to recognize the act of the packagers since delayed recognition of that aspect of the case might be held against the company at a later date as an example of management's arbitrary policies carried out without proper investigation.	T	??	F
10. A general survey should be made to see that plant rules are being obeyed to the letter throughout the department.	T	??	F
11. All the tractor operators in the department should be penalized for wilful neglect and carelessness because of their practice in regard to the inspection rule.	T	??	F
12. The foreman should protect his men by explaining to his supervisor that he had known of and tolerated the limited inspection practice.	T	??	F
13. The foreman was not responsible for the limited inspection practice even though he knew of the rule violation.	T	??	F
14. The foreman should conceal the matter from his supervisor, if possible, since admission of his tolerance of a rule violation would serve only to increase friction and undermine his authority.	T	??	F
15. The company should not permit the foreman and superintendent to admit that an error of hasty misjudgment was made, since that would lower employee morale.	T	??	F
16. The tractor operators as a group had no responsibility in this case because the inspection practice was tacitly approved by the foreman who is management's representative.	T	??	F
17. The responsibility for the occurrence rests solely with the six packagers.	T	??	F
18. This is one of those situations in which the responsibility cannot be fixed.	T	??	F
19. Blame for the occurrence rests solely with the foreman.	T	??	F
20. A foreman should be certain of his information and of all the facts before he takes action against an employee.	T	??	F

203

* R. J. Greenly, "The Case Method in Supervisory Training," American Management Association Personnel Series No. 56, (1942), pp. 30-35.

contracts, and the services of experts in such fields as job analysis and insurance.

It has already been emphasized that some means of measuring the effectiveness of training should be employed. A typical method of measuring the effectiveness of training in company policy is illustrated by supervisory case problems, with related true-false questions, such as the one reproduced in Table XIX on pages 202–203.

The Joe Blake case (the name is fictitious) is an actual case that arose in one industry during one of the conferences on company policy. The answers to the twenty true-false questions obtained from a group of supervisors not only furnish management with a means of knowing how well prepared supervisors are to handle this type of problem but also indicate what areas of company policy should be covered in the supervisory training conferences in order to achieve a unified understanding of company policy on the part of supervision. A series of twenty cases, with twenty true-false questions on each case—from which Case 1 was taken—furnishes management with a 400-item true-false test with which to measure how much the supervisors know about the administration of company policy. True-false or objective questionnaires, formerly considered purely academic in application, have been found to be serviceable as measuring instruments in practical industrial training situations. Similar use may be made of multiple-choice questions dealing with company policy.

Apprentice training

The training of operatives—either old or new employees—can ordinarily be carried on as the need for operatives arises. An immense number—perhaps a large majority—of industrial employees are engaged in semiskilled jobs that require an intensive but not an extensive period of training. Trainees for such jobs can often be prepared in a relatively short period of time—often only two or three weeks. The training of supervisors, on the other hand, requires considerably longer. An adequate understanding of the increasingly complex duties of the modern supervisor ordinarily requires a several months instructional period. Industries must therefore use considerable foresight in anticipating supervisory needs so that training programs may be undertaken in advance of the actual need for supervisors.

Another area of industrial training in which still greater foresight must ordinarily be exercised is the training of skilled tradesmen. This training is usually accomplished by means of an apprentice program. Except for college-trained technical men there is perhaps no other single group of industrial employees who require so extensive a period of training for expert performance as do skilled tradesmen. The federal committee on apprenticeship training specifies that the training period for apprentices shall be not less than 2000 hours, and that the shop instruction shall be accompanied by not less than 144 hours of instruction under public authorities. These stipulations reflect the well-substantiated judgment of those experienced in this field that adequate training of skilled tradesmen requires an intensive and extensive instructional period. These facts make it more necessary for industry to look into the future in the training of skilled tradesmen than in the training of many other types of industrial employees. The various details in the administration of an apprentice program, together with the contractual agreement between the apprentice and the employer, are not of primary concern to the technical psychologist, and therefore will not be discussed here. Psychology, however, may be definitely applied in the use of aptitude and qualification tests for the selection of boys to receive apprentice training. While mass production in industry has reduced the proportion of employees who must be skilled tradesmen, the design, construction, and maintenance of machines has increased so much in complexity that a very high level of capacity is required of the boy who is to become a skilled tradesman. Figures 5 to 8 in Chapter 1 show that the range of ability among applicants for apprenticeships is large indeed. Any program of apprentice training that does not provide an adequate means of selecting trainees according to their capacity to benefit from the training is likely to result not only in a failure to develop expert tradesmen but also in the waste of a considerable company investment in the training given. Those responsible for the administration of an apprentice program should therefore work in close collaboration with the testing division of the personnel office so that trainees will be selected who are able to take full advantage of the opportunity offered.

Other fields or types of training

A complete industrial training program provides for several types of training in addition to those mentioned above. Among these is the training of college graduates. It has long been recognized that the average college man needs help in bridging the gap between the campus and the plant. Every industry has specialized equipment, processes, and methods of production that are quite unknown to the college student at the time he goes to work. A training program that permits him to spend a certain amount of time in each of several departments so as to obtain a background of practical experience which he can relate to his technical training is an indispensable part of an adequate training program for newly inducted college men. This problem is met to some extent by the so-called co-operative systems of higher education in which the student alternates between college and industrial employment, each activity occupying approximately a six-months period. This procedure does not entirely solve the problem, however, partly because the co-operative plan is not in extensive use and partly because even where practiced it acquaints the student only with those industries in which he has had his work experience. Plants differ markedly not only from one industry to another but even from one plant to another in the same industry. Until a student has had an opportunity to learn at first hand the production problems of the plant in which he is later to work he cannot be expected to be a very valuable member of the organization. Thus, special training for college men is nearly always necessary as one phase of a training program.

Related trade training in various forms offered by public-school systems is another type of training commonly used by industry. With the passage of the Smith-Hughes Act in 1917 and the George-Deen Act in 1936, certain funds were made available to school systems through the state offices of education to encourage the development of various forms of vocational education. The particular type of education or training that may be offered by a public-school system can usually be de-termined largely by the needs of local industries, if the industrial men responsible for the training are willing to work in co-operation with the school officials in organizing the courses of study. Under this plan, school systems may give in evening and extension classes technical training in areas related to the jobs of men employed by local industrial plants. This system not only removes from the industry a considerable responsibility in the training of employees in newer developments of their work, but also furnishes a desirable relationship between the schools and the industries.

Correspondence courses furnish another type of training that is often helpful in keeping employees abreast of their jobs and technically prepared to assume more responsible positions. However, certain objections to correspondence courses as a means of training have been raised. These courses, though usually of considerable value in fields that have been well standardized, often do not take into consideration the specific needs of any local industrial situation. It is also true, unfortunately, that often the employees who elect to take the correspondence courses are not the ones who would profit the most from them. As Bird and Paterson [8] have pointed out, correspondence schools could be of much greater service if, instead of selling a course to anyone, they would select students in terms of aptitude and previous training. As it is, only 6 per cent of the group of 305 persons investigated by Bird and Paterson completed the course which they had started.

Some Characteristics of Learning

The problems of industrial training may properly be considered as a branch of educational psychology or the psychology of learning. A great many investigations dealing with the problems of learning have been conducted; from these investigations a set of general principles, part of which are applicable to the industrial situation, has emerged.

The learning curve

Almost every psychological investigation of a learning activity results, among other things, in obtaining a learning curve. Such

[8] C. Bird and D. G. Paterson, "Commercial Correspondence Courses and Occupational Adjustments of Men," *Bulletin of the Employment Stabilization Research Institute, University of Minnesota*, II (1934), 27 pp.

a learning curve for the operation of looping in the hosiery industry is reproduced in Figure 12 on page 16. Learning curves for the operations of trimming, covering, and hemming in the textile industry are reproduced in Figure 68 on page 187.

The learning curve for a given operation shows at a glance the level of skill that has been reached by the average operator after a given period of training or experience on the job. Anyone who is responsible for the training of new employees on a specific job will find that a learning curve obtained from the records of previous employees is of considerable value. From such a curve he will be able to see immediately whether the progress of an operator is up to standard and, if not, how far the performance is below standard at any time in the instructional period. He will also be able to detect immediately whether an employee is maintaining his former level in comparison with the standard curve or is gaining or losing in comparison with other employees. In short, he will have a basis of comparison by means of which he can evaluate the effectiveness of his own instruction and the effectiveness of the learning that is taking place in the new employees. If an employee falls below the curve by a significant amount, and, in spite of every effort of the employee or the instructor to remedy the situation, continues to lose ground in comparison with the curve for the average, it is possible that the employee should be transferred to some other job before too much time and effort have been wasted in training him. It is even desirable, in some instances, to supply each new employee with a copy of the learning curve for the job and allow him to plot his own curve on the same chart, thus giving a graphic record of progress from day to day or week to week.

It should not be inferred from the foregoing discussion that there is any generalized form of learning curve that can be reduced to a mathematical equation and that applies to all learning situations. Many factors determine the form of a learning curve, and these factors vary greatly from one situation to another. Since one of these factors is the method of training, it is not uncommon to find different learning curves for the same industrial operation when different methods are involved. Indeed, a comparison of the resultant learning curves for different methods of training is an excellent way to compare the effectiveness of the methods. But with the various factors, such as method of training, held as constant as possible a reasonably standardized curve results for a given operation for the average person. It is this learning curve that the job trainer should have available if he is to evaluate adequately the effectiveness of his instruction and the progress of the trainees who are under his supervision.

The plateau

In learning any complex task it often happens that, after a certain level of efficiency has been attained, a period of time arrives in which little or no improvement takes place. This period is followed by a later increase in skill. The period during which no apparent improvement occurs is known as a *plateau*. Plateaus are not always present in the learning curves for industrial operations, and when they are present it is sometimes possible to eliminate them by changed or improved methods of instruction. No matter what method of instruction may be in use, however, arrival at a plateau in the learning process often is characteristic of the average learner's performance.

A typical example of a plateau in a learning curve is shown in Figure 12 on page 16. We do not need to concern ourselves here with the cause of the plateau, although it might be mentioned that a considerable amount of psychological investigation has been devoted to this subject and a number of experiments have been made which have identified certain factors that may result in a plateau.[*] If a plateau is characteristic of the average learning curve of an industrial operation it is highly important for the job trainer who is supervising this training to be aware of the situation. Without such knowledge he may feel that his training is inadequate, that the trainees have lost interest or that they have reached the maximum level of which they are capable and therefore need no further training, or that many of the employees should be shifted off the job because they are unable to reach the level of production achieved by experienced operators. If, on the other hand, he is aware of the existence of the plateau, he will continue his instruction, encourage the trainees to stay with the job until the end of the plateau is

[*] W. H. Batson, "Acquisition of Skill," *Psychological Monographs*, XXI (1916), pp. 1–92.

reached, and hold in abeyance his final judgment of the trainees' ability until they have had an opportunity to benefit from the final spurt in production that is certain to follow the plateau if the training is continued.

By analyzing the activities occurring during the plateau period it is often possible to modify the training program so that the plateau may be partially or entirely eliminated. Whether or not the job trainer is able to achieve this result, his knowledge of the existence of the plateau, together with his awareness of the fact that this situation is by no means uncommon in the learning of industrial tasks, will enable him to cope with the situation in a more intelligent manner and to help tide the employees over a period that, at best, is likely to involve a certain amount of discouragement.

Knowledge of results

One way in which training may be, and often has been, given is briefly to explain the work to the new employees and then to "turn them loose," so to speak, to perform the job without systematic or adequate check-up on the quality of their work. Another method is to follow the initial instruction period by frequent and systematic study of job performance and to provide a means for informing the trainees or new employees in exactly what respects they are doing the job correctly or incorrectly. Both experience and experiment have shown that the former method of training individuals in any new task results in a considerably lower level of job performance than the latter method. This principle was first pointed out in connection with the learning of arithmetic among school children. Panlasigui and Knight [10] found that if children are consistently informed of all errors made in arithmetic they show a significantly more rapid improvement in learning the arithmetic computations involved than if they are given exactly the same sets of drills and are not provided with a "knowledge of results." Book and Norvell [11] found the same principle operating in the learning of mental

---

[10] I. Panlasigui and F. B. Knight, "The Effect of Awareness of Success or Failure," *Twenty-Ninth Yearbook of the National Society for the Study of Education*, Part II (1930), pp. 611–619.

[11] W. F. Book and L. Norvell, "The Will to Learn," *Pedagogical Seminary*, XXIX (1922), pp. 305–362.

multiplication. In their experiments the persons in the experimental group watched the record of their progress and attempted at each practice to make a higher score than the score made previously. Persons in the other, or control group, were not

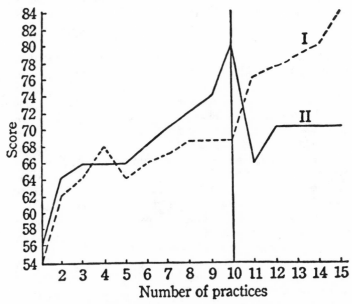

Fig. 71—How knowledge of results affects performance in learning a new task.

informed of their progress. These results are summarized graphically in Figure 71. After the tenth practice period, the conditions were reversed so that the persons formerly receiving knowledge of results were no longer informed of progress. The persons formerly uninformed of accuracy were now given information as to their progress. The curves in Figure 71 show that immediately after the tenth practice the groups changed their relative standing. The group that was given knowledge of results forged rapidly ahead of the other group.

One need not look long in industry to find situations parallel to this experiment. In the investigation of inspectors summarized in Chapter 10 the accuracy of many inspectors was found to be significantly below that of which they were capable and also below the level of accuracy required for satisfactory job performance. It was found that the level of accuracy characteristic of many employees in this department was traceable to the training procedure that had been followed prior to this experimental work. The former training method consisted in placing each new operator between two older operators who were asked to instruct the new employee in the details of the job. Since each of the older employees had a definite amount of work to perform during the day it was only natural that they should spend little if any time in training the new employee. Indeed, it was found in many instances that the older employees resented this additional training load and as a result did not give the new employee adequate training in the details of the inspection job. This method of training resulted in a lack of standardization of inspection practice among the employees and many of the inspectors were overlooking certain defects that they were *able* to detect but which they had not been trained to observe. The new training program instituted in this department included the assignment of specific job trainers to the task of teaching new employees so that they would be able to develop satisfactory standards of performance without guessing at which sheets were satisfactory and which were defective.

The general principle of job training is that new employees will improve very slowly—if, indeed, they improve at all—unless they are provided with systematic and accurate information on the quality of their work. Provision for furnishing new employees with definite knowledge of results should be an integral part of any training program.

Motivation

Ordinarily speaking, people will not learn very much about anything unless they are motivated to do so, that is unless they are supplied with an adequate incentive. Incentives in industry are usually considered under two general heads: financial and nonfinancial. Under financial incentives are considered those that pertain to methods of wage payment, such as an hourly rate *versus* some form of piece work. One of the major problems in industrial management is that of deciding upon a wage payment plan that will result in a satisfactory level of job performance and at the same time will be considered by the employees to be a fair plan. If the plan in use does not place a proper premium upon high production, it often happens that the employees never bother to learn the skill required for a very high level of job performance.

A typical example of this situation is furnished in a study by Kitson.[12] Kitson examined the production records of 40 hand compositors whose experience ranged from one to twenty-seven years with an average of eight years. The average output of these employees was 55 units for a week of work on a scale of efficiency established by time studies. An incentive system of wage payment was installed which permitted the employees to earn a bonus for production over the previous average amount. Within five months these employees were averaging 97 units on the scale and at the end of a year the average output had reached 103 units. This experiment made it clear that the previous method of wage payment did not provide sufficient motivation for these employees to learn the skill necessary for high production, even though they had been on the job a number of years.

Incentives are not limited to financial incentives. A number of investigators of this subject, for example Lee[13] and Miles,[14] have stressed the fact that such factors as recognition of good work, a fair system of promotion, and job security all lead to an attitude of mind on the part of the employee that helps develop a desire to learn the job well and to turn in a satisfactory performance on the job.

Another aspect of motivation upon which the evidence is reasonably clear and convincing is the relative desirability of rewards and punishments. Translated into industrial terms, this question raises the issue as to whether a new employee will learn faster and better if he is complimented for all good job performance or if he is criticized for all poor job performance. Since any new employee will do some things correctly and other things incorrectly, it is quite possible to use either or both of

[12] H. D. Kitson, "Extra Incentive Wage Plans from a Psychological Viewpoint," *Bulletin American Management Association, Production Executive Series*, No. IX (1925), p. 7.

[13] C. A. Lee, "Some Notes on Incentives in Industry," *The Human Factor*, VI (1932), pp. 180–186.

[14] G. H. Miles, "Effectiveness of Labour Incentives," *The Human Factor*, VI (1932), pp. 53–58.

these methods while he is learning the job. Judging from a number of related investigations in the field of experimental psychology, it seems clear that praising satisfactory performance is the more desirable method to follow.[15] Modern industrial practice has largely adopted this point of view, primarily because it results in more satisfactory industrial relations.[16] It is interesting and fortunate that experimental studies in psychology substantiate this judgment for the quite different reason that praise is superior to criticism as a means of inducing the employee to learn.

Attention to specific features of the job

All but the simplest of industrial jobs require several different types of skill or ability. The stenographer must be able not only to take shorthand but also to use a typewriter. The inspector is often required to spot certain defects of appearance visually, other defects by weight or feel, and perhaps still other defects by means of readings taken from special instruments. It often happens that the several aspects of a job are sufficiently independent of each other to necessitate the giving of special training for each. Reference to Table XXVII on page 270 shows that the intercorrelations between accuracy of inspectors in detecting different kinds of defects are in general quite low. This means that the inspectors who are best in detecting certain defects are not necessarily better than average in detecting other defects. To learn an inspection job efficiently new inspectors cannot simply be told to "throw out the defective material." They must be given specific instruction in the nature of the defects and taught what to look for in each specific case. Training must be specific and to the point instead of haphazard and general.

Transfer of training

Does training on one industrial job transfer to another job? Will an employee who has been thoroughly trained in one operation be easier to train in a new operation than an employee

---

[15] E. L. Thorndike, "Effects of Punishment and Reward" (University of Chicago Press, 1932).

[16] J. J. Jackson, "Reprimanding Employees," *Personnel Journal*, XIX (1941), pp. 73–80.

who has not had this previous training? These questions have stimulated a great deal of investigation by psychologists. At one time it was felt (with little or no experimental evidence to support the viewpoint) that training would develop certain general "powers" or "faculties" so that a person trained in one kind of activity would be more able to do many other kinds of activities in which these faculties might be used. It was felt that the memorizing of Latin verbs and conjugations would improve one's memory so that he would be better able to memorize insurance premium tables or grocery price lists. In industrial terms, training in the operation of one machine, it was felt, would improve an employee in ability to operate some other machine with which he had had no direct experience.

This notion—the wholesale *transfer of training*—has been subjected to a great deal of experimental work beginning with that of Thorndike and Woodworth.[17] The conclusion reached by these early investigators—and substantiated by several more recent studies—is that the amount of transfer from one skill or mental function to another is far less than was formerly believed. Indeed, Thorndike [18] has concluded that transfer in a general way does not occur at all and that what is often regarded as transfer is simply due to *identical elements* in the two jobs under consideration. These identical elements may be activities (usually manipulative activities in industry) or methods of work. An example of the former would be any routine assembly operation that is identical with the operation in some other assembly job. An example of the latter would be the methods of laying out work that would be similar from one job to another in the activities of a motion study or layout man.

The conclusion to be kept in mind is that supervisors should not expect more transfer to occur than can be expected in terms of definite similarities in the jobs. Because an employee has been able to learn and successfully perform one job is no guarantee that he will do as well on some unrelated job. On a second job he may succeed or he may fail, but his performance

---

17 E. L. Thorndike and R. S. Woodworth, "The Influence of Improvement in One Mental Function upon Efficiency of Other Functions," *Psychological Review*, VIII (1901), pp. 247–261, 384–385, 553–564.

18 E. L. Thorndike, "Mental Discipline in High School Studies," *Journal of Educational Psychology*, XV (1924), pp. 1–22, 83–98.

is neither limited nor determined by his performance on the first job.

This principle is recognized by many supervisors and personnel men. The frequent shifting of an employee from job to job until one is found that he can perform satisfactorily indicates that the success of an employee on one job does not necessarily indicate his success on another.

Negative transfer or interference

If the individual who has taught himself the "hunt and peck" system on a typewriter decides to learn the touch system, he must give up the use of all, or most, of the habits he has already formed. It is usually as difficult to break old habits as to learn new ones, and sometimes much more difficult. Thus, one who has thoroughly learned the wrong way to do a thing before he is taught the right way has the double task of unlearning old methods and learning new ones.

Unlearning errors is a most wasteful form of learning.[19] It is not surprising, therefore, to find experiments showing that when learners have previously been taught *one* method of doing a task, they have more difficulty in learning a new method than do learners who have had no previous experience on the job at all. This principle is known as negative transfer, interference, or inhibition. Its application to the industrial situation suggests that the time to teach employees the correct way to do a job is when they are placed on the job, not after they have had a few days or weeks of experience in learning incorrect methods.

---

[19] E. L. Thorndike, E. O. Bregman, J. W. Tilton, and E. Woodyard, *Adult Learning* (The Macmillan Company, 1928), p. 183.

8

Work, Fatigue, and Efficiency

CAREFUL consideration of employee aptitude before placing men upon a job followed by a thorough program of training employees on the job will go far toward achieving—but will not guarantee—a satisfactory level of job performance. Other factors besides employee aptitude and training may operate to prevent production from reaching the expected level; and in some cases a proper consideration of these other factors may result in fairly satisfactory production even when little specific attention has been given to employee placement and job training. These other factors have been classified in different ways. They may properly be thought of as related to employee efficiency, job performance, effort expended, or fatigue.

The present discussion will be primarily concerned with the relation of various factors to industrial fatigue. This point of view requires that a definition of industrial fatigue be given and a comparison made between the industrial definition of fatigue and other meanings of this term that are in common use.

The Nature of Fatigue

At least three conceptions of the term *fatigue* are important to our discussion. These are (1) physiological fatigue, (2) psychological fatigue, and (3) industrial fatigue.

Physiological fatigue

It may be readily demonstrated by simple physiological experiments that a muscle undergoing a simple rhythmic contraction gradually loses its ability to make the contraction. Thus, if one squeezes a coiled spring at intervals of two seconds he will find that his squeezes become less and less powerful until finally, if the task is maintained for sufficient time, only very small changes, or no changes at all, in the spring can be noticed. The energy used in the execution of a task of this sort, or any muscular task, comes from potential energy that is stored in chemical form in the muscles. As this energy is expended, the muscles become less and less able to perform their task. This reduction in potential energy available in the muscles may be thought of as physiological fatigue. Starling [1] has stated that the phenomena of fatigue, from this point of view, probably depend upon two factors, namely, the consumption of the contractile material or the substances available for the supply of potential energy to this material, and the accumulation of waste products of contraction. These waste products may be thought of as the chemical result of the muscular activity. Among them lactic acid is probably of great importance, because it is known that fatigue may be artificially induced in a muscle by feeding the muscle with a dilute solution of lactic acid.

To the physiologist, then, fatigue is primarily a matter of chemical changes in the muscle itself or the potential energy available for the muscular contraction. It should be kept in mind that this conception, in and of itself, does not involve a feeling of tiredness on the part of the subject, nor an immediate reduction in the amount of work he is able to do if he is not attempting to do a degree of work that requires more energy than is available at the time.

Psychological fatigue

Entirely aside from the physiological changes occurring in fatigue, it is a matter of common experience that with a repetition of certain tasks one becomes "bored," "uninterested," and in other ways manifests a lessening desire to continue the performance. Or one may simply have feelings of tiredness accompanied by a desire to do something else "for a change." From this point of view, fatigue may be looked upon as the feeling of boredom that often accompanies continued application to any given task.

For one speculating upon the subject of fatigue, it is a temptation to look upon these two aspects of the phenomenon— the physiological and the psychological—as different aspects of the same fundamental change. According to this point of view, feelings of boredom and tiredness occur in proportion as

---

[1] E. H. Starling, *Principles of Human Physiology*, third edition (Lea and Febiger, Philadelphia, 1920), p. 209.

physiological changes in the muscle have taken place; and vice versa, actual changes in the physiological composition of the muscles have taken place to the extent that feelings of tiredness or boredom are experienced by the subject.

If this simple relation were true, the problems of fatigue and its elimination would be greatly simplified. Unfortunately, numerous physiological and psychological experiments have shown that no such simple relationship exists. Indeed, it is necessary to look only at one's own experiences to understand that exceptions to such a relationship are by no means uncommon. Anyone who has driven a car a very long distance to a vacation resort knows that interest in reaching the resort is often maintained long after the body, from the physiological viewpoint, would rather sleep. And everyone who has had a routine, uninteresting, manipulative job to do knows that feelings of boredom often become prominent long before an excessive amount of work in the physiological sense has been performed.

We are thus presented with two contrasting, and in many cases unrelated, conceptions of the term fatigue. Because of the great importance of fatigue among industrial employees and the necessity of discovering ways of reducing or eliminating it, the industrial psychologist has been forced to accept a still different definition, a definition that is concerned primarily with the production or output of the employees.

Industrial fatigue

Fatigue is important in industry not to the extent that it involves physiological changes in the muscles, or feelings of boredom on the part of the employees, but, rather, to the extent that it involves on a long or a short term basis a reduction in the employee's efficiency on the job. Various measures of employee efficiency have been proposed and used for different purposes but, everything considered, the most satisfactory measurement for most purposes is production. The industrialist, therefore, defines *fatigue as whatever changes occur as a result of work that result in decreased employee production.* This does not mean that the industrialist is uninterested in the physiological causes of fatigue nor in the accompanying feelings of boredom. Rather it means that unless these changes result eventually in reduced output, on either a long or a short time basis, he cannot justifiably give very much attention to them. The problems of industrial fatigue, therefore, become essentially problems of determining what such factors as conditions of work, posture, hours of work, or nutrition, contribute toward the maintenance of proper production, and what factors result in, or are accompanied by, an undue reduction of employee output. Vernon [2] has defined industrial fatigue as "the sum of the results of activities which show themselves in a diminished capacity for doing work." Since this definition of fatigue has been found to be most satisfactory in industry, it is the definition that we shall follow.

An acceptance of this definition for industrial purposes does not mean that the physiological or psychological definitions are not of definite value. Rather it means that the industrialist is interested in fatigue in these latter senses only to the extent that it results in lowered production. But, just as the physiological and psychological definitions of fatigue do not always agree with each other, so also the industrial definition does not always agree with either of these two. For example, Arps [3] has pointed out that a production curve can be maintained at a fairly high and constant level if incentives are sufficiently strong even though physiological changes indicate a great or even unwise expenditure of energy. Of course, management is seldom interested in maintaining production by an expenditure of energy that will result in lowered output from a long-time viewpoint. But here again the final criterion as to whether fatigue is really present in the industrial sense is not whether physiological evidences of fatigue can be observed at the time but whether any reduction in output can be noticed, either at the time or in the future, as a result of the activity.

Factors Related to Industrial Fatigue

Illumination

In a number of investigations, such as those reported on page

[2] H. M. Vernon, "Industrial Fatigue in Relation to Atmospheric Conditions," *Physiological Reviews*, VIII (1928), pp. 130–150.

[3] G. F. Arps, "A Preliminary Report of 'Work with Knowledge versus Work without Knowledge of Results,'" *Psychological Review*, XXIV (1917), pp. 449–455.

136, it has been found that an employee's job performance is related to his visual acuity at the work distance. Visual acuity, however, is dependent not only upon the visual mechanism of the employee but also upon the illumination under which the work is done. The relation between visual acuity and illumination has been plotted by Troland[4] according to data published by König.[5] The results plotted by Troland show that acuity increases over a considerable range of variation of intensity in almost direct proportion to the amount of illumination. These results suggest that employees on certain types of industrial work should be provided with sufficient illumination to insure a satisfactory level of visual acuity. Wetzel[6] has pointed out that gains in visual acuity are very perceptible up to about 40 foot candles. A thorough study of the effects of different systems of lighting upon output and accuracy of employees engaged in fine work has been published by Weston and Taylor.[7] The effect of various degrees of illumination upon the output of employees can readily be studied by means of control experiments in which illumination is varied and the production measured under varying conditions. Such experiments often make it possible to increase production by an amount that is worth many times the cost of the extra light.

Visual adaptability to the job

Experiments summarized in Chapter 6 on page 162 show that output of employees on certain types of close work can be definitely increased either (1) by placing on the job only employees who are visually adapted to it or (2) by adapting the employees to the job by means of special occupational spectacles. These experiments may properly be considered as experiments in the reduction of visual fatigue. Indeed, some of the early workers[8]

---

[4] L. T. Troland, "The Principles of Psychophysiology, *Sensation*, II (D. Van Nostrand, New York, 1930), p. 86.

[5] A. König, "Abhangigkeit der Sehschärfe von der Beleuchtungsintensität," Sitzungsber. der Akad. der Wiss., Berlin, Bd. XIII (1897), pp. 559–575.

[6] M. Wetzel, "L'eclairage dans l'industrie," *Recherches et inventions*, VIII (1927), pp. 81–95.

[7] H. C. Weston and A. K. Taylor, "The Effect of Different Systems on Output and Accuracy in Fine Work," *Joint Report of the Industrial Fatigue Research Board and the Illumination Research Committee* (H. M. Stationery Office, London, 1928).

[8] See footnote 20, page 160.

on this subject have considered their work primarily in the field of fatigue. The experiments summarized on page 162 will not be discussed here, but it should be emphasized that the proper allocation of employees according to their visual qualifications is one method of eliminating or markedly reducing visual fatigue. Such reduction often results in an increase or maintenance of satisfactory production.

Temperature and ventilation

The effect of varying temperature upon employee efficiency has not been accurately determined for all types of work, due partly to the fact that the temperature of the atmosphere, or what is ordinarily known as dry-bulb temperature, seldom varies alone. Almost always when atmospheric temperature varies, other conditions, such as humidity and the amount of radiated heat, do not remain constant. However, in spite of the difficulty of controlling conditions, a few studies have shown that temperature is related to employee efficiency. For example, Vernon, Bedford, and Warner [9] found that when temperature was below 70 degrees, only 3 per cent of the time was lost as a result of employee sickness; when temperatures were from 70 to 79.9 degrees, 4.5 per cent of the time was lost; and when temperatures were 80 degrees or more, 4.9 per cent of time was lost as a result of sickness. These findings indicate that the optimal temperature is below 70 degrees. In another investigation Yagloglou [10] found that "the optimum temperature for individuals at rest, or otherwise engaged in light activities in still air and normally clothed" was 64.5 degrees effective temperature. These findings suggest that care should be taken to insure temperature conditions that are not excessively high. Some industries have found that the installation of air-conditioning equipment is a sound investment from the point of view of increased employee productivity.

Although proper ventilation has been found to be more dependent upon circulation of the air than the continual intro-

[9] H. M. Vernon, T. Bedford, and C. G. Warner, "A Study of Absenteeism in a Group of Ten Collieries," *Industrial Fatigue Research Board*, Report No. 51 (1928).

[10] C. P. Yagloglou, "Modern Ventilation Principles and Their Application to Sedentary and Industrial Life," *Journal of Personnel Research*, III (1925), pp. 375–396.

duction of fresh air, ventilation has also been found to be of considerable importance. Wyatt, Fraser, and Stock [11] report an experiment in which suitably placed fans were operated on alternate working days over a period of six weeks during the summer. Their experiments show that when the air is circulated by the fans the production of the employees is significantly higher than when no provision is made for circulating the air. Bedford [12] has pointed out that the sensations of warmth that one experiences depend upon air temperature, air movement, air humidity, and radiation. All of these factors must be considered in insuring optimum conditions for work.

Noise

A great deal has been written concerning the effect of noise upon employee efficiency and fatigue. Often the elimination of noise has been recommended on the grounds that employee efficiency will be greatly improved. Indeed, several experiments, such as the one reported by Scheidt, [13] have shown that noise-proofing the workroom or putting employees in individual booths will improve the quality of their work. To the practical industrialist, however, the elimination of noise presents a serious problem. One can hardly imagine a steel mill in which noise has been eliminated or even very much reduced. In steel, as in heavy industry in general, noise can seldom be avoided. Therefore, even though it is true that fatigue may be lessened by reducing noise, we will not suggest such reduction as a practical method of eliminating fatigue in all situations. Too often it is impossible to reduce the noise. It should be kept in mind, however, that when a high noise level is present, employee efficiency may be affected and that it is often possible to recapture some of the lost efficiency by introducing certain other controls in the form of nourishment, rest pauses, or certain favorable work methods.

---

[11] S. Wyatt, F. A. Fraser, and F. G. L. Stock, "Fan Ventilation in a Humid Weaving Shed," *Industrial Fatigue Research Board*, Report No. 37 (London, 1926).

[12] T. Bedford, "Requirements for Satisfactory Ventilation and Heating," *The Human Factor*, X (London, 1936), pp. 246–254.

[13] V. P. Scheidt, "The Effect of Various Modifications on the Worker," *Kalenda*, XVI (1937), pp. 3–4.

Nourishment

The energy one expends in work comes from the food he eats. Without food, or with food that is insufficient either in quality or amount, one soon loses the ability to withstand physical exertion. Too often the relation between the price of food and its nourishment or energy value is none too high. Some industries have found that a program of employee education dealing with types, caloric values, and vitamin and mineral content of food, and, in general, how to get the most value for one's food dollar, has been of value in improving the diet of employees. A few industries have found that giving extra meals on the job is worth while in terms of increased employee efficiency. Haggard [14] reports that when two extra meals were given, output rose 10 per cent and the workers reported feeling less tired in spite of their greater output. It has also been reported [15] that drinking a one per cent salt solution is effective in reducing industrial fatigue.

Hours of work

During the past fifty years the trend toward a reduced number of hours in the working week as well as a shortened working day has been fairly constant. This change has been due partly to the feeling of labor that life should not be "all work and no play," but it has been also due in no small measure to an increased recognition by management that employees do not reach their greatest efficiency when the number of working hours is excessive. Many experiments have been conducted to determine the relation between the hours of work and employee production. The reduction in hours of work has been largely justified by these experiments. Miles and Angles [16] report that when the hours of work in a plant manufacturing boxes were reduced from 48 to 36 per week the average hourly output increased from 793.5 to 834.0 units of production. In another experiment [17]

[14] W. W. Haggard, "Work and Fatigue," *Mechanical Engineering*, LVIII (1936), pp. 298–301.

[15] A. B. Dill, A. V. Bock, H. T. Edwards, and P. H. Kennedy, "Industrial Fatigue," *Journal of Industrial Hygiene*, XVIII (1936), pp. 417–431.

[16] G. H. Miles and A. Angles, "The Influence of Short Time on Speed of Production, II," *Journal of the National Institute of Industrial Psychology*, II (1925), pp. 300–302.

[17] C. S. Myers, *Mind and Work* (Putnam, London, 1921).

dealing with women engaged in the work of turning fuse bodies, a 68 per cent increase of hourly output and an increase of 16 per cent in total production followed a reduction from 66 to 48.6 in the number of hours worked per week. The general conclusion suggested by these and similar studies is that employee fatigue is lessened and output correspondingly increased if the number of working hours per week does not much exceed 40.

Of course, during a period of emergency production, it is not always possible to achieve maximum efficiency by means of a short working week. At such times it is often necessary to get out maximum production even though by so doing maximum efficiency, from the long-time viewpoint, may be sacrified to some extent. But even during a period of maximum production the question may be raised as to whether real gain can be achieved by excessive lengthening of work hours. Ivy [18] has recently suggested that from the physiological viewpoint we will sacrifice rather than gain, even in terms of short-term production, by increasing the hours of work beyond 56 hours per week for men or 48 hours per week for women.

Rest pauses

A great many investigations on the effect of rest pauses have been conducted. These studies have considered employees on both heavy and light work, and employees paid under a straight hourly rate as well as employees paid under a wage incentive plan. In this field, the work of Vernon [19] and his associates is outstanding. Their studies have shown that rest pauses usually lessen fatigue and increase production in spite of the fact that the rest pause results in some reduction of the actual working time. Typical curves showing the production for a group of employees before and after the introduction of rest periods are shown in Figure 72. These curves are based upon the work of Farmer and Bevington. [20]

We will not attempt a generalization as to how long rest pe-

[18] A. C. Ivy, "The Physiology of Work" (Fourth Annual Congress on Industrial Health, Chicago, January, 1942).

[19] H. M. Vernon, "Industrial Fatigue and Efficiency" (Dutton, New York, 1921).

[20] E. Farmer and S. M. Bevington, "An Experiment in the Introduction of Rest-Pauses," *Journal of the National Institute of Industrial Psychology*, I (1922), pp. 89–92.

riods should be for any given industry, or how frequently they should be allowed during the day. Both the duration and the number of rest periods necessarily vary with such factors as the nature of the work, the effect of a temporary stoppage upon the

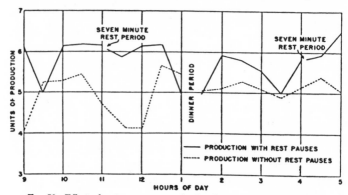

FIG. 72—Effect of rest pauses on production for a typical industrial job.

flow of production, and the availability of suitable rest rooms or other places in which the employees can relax. The duration of rest periods that have proved beneficial has varied from two minutes to fifteen minutes under different conditions, and the number of rest periods during the day has varied from one to five or even more. An excellent summary of representative studies in this field has been given by Viteles [21] and will not be repeated here. Anyone who wishes to consider the introduction of rest pauses for an industrial job should make a careful study of the literature to find an experiment in which rest pauses have been introduced on a similar job. It is sufficient to say here that such a study will almost certainly show the effect of rest pauses on a similar job and will point the way toward the type of rest pause or pauses that may profitably be introduced. In practically every investigation of this subject, some form or type of rest pause or pauses has been found to be worth while both from the point of view of employee comfort as well as that of increased production.

In considering the introduction of systematic rest pauses, it

[21] M. S. Viteles, "Industrial Psychology" (W. W. Norton, New York, 1929), pp. 470–482.

should not be assumed that if no rest pauses are formally allowed the employees will not rest. Several investigations have shown that if formal rest pauses are not allowed, unauthorized rests will be taken by the employees to suit their own convenience.[22] In some cases, such unauthorized rests are as effective in increasing production and allaying fatigue as rest pauses that are officially and formally allowed by management. But in other cases, employees who decide upon their own rest periods may do so in an ineffective manner, or may inconvenience the production schedule by resting at the wrong time. In general, it is a more satisfactory procedure for management to decide upon the proper amount and distribution of rest periods and then formally to allow those rests. Just as a man left to learn a job by himself may, and often does, adopt an inefficient and cumbersome way of performing the job (see page 275), so an employee left to decide upon optimal rest pauses for himself will not always adopt rest pauses that are of maximum value either to himself or to departmental production.

Work methods

If an individual has a pile of rocks to move from one location to another he can do the work with less physical fatigue by using a wheelbarrow than by carrying the rocks one at a time in his hands. This simple fact indicates the almost unlimited possibilities of fatigue reduction by making use of proper work methods. Gilbreth[23] was able to demonstrate more than thirty years ago that the work of the average bricklayer can be increased from 120 bricks per hour to 350 bricks per hour by following a more economical pattern of movement. This early study with its concrete results pointed the way toward an application of this principle—the lessening of fatigue by improved work methods—in a wide variety of industrial jobs. Motion economy has become so important a part of industrial management that every large industry—and many small ones—employ one or more industrial engineers whose major work is concerned with work layout and methods. The proper arrangement of work has been found not only to result in greater efficiency and

[22] R. B. Hersey, "Rests—Authorized and Unauthorized," *Journal of Personnel Research*, IV (1925), pp. 37–45.
[23] F. B. Gilbreth, "Bricklaying System" (M. C. Clark, New York, 1909).

production but also in some cases, as in the work reported by Crowden,[24] to result in temporary rests during the normal work cycle that provide the worker with almost all the advantages of rest pauses.

Financial incentives

People seldom do something for nothing. No one—whether employee or supervisor, executive or clerk, teacher or student—will achieve a very high level of performance on his job unless he is rewarded for doing so. Rewards may be financial payments in proportion to the actual performance on the job, or they may be nonfinancial returns that are desired by the person concerned. With the rise of modern scientific management, industry has devoted a great deal of attention to the subject of financial incentives. Several basic systems have been worked out that operate to pay the employee in accordance with the quantity or quality of work done. The effect of changing a wage-payment plan from a straight hourly rate to some form of incentive system has been shown in many investigations and is well illustrated in a study reported by Kitson (see page 213), in which a marked increase in employee production was found to follow the installation of an incentive plan of wage payment.

It should, of course, be kept in mind that too great a reward for high production may result in an unwise expenditure of energy by the employees. An incentive plan that encourages employees to overdraw their physiological bank account of tomorrow because of large financial payment today is not a sound plan from the point of view of either employees or management. But in many cases, as illustrated by Kitson's experiment, low production is due primarily to a lack of reward for high production. After the installation of an incentive plan the production was practically doubled and no unwise expenditure of physiological energy, either at the time or later, was indicated. The wage incentive plans used by industry may be administered so as to encourage high production up to a certain level and discourage production above that level if such production is likely to result in too great an expenditure of physiological energy.

---

[24] G. P. Crowden, "The Physiological Cost of the Muscular Movements Involved in Barrow Work," *Industrial Fatigue Research Board*, Report No. 50 (London, 1928).

Nonfinancial incentives

Men want, and will work for, many things besides money. On pages 315 and 316 are listed a number of nonfinancial returns that men want from their jobs. It is becoming increasingly apparent to management that without these "other things" no amount of financial reward, in and of itself, will result in complete job satisfaction. Nor will financial payment alone produce satisfactory job performance. Miles [25] has stressed the importance of nonfinancial incentives, and Lee [26] has quite correctly pointed out that financial incentives are not, by themselves, sufficient to produce "the will to work." The major things that employees want from their jobs, other than money, will be discussed in some detail in Chapter 12. For the present we wish only to call attention to the fact that, as Dickinson [27] has suggested, nonfinancial incentives will reduce fatigue and increase production.

Attitude and morale

The importance of employee morale is so great that a later chapter will be devoted to this subject. Dissatisfied or disgruntled employees readily become bored with their jobs, "tire" of doing their work, and in many other ways show evidence of feelings and behavior that result in lowered output. The so-called "fatigue" of such employees is seldom due to excessive expenditure of physiological energy. Rather, it is due primarily to a basic dissatisfaction which, interestingly enough, can seldom or perhaps never be remedied by wage increases alone. Factors that are related to employee morale and suggestions for improving it are discussed in detail in Chapter 12.

Mental abilities and other personality traits

The "born salesman" quickly becomes dissatisfied if he is forced to work by himself on a job that permits little or no contact with other people. The inventive or ingenious employee

[25] G. H. Miles, "Effectiveness of Labour Incentives," *The Human Factor*, VI (1932), pp. 53–58.

[26] C. A. Lee, "Some Notes on Incentives in Industry," *The Human Factor*, VI (1932), pp. 180–186.

[27] Z. C. Dickinson, "American Trends in Industrial Incentives," *Occupational Psychology*, XII (1938), pp. 17–29.

soon becomes bored with a job that involves only routine manipulative assembly.   It has been emphasized in Chapter 1 that
the proper placement of employees consists basically in assigning each employee to a job that is neither above nor below his
basic capacity and is in reasonable conformance to his basic interests.   Definite evidence shows that when employees are not
so placed they neither remain very long on the job (see page
2) nor perform the job very well while they remain on it
(see page 58).   Although such misplaced employees probably
do not become unduly fatigued in the physiological sense, they
do become fatigued in the psychological sense; and the results
of this psychological or mental fatigue are just as serious in
terms of reduced production or lack of attention to the job as
would be the case if the employees actually became physically
exhausted.   Wyatt, Langdon, and Stock [28] have emphasized the
fact that boredom is associated with intelligence, inability to
mechanize certain simple processes, and the desire for creative
work.   A typically bored worker is one who is on a job that is
below his natural level of capacity and ability.   To provide for
the training of such employees for a job that involves responsibility commensurate with their capacity, and to arrange for their
transfer to the new job when the training has been complete, is
a clearcut responsibility of management.   Such a policy of upgrading employees who have the capacity pays dividends both
in terms of improved production of employees on the routine
manipulative jobs and in terms of furnishing a valuable source
of employees for supervisory and other responsible positions.

---

[28] S. Wyatt, J. N. Langdon, and F. G. L. Stock, "Fatigue and Boredom in
Repetitive Work," Report No. 77 (Industrial Health Research Board, London,
1937).

9

Industrial Merit Rating

MERIT rating is a systematic evaluation of an employee by his supervisor or by some other qualified person who is familiar with the employee's performance on the job. Merit ratings are usually made by means of a standardized form that is adapted to the needs of the particular industry. Usually these ratings are made at periodic intervals. A merit rating thus becomes a permanent part of an employee's record with a given company, and, at least in theory, is a part of the record that may be used by management in subsequent promotion, demotion, transfer, or layoff.[1]

The Growth of Merit Ratings

A recent survey,[2] which contacted 64 companies employing from 500 to more than 100,000 employees, reveals that merit rating in some form is now in use by approximately one third of modern industrial establishments. Many factors may tend to increase still further the number of industries using a merit-rating system. Contracts that have been signed by management with labor organizations frequently contain a clause to the effect that an employee has a right to his job at the time of layoff in proportion to the amount of the employee's seniority, if other things such as "job performance, skill, and ability" are equal. Such a clause in a labor contract necessarily involves some method of measuring or evaluating whether the "other things" are equal. Merit ratings have frequently been proposed as one means of meeting this situation. Whether, eventually, merit ratings or some other tool or technique of management will be

---

[1] An excellent summary of practice and experience in industrial merit ratings appears in "Employee Rating: Methods of Appraising Ability, Efficiency, and Potentialities," *Studies in Personnel Policy*, No. XXXIX (National Industrial Conference Board, New York, 1942).

[2] R. B. Starr and R. J. Greenly, "Merit Rating Survey Findings," *Personnel Journal*, XVII (1939), pp. 378–384.

adopted to meet this need, at present an ever-growing number of industries are making a serious attempt to solve the problem with merit ratings. Whatever may be the industrial future of this technique, and however keenly one may be aware of the criticism that may be leveled against many systems of rating now in use, it seems clear that merit rating is likely to remain a sufficiently important part of personnel administration for some time to come to justify our giving rather careful consideration to its discussion.

One point should be made clear immediately: while the term "merit rating" is new, the rating of men by supervisors is by no means new. Such rating has been carried on as long as industry has been in anything like its present mass-production form. Supervisors have *always* rated men, and it is no doubt true that the ratings made in random, slipshod, and unsystematic fashion, unrecorded and undefended, have in the past been just as important, if not more important, in determining whether a given employee should hold his job as any rating made by means of a modern merit-rating chart. The changes that came with systematic merit rating, then, were not changes that involved a making of ratings where none had existed before; rather they were changes that involved the transfer of ratings from haphazard, random, and frequently irresponsible judgments of supervisors made perhaps during the heat of a quarrel, to ratings made calmly, deliberately, systematically, and in a manner that made the ratings, if not completely comparable from one employee to another, at least much more comparable than were the older, haphazard evaluations of employees by supervisors. The question, then, is not whether supervisors should rate their employees—this always has been and probably always will continue to be done—but whether the use of a formal merit-rating system is likely to increase the value of such ratings both to management and employees.

The Content of Merit-Rating Forms

In any discussion of merit ratings, several questions pertaining to the appearance and content of the merit-rating form immediately come to mind. The charts used differ so much from one plant to another that it would be quite unwise or even impossible to propose any single form that would be adapted to the needs of all industrial organizations. The wide variety both in traits rated and in number of traits rated may be seen from an analysis of the merit-rating charts of 18 companies [3] as shown in Table XX. In this table the companies are referred to anonymously by number across the top row of the table. The number of traits included varies from 21 in the case of Company 1, which is analyzed in the first column, down to four traits in the case of

TABLE XX
THIRTY-FIVE RATING ITEMS USED BY EIGHTEEN COMPANIES[4]

A check indicates that the item appears on the company's merit-rating chart. A number following the check indicates the weight assigned to the item. If no numbers appear it is intended to weight all items equally.

NUMBER OF COMPANY

	1	2	3	4	5	6	7	8	9	10	11	12	13	14	15	16	17	18	FREQUENCY
Quality		√8	√	√	√12		√50	√20				√	√	√	√10		√	√50	12
Quantity	√	√6	√	√	√10		√50	√25				√	√	√	√10		√		11
Co-operation	√	√6	√	√			√50	√8	√50	√			√	√	√10				11
Initiative	√	√6	√	√	√10		√50	√6	√50	√	√								11
Dependability	√	√6	√		√			√9	√50	√				√	√10		√		10
Personality	√			√		√	√50		√50	√	√		√		√10	√			10
Health	√	√4	√		√4	√	√50		√50			√				√			10
Safety	√	√6	√		√8		√50	√7	√50				√	√					9
Industry		√6	√	√	√10		√50			√	√				√10				9
Versatility		√6	√	√			√50	√15					√				√		8
Leadership	√	√6	√	√	√10			√5	√50	√									8
Judgment	√	√4					√50		√50	√					√10				7
Intelligence	√	√6	√		√12							√	√			√			7
Attendance		√4	√		√4			√5						√				√10	6
Knowledge of job			√	√			√50			√	√	√							5
Potentiality	√		√							√	√			√					5
Habits		√4			√6	√										√		√10	5
Years of service				√				√15					√					√30	4
Loyalty	√	√4			√														3
Ability to plan	√				√				√50										3
Enthusiasm		√4			√					√									3
Trade skill		√6			√10		√50												3
Technical knowledge		√4	√	√															3
Dependents								√10				√				√			3
Punctuality		√4	√																2
General rating	√								√50										2
Tact	√					√													2
Suggestiveness	√			√															2
Knowledge of costs	√				√4														2
Fairness	√																		1
Knowledge of product	√																		1
Knowledge of equipment	√																		1
Knowledge of company policies	√																		1
Appearance					√														1
Place of residence													√						1
Number of rating items	21	19	15	14	13	12	12	11	10	10	7	7	7	6	6	5	4	4	
Method of rating (C = committee; S = supervisor)	S	—	C	S	S	S	C	C	C	—	S	—	S	S	S	—	S	—	
Explanatory phrases used on rating scale	No	Yes	Yes	Yes	Yes	Yes	Yes	Yes	Yes	Yes	No	No	No	Yes	Yes	No	No	No	

[3] Starr and Greenly, *op. cit.* This article refers to a survey of 16 companies, but the tabulated results show an analysis of 18 merit-rating charts.

[4] From Starr and Greenly, *op. cit.*

the companies analyzed in the last two columns. The median number of traits used is ten; therefore, if any virtue lies in considering the practice of the typical or average industry as indicating the correct practice to follow, ten traits would be the proper number to list in a merit-rating chart. Probably, however, little virtue lies in attempting to fit a merit-rating chart to the average of a typical industry; it would, then, be better in any specific instance to adapt the chart to the industry intending to use it than to make it conform to a given set of characteristics, however representative this set of characteristics might be of industry in general.

There is some reason to believe that with the increasing use of merit-rating charts the tendency will be to rate fewer traits rather than more. The primary reason for this belief is to be found in the existence of the "halo" effect, a phenomenon almost always found in psychological ratings. This effect will be discussed in detail on page 238.

While it is not our purpose to present specific charts in use by industry for comment or criticism, one chart that has been found to function very satisfactorily in practice is illustrated in Figure 73. It is reproduced to clarify a number of principles that will be discussed later.

Some Values of Merit Rating

Regardless of a number of criticisms, statistical and otherwise, that may be directed against any merit-rating system—and which will be discussed on page 238—several values that are to be obtained from such a system are becoming more and more recognized by industrial relations and employment managers.

To obtain these values it is necessary that the results of the merit rating be made available through the proper channel to the employees who have been rated. Whether the "proper channel" should be the supervisor who made the rating, the superintendent of the department, a psychological counselor, or someone else, depends upon many factors. The experience of many industries has been that the employees should be informed of their ratings by some production man—either the foreman himself or the departmental head. However, production men often require special training before they are able to do this smoothly and effectively. Strangely enough, many supervisors who are good production men are perfect bunglers when discussing a man's weak points face to face with the man. To do this successfully calls for tact, objectivity, and a sincere interest in helping the

---

PROGRESS RECORD

Name_____Dept._____Div_____Date_____

Employee's Position_____Job Class_____

Note   This rating will represent in a systematic way your appraisal of the employee in terms of his ACTUAL PERFORMANCE ON HIS PRESENT JOB   In the interests of furthering careful analysis, the following suggestions are offered regarding the use of this form

    1   Consider only one factor at a time

    2   Study each factor and the specifications for each grade

    3   Review upon completion to see that the rating of each factor applies exclusively to the individual's ACTUAL PERFORMANCE ON HIS PRESENT JOB

    4   Comment fully at bottom of page and on reverse side upon any matter which in your opinion needs explanation

PERFORMANCE FACTORS	PERFORMANCE GRADE				
	Far Exceeds requirements of this job	Exceeds requirements of this job	Meets requirements of this job	Partially Meets requirements of this job	Does Not Meet requirements of this job
QUALITY OF WORK Accuracy Economy of Materials Economy of Time (his own and others) Neatness Thoroughness	Consistently superior ☐	Sometimes superior ☐	Consistently satisfactory ☐	Usually acceptable ☐	Consistently unsatisfactory ☐
QUANTITY OF WORK Productive Output	Consistently exceeds requirements ☐	Frequently exceeds requirements ☐	Meets requirements ☐	Frequently below requirements ☐	Consistently below requirements ☐
DEPENDABILITY Follows Instructions Judgment Punctuality and Attendance Safety Habits	Consistently dependable ☐	Dependable in most respects ☐	Ordinarily dependable ☐	Frequently undependable ☐	Consistently undependable ☐
COMPATIBILITY Attitude Towards the Company Attitude Towards Supervisor Co-operation with Fellow-Employees	Inspires others to work with and assist co-workers ☐	Quick to volunteer to work with and assist others ☐	Generally works well with and assists others ☐	Seldom works well with or assists others ☐	Does not work well with or assist others ☐

COMMENTS _____

_____

_____

_____

_____

Fig. 73—A typical merit rating chart used in industry.

man as well as the business. Many industries have found it wise to devote an extended series of training conferences to teaching supervisors how to inform their men of weak spots without offending the men. When this result has been accomplished and when a supervisor is able to talk face to face with his men about their weak as well as their strong points, a long step has been achieved toward solidarity in the working group and toward the upgrading of men who otherwise might, for lack of information, either remain exactly where they are or actually regress.

Prevents grievances

A merit-rating system stimulates supervisors to talk over with their men possible sources of grievance before serious problems have a chance to arise. It is not only sound psychology, but good common sense as well, to "nip in the bud" any situation that may cause friction between two people. Many such situations are certain to arise in a working relationship as close as the one between employee and supervisor. Frankness on the part of the supervisor in making legitimate suggestions is facilitated by a merit-rating system. The spirit of constructive criticism can begin with the construction of the rating scale. Slocombe [5] has suggested that foremen and men to be rated should work together in deciding upon the content of the merit-rating chart. Such co-operation makes everyone concerned with the merit rating become a partner in the enterprise and paves the way for an effective and serviceable use of the system.

Improves job performance

If an employee, either for lack of experience or lack of information, continually performs his job in the wrong way, the supervisor will be doing both the employee and the company, as well as himself, a favor by bringing this matter to the employee's attention in the proper manner. However, unless a supervisor is required periodically to evaluate all of his employees with regard to their ability in various directions, it is quite likely that many aspects of an employee's performance that could easily be improved, and that the employee himself

[5] C. S. Slocombe, "Psychology of Co-operation," *Personnel Journal*, XVI (1938), pp. 325–332.

would like to improve if he were made aware of his shortcomings, will go on from day to day without correction on his part. To inform an employee of his strong and weak points is not only a reasonable and fair thing to do but is also good business for any management that is sincerely interested in having its employees perform their jobs in the best possible way.

Increases analytical ability of supervisors

It is very easy for a supervisor to judge a man as good or bad, strong or weak, desirable or undesirable, without asking himself the question, "Why have I judged this man in this particular way?" But when a supervisor asks himself the question, "Why is a certain employee unsatisfactory?" and when he is assisted in asking this question by a merit-rating chart that lists a number of characteristics in which the employee may be strong or weak, it is often possible to identify immediately a particular weakness that accounts for all, or nearly all, of the employee's undesirability upon a certain job. Perhaps the employee is on a job for which he does not have the necessary dexterity, strength, or adaptability. When one has determined *why* an employee is unsatisfactory on a certain job it is often possible to shift that individual to some other type of job for which he is more adapted and on which his performance will be more acceptable. A merit-rating chart increases the supervisor's consciousness of the need for such analysis of his employees.

Assists management in promotion, demotion, and transfer problems

Another value of merit ratings is that they help to supply an adequate basis for promotion, demotion, and transfer. In any large industry it is necessary to make changes of this type. Often such changes must be made quickly in order to take care of new business or to adapt the personnel of a plant to technological changes. A systematic and periodic record of an employee's rating while he has been on various jobs in the organization greatly simplifies the shifting made necessary by requirements of promotion, demotion, and transfer.

Reveals areas where training is needed

A fifth value of merit rating that is becoming more and more apparent with the growth of industrial "in-service" training is the manner in which such ratings help to locate areas where training can be given to advantage. For example, it is not uncommon to find that in a certain department the average rating of all employees on such a factor as "knowledge of their job" is consistently lower than the ratings of employees in other departments on this characteristic. This situation can often be remedied by the preparation of a job-training manual and the offering of training on those aspects of the job that will upgrade these particular employees. Likewise, a department in which the men are consistently rated lower in "co-operation" than are the other employees in the plant may bring to the attention of management a department in which something is wrong in the relationship between workers and supervisor. To determine whether such a situation is due primarily to the workers or to the supervisor often requires careful study. The difficulty may be due to the fact that the workers cannot get along with the supervisor, in which case perhaps the latter should be changed rather than the workers reprimanded. Whatever may be the cause or the eventual solution, the presence of such a situation is often brought to the attention of management only after a systematic plan of merit rating.

Some Dangers of Merit Rating

Although any merit-rating chart or system should be adapted to the needs of the organization in which it is to be used, certain principles, if followed, will definitely increase the value of the ratings and, if neglected, will cause, at the best, a marked reduction in the value of the ratings and, at the worst, serious trouble in the form of labor difficulties or industrial relations disputes. Several of these principles have been the subject of extensive study by psychologists.

The halo effect

More than twenty years ago Thorndike[*] pointed out on the basis of experimental evidence that a rater has a constant tendency to rate an individual either high or low in many traits because the rater knows (or thinks) the individual to be high or

---

[*] E. L. Thorndike, "A Constant Error in Psychological Ratings." *Journal of Applied Psychology*, IV (1920), pp. 25–29.

low in some specific or particular trait. Thorndike called this tendency the "halo" effect. Applied to the industrial situation, Thorndike's statement means that if the supervisor regards an employee as very satisfactory in terms of his general personality and co-operativeness, he is likely to rate the employee high also in such traits as productivity, ingenuity, inventiveness, adaptability, and perhaps many other traits.[7] In other words, it is difficult for any rater—particularly an untrained rater—to isolate and rate separately the various traits that an employee may possess. We have pointed out that the use of a merit-rating chart is likely to increase the ability of a foreman to make an analytical judgment; but we know that even under the most favorable conditions the halo effect will be present to some extent and that its results will be most prominent where ratings have been made by those unfamiliar with its very existence.

The halo effect can be minimized in several ways. Stevens and Wonderlic[8] suggest having each supervisor rate all of his men on one trait before going on to the second trait, on the second trait before going on to the third, and so on. Since this method causes the supervisor to think of all his men in connection with a given trait rather than to think of each man as a whole, the effect of this general change in point of view is a reduction of the halo effect. This effect can also be minimized by arranging the chart itself so that the desirable end of some traits is on the right-hand side of the scale whereas the desirable end of other traits is on the left-hand side of the scale. This procedure prevents a supervisor from checking down a column on the right-hand side for a generally desirable employee, or down the left-hand side for a generally undesirable employee.

The operation of the halo effect in an actual set of ratings is shown in Figure 74. This figure reveals graphically, for 18 randomly selected men from a large industrial organization, the relationship between ratings on overall job performance, accuracy, safety, and co-operation, on the one hand, and on the other an overall merit rating which included the four traits mentioned

_____

[7] A discussion of the halo effect in the industrial application of merit rating is given by R. S. Driver, "A Case History in Merit Rating," *Personnel*, XVI (1940), pp. 137–162.

[8] S. N. Stevens and E. F. Wonderlic, "An Effective Revision of the Rating Technique," *Personnel Journal*, XIII (1934), pp. 125–134.

above along with eight others that need not be identified. The 18 men are arranged in rank order from left to right according to their overall merit rating. These ratings are indicated by the heavy black line. The ratings of the 18 men on the other four

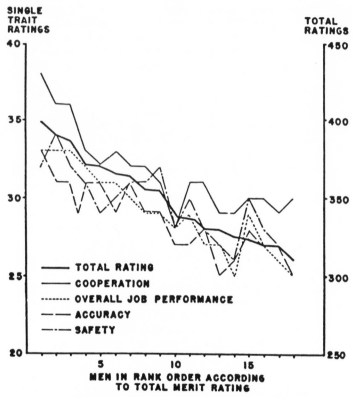

Fig. 74—Operation of the "halo effect" in industrial merit rating.

traits are indicated by the remaining lines. It will be seen from an inspection of Figure 74 that those individuals who tend to rate high in any given trait, say co-operation, are also rated about equally high on all of the other traits shown. Of course, it may theoretically be possible that the individual high in one trait is actually high in all of the other traits, but it seems much more likely that the halo effect, rather than any real relationship among the traits, is operating here.

Further evidence of a more extensive statistical sort of the existence of the halo effect has been obtained from a factor analysis of approximately 1100 ratings selected at random from a plant in which about 9000 employees had been rated.[*] The chart used involved ratings on twelve separate traits. These traits and the intercorrelations between the ratings for each pair of traits are shown in Table XXI. Such a correlational matrix containing correlations in general as high as those shown in Table XXI is sufficient in itself to indicate that a common factor is operating

TABLE XXI

INTERCORRELATIONS OF THE TRAITS IN A TWELVE-ITEM MERIT-RATING SCALE

Traits	1. Safety	2. Knowledge of Job	3. Versatility	4. Accuracy	5. Productivity	6. Overall Job Performance	7. Industriousness	8. Initiative	9. Judgment	10. Co-operation	11. Personality	12. Health
1. Safety												
2. Knowledge of job	.61											
3. Versatility	.52	.81										
4. Accuracy	.63	.85	.80									
5. Productivity	.55	.79	.72	.81								
6. Overall job performance	.60	.82	.80	.67	.86							
7. Industriousness	.49	.78	.71	.80	.86	.85						
8. Initiative	.54	.78	.78	.78	.80	.83	.82					
9. Judgment	.62	.80	.82	.84	.81	.88	.84	.86				
10. Co-operation	.61	.67	.68	.74	.81	.80	.80	.72	.76			
11. Personality	.55	.67	.63	.70	.73	.74	.67	.72	.75	.80		
12. Health	.25	.52	.50	.84	.45	.60	.53	.77	.43	.52	.71	

to influence most, if not all, of the ratings. The results of a factor analysis of these ratings quite definitely justify this judgment. Factor analysis is a statistical technique that reduces a set of measurements (such as test results or merit ratings) to the

[*] Edwin Ewart, S. E. Seashore, and Joseph Tiffin, "A Factor Analysis of an Industrial Merit Rating Scale," *Journal of Applied Psychology*, XXV (1941), pp. 481–486.

minimum number of basic variables or factors that will account
for the variations in the original data. The factor analysis of
the merit ratings revealed three basic factors, factor loadings
for which are given in Table XXII. In interpreting the importance of the different merit-rating items as they enter into
each of the three factors, we should bear in mind that the

TABLE XXII
Factor Loadings after Rotation

	Factor Loadings			h^{2*}
	I	II	III	
1. Safety	.633	.245	−.039	.462
2. Knowledge of job	.841	.337	−.002	.821
3. Versatility	.795	.325	.030	.739
4. Accuracy	.826	.448	.297	.971
5. Productivity	.913	.039	−.042	.837
6. Overall job performance	.961	−.080	−.064	.934
7. Industriousness	.906	.009	.007	.821
8. Initiative	.887	.094	.252	.859
9. Judgment	.897	.265	−.036	.876
10. Co-operation	.881	−.025	.042	.779
11. Personality	.815	.009	.259	.731
12. Health	.573	−.016	.836	1.027

* Communalities.

amount of the factor loading indicates the extent to which that
item is related to the factor in question. An inspection of the
merit-rating items entering into Factor I reveals that overall
job performance is loaded the most heavily; productivity, second; industriousness, third; judgment, fourth; and so on down
the list. If we were to attempt to name this factor, probably the
best name available would be "Ability to Do the Present Job."
In other words, this factor seems to be a job-performance factor.
Since the factor loadings on all of the traits entering into Factor I are high, compared with the loadings on Factors II and III
(except Health in Factor III), we infer that this factor is by far
the most important of the three in determining the overall merit
rating and that, since all of the heavily loaded traits entering
into Factor I deal rather specifically with ability on the job, it
would seem safe to identify this factor as a job-performance
factor.

Factor II contains no elements so heavily loaded as are those entering into Factor I. However, those most heavily loaded in Factor II are accuracy, knowledge of the job, and versatility. Judgment and safety are the fourth and fifth, respectively, but they are not so highly related to Factor II as are the first three traits named. If we attempt to name Factor II, a name must be found which combines the five traits as they are all related to the unnamed factor. Since none of the loadings for this factor is high in comparison with those for Factor I, we must conclude that none of the twelve items of the rating scale "taps" this factor very well. We are faced then with the task of naming this factor although we know only the following facts: (1) accuracy correlates with it .44, (2) knowledge of the job correlates with it .34, (3) versatility correlates with it .33, (4) judgment correlates with it .27, (5) safety correlates with it .25, and (6) no one of these items from the rating chart is a satisfactory name for the factor because no one of them correlates highly with the factor.

From this evidence it would seem that Factor II may deal with the *quality* of performance on the job. Skill and accuracy are also suggested as possible names. Since knowledge of the job has the second highest factor loading, perhaps promotability or likelihood of being promoted would be an appropriate identification of this factor. Whatever we may choose to call it, certainly this second factor is not the same as Factor I and it does not have as much influence on the total ratings, under the system which had been in use when these merit ratings were obtained, as does Factor I.

Factor III was found to be significantly loaded with only one element, namely, health. In other words, this factor was related to the health ratings and to nothing else. It should be mentioned at this point that the reliability of the ratings of the various traits had previously been obtained and, of all the traits, the one rated with the least reliability was *health*. Indeed, the reliability of the health ratings was only .37, and yet here we are presented with a situation in which the factor analysis shows a trait whose internal reliability is only .37 to have a factor loading on the third factor of .84. This would mean that a trait that correlates with itself only to the extent of .37 nevertheless correlates with something else (Factor III) to the extent of .84. Now, there is an axiom of statistical studies of reliability that no trait or measurements or rating can correlate with anything—except by chance—higher than it will correlate with itself. We are, therefore, presented with the paradoxical situation of explaining how ratings on a certain trait (health) are able to correlate .84 with Factor III when their reliability is only .37. The answer to the paradox is that the unknown factor identified in Factor III can be nothing but the unreliable health ratings themselves. The analysis reveals a third factor to account for these health ratings for the same reason that any unreliable, inconsistent, and random measurement would necessarily come out in a factor analysis as an independent factor. Such a factor would correlate with nothing else.

This evidence provides quite sufficient grounds for disregarding the health ratings as indicating anything except random and relatively worthless judgments of the moment. A further reason (if one were needed) for disregarding the health ratings would be the fact that an employee's health is, of all things, something that should be determined scientifically by a physician and not by the judgment of his foreman or supervisor.

The logical conclusion one would reach from the foregoing discussion is that the merit-rating chart in question should be reduced to only two traits and that these traits should be identified so as to cover as well as possible the two factors that the analysis revealed. The Western Electric Company, an organization entirely separate from the one in which the above analysis was made, acting upon the results of analyses made of its own merit-rating plan, has done exactly that. This company has reduced the number of traits rated to two. The plan now in use by this organization involves having each employee rated, first, upon his ability to do his present job, and second, upon his likelihood of being promoted. No further ratings of the men by their supervisors are asked for, and the management of this organization feels that it obtains more serviceable results from ratings limited to these two important traits than it had previously obtained from more analytical ratings. This case is cited as one indication of the fact that, insofar as the employee's overall merit is concerned, it seems clear that such a reduction in number of traits rated involves no sacrifice in either reliability or accuracy. However, it may well be that certain other advantages that accrue from merit rating—such as increasing the analytical viewpoint of the foreman and the identification of the employee who needs help or training—can be achieved by a more detailed type of merit-rating chart. Here again the problem must be solved by each industry in the light of the evidence and after a careful consideration of the needs of the particular plant.

It should be stated that the presence of only two factors in the ratings on twelve traits may be a reflection of inadequate training of the supervisors in the general principles of rating employees. One recent study [10] of a similar set of ratings obtained from supervisors who had been given seven hours of intensive training in rating methods revealed much lower intercorrelations than those shown in Table XXI.

The general conclusion with regard to the halo effect is that unless supervisors have been trained very carefully they may allow one trait of an employee greatly to influence their ratings of that employee on many other traits.

The "weighting" of traits

After a decision has been reached in regard to the particular traits that are to comprise a merit-rating chart, many industries have felt it desirable to weight each of these traits according to what seems to be the relative importance of each for success of employees in that particular organization. Thus, one industry might weight initiative twenty points and safety five points whereas another organization might reverse this weighting of items. Table XX shows that of the 18 charts analyzed, four, or 22 per cent, incorporated some sort of differential weighting for the various items. The remaining charts use either equal weightings or no weightings at all. Either of these methods is presumably intended to give the same importance to the several traits included on the chart.

At least two difficulties arise in connection with weighting of items on a merit-rating chart. The first of these is that items are not necessarily weighted equally when all are given the same maximum numerical value, nor are they necessarily weighted in the way intended when a predetermined set of maximum values for each is used. In combining scores—whether they are merit-

[10] Unpublished Study by R. S. Driver, Atlantic Refining Company, Philadelphia.

rating items, test scores, production records, or any other set of values—the scores weight themselves automatically in proportion to their respective variability. Expressed in statistical terms, the scores weight themselves in proportion to their respective standard deviations. Therefore, if the variability of all employees on one rating item, say health, is twice as large as the corresponding variability of all employees on some other item, say initiative, a direct combination of ratings for any employee on these two traits is actually weighting the health ratings twice as heavily as the initiative ratings. It might, of course, be the wish of management to weight those two items in this proportion, but it is unlikely that the chance weights that creep into a set of ratings as a function of their respective variabilities will weight the various traits in the manner desired by management.

The statistical reason for weights being determined by variability of the ratings is discussed in some detail in Appendix A, page 347. An example here may further clarify the principle.

Suppose that 1000 men have been rated on two traits, namely, health and initiative. Each man has been rated on each trait on a 50-point scale. Suppose, for the present illustration, that all of the men have received ratings on initiative of between 30 and 35 points. Suppose, further, that the health ratings vary from 25 to 45. If we now combine for each man his rating on initiative and his rating on health we will obtain a combination rating in which it has often been assumed (because each trait was originally rated on a 50-point scale) that the two ratings are weighted equally. Under these circumstances, however, the traits are not weighted equally at all. The health ratings, which vary over a range of 20 points—from 25 to 45—will have approximately four times as much effect on the total rating as the ratings on initiative, which vary over a range of only 5 points —from 30 to 35. A method of combining the ratings so that they may be weighted equally is described in Appendix A. If this method seems rather complicated, it can only be said that the rating of human personality traits is complicated and is difficult enough to accomplish satisfactorily even when all statistical safeguards are followed.

The fact that unknown weights for the various items on a merit-rating chart not only may but *do* creep in, if not guarded against statistically, is proved by an analysis of the merit ratings

of 1000 employees in a steel mill. The variability of the ratings
on each of twelve traits was computed and the standard deviations are shown in Table XXIII.

TABLE XXIII

Standard Deviations of Ratings of Employees in Twelve Traits [11]

Trait	Standard Deviation	Relative Weight
1. Safety	2.24	1.00
2. Knowledge of job	2.77	1.24
3. Versatility	2.88	1.29
4. Accuracy	2.69	1.20
5. Productivity	2.58	1.15
6. Overall job performance	2.63	1.18
7. Industriousness	2.96	1.32
8. Initiative	3.08	1.38
9. Judgment	2.68	1.20
10. Co-operation	2.72	1.22
11. Personality	2.51	1.12
12. Health	3.14	1.40

The employees had been rated on each of these traits on a
50-point scale, and it was assumed that this procedure resulted
in total ratings that were influenced in an equal amount by each
trait. Actually, the health ratings, which had the largest standard deviation, were exercising 40 per cent more effect on the
total ratings than the safety ratings, which had the smallest
standard deviation. Next in importance were the ratings on
initiative, which were exercising 38 per cent more effect than the
safety ratings. The relative weights actually exercised by each
of the twelve factors are given in the final column of Table
XXIII. It is doubtful whether the management of this company would have agreed upon this weighting of items if the matter had been discussed when the chart was constructed.

The simple adding of ratings for several traits not only fails
to weight the traits equally (except occasionally and by chance)
but also fails to give them any preassigned weights that might
have been decided upon and crystallized in the form of a maximum value that each trait may receive. Suppose, for example,
that management has decided that accuracy is twice as important as production and therefore has adopted a chart in which
accuracy is rated on a 40-point scale and production on a 20-
point scale. This arrangement will not necessarily result in ac-

---

[11] This table is from an unpublished study at Purdue University by Wayne
Musser.

curacy being weighted twice as heavily as production, for *the relative weights of the traits are determined by the variability or spread of each and not by the maximum values assigned to each*. It would be quite possible in the above situation for the production ratings to assume the heavier weights if the original ratings were directly added.

A second hazard related to the matter of weighting items on a merit-rating chart, even when proper steps have been taken to insure the functional operation of the weights decided upon, deals with the differential weighting of traits for employees on different jobs.

Suppose that a system is set up to weight experience twenty points and education five points. Let us say that an older man who has been on his present job for many years is now to be compared with a research man who has recently been employed. The older employee, because of his extensive experience, will receive practically the maximum amount of rating points for experience, but, because of lack of education, will receive little on that trait. Let us say that he gets the full twenty points for experience but only one or two points for education, giving him a total merit rating of 21 or 22 points. The research worker, on the other hand, having only recently joined the organization, receives a minimum of points on the experience rating but the maximum points on the education rating. Let us say that he receives three points for experience and the maximum, or five points, for education. His total merit rating would therefore be eight points which, compared with the 22 points received by the older employee, would seem on the surface to indicate that the older worker is a considerably more valuable individual to the organization than the research worker. Now it is entirely possible that the older worker is of more value to the company than the research worker, but it is by no means certain that he is. The point being made here is that a merit-rating system that weights the items as we have mentioned above is almost certain to give the worker of longer experience a higher total rating than the younger man.

It may be suggested that this difficulty may be eliminated by weighting all items equally. However, this procedure assumes that for all jobs on which the merit-rating system is to be applied the various traits included in that merit-rating system are of equal importance. This plan also involves an error in many situations. Consider, for example, the case of rating two clerics, one a receptionist secretary and one a private secretary to the plant superintendent. In many organizations the receptionist secretary, in order to do her job efficiently and satisfactorily, needs a maximum of appearance, poise, tact, and friendliness, and very little, if anything at all, of such traits as originality, versatility, and intelligence. The private secretary, on the other hand, needs all of these latter traits, although she perhaps does not need to be quite so personable on first appearance as does the receptionist secretary.

Several traits might well operate to give a total overall rating to the receptionist secretary considerably lower than that of the private secretary; and yet this receptionist secretary might possess the one or two characteristics that such a job requires so that she is not only highly satisfactory but actually is able to do this job even better than the private secretary would be able to do it if she were transferred to it. A supervisor in rating an individual in terms of his or her ability to do his present job tends to take all of these factors into consideration in an unconscious general evaluation. In the situation referred to above, it is quite likely that the receptionist secretary would be rated in terms of her present job as highly as the private secretary is rated in terms of her job. But if the merit-rating chart is so set up that it is necessary to rate each individual on a number of specific points and then to determine the total merit rating from some combination of these several ratings, it would be quite likely that an overall result not compatible with the facts would be obtained. Here, then, we are presented with a situation in which we must be careful about judging an employee's fitness on his present job by adding the results of several merit-rating items. From this point of view, the halo effect, as Bingham [12] has pointed out, may be the saving grace of a fractionated merit-rating system. In other words, when a supervisor begins to rate any given employee, he may, and probably does, first of all center his attention upon the particular trait or traits that are necessary for the employee on his particular job. After these traits have been rated, all of the remaining traits on the chart

[12] W. V. Bingham, "Halo, Invalid and Valid," *Journal of Applied Psychology,* XXIII (1939), pp. 221–228.

automatically fall in line in terms of where the key traits have been rated. But the old axiom that one cannot eat his cake and have it too prevails in the use of an itemized versus an overall merit-rating system. To the extent that the merit-rating system really does fractionate an employee's charactertistics, it is unlikely to give an accurate indication of the employee's ability on his present job; whereas to the extent that the system fails to fractionate the traits due to the halo effect, it is likely to work well in terms of giving an adequate overall indication. Some industries have solved this problem by using a dual system, that is, one in which the employee is first rated on overall ability on his present job before further ratings of a fractionated sort are obtained. Such a dual system will accomplish both results with little more labor on the part of supervisors than is included in any of the systems now in use.

Pooling unreliable with reliable ratings

It has been shown by psychological research that the reliability of ratings is increased when it is possible to pool the ratings of several raters. Such pooling, however, assumes that the various raters are all competent to rate the employee in question. It is not necessary that the raters be equally competent or equally familiar with the employee, but it is necessary that they have enough knowledge of the employee so that their rating is not based largely on chance. Acting on this premise, many industries have installed a system that involves pooling of two or three or even more ratings before a final overall rating of an employee is obtained. However, the very organization of a modern industrial establishment is such that the more ratings one attempts to obtain on a given employee, the further away from that employee in terms of contact with him one must go in order to obtain the additional raters. Unfortunately it is not necessary to go very far before one has brought in raters who are so far away from the actual observation of the employee on his job that their ratings of him are not only relatively worthless in themselves, but, what is worse, are also so inaccurate that when averaged with the ratings of the foreman in direct contact with the worker the result is to decrease whatever validity the foreman's ratings may possess. One rotten apple may spoil a bushel of good ones, and it is even more likely to spoil one or two good ones if those one or two happen to be in close contact with the spoiled one. Thus there is considerable danger in assuming that, because pooled ratings are known to have more reliability than individual ratings, pooling will automatically increase the validity of merit ratings. This result will not be accomplished if the pooling necessitates pooling unreliable with reliable ratings. An adequate merit-rating system should make provision for the rater to state how well he is acquainted with the employee and under what circumstances he has had an opportunity to judge him. This makes it possible to pool ratings when such pooling is likely to increase their value, and to avoid the pooling if by so doing the ratings would be made less valid.

Failure to determine the reliability of ratings

The general concept of reliability has been discussed in some detail on page 30 in connection with industrial-selection tests. It should be kept in mind that this concept is also directly applicable to merit rating. Only to the extent that repeated ratings will tend to give an individual the same rating, assuming that in the meantime he has had no opportunity to change, are we justified in allowing those ratings to influence our judgment of employees. The implication of this statement is that the more unreliable the ratings are the greater must be the change in an employee from one rating to another before we are justified in assuming that the change in rating actually indicates a corresponding shift in the employee's merit. One study by Reymert and Kohn [13] revealed the reliability for a nine-item scale to be .59 when two judges were used. This figure is rather typical of the reliability that may be expected of any merit-rating system based on two or three competent raters. When a ranking procedure rather than a rating chart is used in making the ratings, higher reliability (sometimes as high as .85 to .95) have been obtained. [14]

Data on the reliability of ratings on each item of a twelve-item rating chart, as well as the reliability of the total rating, are given in Table XXIV.

[13] M. L. Reymert and H. A. Kohn, "The Mooseheart Graphic Rating Scale for Housemothers and Housefathers," *Journal of Applied Psychology*, XXII (1938), pp. 288–294.

[14] Personal communication from Dr. H. C. Taylor of the Western Electric Company.

TABLE XXIV

RELIABILITY OF EACH ITEM OF A TWELVE-ITEM MERIT-RATING SCALE, AND
TOTAL RATING BASED ON THE SUM OF ALL TWELVE ITEMS

Trait	Reliability
1. Safety	.35
2. Knowledge of job	.46
3. Versatility	.47
4. Accuracy	.45
5. Productivity	.46
6. Overall job performance	.46
7. Industriousness	.47
8. Initiative	.48
9. Judgment	.45
10. Co-operation	.37
11. Personality	.39
12. Health	.36
Total	.55

The reliability coefficients shown in Table XXIV were obtained by correlating results from pairs of raters who had rated the same employee. The data are based on a total of 92 raters and 4,500 rated employees. While somewhat higher reliabilities might be obtained in other industries by means of a different merit-rating chart, it does not seem reasonable to expect the reliability of any ratings based on only two or three raters to reach a much higher level than the figures here cited. It is unwise to place too much confidence in any measurement that has a reliability no higher than .55, the value obtained for the summation of items on the chart.

Another factor that often tends to make the ratings more consistent from one year to another than the facts of the situation justify is the supervisor's memory of his previous ratings of the employees. It is only reasonable to expect that when a supervisor rates a man twice the second rating will be similar to the first if no marked new factors have arisen during the intervening period that might cause the supervisor to change his estimate of the man. The extent to which this memory element influences the consistency of ratings has been studied by determining the correlation between ratings on successive years for groups of employees who were rated by the same and different raters on the two occasions. The findings of this analysis are summarized in Table XXV. An inspection of this table reveals a consistent decrease in the size of the correlation from the situation at the top of the list, where the same three raters were involved during

TABLE XXV

CORRELATIONS BETWEEN RATINGS ON SUCCESSIVE YEARS OF EMPLOYEES
WITH SAME AND DIFFERENT RATERS

	Correlation
Same three raters both years	.65
One new rater second year	.59
Two new raters second year	.46
Three (all) new raters second year	.49

the two successive years, to the bottom of the list, where two or three new raters were involved the second year. These correlations should not, of course, be interpreted as reliability coefficients because the ratings were separated by an interval of a year, for during a period of that length many employees might actually change in such a way as to justify a change in the rating given them. However, the fact that a rather marked difference exists between the situation in which the same raters are involved and that in which one or more raters have been changed indicates that the constancy of the rater does affect the consistency of the rating.

All of these facts considered together indicate that merit ratings do not have a particularly high reliability. This does not mean that the ratings are of no value, but it does mean that one should be aware of their reliabilities and should not attempt to use merit ratings in a way that presupposes a higher reliability than they actually possess.

In proportion as ratings are unreliable it is not a valid procedure to consider a slight change in rating from one time to another as indicating a real change in the merit of the employee. By means of a simple statistical procedure, it is possible to obtain for merit ratings what is known as the probable error of measurement. Unless an employee's rating changes by at least four probable errors of measurement from one rating to another, it is unsafe to assume that any real change has occurred. In the case of the ratings that were used in determining the reliability coefficients summarized in Table XXV, the probable error of the total rating was fifteen points. This means that an employee must shift up or down by approximately sixty points before management is reasonably certain that an actual change in the employee's merit has occurred. It is therefore very important for management to know the reliability of the ratings that are used. Only through such knowledge is it possible to know whether the ratings indicate a real difference between two employees or a real change in an employee from one time to another.

Giving numerical values of ratings to employees

In one set of ratings studied, the numerical values, obtained by adding the points contributed by the twelve items comprising the scale, varied from 150 to 500. The reliability of this set of ratings as discussed in the preceding section was such that two employees must differ by at least 60 points before it can safely be assumed that a real difference between the two employees exists. In the light of this situation it is unwise to give the employees exact numerical statements of their ratings. One learns early in life that the figure 400 is larger than the figure 399. Therefore, if two employees should receive ratings represented by these numbers, one is likely to feel elated and the other depressed, though there is no reason at all for assuming that such a slight difference represents any real difference between the two employees. It is much safer to divide the range of ratings into four or five categories and to tell each employee only in which category he is located rather than exactly where he stands in that category.

A second problem in giving out numerical ratings arises when an employee compares his rating with a rating given him at some previous time. Suppose, for example, an employee's rating in 1940 is 350. He is not satisfied and makes every effort during the following year to improve his performance on the job. Possibly he attends night school, reads material related to his job, and in other ways makes a sincere effort to upgrade himself. At the end of the year the ratings are repeated and he finds that this time his numerical rating is only 345. One familiar with the fact that ratings are none too reliable even at the best would certainly not consider such a slight decrease from one year to another as indicating a drop in the employee's merit. But the employee himself, if these numerical figures have been given out, is very likely to adopt the policy, "What's the use?" If he has done everything possible during the year to improve himself, and finds at the end of that time that he has decreased in value to the company, he is unlikely to make any serious attempt in the future to improve his ability. This difficulty can be largely eliminated by giving out only general classifications such as A, B, C, and D. A "B-grade" employee is not likely to be depressed if at the end of the year he is still a "B-grade" employee, but he is very likely to be disappointed if, in terms of a numerical rating, he has dropped by even so much as one or two points.

Failure to consider departmental differences in rating

It often happens that the merit ratings turned in from different departments in a given plant differ markedly from one de-

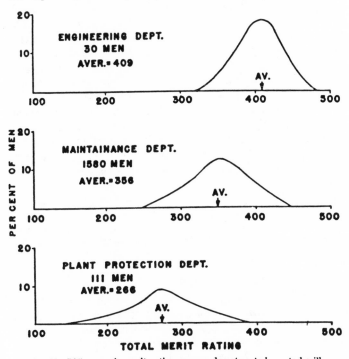

Fig. 75—Differences in merit ratings among departments in a steel mill.

partment to another. This may be due in part to actual differences in the merit of employees in the various departments, but it may also be due in part to differences in standards or interpretation of the merit-rating scale among the departments. Whatever may be the cause, when such differences do occur it is usually desirable to evaluate a given employee's rating in terms of the other ratings from the department in which he is working rather than in terms of the ratings obtained from the plant as a whole. This situation is graphically illustrated in Figure 75, which shows the distributions of total merit ratings obtained from three departments of a plant made up of 14 departments and employing approximately 10,000 men. The three departments selected for illustration are engineering, maintenance, and plant protection. These three have been selected to show the marked differences which may be found in ratings from one department to another. The difficulty of interpreting the significance of a merit rating without reference to the department from which it was obtained may be readily seen from inspecting Figure 75. For example, a merit-rating score of 350 would be a very low rating for a man in the engineering department. The same rating would be approximately average for a man in the maintenance department, and it would be very high for a man in the plant-protection department. Since one major function of a merit rating is to indicate how well—in relation to other employees—an employee is doing his present job, a fair and reasonable basis for comparison of ratings of different men must be employed. When ratings differ markedly from one department to another, evaluation of any rating should be in terms of the department from which it was obtained. The difficulty inherent in this problem can be largely eliminated by using separate norms for different departments.

Failure to consider job differences

Another source of possible difficulty closely related to the matter of departmental differences is the variation in rating often found from one job to another. When employees on any given job are consistently given higher merit ratings than are employees on other jobs, such job differences should be considered in evaluating the rating of any given employee. Figure 76 illustrates this situation for 51 jobs in a Sheet and Tin Mill. The 51 jobs studied are arranged in order from the one receiving the highest average rating (tinner) at the top to the one receiving the lowest average rating (opener and examiner) at the bottom. It will be noted that there is a variation from 280 to 385, or 105 points, in average merit rating from the lowest to the highest average rating. From these differences it is clear that a rating of 300 is very high for an employee who is on one of the jobs located near the bottom of the list, but that 300 is very low for an employee on one of the jobs near the top of the list. The

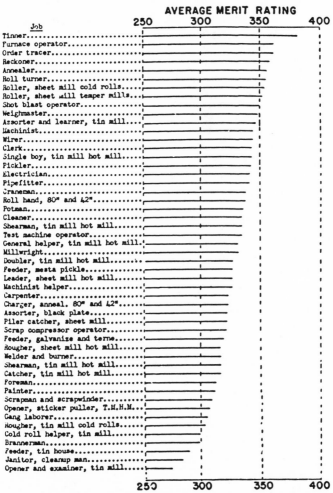

Fig. 76—Differences in average merit rating of employees on 51 jobs in a steel mill.

implication of this is that the merit rating of an employee should be evaluated in relation to the ratings of other employees on the same job or on jobs that are given approximately the same average merit rating.

Failure to consider the age of an employee

The age of an employee is another factor that is often related to the rating an employee receives. In one set of approximately 9,000 merit ratings obtained from a single industrial plant, the

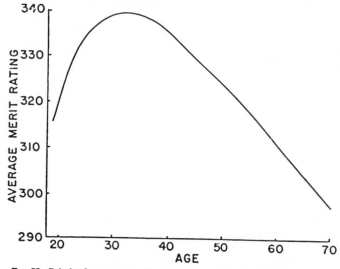

FIG. 77—Relation between age and average merit rating for 9000 steel workers.

relationship between total rating and age is graphed (Figure 77). This figure shows that an employee between the ages of 30 and 35, other things being equal, is likely to get a higher merit rating than an employee who is either older or younger. Figure 77 also shows that after this high point is reached a progressive decrease in merit rating takes place as age increases. It is clear from this chart that an employee with a merit rating of 330 would be definitely below average if he is in the age range from 30 to 35, but that he would be well above average if he is in the age range from 55 to 60.

Failure to consider other factors that may affect merit ratings

The preceding factors that should be considered in evaluating the merit rating of employees have been mentioned as illustrative of the kind of factors that have been found in a number of investigations to be related to merit ratings. Still other factors exist that may affect merit ratings in any given plant. Figure 78, for example, illustrates the relationship found in one plant between merit ratings and length of service on the present job.

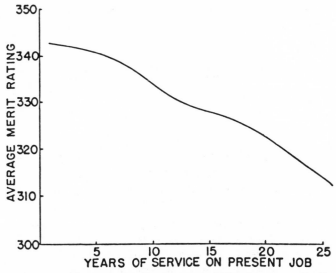

FIG. 78—Relation between years of service on present job and average merit rating for 9000 steel workers.

In definite contradiction to the opinion of management before these results were obtained, this chart shows a progressive lowering of merit ratings as the length of service on the job continues. In other words, the longer a given employee remains on a certain job, the lower the merit rating he is likely to receive from his supervisor. Probably the explanation for this relationship is that only those employees who are ineligible for promotion or transfer to another or more important job are likely to remain on their present jobs for a long period of time. Or perhaps, in this particular plant, the employees with longer service on their present jobs are in general older employees and may be unable to do the work as effectively as younger men. Whatever may be the cause of the relationship, it is clear that it exists and that it should, therefore, be considered in evaluating a given employee's rating. A rating, such as 335, that might be well below average for an employee of short service on the job, would be well above average for an employee who has been on the job 15 or 20 years.

Figure 79 graphs the relationship between merit rating and total service in the plant. It is clear that the drop-off or decrease

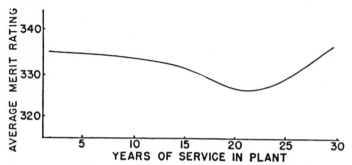

Fig. 79—Relation between years of plant service and average merit rating for 9000 steel workers.

in merit rating with total plant service is much less marked in the case of this relationship than in the case of the relationship with length of service on the present job. But here also a slight decrease in total rating seems to occur as the total plant service increases.

It is not meant to imply from the results summarized in the preceding sections that the relationships found in the studies reported exist in exactly this same form in all industries. Indeed, there is every reason to expect that these relationships are not universal and that opposite trends may occur in many plants. The point to be emphasized is not the universality of the trends discussed but the fact that no company can properly interpret the results of the merit ratings in its own plant or plants without definite knowledge of what trends and extraneous factors influence these ratings in that particular organization. The only way an organization may determine this is to make a set of analyses similar to those reported in the preceding sections. Such a procedure may be objected to on the grounds that it would involve more labor, and perhaps expense, than merit ratings are worth. It is entirely possible that this is true. But, if one is to obtain merit ratings that are to be used in evaluating employees, it is not fair either to management or to the employees rated to use ratings when it is not known definitely what factors have influenced them. If it is not possible to determine what these several factors are in any given organization, it might be a wiser policy to discard the ratings altogether than to attempt to use them without this information.

10

Industrial Inspection[1]

NEARLY all industrial products undergo some form of inspection. Sometimes inspection is accomplished by mechanical or other automatic devices, but often it consists of an inspection for appearance and is therefore dependent upon the visual and manipulative skills of the inspectors. The skills and capacities necessary for accurate inspection may be measured by means of certain psychological tests, and the training program that is given to new inspectors may also function more efficiently if the instruction is organized around basic psychological principles of learning.

This chapter describes certain procedures that have been found helpful in the selection and training of tin plate inspectors. It is recognized that the specific conclusions reached with regard to this one type of inspection may not apply directly to inspection of other products; but the methods described, which have been found to result in definite improvement both in the selection and training of these inspectors, apply with very little modification to the problems of selecting and training employees for any inspection job. It should be emphasized that the present discussion deals with *methods*. Application of these methods to tin-plate inspection has been chosen as a means of describing these methods because several years of first-hand experience in their application on this job have given direct evidence of their practicability.

The job of tin-plate inspecting, ordinarily called assorting, is essentially an inspection for appearance that is made while the inspector turns the sheets of tin plate from one stack to another. As the sheet is turned, the inspector makes a decision from the

[1] This chapter is based largely upon data previously published by Joseph Tiffin and H. B. Rogers "The Selection and Training of Inspectors," *Personnel*, XVIII (1941), pp. 14–31.

appearance and feel of the sheet as to whether it is a prime or a second or contains one of a number of possible defects. The standard size sheet is approximately 28 by 30 inches, though this varies with the specific order. In the plant studied, the work is done by women assorters.

Supervisors have generally felt that inspectors on this job do not reach their maximum performance until they have had approximately six months of experience. The inspectors are paid on a straight and uniform hourly rate. At the time of these experiments approximately 300 girls were employed in this operation.

Measuring the Accuracy of Inspectors

In many production jobs it is possible to determine the relative efficiency of a group of employees from records of production or earnings. Likewise, in some inspection jobs a reinspection of samples of material is often used to check the accuracy of the original inspectors. On the inspection job of the present study, however, neither of these indications of employee efficiency was available. The inspectors were paid on a straight hourly rate and the mechanics of wrapping and shipping made it impractical to reinspect samples of the material.

It was therefore necessary to devise a method of measuring the accuracy of the present inspectors. Since this problem often arises in an inspection department, we will give a fairly detailed description of the method used. This method resulted in a criterion of job performance that was used later in the investigation.

After considerable preliminary experimentation, a coded stack of tin plate containing 150 sheets was assembled. This stack was assorted (inspected) by 150 operators. This coded stack was made up of 61 prime sheets (sheets satisfactory in every respect) and second sheets (sheets containing a minor surface blemish or uneven coating of tin), 30 sheets containing appearance defect No. 1, 26 sheets containing appearance defect No. 2, 13 sheets containing appearance defect No. 3, and 20 sheets containing a weight defect. The prime and second sheets were included in a single category for the purpose of the experiment because with repeated assortings the prime sheets tend to become scratched and thus to become seconds. The other defective plates included in the coded stack remained the same regardless of the number of times the stack was assorted.

The defects will be referred to by number rather than by name because it is the method of measuring the accuracy of the inspectors rather than their accuracy on specific defects that is of primary importance.

Each sheet included in the coded stack was carefully selected in advance and was known definitely to be either a prime or a second, or to contain one of the defects selected for study. The 150 sheets were numbered in random sequence. As the inspectors assorted the sheets, they called aloud their judgment of each sheet as to whether it was a prime or a second or contained one of the defects, and, if so, which one.

As each operator assorted the 150 sheets her judgments were recorded by an observer. She was also timed with a stop watch. This procedure resulted in data from which it was possible to determine both the speed and the accuracy of the assorters studied.

The coded stack was scored for each girl according to the total accuracy on the 150 sheets and also for the accuracy on the specific defects. This resulted in five specific measurements of accuracy for each girl. It also resulted in a measurement of the reliability of each of the five methods of scoring the coded stack test. The five resulting measurements with their respective reliabilities are summarized in Table XXVI.

TABLE XXVI

THE FIVE MEASUREMENTS OF ACCURACY YIELDED BY THE CODED STACK, WITH THE RELIABILITY OF EACH

Method of Scoring	Reliability
Mixed sheets	+ .90
Appearance defect No. 1	+ .86
Appearance defect No. 2	+ .87
Appearance defect No. 3	+ .68
Weight defect	+ .74

The reliability figures given in Table XXVI were obtained by correlating correct inspections on odd versus even items for each defect, as described on page 32. The reliability indicates the extent to which repeated or duplicate measurements of each girl by means of the coded stack test would result in the same score for her for the defects in question. If repeated measurements would give exactly the same score to all of the girls on repetition of a given test, the reliability of that test would be + 1.00. If, on the other hand, the present scores given to the girls were entirely the result of chance and would, therefore, bear no relation at all to repeated measurements on the coded stack test, the reliability would be .00. It may be seen from Table XXIV that the reliabilities vary from .68 to .90. While these reliabilities are not as high as might be desired, they compare favorably with the reliabilities of many other industrial criteria that have been used to measure the successfulness of employees.

As the inspectors assorted the coded stack, they were allowed to set their own speed or rate of inspection. This resulted in very great differences in speed. The time required for the various girls varied from eight to forty-eight minutes. It was first thought that this uncontrolled time factor would be a marked handicap to this method of measuring inspector accuracy. After careful consideration, however, it was thought best to retain an indefinite time limit procedure because only under such circumstances would it be possible to determine for each girl the maximum accuracy of which she was capable. In other words, the coded stack test was deliberately given under conditions that would cause every girl to bring to bear every bit of inspecting knowledge she had and that therefore would allow her to reach a level of accuracy that was close to, if not equal to, the maximum accuracy of which she was capable.

The results of the coded stack test as administered to the 150 girls are summarized in graphic form in Figure 80. The six curves shown in this figure are frequency distributions obtained from the 150 inspectors.

The time curve in the upper left-hand corner indicates the number of girls completing the 150 sheets of tin plate in each of the times specified along the base line. The most rapid assorter, it will be noted, completed the test in 8 minutes, whereas the slowest required 48 minutes. The curve is highest over the region of 14 to 21 minutes, indicating that a plurality of the girls required between 14 and 21 minutes to assort the 150 sheets under the conditions of the test. The average time required, as indicated in Figure 80, is 20.1 minutes.

In the curve immediately below this the ordinate again represents the number of girls and the base line represents the percentage of accuracy for the entire stack of 150 sheets. The average accuracy for the 150 sheets under the conditions of this test was, as shown in Figure 80, 78.5 per cent. This does not mean that the accuracy of these assorters in a normal assorting

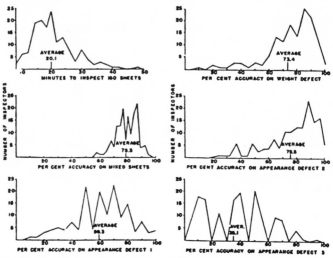

Fig. 80—Distributions of results on a coded stack test of 150 tin-plate inspectors.

situation is only 78.5 per cent. The assorting skill required to inspect the coded stack is greater than that required in a normal assorting situation, because more defective plates of various types were included in the test than are found in the run of the mill and the defective plates were not included in any sequence or groupings. The test as given measures differences among the girls in their skill on this job but probably gives to each girl a somewhat lower score, that is, a poorer accuracy, than she customarily reaches in routine daily assorting.

The remaining four curves in Figure 80 give similar distributions for the four specific defects studied. Figure 80 shows, among other things, that for the four defects studied the average inspector is most accurate on appearance defect No. 2 (75.5 per cent), and least accurate on appearance defect No. 3 (35.1 per cent). The data also show a great variation among the various girls in their accuracy on any specific type of defect. For example, 8 girls out of the 150 detected only 5 per cent of appearance defect No. 3, whereas one girl spotted 95 per cent of the sheets containing this defect. There is nearly as wide a variation in accuracy for the other four defects studied.

Inspection of Figure 80 also reveals that the amount of variation among the girls, that is, the range from the poorest to the best, is smaller for the curve representing total accuracy than for the several curves representing accuracy on specific defects. The reason for this is that only a slight relationship exists between accuracy in detecting any one defect and accuracy in detecting other defects. Thus, if a girl is far above average in detecting one defect she is likely to be at average, or possibly below average, in detecting other defects. This fact tends to give scores for the total 150 sheets of mixed plate more nearly alike than the scores for the various individual defects.

It will be noticed that the average accuracy on mixed plate is higher than the accuracy on any specific defect. This difference is due to the fact that a majority of the sheets included in the coded stack were primes or seconds and that the acceptable sheets were seldom called defective, whereas the defective sheets were frequently called primes or seconds. In other words, there was a tendency to overlook the defects. Hence, the accuracy for the total stack, which included a majority of primes and seconds, and a minority of defective sheets, was found to be higher than the accuracy on any specific defect studied.

The next question investigated was the relation between speed and accuracy in detecting the different types of defect. The results for this part of the investigation are summarized in graphic form by the curves in Figure 81. Each of the curves in this figure is a logarithmic curve of best fit [2] representing the relationship between speed and accuracy. The equations of the curves shown in Figure 81 are as follows:

Percentage accuracy on appearance defect $1 = 24.0 + 33.2 \log_{10}$ (Time—7.5)
Percentage accuracy on appearance defect $2 = 55.5 + 19.5 \log_{10}$ (Time—7.5)
Percentage accuracy on appearance defect $3 = 9.4 + 28.4 \log_{10}$ (Time—7.5)
Percentage accuracy on weight defects $= 72.7 + 5.6 \log_{10}$ (Time—7.5)

In using these equations, it should be remembered that the word "Time" refers to the number of minutes used in assorting 150 sheets. It is understood that the percentages of accuracy

---

[2] The curves were fitted according to the mathematical criterion of least squares.

that the equations yield are for the conditions under which the coded stack test was given.

It is interesting to note that in detecting off-weight sheets the accuracy is about the same whether the test is completed in 10

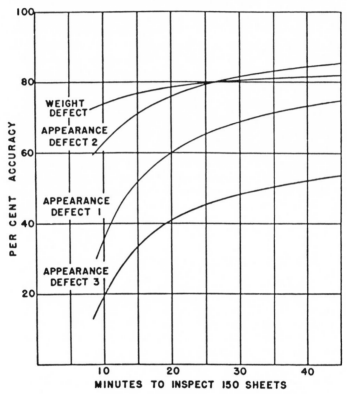

Fig. 81—Relationships between speed of inspection and accuracy in detecting four defects.

minutes or in 40 minutes. In other words, accuracy in detecting off-weight sheets for the 150 girls tested is not appreciably affected by speed of inspecting within the time limits found for these girls. To some extent the same general situation is true for appearance defect 2, although in detecting this defect we note a beginning tendency for accuracy to decrease with increased speed. This tendency is still more pronounced in the case of appearance defects 1 and 3. For example, we find that when the stack is assorted in 10 minutes, only 20 per cent of the sheets containing appearance defect No. 3 are spotted and only 35 per cent of those containing appearance defect No. 1.

On many inspection jobs, certain defects may be spotted equally well at either fast or slow rates of inspection, but other defects cannot be spotted with satisfactory accuracy above a certain inspection speed. These curves clearly reveal this situation for this inspection job. Defects of weight are noted almost as well when the 150 pieces are inspected in 10 minutes as they are when 40 minutes are used to inspect this number of sheets. It is important for the head of an inspection department to know how accuracy is affected by varying speed. When he possesses this information he is more able to set the speed of inspection so as to achieve satisfactory quality without wasting time in overcareful inspection.

The coded stack used in this study not only furnished a means of measuring the accuracy of the inspectors but also furnished data from which the relationships between speed and accuracy plotted in Figure 81 were determined.

The Determination of Tests for the Placement of Inspectors

The tests selected for tryout consisted of a series of vision tests,[3] the Zeigler Rate of Manipulation Test,[4] the Purdue Hand Precision Test,[5] and, in addition, measurements of reaction time, strength of grip, height, weight, and age.

Table XXVII summarizes the interrelations of the several tests in terms of the correlations[6] between them. According to the technique used for computing these correlations, the maximum value the figure theoretically could reach is $+1.00$. This would be reached in the case of a perfect positive relationship between the two variables under consideration. The minimum figure the correlation could reach is -1.00, which would represent a perfect negative relationship.

---

[3] See page 131.
[4] See Table VI on page 86.
[5] See page 82.
[6] The correlations in Table XXVII are product moment correlations, computed as described in Appendix A, page 353.

TABLE XXVII

CORRELATIONS OF TEST RESULTS OF 150 TIN PLATE INSPECTORS

	Speed	Mixed sheets	Appearance defect 1	Appearance defect 2	Appearance defect 3	Weight defect
Mixed sheets...............	−.49					
Appearance defect 1.........	−.42	+.80				
Appearance defect 2.........	−.49	+.68	+.24			
Appearance defect 3.........	−.36	+.58	+.35	+.21		
Weight defect..............	−.05	+.29	+.22	+.02	+.12	
Visual discrimination (distance)...................	−.26	+.22	+.28	+.16	+.19	+.02
Visual discrimination (near)..	.00	+.09	+.08	+.13	+.15	−.10
Vertical balance of the eyes..	−.43	+.03	+.25	−.13	+.08	+.01
Height.....................	−.07	+.21	+.05	+.02	+.10	+.13
Weight.....................	−.20	+.25	+.09	+.14	+.04	−.05
Age........................	−.11	−.16	−.09	+.03	−.12	−.21
Experience.................	+.05	−.05	−.07	.00	+.06	−.16
Strength of grip.............	+.02	+.17	−.05	+.19	−.07	+.14
Minnesota Rate of Manipulations...................	+.01	+.06	−.10	−.03	+.03	+.14
Speed of Reaction...........	−.02	+.12	+.05	+.10	−.07	+.03
Purdue Hand Precision.......	+.05	−.13	−.06	+.12	+.01	+.34

The first figure mentioned in the table, it will be noted, is −.49, which indicates the relation between speed and accuracy on mixed plate. This means that there is a tendency for those who are above average in speed to be below average in accuracy, and vice versa. It will be noted further that the correlations between speed and accuracy for the various specific defects are all negative and that the amount of negative relation between speed and accuracy on off-weight plate is the smallest found in the group. The intercorrelations between accuracy for the various specific defects are all small, the largest being only + .35. This finding substantiates the statement previously made that there is no decided tendency for girls who are above average in detecting one type of defect to be above average in detecting other types of defects.

The general conclusion that may be drawn from the correlations between the vision tests and the specific ways of scoring the coded stack is that the vision tests clearly tend to pick the girls who are the most accurate on the job. Although two correlations are slightly negative, the remaining thirteen are positive. The distance discrimination test gave the highest positive correlations with accuracy in detecting all three appearance defects.

Table XXVII also shows correlations between accuracy, as revealed by the coded stack test, and the height, weight, age, and experience of the operators. It will be noted that the taller girls tend slightly to be somewhat slower than the shorter girls (correlation between height and speed is − .07). Taller girls, however, tend to be more accurate on the several phases of the coded stack test, as indicated by the fact that the remaining correlations in this row are all positive. Likewise, in considering body weight we note that the heavier girls are somewhat slower but more accurate on everything but the off-weight sheets. The older girls, however, are not only slower but less accurate on everything but appearance defect 2. The more experienced girls are slightly faster but less accurate on nearly every defect.

Correlations between the remaining tests and the various ways of scoring the coded stack are given in the last four rows of Table XXVII. While the correlations shown in the remaining rows are somewhat inconsistent, at least one value is high enough to indicate a definite and real relationship. This value is the correlation of + .34 between the Purdue Hand Precision Test and accuracy in detecting off-weight plate. The hand precision test is recommended, therefore, for inclusion in a battery of employee placement tests as discussed in the last section of this chapter.

The student may wonder why correlations have been included in Table XXVII that are so low that no appreciable relationships are indicated. The reason for including these low correlations in this table is to emphasize again the fact that in setting up any battery of employee tests it is always necessary to start with more tests than one expects finally to retain. Many of one's guesses are likely to be wrong. In the present experiments, the tests that were found of no value were strength of grip, Zeigler Rate of Manipulations, and reaction time. These represent the bad guesses in finding aptitude tests for the job. However, it should not be assumed that these tests are generally of no value, for they might be the very ones to "come through" best on some other job.

The following general conclusions from the test results will give some indication of the kind of results such a procedure may yield:

1. By means of a coded stack of material, it is possible to measure the accuracy of inspectors.

2. These measurements reveal whether any relationship exists between speed and accuracy of inspection, and, if so, how much relationship.

3. Results of this procedure also reveal whether a good inspector is accurate on all types of defect or more accurate on some defects than on others. Such information is of value in training or re-training inspectors.

4. The procedure also reveals which defects are most difficult for inspectors to detect. This information is also of value in a training program.

5. A battery of vision tests was found to be of importance in placing persons on this job of inspection for appearance. It is probable that the same tests would be of value in placing employees on any other job of inspection for appearance.

A Battery of Placement Tests for the Inspectors

A study of the correlations shown in Table XXVII resulted in setting up four qualifications that a girl must meet before being trained as a tin-plate inspector. These requirements were:

1. Pass the near and far visual discrimination tests and the vertical balance test.

2. Be at least 5 feet 2 inches tall.

3. Weigh at least 118 pounds.

4. Score not over 2.00 on the Purdue Hand Precision Test. (See page 82.)

An indication of the effect of placing inspectors upon the basis of these recommendations may be seen from Table XXVIII, which is based upon data gathered in this investigation.

The inspectors meeting the qualifications, though 5 per cent slower on the coded stack, were from 4 per cent to 15 per cent more accurate in detecting the several defects. It might be suspected that, since the inspectors in the qualifying group were slower by 5 per cent on the coded stack than the average of all inspectors, the greater accuracy of this group is simply a reflection of this slower speed. However, reference to the equations showing the relation between speed and accuracy (see page 267)

TABLE XXVIII

A COMPARISON OF THE JOB PERFORMANCE OF 150 INSPECTORS SELECTED AT RANDOM
WITH THE JOB PERFORMANCE OF 28 INSPECTORS WHO MET FOUR
BASIC REQUIREMENTS

	Average of all 150 inspectors	Average of 28 inspectors who met qualifications on four tests	Difference in favor of inspectors passing tests
Time to assort 150 sheets.....	20.1 min.	21.1 min.	5% slower
Accuracy on mixed sheets ...	78.5 min.	81.7 min.	4.1% more accurate
Accuracy on appearance defect 1	59.3 min.	68.4 min.	15.3% more accurate
Accuracy on appearance defect 2	75.5 min.	83.1 min.	10.1% more accurate
Accuracy on appearance defect 3	35.1 min.	38.0 min.	8.3% more accurate
Accuracy on weight defect ...	73.4 min.	76.4 min.	4.1% more accurate

and the curves of these equations, plotted in Figure 81, shows
that the speed differential would account for a maximum of
only 1.1 per cent difference in accuracy, and that this is considerably less than the difference in accuracy on any one of the
defects. It seems conclusive, therefore, that the greater accuracy
of the qualifying group is due primarily to the visual and other
test characteristics of this group rather than to the fact that
they inspected at a slightly slower speed than the average of all
inspectors studied.

Relation between Psychological and Motion Study Analysis of the Job

The discussion thus far has dealt chiefly with the statistical
analysis of the data obtained from supervised tests on the coded
stack and from various psychological tests. It seemed desirable
to check these results with records of performance under actual
shop conditions, and for this purpose micromotion studies of
representative operators were made.

Motion pictures were taken, at 1,000 frames per minute, of
twelve inspectors selected from those who had taken the coded
stack test. In this group were two who had been rated as fast
and accurate, two fast but inaccurate, two slow and accurate,
two slow and inaccurate, and four rated as average in both
speed and accuracy according to the test stack data. The pictures were taken in the shop under normal working conditions,
and because of the general noise and shop activity, the operators

were not aware of the exact moment at which the pictures were taken.

Obviously the pictures did not reveal the accuracy with which the inspector detected the defects. However, they did show the normal speed of the operator, the relative body activity or exertion, the various methods used in grasping and moving the sheets, and the disturbance in the rhythm whenever a defective sheet was found. In general the speeds indicated by the analysis of these films correlated fairly well with the speeds indicated by the test stack.

The pictures were analyzed in an attempt to detect individual motion characteristics that might indicate causes for differences in accuracy. Since the detection of all but one class of defects depends upon vision, the eye fixations were plotted in relation to the positions of the hands and the positions of the sheet.

In the normal handling of the sheets the several stacks of sheets that have not been inspected, the sheets of first quality, those of second quality, and those containing various types of defects are aligned along a bench. The operator picks up a new sheet from the pile at her left and turns it over toward the right onto the adjacent pile of first-quality sheets where it normally remains. If a defect is discovered, the sheet is moved to the proper pile farther along the bench.

For most of the operators it was found that the eyes tend to follow the movements of the hands. Thus as the hands move toward the left to grasp a new sheet, the eyes attempt to scan the full top surface of the sheet within the very short period of time required for the grasp. As the sheet is picked up and turned over onto the adjacent stack, the eyes tend to follow the movement of the sheet which, in the upright position, presents only one edge toward the eyes. As the sheet approaches the right-hand stack, the eyes attempt to scan completely the second surface of the sheet; but as the release period is very short in duration, the scanning period is likewise very brief.

In this sequence, the eyes are attempting to see an object that is almost continually in motion, and it was found that the operators who most nearly followed this pattern had the lowest accuracy ratings in the test-stack data. This is logical since it is more difficult to see a moving object and the continual attempt to do so reduces the accuracy of the operator.

On the other hand, the accuracy ratings were higher for those inspectors whose eye movements were more nearly opposite the above sequence. For example, the inspector mentioned above, who was both fast and accurate according to the films and actual production records, used the following cycle of eye movements. As the hands moved to the left to pick up a new sheet, the eyes were scanning the second side of the previous sheet. The fact that this previous sheet was not in motion contributed to the ease of seeing possible defects, and the scanning period was increased to include nearly the full handling time of the next sheet. When the next sheet approached the second pile to the right of the operator, the eyes quickly shifted toward the left, to the first side of the top sheet on the new pile where the scanning period included the time for disposal of the previous sheet (see Figure 82).

In this second cycle of eye movements, the eyes move quickly from one motionless object to the other and thus gain greatly increased scanning periods for detecting the defects. Accuracy data both from the test stacks and from production records correlated very closely with the eye-movement patterns of the twelve inspectors thus analyzed.

It has been demonstrated experimentally that the eyes can see a motionless object more accurately than one that is in motion, and the longer the scanning period, the greater the opportunity to observe defects. If the increased scanning periods are longer than necessary for effective inspection, the operator tends to handle the sheets faster. It is logical, therefore, that the girl who, accidentally or otherwise, has acquired this improved routine shall be both fast and accurate.

This cycle is opposite the more natural cycle of following the hands with the eyes; but as in many other operations, the natural way is not necessarily the best way. This less natural, but more effective co-ordination of the eyes and hands is simple to learn, but because it is less natural, its technique must be explained and taught to the operator along with the other requirements of the job. This might be classed as one of the "tricks of the trade" not readily discovered without adequate instruction.

The Training of Inspectors

Several specific needs for training came out of the above ex-

THE "NATURAL" WAY
IS WRONG

THIS LEARNED WAY
IS RIGHT

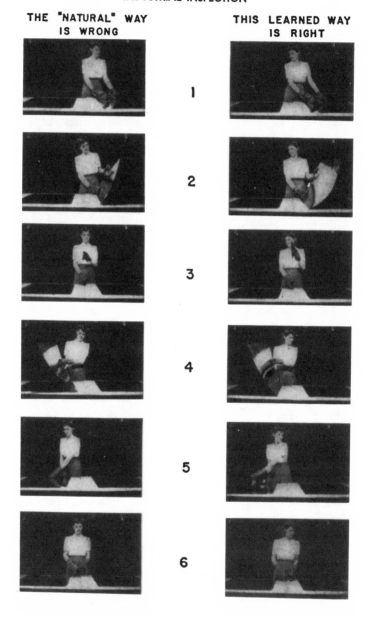

perimentation. In the first place, the accuracy of inspectors on the job was found to be far from the level of satisfactory performance that management considered desirable. Reference to Figure 80 shows that, in the case of some of the defects, an appreciable number of the present employees were unable to spot over 10 or 20 per cent of the defective material. The relationship discovered between accuracy and visual capability resulted first of all in the recommendation that those girls low in accuracy on defects of appearance immediately see an eye specialist. Subsequent study of the inspectors in the plant revealed that those girls who had received professional eye care that improved their performance on the vision tests were doing a more satisfactory job of inspection than those girls who still were unable to pass all of the vision tests.

A second effort made to upgrade the performance of employees on the job consisted of a series of inspectors' conferences. The inspectors were brought into conference in groups of approximately 20, on company time. The first thing done in each of these conferences was to pass out a slip to each girl on which was printed her accuracy on the coded stack as a whole and on each of the four specific defects studied. This information gave each girl a clear indication of her weak as well as her strong points and resulted, in most cases, in a definite desire on her part to improve her level of performance. The fact that little correlation was revealed between accuracy on the different kinds of defects resulted in the fortunate circumstance that a girl who was very low in accuracy on one defect, or possibly even two defects, was likely to be average, or even above average, in accuracy on the other defects. This fact, coupled with the further fact that most of the girls were low in accuracy on at least one defect, prevented any employee from feeling that she had been singled out because of her low-quality work. Each inspector attended two of these training conferences, which lasted an hour and a half each and were separated by a period of two weeks.

FIG. 82—Sequence of sheet movements and eye-movement patterns in inspecting tin plate. In the "Natural" way the eyes follow moving objects. The inspector thus sees the full sheet only in steps 1 and 5; she tries to see it while it is in motion in steps 2 and 4; she sees only the edge in step 3; and merely watches her hands in step 6. In the Right Way, which must be learned, the inspector sees a motionless sheet during all 6 steps. This way nearly doubles the available inspection time.

The time was spent in thorough discussion and demonstration of the various kinds of defects found in tin plate.[7] The demonstration also included a review of the micromotion films and an explanation of differences between the patterns of eye movements with respect to the moving sheet. The films illustrated these eye-movement patterns and provided a means of teaching the most effective sequence of visual fixations. General improvement in performance following these conferences was noted.

The second innovation of training procedures that directly resulted from this investigation dealt with the training of new employees. The procedure followed in the past consisted in placing a new girl between two experienced inspectors. The expectation was that new employees would be able to ask questions of the more experienced employees. The present results indicated that this procedure had not resulted in adequate training of new inspectors. Since hindsight is often better than foresight, it was easy to conclude after the investigation that experienced operators do not wish to be bothered with stopping frequently to answer the questions of a new girl. This knowledge resulted in each new employee finally setting up her own methods and standards of performance. It is not surprising that under such circumstances the standards varied markedly among the employees on the job.

The new procedure consisted in assigning an experienced and capable inspector as an instructor to each group of four new employees. The old employee was taken off the job of inspection, and since she had no assigned inspection work to perform she was able to devote all of her time to instruction of the new employees. This procedure resulted not only in much more uniform standards of inspection among the newer employees than had heretofore existed but also in a marked reduction of the time necessary for bringing a new girl up to a satisfactory level of performance. As the newer girl became more adjusted to the job, less and less time of the instructor was called for; and after a certain level of efficiency was reached, the instructor automatically resumed her former work. Under this system the older employees assigned as instructors took considerable pride

---

[7] This procedure has been suggested by J. H. Mitchell, "Subjective Standards in Inspection for Appearance," *The Human Factor*, London, IX (1935), pp. 235–239.

in the fact that they had been selected for the job of breaking in the newer inspectors, and the method was favorably received both by the older employees and the newer employees, as well as by the management.

The general conclusions from this work are that if adequate inspectors are to be obtained they must be selected with scientific precision and trained with corresponding thoroughness. No amount of desire on the part of a new employee to be a good inspector will result in satisfactory job performance if the employee does not have the visual qualifications, the necessary eye-hand co-ordination, or the physical stamina that experiments show to be necessary for the job. And in like manner, no amount of qualification for the job will result in satisfactory performance without a systematic training program covering standards and procedures as well as "tricks of the trade."

11

Accidents and Safety

ACCIDENTS do not just happen. In dealing with them nothing is gained, except a temporary dodging of responsibility, by ascribing them to bad luck or chance. The concept of luck is used in explaining human behavior only when the really causative factors are unknown or when, for some reason, we have been unable to exercise adequate control over known factors. As those factors that are related to industrial accidents become more and more clear in the light of statistical investigation, the use of the concept of luck or chance becomes less and less necessary. In the light of such causative factors as are now known definitely to exist, Heinrich [1] has estimated that around 98 per cent of industrial accidents are preventable. Of these, around 88 per cent involve such things as faulty inspection, inability of the employee, poor discipline, lack of concentration, unsafe practice, and mental or physical unfitness for the job. These factors may be eliminated or greatly reduced by adequate supervision and proper job placement by employers. The importance of what might be called the psychological or personal factors in causing accidents is firmly attested by Heinrich's conclusion that only around 10 per cent of industrial accidents are due to distinctly physical causes such as faulty equipment or bad building conditions. He further estimates that a reduction of approximately 50 per cent is often possible when adequate consideration is given to the underlying and basic causes.

General Considerations

Psychological versus physical conditions as causes of accidents

It is the purpose of this chapter to point out a number of essentially psychological factors that have been found by experimental and statistical investigation to be definitely related to

---

[1] H. W. Heinrich, *Industrial Accident Prevention* (McGraw-Hill, 1931).

industrial accidents. It is not meant, however, to imply that all accidents are related to, or can be explained by, the psychological factors involved. The importance of such external conditions as machinery safeguards and working conditions is fully attested by the favorable safety records that have so often followed the installation of a program that deals primarily with these factors. The present discussion is limited primarily to the psychological aspects of safety, not because we fail to recognize the importance of the other aspects, but because this discussion is primarily intended to bring out the mental and personal features of a safety program.

Different factors cause lost-time and minor accidents

Any investigation intended to discover the causes of accidents must consider the severity of the accidents. The reason for this is that the same factors do not operate in causing first-aid or minor accidents and lost-time or more serious accidents. This fact is strikingly revealed in Table XXIX, which shows the relative frequency of lost-time accidents and first-aid accidents for eleven departments of a steel mill for the year 1940. For both types of accidents, the figures are given in terms of acci-

TABLE XXIX

ACCIDENT DATA FROM A STEEL MILL FOR ONE FISCAL YEAR

Department	Lost-Time Accidents per Million Hours	First-Aid Accidents per Million Hours
1	5.91	433
2	3.30	660
3	2.36	574
4	2.34	485
5	8.37	496
6	2.62	392
7	4.18	930
8	2.45	725
9	2.65	504
10	2.26	534
11	.50	242

dents per million man hours. A large difference in the relative frequency of accidents of the two types will be noted, the first-aid accidents far exceeding in number the lost-time accidents. A rather great difference in the order of importance or frequency of these accidents in the different departments will also be noted. For example, Department 7, which stands at the top in terms of first-aid accidents with 930 such accidents per million man hours for the year in question, is third from the top in lost-time accidents with 4.18 per million man hours. Department 5, which stands at the top in lost-time accidents with 8.37 per million man hours, is seventh from the top in first-aid accidents with 496 per million man hours. The rank order coefficient of correlation between frequency of these two types of accidents for the eleven departments studied was only .21. The conclusion indicated by this low correlation is that only a very slight relationship exists between the hazard of a given department with respect to the possibility of lost-time accidents and the hazard of that same department with respect to more minor accidents. Thus, the factors that result in a large number of first-aid or minor accidents do not necessarily result in a correspondingly large number of lost-time accidents, and vice versa. Throughout the discussion of this subject, therefore, we shall identify in the case of each statistical summary whether the data refer to lost-time or minor accidents.

The distinction between lost-time accidents and first-aid injuries is one of degree rather than of kind. In drawing the line that separates these two categories, some variation from one plant to another will be noted. Usually, however, a lost-time accident is one that involves not only lost time by the employee but also the payment of compensation by the company.

The importance of reducing lost-time accidents is indicated by the fact that the plant from which a number of the investigations reported in this chapter were obtained has estimated that a lost-time accident involves a minimum cost of $2000 to the company. First-aid injuries, on the other hand, are considerably less expensive both in time lost and inconvenience. However, no actual figures on the exact cost of these latter injuries are available.

Accident proneness

When industrial safety first began to be given serious consideration by management, opinion differed considerably as to the relative importance of factors within the individual and working conditions as causes of accidents. It is obvious that a safety program within a plant must depend upon specific knowledge of whether these factors are both operating, and, if they are, of what their relative importance is for the plant in question. The concept of accident proneness is concerned with whether each employee tends to retain a given accident rate in comparison with other employees regardless of changes in the general physical condition of the machinery and working conditions within the plant. To the extent that each employee does tend to retain his same relative accident rate from one time to another, we may conclude that personal factors, peculiar to that individual, are affecting his accident record. This situation has been called *accident proneness.*

The relative importance of working conditions and accident proneness as causative factors varies from one plant to another. In plants where the machinery used is unavoidably dangerous in itself, the former is of greater importance. In plants where the working conditions in and of themselves are not hazardous, the latter factor is of greater importance. When individual or personal factors are causing the trouble, it is clear that an adequate safety program must make provision for the individual handling of the high accident rate or accident-prone employees. It is, therefore, of vital importance for the safety director of a plant to know the extent to which his own employees are affected by accident-proneness factors.

In nearly every investigation of industrial accidents, accident proneness has been found to be a factor, and in some cases, a vitally important factor. The work of Greenwood and Woods,[2] Marbe,[3] and others whose work has been summarized by Viteles [4] tends to support the statement that "accidents do not distribute themselves by chance, but they happen frequently to some men and infrequently to others as a logical result of a combination of circumstances." [5] Several more recent investigations substantiate this general conclusion. The work of Slocombe,[6] for example, revealed a correlation of .51 between accidents for two successive years. Slocombe concluded, among other things, that the acci-

---

[2] M. Greenwood and H. M. Woods, "The Incidence of Industrial Accidents, With Special Reference to Multiple Accidents," *Industrial Fatigue Research Board*, No. 4 (1919).

[3] K. Marbe, Praktische Psychologie der Unfälle und Betriebschäden (Munchen, 1926).

[4] M. S. Viteles, *Industrial Psychology* (W. W. Norton, 1932).

[5] *Ibid.*, page 334.

[6] C. S. Slocombe, "Consistency of Operating Efficiency," *Personnel Journal*, VIII (1930), pp. 413–414.

TABLE XXX

FREQUENCY OF HOSPITAL VISITS FOR TWO CONSECUTIVE YEARS IN ELEVEN DEPARTMENTS OF A STEEL MILL

| Department | Freq. 1938 | Freq. 1939 | Freq. 38–39 | Average Number of Hospital Visits in 1939 for Men With 0, 1, 2, etc. Visits in 1938 | | | | | | | | | |
| | | | | Number of Visits in 1938 | | | | | | | | | |
				0	1	2	3	4	5	6	7	8	9
1	.66	.85	.75	.61	1.05	1.54	1.14	1.64	2.20	5.00	2.50	....	3.50
2	1.13	1.31	1.22	.68	1.31	1.60	2.35	3.63	3.27	3.00	4.33	....	7.00
3	.81	1.03	.96	.63	1.14	1.56	2.16	2.56	4.50	3.00	1.00	....	....
4	.89	.81	.94	.55	.87	1.06	1.54	1.86	1.78	2.66	4.25	5.00	....
5	1.01	.99	1.00	.68	.95	1.00	1.94	2.23	1.60	3.33	5.00	....	....
6	1.20	1.27	1.23	.74	1.24	1.56	1.98	1.82	3.63	3.63	5.00	....	7.00
7	1.12	1.26	1.19	.81	1.15	1.45	2.00	2.29	3.44	3.21	11.00	4.00	5.00
8	1.32	1.21	1.26	.64	1.04	1.35	2.34	2.28	2.61	3.36	4.00	6.50	4.70
9	.71	1.05	.88	1.03	1.11	1.43	1.48	3.15	4.50	7.00	....	....	....
10	.91	1.16	1.03	.53	1.26	2.05	2.41	3.18	3.50	4.25	4.50	7.00	8.00
11	.58	.88	.73	.71	1.22	1.47	1.14	3.00	5.50	....	....	....	....
Average for All Depts..	.94	1.07	1.01	.69	1.12	1.46	1.86	1.91	3.32	3.84	4.62	4.91	5.14

dent-prone men, as identified from their record for a given period of time, will subsequently experience more accidents than the average in 76 per cent of the cases. It is not our intention here to resummarize the excellent digest of the literature on this subject already published by Viteles. Our purpose, rather, is to present certain statistics not previously published that have a direct bearing on this topic. These statistics both strengthen the case for the concept of accident proneness as a causative factor of industrial accidents and answer certain questions which previous investigations have not particularly considered.

Table XXX summarizes certain facts pertaining to hospital visits from the employees of eleven departments of a sheet and tin mill employing around nine thousand employees for the years 1938 and 1939. The second, third, and fourth columns reveal respectively the average number of hospital visits per man for the year 1938, the year 1939, and for the two years combined for each of the eleven departments, as well as for the mill as a whole (in the bottom row). In the remaining columns of this table the average hospital visits per man for the year 1939 are given for the employees who had previously been classified according to the number of hospital visits experienced in 1938. Thus, for Department 1, the individuals with no hospital visits during 1938 averaged .61 hospital visits in 1939, whereas in this same department the employees with seven visits in 1938 averaged 2.50 visits in 1939. Although some inversions of the data from one category to the next occur, particularly in departments where the total number of men was not large, the general trend in all departments is toward an increase from left to right. When attention is turned to the data summarizing the mill as a whole, which are tabulated in the lower row, this trend is seen to be still more pronounced. For the mill as a whole, no inversions whatever are found in the tendency.

These data for the entire mill are shown graphically in Figure 83. In this figure the number of hospital visits for 1938 are plotted along the base line or abscissa and the corresponding number of hospital visits for the following year of 1939 along the ordinate. From these data we may confidently state that the average employee tends to retain approximately his same relative position with regard to hospital visits for any two successive years.

Accident proneness versus the job as causes of accidents

The question may be raised as to why those employees who had nine hospital visits during the first year did not, on the average, have nine such visits during the second year instead of 5.14

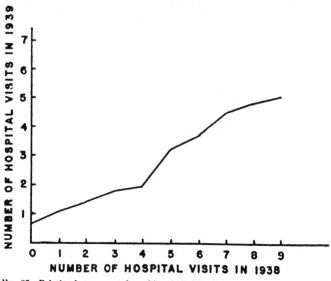

Fig. 83—Relation between number of hospital visits for two successive years among approximately 9000 steel workers.

visits as revealed by the data. It may be argued that if factors within the individual or accident proneness are the sole cause of hospital visits, then the employees with nine hospital visits during 1938 should have also on the average nine such visits during 1939. The answer is that if accident proneness were the sole cause of accidents, this group would have nine visits during 1939. The discrepancy between the nine visits experienced by employees in this group during 1938 and the 5.14 average visits experienced by these same employees in 1939 may be taken as a measure of the relative importance of accident proneness versus external factors in causing hospital visits in the mill in question. In other words, we may say roughly that of every nine hospital visits made by the most accident-prone group slightly more than five are essentially related to the accident proneness of these individuals and the remaining four cannot be related so clearly to individual factors within the employees. To prove the importance of the accident-proneness hypothesis, it is not necessary that the high-accident group for any year retain the same level of accidents for a subsequent year, but only that this group account on the subsequent year for a number of accidents significantly greater than the average of the plant. As revealed in Table XXX, this situation is clearly the case for the mill in which these statistics were gathered.

An objection may be raised to the above results as evidence of the fact that an individual or personal factor operates in the causation of accidents. This objection is that the job to which each employee is assigned may involve a specific accident hazard which, remaining the same or relatively the same from one year to another, results in a consistency of accidents for each employee from year to year, a consistency due more to the accident hazard of a given job than to any factors within the individual. It must indeed be admitted that each job has a relatively constant accident hazard and that this hazard clearly varies by rather marked amounts from one job to another. This fact is brought out in Table XXXI which gives the average number of hospital visits per year for employees on eleven specific jobs in a steel mill. It will be noted that the average number of hospital visits varies from 3.55 in the case of cranemen down to .47 in the case of roll turners. It might reasonably be expected that this ratio of 7 to 1 found among this sampling of eleven jobs would be still larger if a larger sampling of jobs had been included in this survey. The table will suffice, however, to set forth clearly the fact that a specific hazard on different jobs does exist and that this hazard is likely to vary by a rather large amount from one job to another.

This situation makes it necessary to rule out the element of job hazard in evaluating the concept of accident proneness. This was done in Table XXXII by reassorting the data according to specific jobs. Table XXXII is similar to Table XXX in general interpretation. In it, however, the employees are divided according to the particular job they are on rather than the department in which they are working, as was done in Table XXX. Thus, all openers, regardless of the department in which they are working, as we move from left to right across any

TABLE XXXI

VARIATION IN AVERAGE NUMBER OF HOSPITAL VISITS PER YEAR
AMONG EMPLOYEES ON ELEVEN DIFFERENT JOBS

Job	Average number of hospital visits per year
Craneman	3.55
Opener	3.54
Reckoner	2.96
Machinist helper	2.77
Leader	2.75
Sheet inspector	2.54
Shear helper	2.40
Assorter	2.36
Potman	2.10
Foreman	1.16
Roll turner	.47

row, are exposed to approximately the same accident hazards. It may be seen in Table XXXII that for nearly every job the average number of hospital visits for 1939 shows a progressive increase. The combined data for the eleven jobs considered are summarized in the bottom row of Table XXXII and are portrayed graphically in Figure 84. We note nearly as definite a relationship between accidents of two successive years in Table XXXII and Figure 84, when the element of job hazard has been essentially eliminated, as we previously noted in Table XXX and Figure 83 when the job-hazard element might conceivably have had a significant effect upon the results. From the data, it seems safe to conclude that accident proneness, or individual accident susceptibility, is one important cause of the type of accident that results in hospital visits for the plant studied.

It is one thing to determine, as the above data demonstrate, that an appreciable number of hospital visits are due to accident proneness or factors within the individual. It is quite another thing, however, to identify the particular factors within the individual that determine accident proneness. In other words, once the concept of accident proneness has been established as an operating factor, the next question that arises is: What are the particular factors within an individual which tend to give him the particular degree of accident proneness that he is known to possess? It is obvious that two men could be equally prone to accident for entirely different reasons. Theoretically, at least, one man may be constantly getting into accidents because he is

TABLE XXXII

ACCIDENT PRONENESS FOR MEN ON JOBS WITH SIMILAR HAZARDS

Job	Average Number of Hospital Visits in 1939 for Men with 0, 1, 2, etc. Visits in 1938									
	Number of Visits in 1938									
	0	1	2	3	4	5	6	7	8	9
Craneman	.46	.92	.78	2.20	1.00	1.00	3.00	....	....	....
Opener	1.00	1.54	1.50	1.83	2.33	2.00	6.00	7.00	2.00	5.00
Reckoner	.65	1.42	1.40	2.00	3.20	3.00	....	6.00	8.00	....
Machinist helper	1.19	1.36	3.67	3.75	3.00	3.66	....	....	....	....
Leader	1.38	1.38	2.00	3.00	6.00	....	....	....	....	....
Sheet inspector	.50	1.85	.78	....	....	....	....	....	....	....
Shear helper	1.63	1.40	1.72	2.25	....	5.00	....	....	....	....
Assorter	1.48	1.10	1.75	2.60	2.80	2.00	3.41	1.50	2.00	3.00
Potman	.40	3.00	1.30	....	....	....	....	....	....	....
Foreman	.48	1.05	1.42	1.08	2.75	....	....	....	....	....
Roll turner	.48	.45	....	....	....	....	....	....	....	....
Average for all	.85	1.40	1.63	2.33	3.01	2.78	4.14	4.83	4.00	4.00

blind or nearly blind, while another man with perfect vision may find himself equally often involved in unsafe practices because of an unconscious desire on his part to escape certain responsibilities by experiencing occasional minor injuries. The remedy

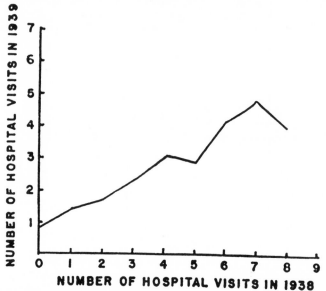

FIG. 84—Relation between number of hospital visits for two successive years among steel workers when hazard of the job is eliminated as a determining factor.

in the first case might be as simple as obtaining a new pair of adequately fitted spectacles. The remedy in the second case, if it could be effected ·at all, might involve an extended and expensive series of psychiatric treatments. The point is that the specific factors underlying accident proneness must be determined before the plant management is in a position to make a really effective effort in the direction of reducing accident proneness of the high-accident employees.

External Factors Related to Accident Proneness

It is a recognized fact that many nonpsychological factors influence the accident rate and, to some extent, determine an employee's accident proneness. For example, it has been pointed out by Vernon [7] that the accident rate increases during the latter part of the working day. According to Vernon's results, this tendency is so marked that during a 12-hour working day women experienced 2½ times as many accidents as during a 10-hour day. Although fatigue has often been considered the cause of this increase, the fact that the time of greatest accident rate as compared with hours worked is reversed on the night shift indicates that psychological rather than physiological factors are at fault. Although Vernon's results attach somewhat more importance to the length of working day than do other investigations of this subject, it is quite commonly agreed that accidents do increase as the working day is lengthened in greater proportion than the actual increased number of hours worked.

The job itself, as we have already noted, accounts for a part of accident proneness. Table XXXIII shows the hospital visits for ten departments of a sheet and tin mill. It will be noted in the last column of this table that the hospital visits per man per year vary from a minimum of .55 to a maximum of 1.26. This difference clearly reflects the hazard of working in the different departments. A good many other nonpersonal factors, such as heat, ventilation, and humidity have been pointed out by various investigators as causative factors in industrial accidents. Osborne and Vernon [8] report, for example, that whenever the temperature increases or decreases above or below a normal and comfortable level of around 70 degrees, the accident rate becomes correspondingly higher.

TABLE XXXIII

DEPARTMENTAL DIFFERENCES IN HOSPITAL VISITS RATE

Department	Number of Men	Number of Accidents for 1939 & 1940	Accident per Man per Year
1	811	902	.55
2	573	1,144	1.26
3	480	723	.75
4	1,099	1,599	.73
5	336	555	.67
6	582	1,123	.96
7	624	1,238	.98
8	1,192	2,266	.94
9	373	529	.65
10	1,101	1,945	.88

[7] H. M. Vernon, "An Experience of Munition Factories During the Great War," *Occupational Psychology*, XIV (1940), pp. 1–14.

[8] E. E. Osborne and H. M. Vernon, "The Influence of Temperature and Other Conditions on the Frequency of Industrial Accidents," *Industrial Fatigue Research Board*, Report No. 19 (1922).

It is also quite commonly accepted among safety men that an increase in the accident rate usually accompanies a step-up in production. Although this situation undoubtedly occurs in many individual plants when an attempt is made to step up production without adequate expansion of plant facilities, it is interesting to note that in a thorough study of the relationship between safety and production reported by the American Engineering Council [*] it was found, on a country-wide basis and over a period of years, that increased production in nearly every industry was accompanied by a decrease in the accident rate. This means that there is nothing inherently characteristic of a high-production rate that tends to make automatically for a high-accident rate. Rather it means that, as high production is achieved in the normal course of events by improved machinery and capacity for output, the accident rate will be likely to decrease along with the technological improvements and plant expansion. In any event, the effect upon safety of increased production, like the effect of temperature or job hazard, is essentially a physical rather than a psychological matter; and thus, important as this circumstance may be for the safety engineer who is interested in all angles of industrial safety, it is not primarily of psychological interest.

Psychological Factors Related to Accident Proneness

In contrast to the above-mentioned factors which partly determine accident proneness, certain factors related to accidents exist which are concerned primarily with the individual employee. Since in many cases these factors may be modified or even eliminated by methods that deal exclusively with the employee, they may properly be considered in the sphere of psychological factors that affect safety.

Vision

In spite of the fact that nearly every industry administers some form of vision test as a part of its employment procedure, vision surveys conducted among present employees in a number of industries reveal astounding differences in visual performance.

---

[*] American Engineering Council, *Safety and Production: An Engineering and Statistical Study of the Relationship Between Industrial Safety and Production* (Harpers, 1928).

(See page 134.) These differences are due in part to original differences among applicants that are not disclosed by rough visual screening tests; in part to the changes in vision that occur with increasing age; and in part to the fact that an injury or deterioration of an employee's vision after he has been employed often may go unnoticed unless the injury takes place on company property and during working hours. There are many reasons for insisting upon a visual check-up of employees, but by no means the least of these reasons is the relation that has been discovered between satisfactory vision and the frequency of accidents. A discussion of this relationship for two plants embracing a total of more than 13,000 employees has been covered in Chapter 6 on page 142.

Entirely aside from the extent to which the importance of vision is revealed by this individual study of the accident records, the study strongly suggests a relationship between visual performance and safety. When these statistics were first shown to safety men from the plants in question, a thorough study was made of the individual case records of the various lost-time accidents. Nowhere in the description of these accidents, which had been written at the time of the accident by persons familiar with the background of each mishap, could there be found reference to the fact that faulty vision had played a part in causing the accident. These individual case studies did not reveal a deficiency of vision of the employee responsible for the accident. Yet the statistics show that the visual factor is operating. On an actuarial basis, it can be predicted that, if all plant employees had been required to pass the four critical vision tests, the lost-time accident rate among the employees at present failing these tests would have been reduced at least 25 per cent. The uncovering of the importance of this factor by statistical investigation, which had long escaped notice through ordinary case study of accidents, is a striking illustration of the value of the statistical approach in revealing hidden causative factors in any phase of human behavior.

No one should conclude from these statistics, however, that faulty vision is the *sole* cause of industrial accidents. Just as all kinds of factors may cause disease, so all kinds of factors may cause accidents. But the statistics do prove that faulty vision is *one* cause of accidents and a very important one. Certainly this factor is sufficiently important to deserve much more attention than it has received in many industrial plants in the past. Programs for such attention have been discussed in detail in Chapter 6.

Age and plant service

A number of the investigations of the relationship between accident rates and plant experience or job experience of the employee have been reported. As might be expected, these investigations do not reveal entirely consistent results from one plant to another or from one industry to another. In most of these studies it has been found that the accident rate is higher among the younger, more inexperienced employees. This is the conclusion reached by Hewes,[10] Gates,[11] Schmitt,[12] and Lipmann.[13] Previously unpublished data obtained in a sheet and

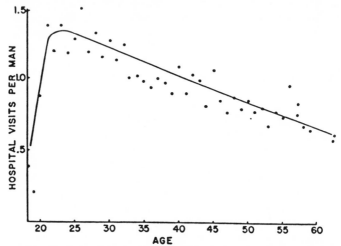

Fig. 85—Relation between age and hospital visits per man per year among 9000 steel workers.

[10] A. Hewes, "Study of Accident Records in a Textile Mill," *Journal of Industrial Hygiene*, III (1921), p. 6.

[11] D. S. Gates, "A Statistical Study of Accidents in Cotton Mills, Print Works and Worsted Mills of a Textile Company," *Journal of Industrial Hygiene*, II (1920), p. 8.

[12] E. Schmitt, "Unfällaffinität und Psychotechnik im Eisenbahndienst," *Industrielle Psychotechnik*, III (1926), pp. 144–153; 364–366.

[13] O. Lipmann, Unfällursachen und Unfällbekampfung (Berlin, 1925).

tin mill also show a drop-off in the accident rate with the age of
the employees, their years of service in the plant and their years
of service on their present jobs. These relationships are shown
graphically in Figures 85, 86, and 87. Except for a low point of

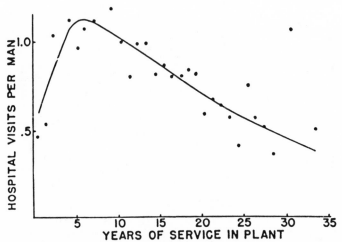

Fig. 86—Relation between years of service in the plant and hospital visits per man
per year among 9000 steel workers.

the curves for the very young or very inexperienced employees,
there is a continuous decrease in hospital visits with increasing
age or increasing plant or job experience.

Several possible explanations for the trends shown in Figures
85, 86, and 87 have been offered. It has been suggested that the
younger employees are placed on the more hazardous jobs and
that, as they become older and more "plant wise," they tend to
get themselves transferred to jobs of greater relative safety. It
has also been suggested that the younger employee, who, in general, has relatively few family responsibilities, is less cautious
and more likely to take chances than the older employee and
therefore becomes involved in a greater proportion of industrial
accidents. It has been further suggested that the younger employee is less acquainted with the possible dangers that exist in

connection with the different machines and is thus more likely to subject himself to situations in which an accident is likely to occur. Any or all of the above factors (and possibly other factors which have not been mentioned) may account for the re-

Fig. 87—Relation between years of service on present job and hospital visits per man per year among 9000 steel workers.

sults found. Whatever may be the cause or combination of causes, it is clear that in the plant studied the younger employee accounts for far greater than his share of accidents. An adequate safety program must therefore take into account the age and service differential in accident susceptibility. This can be done by safeguarding the younger employee while he is becoming experienced on the job, by organizing safety conferences with particular reference to these employees, and by making other efforts to instill in this high-accident group those habits of work and methods of thought which tend to reduce the hazard.

It should be emphasized, however, that the above relationships are not necessarily true of industry in general and that in certain other investigations a reversed type of relationship has been found. Stevens,[14] for example, found in the plants which

---

[14] A. F. Stevens, Jr., "Accidents of Older Workers: Relation of Age to Extent of Disability," *Personnel Journal*, VIII (1929), pp. 138–145.

he studied that frequency of accidents increased with age and that the mature workman is disabled for a longer period than is the younger man when an accident does occur. Shrosbree [15] also reports statistics from one industry to show that workers of longer service are a greater hazard. This is due, according to Shrosbree, to their becoming accustomed to danger and hence less careful than the less experienced employee. Although the general rule seems to be a decrease in accidents with age, the last two studies cited indicate that this is not an invariable rule and that, occasionally, even the reverse principle may exist. The important thing to realize is not that a single rule necessarily applies to every industry, but that in any given industry the working conditions and other factors probably result in some sort of relationship. It is important for a safety director to know what relation exists in his plant and to direct his safety program specifically to that particular group of employees, young or old, who are working under the greatest accident hazard. Data of the type reported here are relatively easy to obtain in any industrial organization. Such data should definitely be in the hands of the safety director in formulating and administrating his safety program.

Emotional factors

Two emotional factors which have been found to be related to employee accidents are general emotional maturity and the emotional state at the time of the accident. An analysis of the causes of accident susceptibility among fifty motormen of the Cleveland Railway Company, published by the Metropolitan Life Insurance Company, is reproduced in Figure 88. In this analysis four single items, namely, faulty attitude, impulsiveness, nervousness and fear, and worry and depression, account together for 32 per cent of the accidents among the group studied. Since these four items are essentially emotional in nature, it may be inferred that emotional conditions account for a considerable proportion of accidents. It is well accepted psychologically that many individuals vary in their general emotional state between a "high" and a "low" condition. These conditions are often fairly regular in their occurrence and appear in a cycle from one extreme to another. This situation is readily recog-

---

[15] G. Shrosbree, "Relation of Accident Proneness to Length of Service," *Industrial Welfare* (1933), pp. 7–8.

nized in its extreme form as it results in the so-called manic-depressive psychosis. In a minor form, however, it characterizes many people who are in no sense of the word psychotic but who do, nevertheless, experience definite "ups and downs" in their

PRIMARY CAUSES OF ACCIDENT-PRONENESS

Percentage Distribution Among Fifty Motormen

WOODHILL DIVISION, THE CLEVELAND RAILWAY COMPANY

PERCENT

Faulty Attitude	14	
Failure to Recognize Potential Hazards	12	
Faulty Judgment of Speed or Distance	12	
Impulsiveness	10	
Irresponsibility	8	
Failing to Keep Attention Constant	8	
Nervousness or Fear	6	
Defective Vision	4	
Organic Diseases	4	
Slow Reaction	4	
High Blood Pressure	2	
Senility	2	
Worry or Depression	2	
Fatigability	2	
Improper Distribution of Attention	2	
Inexperience	2	
Miscellaneous	6	

0   3   6   9   12   15

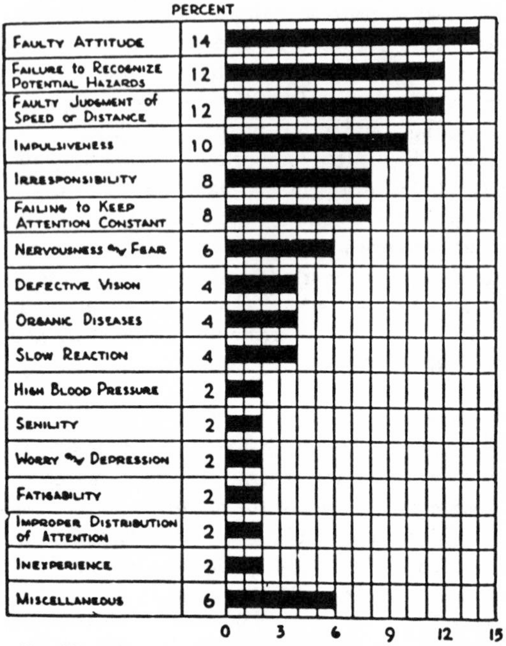

Fig. 88—Primary causes of accident proneness according to a survey among 50 motormen of the Cleveland Railway Company.

general emotional state. The relationship between these emotional cycles and the frequency of accidents has been shown in an investigation by Hersey,[16] who found that the average worker is emotionally low about 20 per cent of the time and that more than half of the four hundred minor accidents studied occurred

[16] R. B. Hersey, "Emotional Factors in Accidents," *Personnel Journal*, XV (1936), pp. 59–65.

during these low periods. According to chance alone only 20 per cent of the accidents would have occurred during such periods; the differential may therefore be taken as indicating the effect that an emotional depression has upon an employee's safety.

The general importance of the employee's emotional condition is further attested by another study by Hersey[17] in which it was reported that the production of industrial workers is around 8 per cent higher during periods when the men are elated, happy, hopeful, and co-operative than when they are suspicious, peevish, angry, disgusted, pessimistic, apprehensive, or worried. A favorable emotional condition thus not only is desirable from the standpoint of safety but also from the standpoint of plant productivity.

Supervisors and others dealing with human relations problems have long been aware of the fact that certain individuals vary from day to day in their agreeableness or ability to get along with others. Too often it has been the practice to dismiss such individuals either with a sharp reprimand or a general comment to the effect that so and so has a "grouch on" today. An employee who periodically gets a "grouch on" very likely is one who is afflicted with more than the average amount of cyclic fluctuation in his emotional state. To reprimand such an employee usually does about as much good as to reprimand a man with a broken arm for not getting out his full share of work. Such an individual should be dealt with clinically to unearth the cause of his emotional condition. If this is impractical, he should be kept off of a job that is in any way hazardous for the duration of his unsatisfactory emotional state. It should be emphasized that an employee who suffers from extreme variations in mood is not doing so for the fun of it. He cannot help himself and he, himself, is unhappier as a result of his condition than are any of the people who are in contact with him.

Aside from the fairly common fluctuations in temperament that are quite certain to be found among a few at least of any large group of employees, there is the matter of general emotional maturity in responses which varies considerably from one person to another. It is entirely possible for an individual to be

---

[17] R. B. Hersey, "Rates of Production and Emotional State," *Personnel Journal*, X (1932), pp. 355–364.

fifty years old by the calendar and yet be only five or six years old in terms of the level of his emotional behavior. A certain level of emotional development characterizes each state of the normal growth process. The baby cries and sleeps, the two-year-old kicks and screams, the eight-year-old fights, the adolescent sulks. The normal adult seldom indulges in any of these kinds of behavior; instead he has matured to a point where he recognizes and practices other more social ways of gaining his end. Occasionally, however, we find a supposedly mature individual who has not grown up emotionally. He curses and fights like a child, sulks like an adolescent, and even occasionally cries like a baby. Such behavior obviously does not result in the degree of carefulness and responsibility that is necessary for safe practice in a modern industrial plant.

For an employee of this type who is interested in gaining greater insight into his own condition, a simple test, such as the Frederick Test for Emotional Maturity, is recommended. This test is reproduced below.

THE FREDERICK TEST FOR EMOTIONAL MATURITY [18]

1. Do I get discouraged rather easily and have moods and occasional fits of depression?   Yes   No
2. Am I rather fond of "cutting a dash" with my clothes, and do I enjoy attracting attention to myself with my dress and manner?   Yes   No
3. Am I cool or self-possessed in emergencies?   Yes   No
4. Am I inclined to being very positive, irritable, or dogmatic when I am arguing a question against strong opposition?   Yes   No
5. Is solitude or being alone enjoyable to me?   Yes   No
6. Do I often say things which I later regret?   Yes   No
7. Are my relations with my family peaceful and sweet?   Yes   No
8. Do I frequently take offense at the words or actions of others?   Yes   No
9. Do I readily admit I am wrong when I know I am wrong?   Yes   No
10. Am I inclined to blame others for my faults and mistakes?   Yes   No
11. Do I place myself first in nearly all my relationships?   Yes   No
12. Is it my idea that I haven't had a very good "break" from life?   Yes   No

---

[18] J. G. Frederick, "What is Your Emotional Age? A Book of 65 Amusing Psychological Tests" (Business Bourse, 1928).

13. Am I inclined to live beyond my means?   Yes   No
14. Have I an underlying sense of inferiority or lack of
    confidence in myself which I try to hide?   Yes   No
15. Do I incline toward tears when attending an emo-
    tional play?   Yes   No
16. Do little annoyances tend to "get my goat"?   Yes   No
17. Am I inclined toward impressing my superiority on
    other people?   Yes   No
18. Am I domineering?   Yes   No
19. Am I frequently looking for sympathy from others?   Yes   No
20. Do I have tantrums when I am upset or displeased?   Yes   No
21. Am I a good hater, with active dislikes for some
    people?   Yes   No
22. Do I get pangs of envy and jealousy when others have
    success?   Yes   No
23. Am I very considerate of the feelings of other people?   Yes   No
24. Do I get angry or peeved frequently and have "tiffs"
    with people?   Yes   No
25. Have I ever thought of murdering someone, or com-
    mitting suicide?   Yes   No

SCORING SYSTEM AND NORMS

VALUES			VALUES			VALUES			VALUES		
Number	Yes	No	Number	Yes	No	Number	Yes	No	Number	Yes	No
1	11	21	7	31	9	13	13	26	19	7	24
2	7	20	8	11	20	14	7	25	20	5	20
3	26	7	9	26	10	15	5	30	21	7	21
4	12	30	10	7	26	16	11	28	22	11	21
5	40	8	11	6	25	17	7	25	23	22	7
6	10	20	12	11	29	18	12	30	24	10	20
									25	5	20

The score on this scale is obtained by finding the total of the
encircled *yes* and *no* answers and dividing this total by 25. Scores
so obtained may be interpreted as follows:

25	Perfect emotional maturity.
21–24	Very good emotional maturity.
17–20	Average emotional maturity.
13–16	Adolescent emotional development.
10–12	Childish emotional development.
9 or below	Infantile emotional development.

A test of this type is of value only for those employees who are interested in obtaining increased insight into their own emotional development. Such a test is of no value for measuring emotional maturity in an individual who does not want to be measured. Unfortunately, an unwillingness to be measured is often found in the very employees who are most in need of emotional development. The unwillingness itself is often a symptom of emotional maladjustment. Such cases require definite therapeutic measures of the type described by Anderson [19] and Wright.[20] Anderson describes several points to be followed in making a psychiatric study of an employee who has had emotional difficulties. Wright describes in some detail the counseling plan that has been in operation for a period of years in several plants of the Western Electric Company. The essential feature of this plan is that provision is made for individual study and counseling of problem employees by professionally trained counselors. Sometimes a counselor will spend only a single period of a few minutes with an employee and will find that the problem of the employee has been satisfactorily solved. But often the counselor will find it necessary to devote a number of periods of one hour or even longer to a single employee before the trouble is really unearthed and the way made clear for a satisfactory solution. The work of these counselors might be described as a sort of applied psychoanalysis, although it differs in many ways from a really psychoanalytic treatment.

Some type of individual study and treatment seems definitely to be necessary in the case of those employees who are handicapped by severe emotional problems. Such treatment, while clearly of personal value to the employee, need not be looked upon by management as a sheerly paternalistic venture; on the contrary, it should be viewed primarily as a financial and business venture. The solution of the emotional problems of employees is a paying proposition in terms of reduced accidents and increased production.

Mental ability

Numerous investigations have shown that a certain minimum

---

[19] V. V. Anderson, "The Problem Employee, His Study and Treatment," *Personnel Journal*, VII (1928), pp. 203–225.

[20] H. A. Wright, "Personal Adjustment in Industry," *Occupations*, XVIII (1940), pp. 501–505.

mental ability is required if an employee is to escape the hazards that are to be found in any industrial plant. Chambers [21] found that very few accident-prone individuals were above average in handwork, intelligence and learning ability, dependableness, and industry. The accidents for the most part were contributed by individuals who were relatively low in the traits associated with mental ability. In another investigation, Henig [22] found a definite relation between accidents in the Essex County Vocational School at West Orange, New Jersey, and scores on the Army Alpha Mental Test. The rapidly increasing use of some form of mental ability test as a standard part of employment procedure in many personnel offices is quite likely to be followed, as a secondary but very valuable result, by a reduction in accidents as well as an increase in general worker efficiency. The ever-increasing mechanization of modern industry is more and more increasing the importance of keeping away from the machine those individuals whose mental capacity renders them unable to recognize fully the dangers that are always present if unsafe practices are followed.

In apparent contradiction to the above results, a few investigators, for example Farmer and Chambers, [23] have found no correlation between degree of intelligence and accident liability. The disagreement is more apparent than real, however, for investigations of this latter type have attempted to correlate the degree of intelligence with accidents among employees who are above a certain minimum intelligence level. It seems clear that above a minimum critical mental ability level little, if any, relationship exists between further amounts of mental ability level and susceptibility to accidents. But it still remains quite necessary for an employee to possess this minimum amount of mental ability. Those who lack it are quite likely to be hazardous employees. It is primarily for the identification of this extremely low group that the use of mental ability tests is rec-

---

[21] E. G. Chambers, "A Preliminary Inquiry into the Part Played by Character and Temperament in Accident Causation," *Journal of Mental Science,* LXXXV (1939), pp. 115–118.

[22] M. S. Henig, "Intelligence and Safety," *Journal of Educational Research,* XVI (1927), pp. 81–87.

[23] E. Farmer and E. G. Chambers, "A Psychological Study of Individual Differences in Accident Rates," *Industrial Fatigue Research Board,* Report No. 38 (1926).

ommended as an important part of any accident-prevention
program.

Ratio between perceptual and muscular speed

An interesting hypothesis which seems to account for at least
a part of the cause of accident proneness has recently been ad-
vanced by Drake.[24] Drake administered to a number of accident-prone and safe individuals a series of psychological tests.
The tests were roughly divided into two groups, namely, those
dealing with perception and those dealing with muscular responses. The perceptual tests were primarily concerned with
visual discrimination and the muscular tests with the speed of
executing a number of routine manual activities. In the course
of examining these test results it was observed that the accident-
prone persons tended to have motor test scores which were relatively higher than their scores on the perception tests. It was
also observed that the safer employees or accident-free individuals tended to have motor test scores which were lower, relatively,
than their scores on the perception tests. Following this cue, a
combination test score was obtained as follows:

Test score = spiral test score − turning test score.

In this formula the spiral test consisted of a hundred small
aluminum spirals each of which had been punched with a small
hole near one end. Fifty were punched "standard," that is, they
contained the punched hole two and one half turns from the
end. The remaining fifty were punched "off-standard," that is,
the hole was punched at a distance from the end different from
the·two and one half turns of the standard punch. The person
tested was required to separate the standard items from the
others. Although an element of muscular dexterity was required
in selecting these pieces, the test is primarily a measure of the
individual's rapidity of perceptual discrimination in detecting
the differences between the "standard" and "off-standard"
pieces. The turning test referred to in the formula, on the other
hand, involved the turning of ten pairs of machine screws into
threaded holes in a vertical steel plate. This test, therefore,
was largely one of speed of manual activity. The scores of both

---

[24] C. A. Drake, "Accident-Proneness: a Hypothesis," *Character and Personality*,
VIII (1940), pp. 335–341.

tests were first converted into comparable standard scores and then recomputed into a single final score according to the formula. It is clear from this formula that a positive final score results when the perceptual test score is higher than the muscular

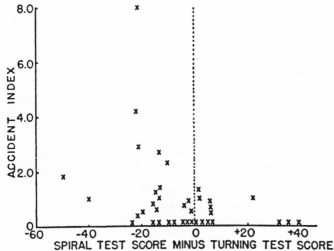

FIG. 89—Relation between accident proneness and test scores dealing with perceptual and muscular speed.

test score, and a negative final score results when the opposite situation with reference to the two initial tests prevails.

After the composite test score obtained in this manner had been obtained for each of thirty-eight employees, the accident index of each employee was computed according to the following formula:

$$\text{A.I.} = \frac{\text{Number of Accidents} \times \text{Severity}}{\text{Length of Service in Months}}$$

The next step was to plot the accident indices so obtained for the 38 employees against the composite test score. This has been done in Figure 89. The general trend of the relationship is clear. Though it is not a straight line or linear relation, individuals with negative composite scores show a definite tendency to be among those with the high accident indices, whereas those with the positive composite scores are relatively free from accidents. Drake's statement of the principle involved, as illustrated in Figure 89, is that "Individuals whose level of muscular action is above their level of perception are prone to more frequent and more severe accidents than those individuals whose muscular actions are below their perceptual level. In other words, the person who reacts quicker than he can perceive is more likely to have accidents than is the person who can perceive quicker than he can react."

Other psychological factors

Other attempts have been made to identify the accident-prone employee by means of tests; notable among these is the work of Farmer and Chambers.[25] These investigators administered to a number of industrial employees a group of muscular tests (dotting tests, reaction time tests, and pursuit meter tests), a group of what was called temperamental instability tests (including muscular balance, rate of tremor, and psycho-galvanic reflex), and tests of the higher thought processes (which included intelligence and a number-setting test).

Follow-up studies were then made to determine whether employees who were above average in these tests were, in general, more free of accident records than employees whose test scores were below average. For six separate groups of employees, it was found, those whose performance on the dotting tests was better than average had a more favorable safety record than the poorer testing employees. Apparently the muscular skill required to obtain a favorable score on the dotting test is, in some way, of value to an employee in helping him to avoid accidents in the plant.

No one would contend from the preceding studies that any single one of the factors discussed is wholly the cause of industrial accidents. But the analyses indicate that each factor plays some part in causing accidents and that, together, these identifiable factors clearly account for a significant proportion of plant accidents. It seems clear, then, that individual safety can never be fully attained by improvement of working conditions and safeguarding the machines. No matter how safe a machine is, the accident-prone employee may find himself injured by it. An employee whose vision is unsatisfactory can severely injure him-

---

[25] Farmer and Chambers, *op. cit.*

self on a machine that is perfectly safe to an employee with normal vision; and an employee whose emotional condition is in the depths of a "devil-may-care" condition will unconsciously *find* a way to injure himself on the safest machine imaginable. The individual must be considered. He, himself, is the cause of many accidents and the adequate handling of the accident-prone employee is just as important a part of the safety engineer's job as is the installation of machinery safeguards.

How to Reduce Accident Proneness

Several ways to reduce the proportion of accident-prone employees among newly hired employees and to reduce the degree of accident proneness among present employees may be seen to follow logically from the foregoing statement of factors that determine accident proneness.

Psychological tests at the time of employment

When it has been found that accident-prone employees and safe workers make significantly different scores on a psychological test, that test may safely be used at the time of employment to detect and reject those applicants who are in the unsafe or accident-prone category. Rigid adherence to such a policy of hiring in the employment office is as beneficial to the rejected employees as to the management. No employee would willingly take a job on which, because of his own particular psychological makeup, he would be demonstrably more likely to suffer an accident than would an employee whose psychological makeup differs from his. Yet, when employees are hired without reference to those psychological and personal factors that affect accident proneness, the end result is the placement of employees in such a manner that an unnecessary number of accidents will occur. For example, it has been demonstrated (see page 142) that employees failing certain vision tests are definitely more likely to experience industrial accidents than employees passing those tests. Therefore, the hiring of employees without regard to their scores on vision tests is almost certain to be followed by a poorer safety record than could easily be obtained if certain critical scores on these tests were made one of the requirements for employment. Many, perhaps most, industries give some sort of vision test as a part of employment procedure. But often this test consists only of the Snellen Chart at twenty feet, and this test measures no more than visual acuity at that distance. Among employees passing this test are many who experience accidents because of visual trouble (such as lateral or vertical phorias) that is not detected by the Snellen test. A comprehensive visual performance test is necessary as a part of employment procedure if the employees who are accident prone for visual reasons are to be identified. Many, if not most, failures on visual performance tests can be remedied by proper professional attention. But without the stimulus of vision tests at the time of employment, many applicants would be quite willing to go to work with vision entirely inadequate for safe conduct within the plant.

Other tests dealing with such factors as mental ability and muscular speed may also be used to advantage, particularly in selecting employees for the more hazardous jobs. The several investigations summarized on the relation between mental ability and accident experience all point to the general conclusion that a minimum score on an adequate mental ability test should be required of employees who are to be exposed to the normal hazards of a modern industrial plant. This does not mean that a particularly high critical score need, or should, be required for many jobs; but it does mean that a reasonable minimum score should be required and that an applicant who is so low in mental ability as to fall below that score should not be employed.

Safeguarding and training inexperienced employees

The fact that young or inexperienced employees ordinarily experience more than their share of industrial accidents suggests the need for special care in building up a "safety consciousness" in the members of this group. This may be done in several ways. New employees often may be placed for a time on jobs that are not hazardous but that are close enough to those jobs where great care must be exercised that the new employee will have an opportunity to learn by observation something about the machinery with which he later will be in contact. This procedure enables the new employee to have a "breathing spell" during which he can adjust himself to the plant and overcome whatever feelings of uncertainty and anxiety he may have immediately after going to work in a strange (and, to him, often awesome) industrial plant.

Another method of helping the new employee is to assign him to periodic safety conferences. Conferences of this type are becoming more and more widely used as a tool of management, particularly on a supervisory level, and more is said about the general nature and purposes of such employee conferences on page 198. These conferences are of real value as one means of assisting the new employee in his task of becoming familiar with the hazards of his job. Every safety engineer has available a list of unsafe practices that apply to the several departments and operations of his plant. These unsafe practices are usually fairly well known to experienced employees who have seen men hurt when the safety rules were not followed, and who, therefore, are likely to avoid the unsafe practices with reasonable care. But the new employees, who often do not know what the unsafe practices are, are likely to endanger themselves not because they are essentially careless or foolhardy, but simply because they do not know *how* to be safe.

Posters and placards may help the new employee to some extent, *if* the posters tell him specifically *what* to do and what *not* to do, and *if* he reads the posters and remembers what he reads. But too often posters simply show an accident and, in large type, say "Be Careful." Now we can be assured that no employee, old or new, will voluntarily hurt himself. The degree of carefulness of every employee is determined by (1) what he knows of safe and unsafe practices, and (2) how important he thinks it is to follow his knowledge on the subject. In other words, some employees follow unsafe practices because they actually do not know any better. The need in such cases is for specific information on what to do and what not to do. A systematic and comprehensive series of conferences covering this specific information is a much more effective means of informing the employees than is the chance and casual learning obtained from posters or from observations that employees may (or may not) make. Once the information has been given to the employees, still further education is necessary to make sure that they *believe* as well as *know* that certain practices are unsafe.

Personal protection

The use of recommended safety measures, such as safety goggles and safety shoes, might be considered primarily as physical rather than psychological equipment, if it were not for the fact that the use an employee makes of such safeguards is so often determined by his own personal beliefs, attitudes, and, sometimes, prejudices. Many men believe that safety goggles are unnecessary even on jobs that are demonstrably dangerous because "they have never had an accident." This is one instance in which neither management nor employees can safely follow the adage that experience is the best teacher. Those who wait for experience to teach them that goggles should be worn to protect their eyes may have no eyes to protect after they have learned the lesson. The adequate utilization of safety measures requires not only that such measures be made available to the employees but also that the employees be educated in the use of these measures and *convinced* of their value. It is just as much a part of management's job to insure the success of the educational part of the program as to supply the safety measures.

Job analysis and accident records often reveal that employees on certain jobs are particularly liable to visual injury. However, until such studies have been made, management is not always aware of the particular departments or jobs in which a visual hazard is most likely to exist. Table XXXIV shows a breakdown by departments of the relative frequency of seven different types of minor injuries experienced during two years by approximately 9000 employees in a steel mill. It was noted that in one of the ten departments, Department 7, visual injuries were more frequently experienced than any other type of accident. In eight of the ten departments visual injuries were second in frequency, and in one department the visual injuries were third in order of frequency. For the plant as a whole, eye injuries were second in importance, being exceeded in frequency only by cuts and bruises. Many of the eye injuries reported were of course of a minor nature, perhaps involving little more than careful removal of a foreign body from the eye. However, even injuries of this nature would be better prevented, for they involve not only loss of time for the employee and the company but also the possibility of serious complications requiring compensation and rehabilitation.

Influenced by such evidence as that presented in Table XXXIV, many industries have adopted a mandatory safety-goggle program. Such a program requires the wearing of safety goggles by everyone in the plant at all times and regardless of

TABLE XXXIV

DEPARTMENTAL DIFFERENCES IN TYPE OF ACCIDENTS

DATA BASED ON MINOR ACCIDENTS FOR ONE YEAR IN A STEEL MILL

Type of Injury	Department									
	1	2	3	4	5	6	7	8	9	10
Eye Injuries	14.4%	13.8%	14.1%	11.3%	25.5%	19.4%	38.8%	12.7%	20.4%	24.8%
Strains	3.5	3.3	2.9	2.6	3.4	2.6	3.7	3.2	3.5	2.7
Fractures	1.5	0.4	0.3	0.1	1.1	0.5	0.8	0.8	1.2	0.1
Heat	1.8	0.7	15.7	0.6	1.2	0.3	5.3	0.9	0.1	0.1
Burns	4.9	3.5	9.7	4.1	5.2	3.7	9.1	3.7	5.2	6.5
Cuts & Bruises	64.3	71.3	50.0	73.6	54.1	66.5	37.1	70.7	60.0	55.7
Miscellaneous	9.6	7.0	7.6	7.4	9.7	7.1	5.5	8.0	9.6	10.1
Total Number of Hospital Visits 1938–1939 (Minor Injuries)	1217	1390	861	1852	652	1416	1433	3000	657	2269

his job. The experience of organizations that have adopted such a program, such as the Pullman Company,[26] has been highly favorable. Indeed, these companies report a marked financial saving that is directly traceable to the reduction in eye accidents effected by the safety-goggle program.

Immediate attention to injury

Management finds it a paying proposition to be sure that every injury, no matter how slight, receives prompt and adequate attention. It is not enough to have hospital or first-aid service available for an employee to make use of if he wishes to do so. Means must be found to insure his making use of such facilities. Very often factors that have been totally overlooked by management effectively prevent many employees from taking advantage of available first-aid facilities. In one mill, for example, two machine shops contained identical machinery, employed approximately the same number of men, and turned out the same kind of work. An analysis of the accident records at the end of a year showed that the employees in one of these shops averaged 1.73 hospital visits per man for the year, whereas the employees in the other shop averaged only 1.10 hospital visits per man for the same period. So great a difference in the apparent hazards of the two shops was entirely unexplainable in terms of the men, the work, or the shops themselves. After much thinking about the problem, it was remembered that the hospital in which first aid and treatment were administered was next door to one of the machine shops but was about five hundred yards from the other. The men in the shop close to the hospital took advantage of the service in nearly 60 per cent more cases of minor injury than did employees in the more distant shop. The solution to this problem is one of educating the employees in the latter shop to walk five hundred yards to receive treatment when treatment is needed or one of locating another emergency first-aid station closer to these men. Management should not and cannot take the point of view that the service is there and that employees who do not take advantage of it are on their own responsibility. Management must see that the service is utilized if a satisfactory safety record is to be obtained.

---

26 H. Guilbert, "No One Enters This Plant Without Goggles," *Factory Management and Maintenance*, XCVI (1938), pp. 83–85.

12

Attitudes and Morale

IN an army, a school system, or an industrial plant there is no substitute for morale. The main difference between men and machines is that the productivity of a man is determined very largely by the way he feels about his job and his attitude toward the company that employs him. There is an old saying that loyalty has no price. One can hire "hands" but the "hands" are of little value if the man who owns them feels that he is not being treated fairly by the management.

The very use of the term *hands* in referring to employees reflects a mistaken viewpoint by management, as man's hands alone are never hired. The whole man is always hired, and the whole man brings to work a good many things besides his hands. He brings the effects of too many or too few spankings as a child; of whether he won or lost in last night's card game; of whether his wife sent him to work with a scolding or a kiss; of whether or not the company "docked" his wages when he was home last week with a sick child. Such things as these are of vital importance in determining an employee's real value to a company. And such things as these, considered together for the whole working force, determine the morale of an industrial plant.

Morale cannot be legislated or induced by logical argument; neither can it be bought for a price. The employees of many industries with wage scales above average for the locality are constantly bickering because they feel that "they are not being treated fairly by the company." Management has often made the mistake of assuming that high wages and short hours are what men want most from their jobs. Acting on this assumption, management has often made an effort to remedy the situation by raising wages still higher or shortening the hours of work, or both. And then management has been amazed by a continuation of the discontent and often has been quite unable to understand why the men do not return happily to work.

Nor has the lack of understanding what men really want from their jobs been limited to management. M*ny employees are themselves unaware of what is needed to make them satisfied with their jobs. This does not mean that the employees are unintelligent or that they have any special disability to analyze their true motives. It simply illustrates a well-established principle of normal human behavior, namely, that it is difficult for anyone to identify in clear and unmistakable terms the forces that underlie his feelings and his actions. Everyone has observed the employee who, under one supervisor, continually sulks on the job because "the company doesn't pay him what he is worth," and, under another supervisor, works in a contented and industrious manner for exactly the same wage. It is not unusual to watch a man's attitude shift from one of chronic discontent to one of complete satisfaction following a shift from a job of low status to one higher in this intangible quality, even though the change in jobs involved no appreciable increase in wages.

Every impartial study of what industrial employees want from their jobs has shown that many things besides high wages and short hours are desired. Such studies have shown, also, that some employees consider these other things even more important than wages and hours.

What Men Want from Their Jobs

Typical of studies on this subject is one by Houser,[1] who found that the nonselling employees (including unskilled labor) of a large merchandising organization considered the factors shown in Table XXXV to be the things they wanted from the company. The order in which these factors are listed in Table XXXV shows the relative importance attached to the factors by the employees. It is interesting to note that the employees of this company ranked the items concerned with pay twenty-first and twenty-second in importance.

Though studies of other employees in other plants do not consistently show the financial incentive to be so far down the list as it appears in Houser's study, other studies do almost univer-

[1] J. D. Houser *What People Want from Business* (McGraw-Hill Book Company, 1938), p. 29.

TABLE XXXV

RELATIVE IMPORTANCE OF 28 FACTORS TO THE NONSELLING EMPLOYEES OF A
LARGE MERCHANDISING ORGANIZATION

Rank

Receiving help necessary to get results expected by management..........	1
Being encouraged to offer suggestions and try out better methods..........	2
Being able to find out whether work is improving.......................	3
Reasonable certainty of being able to get fair hearing and square deal in case of grievance...	4
Certainty of promotions going to best qualified employees...............	5
Encouragement to seek advice in case of real problems..................	6
Being given information about important plans and results which concern the individual's work..	7
Being given reasons for changes which are ordered in work..............	8
Not being actually hampered in work by superior.......................	9
Getting contradictory or conflicting orders............................	10
Being given to understand completely the results which are expected in a job	11
Pay—*Assurance of increases when deserved*............................	12
Being invited to offer suggestions when new plans are being considered.....	13
Feeling that superior understands all about the difficulty of the individual's job...	14
Being given to understand completely the general methods which the superior wants followed...	15
Complete definition of duties...	16
Not being responsible to too many superiors............................	17
Knowledge of other jobs in the organization which the individual feels capable of handling and would prefer.................................	18
Knowledge of other jobs preferred, even at same pay....................	19
Red tape in the organization, preventing best work....................	20
Pay—*compared to that of other jobs of equal importance in the organization*	21
Pay—*compared to that of similar work in other organizations*.............	22
Treatment when being employed...	23
Knowledge of lines of promotion.......................................	24
Value of Mutual Benefit Association....................................	25
Being permitted to make important decisions in work....................	26
Regularity of amount of work..	27
Service of Medical Department...	28

sally show other factors to be of significant importance. Hersey,[2] in a study of union and nonunion employees, found that fourteen factors were considered "most important" by the percentages of employees tabulated in Table XXXVI.

Hersey did not find the financial aspect of the job to be quite so unimportant, in comparison with other factors, as did Houser in his study. Yet Hersey did find two things of importance. First, he found that amount of pay was not considered most important by most employees in either the union or the nonunion group. "Steady employment" was checked by more em-

---

[2] R. B. Hersey, "Psychology of Workers," *Personnel Journal*, XIV (1936), pp. 291–296.

TABLE XXXVI

PERCENTAGE OF UNION AND NONUNION EMPLOYEES WHO CONSIDERED THE LISTED
ITEMS AS "MOST IMPORTANT" AMONG FACTORS RELATED TO THEIR JOBS

	Per Cent of Union Employees Checking Item as "Most Important"	Rank of Item	Per Cent of Non-Union Employees Checking Item as "Most Important"	Rank of Item
1 Employee stock subscription...	5	11.5	2	13.5
2 Voice or share in management.	13	9.5	6	11.0
3 Fair adjustment of grievances.	80	1.0	24	7.0
4 Chance of promotion	28	6.0	47	3.0
5 Steady employment	65	2.0	93	1.0
6 Medical and dental service....	0	13.5	6	11.0
7 Safety	57	3.0	21	9.0
8 Amount of pay	49	4.5	51	2.0
9 Working conditions	49	4.5	45	4.0
10 Hours of work	13	9.5	23	8.0
11 Type of man in charge	18	7.5	38	5.0
12 Methods of pay	0	13.5	2	13.5
13 Insurance systems and pensions	18	7.5	36	6.0
14 Chance to show intiative	5	11.5	6	11.0

ployees as a most important factor in both groups and, in the
union group, the factors of "fair adjustment of grievances" and
"safety" also outranked "amount of pay." Second, Hersey
found that still other factors, though admittedly of somewhat
lesser importance than amount of pay to the majority of employees, are considered of first importance by a sufficiently
large percentage of employees to justify definite attention
by management.

Another investigation dealing with the factors that appeal to
factory workers has been reported by Wyatt, Langdon and
Stock.[2] In this study, ten factors were ranked by the 325 employees in the order of importance shown in Table XXXVII.

TABLE XXXVII

RANKING OF TEN ITEMS IN ORDER OF IMPORTANCE BY 325 FACTORY WORKERS

Rank	Factor
1	Steady work
2	Comfortable working conditions
3	Good working companions
4	Good boss
5	Opportunity for advancement
6	High pay
7	Opportunity to use your ideas
8	Opportunity to learn a job
9	Good hours
10	Easy work

In this report, as in those mentioned before, many factors be-

[2] S. Wyatt, J. N. Langdon, and F. G. L. Stock, "Fatigue and Boredom in
Repetitive Work," *Industrial Health Research Board*, Report 77 (1937).

sides those of a monetary nature are considered of real importance by the industrial employees studied.

Hoppock [4] has published the results of an interesting investigation into the problem of job satisfaction and the conditions that favor it. In one part of the study, eighty persons representing a wide range in age, intelligence, occupations, and earnings were interviewed. From these results Hoppock states that no conclusions are drawn except "that what happened in these cases can happen." However, the interview case studies corroborate the general conclusion reached above, that is, that job satisfaction is related to a good many things besides financial return. Some of these factors, as summarized by Hoppock, are "relative status of the individual within the social and economic group with which he identifies himself, relations with superiors and associates on the job, nature of the work, earnings, hours of work, opportunities for advancement, variety, freedom from close supervision, visible results, the satisfaction of doing good work, opportunities for service to others, environment, freedom to live where one chooses, responsibility, vacations, excitement, opportunity for self-expression, competition, religion, opportunity for or necessity of traveling, fatigue, appreciation or criticism, security, and ability to adjust oneself to unpleasant circumstances."

These studies should not be interpreted by management as meaning that the average employee has no interest in his pay check or that he wants to be "fathered" or "mothered" or in any other way made the beneficiary of a paternalistic system. The average employee wants to take care of himself. He does not want the company to pay his medical or dental bills (see item 28 in Table XXXV and item 6 in Table XXXVI), nor is he particularly interested in being given a voice in the management of the plant (see item 26 in Table XXXV and item 2 in Table XXXVI). He wants the opportunity to do a job for a reasonable wage, to have an impartial hearing if he thinks he has been treated unfairly, and to be reasonably sure of holding his job as long as his work is satisfactory. In one investigation, [5] the last-mentioned point, job security, was found to be more important

---

[4] R. Hoppock, *Job Satisfaction* (Harper & Brothers Company, 1935).

[5] D. McGregor, "The Attitudes of Workers Toward Layoff Policy," *Journal of Abnormal and Social Psychology*, XXXIV (1939), pp. 179–199.

than any other factor. These are the things that must be considered by management if employee morale is to be kept on the high level that efficient plant operation requires.

The Measurement of Morale

Morale cannot be weighed on a scale, like a pound of butter; it cannot be measured with a rule, like a strip of carpet; it cannot be gauged with a thermometer, like the temperature of a room. Yet, though it is intangible, it can be measured. Thorndike long ago pointed out that whatever exists, exists in some amount, and whatever exists in some amount can be measured. Certainly morale does exist. It is a characteristic of a group of employees that makes for success or failure of the plant as a business enterprise. Until recently, management attempted to keep in touch with the morale of the working force only through such factors as chance remarks by employees, appearance and behavior of the men at work, and occasional reports by supervisors. These methods were none too satisfactory. It is one characteristic of an employee whose morale is poor that he is likely to keep his attitude to himself, particularly if he feels that he personally is likely to be identified with a condition of dissatisfaction. Therefore, if morale is to be gauged or measured, means must be found to encourage employees to express their honest feelings and reactions. The most satisfactory method of doing this is by means of an anonymous attitude survey or labor audit. Such a survey makes use of a questionnaire adapted to the needs of the investigation. The employees are asked to check such a questionnaire and drop it in a ballot box. No one knows how any particular employee checked the questionnaire, but from the average results, a comprehensive picture of general employee reactions is often obtained.

A typical example of an attitude scale that may be used to determine the general attitude of employees toward their company is shown in Table XXXVIII. This scale is taken from an article by Bergen.[6] The theory of such scales and detailed instructions for their construction have been described by Thurstone and Chave.[7] Such a scale requires that numerical values

[6] H. B. Bergen, "Finding Out What Employees Are Thinking," *The Conference Board Management Record*, April, 1939.

[7] L. L. Thurstone and E. J. Chave, *The Measurement of Attitude* (University of Chicago Press, 1929).

be found for each of a series of statements that express a thought (favorable, unfavorable, or indifferent) about the subject of the attitude survey.

TABLE XXXVIII

STATEMENTS USED IN BERGEN'S SCALE FOR MEASUREMENT OF ATTITUDE OF EMPLOYEES TOWARD THEIR COMPANY

	Scale Value
I am made to feel that I am really a part of this organization........	9.72
I can feel reasonably sure of holding my job as long as I do good work	8.33
I can usually find out how I stand with my boss.....................	7.00
On the whole, the company treats us about as well as we deserve......	6.60
I think training in better ways of doing the job should be given to all employees of the company....................................	4.72
I have never understood just what the company personnel policy is...	4.06
In my job I don't get any chance to use my experience...............	3.18
I can never find out how I stand with my boss......................	2.77
A large number of the employees would leave here if they could get as good jobs elsewhere..	1.67
I think the company's policy is to pay employees just as little as it can get away with...	.80

The numerical values assigned to the statements in Table XXXVIII are not determined arbitrarily. They are obtained from a careful series of experiments conducted during the construction of the scale. In the scale construction, the first step is to write out a large number of statements, perhaps a hundred or more, each of which expresses a viewpoint of some kind toward the company. An effort should be made to have these statements express all possible attitudes from extremely favorable to extremely unfavorable. Each of these statements is typed on a separate slip of paper and a judge is asked to place each statement in one of ten piles, ranging from statements showing the least favorable viewpoints, in pile one, to statements expressing the most favorable viewpoints, in pile ten. When the judge has allocated all statements, a tabulation is made of where he placed each one, and the statements are shuffled and given to another judge. This procedure is repeated until the statements have been separately allocated to the various piles by approximately one hundred judges. It should be emphasized that the hundred judges used as described above are assisting in the construction of the scale. They are not having their own attitude measured. To measure attitudes with the scale is not possible until the scale has been constructed, and the allocation of statements to the several piles is a part of the process of constructing the scale.

The purpose of the allocation is to determine the scale values of the various statements. If all judges tend to place a statement in piles toward the favorable end of the continuum, we may safely conclude that that statement expresses a favorable attitude toward the company. If a statement is generally placed by the judges in piles toward the unfavorable end of the series, we may likewise conclude that an unfavorable attitude is expressed by that particular statement. *The scale value of each statement is thus determined by finding the average pile in which it is placed by the judges.* By starting with many more statements than need be retained for the final attitude scale, it is usually possible to pick from ten to fifteen statements that are spread over the entire attitude range. The statements so selected, together with their scale values as shown in Table XXXVIII, comprise the final material for the attitude scale.

One might think that the attitudes or feelings of the judges who are used in the construction of the scale would have an effect on the scale values obtained. In other words, it might be felt that one set of scale values for a series of statements might be obtained if the judges were, in general, *favorable* toward the company, while a different set of values might be obtained if the judges in general were unfavorable or indifferent toward the company. This possibility has been subjected to experimental test, and it has been found that the attitudes of the judges do not significantly affect the scale values obtained from them.[*] This fact increases the possibilities of use for such scales in industry because it often happens that the persons who are most conveniently available for use as judges in constructing a scale may be more favorably disposed toward the company than certain groups of employees with whom the scale is to be used after it is constructed.

In the practical administration of an attitude scale, statements are printed on a sheet in random order, without the scale values appearing in Table XXXVIII. Each employee is given one of these sheets and is requested to check all statements that he agrees with or believes to be true. The sheets are then turned in without being signed. The attitude of an employee toward the company is defined as the average scale value of the

[*] E. D. Hinckley, "The Influence of Individual Opinion on the Construction of an Attitude Scale," *Journal of Social Psychology*, III (1932), pp. 283–296.

statements he has checked. For example, an employee checking statements one, three, and five of those shown in Table XXXVIII would have an attitude of $\frac{9.72 + 7.00 + 4.72}{3}$ or 7.15. On a scale of ten (ten being the most favorable end and zero the least favorable end) an attitude of 7.15 would be one somewhat toward the favorable end of the scale. On the other hand, an employee checking statements seven, eight, and ten would have an attitude represented by $\frac{3.18 + 2.77 + .80}{3}$ or 2.25. This would be a much less favorable attitude toward the company than the one described above.

The attitude scale reproduced in Table XXXVIII is by no means the only set of statements that might be constructed to fulfil the requirements of a suitable scale. Uhrbrock,[*] in a comprehensive study of the attitudes of 3934 factory workers, 96 clerical workers, and 400 foremen, used a different scale, but one

TABLE XXXIX

STATEMENTS USED IN UHRBROCK'S SCALE FOR MEASURING ATTITUDE OF EMPLOYEES TOWARD THEIR COMPANY

Statement	Scale Value
I think this company treats its employees better than any other company does	10.4
If I had to do it over again I'd still work for this company	9.5
They don't play favorites in this company	9.3
A man can get ahead in this company if he tries	8.9
I have as much confidence in the company physician as I do in my own doctor	8.7
The company is sincere in wanting to know what its employees think about it	8.5
A wage incentive plan offers a just reward for the faster worker	7.9
On the whole the company treats us about as well as we deserve	7.4
I think a man should go to the hospital for even a scratch, as it may stop blood poisoning	6.3
I believe accidents will happen no matter what you do about them	5.4
The workers put as much over on the company as the company puts over on them	5.1
The company does too much welfare work	4.4
Soldiering on the job is increasing	4.1
I do not think applicants for employment are treated courteously	3.6
I believe many good suggestions are killed by the bosses	3.2
My boss gives all the breaks to his lodge and church friends	2.9
I think the company goes outside to fill good jobs instead of promoting men who are here	2.5
You've got to have "pull" with certain people around here to get ahead	2.1
In the long run this company will "put it over" on you	1.5
The pay in this company is terrible	1.0
An honest man fails in this company	0.8

[*] R. S. Uhrbrock, "Attitudes of 4430 Employees," *Journal of Social Psychology*, V (1934), pp. 365–377.

constructed as explained above to measure the general attitude of employees toward the company. Some typical statements, with their scale values from Uhrbrock's scale, are reproduced in Table XXXIX.

The fact that scales such as those illustrated in the Tables XXXVIII and XXXIX may be used independently to measure the attitude of employees toward their company illustrates several points concerning the use of such scales. It will be noticed that the statements comprising the two scales are not the same, yet both scales measure essentially the same thing. Thus, the use of such scales does not require including any specific statements which, from an industrial relations viewpoint, might seem undesirable. A scale can be "tailor made" for a given plant and deliberately kept free of statements that may seem to pack dynamite without sacrificing the validity of the scale. The use of different statements in scales measuring the same attitude also facilitates checking of results by a repeat test in order to be sure of conclusions reached and to measure the effectiveness of systematic company efforts to improve employee morale.

Attitude scales are not perfect instruments for the registering of employee feelings, but they are considerably better than guessing or relying on chance (and often biased) individual reports.

Factors Affecting the Attitude of Employees

Attitude scales are of no practical value unless investigations making use of this technique are successful in identifying factors that affect employee morale and point the way toward changes that may be instituted by management to improve morale. A number of investigations of this type have been conducted and several determining factors have been isolated. Some of these can be easily changed by management; others are more difficult to modify. In any event, a statement of those factors that have been found to influence employee morale will indicate something of the value of this method as a tool by means of which management may keep in touch with the pulse of employee feelings toward the company.

Job or rank of employees

In Uhrbrock's study [10] it was found that foremen are more

---

[10] *Ibid.*

favorably disposed toward the company than are clerks, and clerks more favorably disposed than are factory workers. The distributions of attitude scores for the three groups are shown in Figure 90. This finding is in accord with what one might ex-

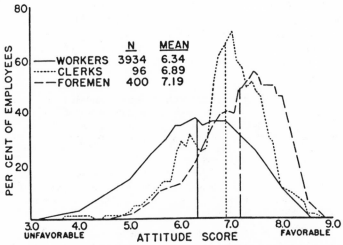

Fig. 90—Distribution of attitude toward the company of three groups of employees.

pect, and it may be considered as an added indication of the validity of the attitude-scale method of measurement. Many companies have employees on jobs that lack status. The identification of such jobs and the means of improving morale of the employees assigned to them is one practical value of an attitude survey. Often a marked improvement of morale can be effected by a slight change in job status. Super[11] has found that the *amount* of change in status is of little importance in effecting an increase in job satisfaction, but the *direction* of change is of vital importance. Those departments having employees whose morale would be helped by such measures can be readily identified by means of an anonymous attitude survey, provided only that the employees identify their department and job.

Success of the employee

The old maxim that "nothing succeeds like success" applies to

---

[11] D. E. Super, "Occupational Level and Job Satisfaction," *Journal of Applied Psychology*, XXIII (1939), pp. 547–564.

employee morale. Those employees who are doing a job well and are made to feel that they are doing a job well have good morale. If they are failing, or made to feel that they are failing, morale suffers. For high morale to exist, the job does not have to be one of vital importance to the plant. It can be quite an ordinary job and yet accomplish the desired result. In other words, it is not so much the job as how the employee feels about it and how the boss regards the employee that determines the latter's morale. Glen Gardiner [12] has given an excellent illustration of this principle:

Riding on a freight elevator with the superintendent of the U. S. Gypsum Company on Staten Island, I was impressed by this incident. As we stepped on the elevator the superintendent said, "I want to introduce you to Tony who has been running this elevator for more than eight years and has never had a single accident of any kind, which is a record we're proud of."

The way Tony grinned and stuck out his hand made one realize that he appreciated the credit being given him and that he was 100 per cent sold on the idea of running that elevator for many years to come without any accidents.

Comprehensive statistical studies have been made which show that the morale of the successful employee is better than that of the employee who is struggling with his job. For example, Kolstad [13] found that the morale scores of low-selling employees in a department store were significantly lower than the corresponding scores of the high-selling employees. It seems clear that employees should not be placed nor kept on jobs in which they are unable to achieve a reasonable degree of success.

Supervision

Everyone recognizes the fact that a man may work contentedly for one boss and complain bitterly when asked to work for another. Probably few things exert so unfavorable an effect on employee morale as the blustering, bully type of "straw boss." This has been emphasized by McMurry [14] and it is attested by

---

[12] Glen Gardiner, "Reaching the Individual Worker," Address before the Second Annual Greater Philadelphia Safety Congress, May 27, 1935.

[13] A. Kolstad, "Employee Attitudes in a Department Store," *Journal of Applied Psychology*, XXII (1938), pp. 470–479.

[14] R. N. McMurry, "So You Handle People," *Society for the Advancement of Management Journal*, II (1937), pp. 168–172.

the personal experience of everyone. In the past, management has too often selected the supervisor from the working group primarily because the man chosen was a good worker or a high producer. We now know that ability to produce well on the job is no guarantee whatever of ability to supervise other men on the job. The supervisor chosen because of his production record is as likely as not to be a failure in handling men; and we might add that he will almost certainly fail unless he is given specific training in how to handle men. Industry today recognizes this situation and is not only considering many factors besides production ability in promoting a man to a supervisory position, but also is training supervisors in the solution of problems unique to the supervisory job. Evidence shows that when supervisors and others in positions of authority are correctly trained, the guidance which they may give has a favorable effect on employee morale.[15]

Working conditions

Employee morale is lowered by unfavorable working conditions. This situation is the more serious because often the employees who are affected are unaware of the true cause of their grouchiness and dissatisfaction. Collier[16] has pointed out a number of specific relationships found between reactions of employees and the physical working conditions of several jobs. He states that the feelings of uneasiness and unrest found among spray painters were removed by the installation of a new air exhaust. He also found that the presence of methylene chloride produces bad temper, irritability, and sleeplessness. Needless to say, the employees so affected were unaware of the real cause of their mental discomfort and therefore probably tended to attribute their feelings to imaginary causes. Other effects reported by Collier were that mercury produces irritability, anxiety, depression, and sleeplessness, while manganese produces languor, lethargy, muscular cramps, and abnormalities of gait.

These findings indicate that the physical surroundings of a job may result in a general lowering of employee morale in a

---

[15] J. F. Murphy, O. M. Hall, and G. L. Bergen, "Does Guidance Change Attitudes?" *Occupations*, XIV (1936), pp. 949–952.

[16] H. E. Collier, "The Mental Manifestations of Some Industrial Illnesses," *Occupational Psychology*, XIII (1939), pp. 89–97.

way which is not revealed by ordinary questioning of the men. Questions, or better still, an attitude survey, will reveal the low morale, but it will not identify the cause. The conclusion we may draw is that when an unfavorable morale condition is found to exist, it is wise to examine carefully the physical surroundings to determine whether some unnatural condition may be at fault.

Some evidence indicates that a deliberate effort to create favorable working conditions (as opposed to the elimination of definitely unfavorable surroundings) will be followed by an improvement of morale. For example, Tindall [17] reports that the presence of music on the job speeds up production, improves morale, pacifies labor unrest, creates good will, lessens labor turnover, and reduces errors. While the several favorable effects found in this study suggest the desirability of keeping the working conditions as pleasant as the nature of the work will permit, we should hardly conclude that the use of music is either possible or desirable in all instances. In many cases (namely, in a steel mill) music would be out of the question, because the general noise level is so great that no one could hear it.

Salary reviews and praise

A fact not realized by many hopeful college graduates is that it is entirely possible for an employee to become lost and buried in a large industrial plant, *even while he is doing his job well.* Indeed, the very fact that he is doing a routine job well may prevent him from being brought to the attention of anyone who has the authority to promote or demote him. Obviously, the permanent or semipermanent location of an employee on a job from which he hoped to advance is not conducive to high morale. Many industries are solving this problem by a scheme for systematically reviewing, at stated intervals, the job and salary of every employee. Such a scheme does a great deal to prevent a capable employee from being "lost in the mill." The advisability of such a scheme has been stressed by Shepard [18] in his emphasis of the fact that workers are happier as well as more valuable if they are praised and given regular salary reviews.

---

[17] G. M. Tindall, "Rhythm for the Restless," *Personnel Journal,* XVI (1937), pp. 120–124.

[18] J. L. Shepard, "Recognition on the Job," *Personnel Journal,* XVI (1937), pp. 111–119.

The matter of praise, also, is sometimes given too little consideration by management and supervision. If we are willing, temporarily, to oversimplify a very complex problem, we might say that there are in general two ways of motivating people: to praise (or reward) for doing the desired thing, and to reprove (or punish) for doing the wrong thing. Much thought and considerable experimentation have been concentrated on this problem in an effort to determine which of these methods of motivation achieves the best results. Unfortunately, a general conclusion that is universally applicable in all situations has not been reached; but the preponderance of evidence clearly favors the praise over the reproof method. This was the conclusion reached by Hurlock [19] in his studies of learning in school children, and there seems to be every reason for expecting the results to apply in a general way to the behavior of industrial employees. One should not infer from Hurlock's study that praise is always superior to reproof or that reproof should never be used. His investigations, indeed, show that reproof for failure accomplishes better results than no comment at all. And in practical situations, it seems obvious that situations arise which clearly call for some kind of reproof. The general principle that we emphasize here is that praise and rewards are in many (if not most) cases more potent than reproof as a motivating factor and will *almost always have a better effect on employee morale.* Supervisors will do well not only to *know* this, but to *use* it in their day-by-day operations with their men.

Wage payment methods

Entirely aside from the *amount* of money earned by an employee, the *method* by which his wage is computed may be a source of employee complaint. Wage incentive plans are ordinarily installed for the purpose of motivating the worker to reach a reasonable output and at the same time of rewarding the employees who reach such an output in proportion to the actual amount of work done. A discussion of the various wage incentive plans in use by modern industry does not fall within the scope of this volume; but it should be said here that such plans are often somewhat complicated in operation and are therefore

---

[19] E. B. Hurlock, "An Evaluation of Certain Incentives Used in School Work," *Journal of Educational Psychology*, XVI (1925), pp. 145–159.

not always understood completely by the employees who are affected by them. An employee wants to know how to figure his own check. If no one has explained the wage payment plan to him, or if it has been explained but he has not understood the explanation, he is very likely to be suspicious of the whole system. An employee who figures that the company owes him $26.60 but who receives a check for only $26.50 is disgruntled out of all proportion to his imagined loss of ten cents. When management installs a wage incentive plan, the job is only half done; there remains the job of *explaining* the plan to the employees who are to work under it, of being sure that they *understand* it, and of *selling* it to them. Modern management no longer tells its employees, "This is the way we are going to do it, and you can like it or quit." Management today realizes that it is good business to help every employee to feel that he is part of the business. Such a feeling cannot be developed if an employee cannot even compute his own pay check.

A wage incentive plan is usually based upon a job analysis of the various jobs so that equal skill, industry, and effort on the different jobs will be paid equally well. Such job analyses always involve some subjective element in rating the different jobs; and it is a rare case where the first installation of a wage incentive plan is not found to contain a few jobs that are "out of line," that is, are set too high or too low in comparison with other jobs. It is very important to keep a constant lookout for such cases and to correct them at the first opportunity. Both in factory work and office work, jobs that are "out of line" in rate or salary are a significant source of employee unrest.[20]

Other factors affecting morale

Several other studies have identified still additional factors which, at least in certain cases, have an effect on employee morale. In Uhrbrock's investigation it was found that the attitude toward the company of the male employees was significantly less favorable than that of the female employees. Apparently some factor, or combination of factors, which had been unnoticed by

[20] H. B. Bergen, C. E. Haines, L. G. Giberson, F. L. Hallock, and C. S. Coler, "Attitudes and Emotional Problems of Office Employees," *Office Management Series*, No. 87, p. 34.

P. Hall and H. W. Locke, *Incentives and Contentment: A Study Made in a British Factory* (Pitman, London, 1938).

management was operating in this particular company to give the women a better feeling toward the company. The forces at work may have been seemingly trivial *to management*, but factors that seem trivial to management often seem quite important to employees. In fact, as Schultz [21] has pointed out, employee attitudes are often affected more by little things than by broad management policies.

It should be mentioned also that employee attitudes are often made up of a combination of attitudes toward different aspects of the total situation. Employees may be favorable toward some, and unfavorable toward other, aspects of their jobs. Geiger, Remmers, and Greenly [22] found that little relationship exists between the attitude of apprentices toward their job proper, fellow employees, foremen, opportunity for promotion, related instruction, and management. This study includes the development of a diagnostic scale which indicates how differential attitude toward different aspects of the job may be measured.

It is not intended to imply that the factors listed above are *all* of the factors that may affect employee morale. The list is only illustrative of factors that have been found operating in certain plants and that may give cues to the alert plant superintendent in analyzing his own particular situation. Although we may confidently expect that future developments in applied psychology will make this problem easier to cope with than it is today, sufficient evidence already exists to show that the judicious use of attitude scales and of techniques now available will aid in the solution of many industrial relations problems. Departments in which unsatisfactory relations exist between employees and their supervisor can be located. Company policies that are not satisfactory to employees can be identified. Employee reaction to such topics as method of wage payment, insurance programs, and plans for promotion and transfer can be determined. The attitude survey is of real value in the solution of such problems and has become a powerful tool of management in the prevention of industrial relations disputes.

---

[21] R. S. Schultz, "Psychology in Industry," *Personnel Journal*, XVI (1937), pp. 221-223.

[22] H. E. Geiger, H. H. Remmers, and R. J. Greenly, "Apprentices' Attitudes Toward Their Training and the Construction of a Diagnostic Scale," *Journal of Applied Psychology*, XXII (1938), pp. 32-41.

Appendices

Appendix A
Elementary Statistical Procedures

WHEN many measurements, such as scores or other data, are to be summarized or interpreted, the use of some form of statistical procedure is usually desirable. If a considerable amount of raw data is involved, a simple listing of the data is of little value. Such a listing will not tell us, for example, how the data are distributed, how much they vary, or where in the total distribution they tend to cluster. Further, such a listing is of little value in indicating how the data compare with, or are related to, other sets of data collected under other circumstances. Before a meaningful interpretation of the data can be made it is necessary to reduce them to a *chart or to one or two single numbers which may represent the data as a whole.*

Graphic Representation of Data

The frequency distribution and polygon

A frequency polygon, constructed from a frequency distribution, is a graphic representation of a set of data. The construction and interpretation of a frequency polygon may best be explained by an example. Suppose 60 employees on an inspection job have detected the following number of flaws of a certain type during one week of work:

TABLE XL

NUMBER OF FLAWS DETECTED BY EACH OF 60 INSPECTORS DURING ONE WEEK OF WORK

15	36	40	37	32	13	35	20	33	36	33	16	38	19	33	34	24
36	25	29	27	39	42	31	21	26	28	53	23	51	21	26	39	28
30	31	32	30	29	49	39	30	44	34	37	35	38	35	41	37	43
42	38	45	22	46	41	47	45	34								

From a gross, or even a detailed, inspection of these 60 values one cannot answer such questions as: What is the typical number of defects spotted by an average inspector in a week? How much difference is there between the best and poorest inspectors in spotting defective material? Is there any preponderance of good, poor, or average ability represented in the performance of these inspectors?

Such questions as these may be answered at a glance if the data are grouped and presented in a chart. One variety of such a chart is a frequency polygon. The steps involved in constructing a frequency polygon are as follows:

1. Determine the range of the values in the raw data. Quickly glance through the data to determine the *highest* and the *lowest* values. The range is the difference between these values. In the case of the 60 inspector records, the highest figure is 53 and the lowest is 13. The range is therefore $53 - 13 = 40$.

2. If we find that the range of the data is large (that they are widely spread), it will be more convenient to group them by intervals (class intervals, abbreviated c. i.) with a range in each c. i. of more than one unit. The c. i. is a group of adjacent scores of such a size that from 12 to 18 c. i.'s cover the range of the whole distribution or all of the data. With a range of 40, a c. i. of 2 would require 20 groups; a c. i. of 3, 14 groups; and a c. i. of 4, 10 groups. In our illustrative problem, a c. i. of 3 is therefore the proper size to use.

A simple rule of thumb which is helpful in deciding upon the correct size of the c. i. is to divide the range by 15 (15 because, on the average, this is the most desirable number of c. i.'s) and take as the c. i. the whole number nearest to the quotient. In our problem, the range divided by 15 would be $40 \div 15 = 2.66$. As 3 is the whole number nearest to 2.66, 3 would be the size of the c. i. to be used.

3. Arrange the adjacent c. i.'s in a column, leaving a blank space immediately to the right of this column. The arrangement of the c. i.'s preparatory to the construction of a frequency distribution appears as follows.

TABLE XLI

CLASS INTERVALS TO BE USED FOR ILLUSTRATIVE DATA IN TABLE XL

51–53
48–50
45–47
42–44
39–41
36–38
33–35
30–32
27–29
24–26
21–23
18–20
15–17
12–14

4. Place a tally mark for each value in the original list of raw data opposite the appropriate class interval. As the first value among the 60 listed in Table XV is 15, the first tally mark should be in the 15–17 c. i. The second value, 36, is represented by a tally mark in the 36–38 c. i. Usually it is advisable to tally the fifth entry in each c. i. with a line across the preceding four tally marks. This simplifies the counting of tally marks at a later time. When all entries have been made, that is, all data tabulated, the frequency di 'bution appears as in Table XLII.

5. Lay off appropriate units on squared (cross section or graph) paper so that a graph may be constructed on which the midpoints of the c. i.'s are plotted on the base line and the frequencies or number of cases in each c. i. on the vertical axis. When this is done, the frequency polygon shown in Figure 91 is obtained.

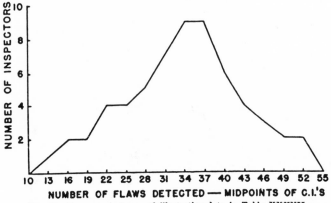

Fig. 91—Frequency polygon of illustrative data in Table XXXVII.

TABLE XLII

CLASS INTERVALS, TALLY MARKS, AND FREQUENCIES (f.) FOR ILLUSTRATIVE
DATA IN TABLE XL

Class Intervals (c. i.)	Tally Marks	Frequency (f.)
51–53	//	2
48–50	//	2
45–47	///	3
42–44	////	4
39–41	⎤⎤⎤ /	6
36–38	⎤⎤⎤ ////	9
33–35	⎤⎤⎤ ////	9
30–32	⎤⎤⎤ //	7
27–29	⎤⎤⎤	5
24–26	////	4
21–23	////	4
18–20	//	2
15–17	//	2
12–14	/	1
		Total = 60

To one familiar with the concept of a frequency polygon, the graphic illustration in Figure 91 is a much more meaningful representation of the data than the list of values shown in Table XL, or the frequency distribution shown in Table XLII. The frequency polygon makes apparent at a glance that the typical or average inspector detected around 35 defects during a week of work, that the operators range or vary from some who detected only 13 defects to others who detected 52, and that a majority of the operators are fairly near the average in ability (that is, that not so many are very high or very low as are near the average). In summarizing psychological data it is a definite advantage to be able to present all of the major facts in a single graphic presentation of this type.

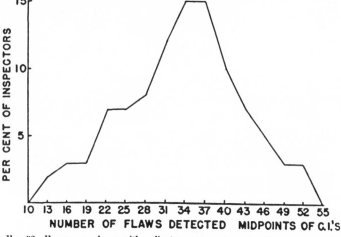

FIG. 92—Frequency polygon with ordinates as percentages for illustrative data in Table XXXVII.

In a frequency polygon such as the one shown in Figure 91, the area between the curve and the base line is determined by the number of cases (called N) which the graph represents. Thus, a curve portraying 120 cases would cover twice the area of the curve shown (if the c. i.'s are the same for both distributions), and a curve portraying 600 cases would cover ten times this area. This is no disadvantage in many cases, but situations sometimes arise in which it is desirable to keep the total area under the curve the same, regardless of N or the number of cases. To meet this situation we may plot the *percentage* of cases rather than the *number* of cases falling in each c. i. This may be accomplished by dividing each f value in Table XLII by the total number of cases in the distribution. Each quotient thus obtained indicates the percentage of cases from the total falling in the respective c. i. These computations are indicated in Table XLIII.

If the percentages shown in the last column of Table XLIII are now plotted as the ordinates (vertical axis points) of a frequency polygon, the chart shown in Figure 92 is obtained.

When a frequency polygon is to be compared with a number of other polygons, and when the important facts to be compared deal with the central tendencies and general form of the distributions rather than with the different number of cases plotted in each, the "percentage method" of plotting a frequency distribution is preferred to the "total-number-of-cases method."

We may define a frequency polygon, in the light of the above description, as *a curve which portrays data graphically and which is so drawn that the base line represents the varying values of the original data and the ordinates represent the number of cases (or percentage of cases) at each of the raw data values.*

TABLE XLIII

FREQUENCY AND PERCENTAGE OF CASES IN EACH C. I. FOR ILLUSTRATIVE DATA IN TABLE XL

Class Intervals	f	Calculation of Percentage	Percentage
51–53	2	$\frac{2}{60}$ = .033	3
48–50	2	$\frac{2}{60}$ = .033	3
45–47	3	$\frac{3}{60}$ = .050	5
42–44	4	$\frac{4}{60}$ = .066	7
39–41	6	$\frac{6}{60}$ = .100	10
36–38	9	$\frac{9}{60}$ = .150	15
33–35	9	$\frac{9}{60}$ = .150	15
30–32	7	$\frac{7}{60}$ = .117	12
27–29	5	$\frac{5}{60}$ = .083	8
24–26	4	$\frac{4}{60}$ = .066	7
21–23	4	$\frac{4}{60}$ = .066	7
18–20	2	$\frac{2}{60}$ = .033	3
15–17	2	$\frac{2}{60}$ = .033	3
12–14	1	$\frac{1}{60}$ = .017	2
Total =	60		100

The normal distribution

The shape of the frequency polygons shown in Figures 91 and 92 is typical of the kind of distribution usually found when data obtained from a group of people are plotted. It will be noted that the curves are approximately "bell-shaped," that is, they are high in the center and taper off toward the base line at both ends. If we were to divide the area under such a curve by drawing a perpendicular line from the central high point to the base line, the two parts would be approximately equal in area and would be bilaterally symmetrical in shape. It is well recognized that all, or nearly all, measurements of human traits and abilities result in distributions of approximately this form. Such distributions are called *normal distributions.* A strictly normal distribution conforms to a symmetrical bell-shaped curve that is defined by a mathematical equation, the derivation of which is beyond the scope of the present discussion.[1] It will suffice for the beginning student to know that:

---

[1] The interested student is referred to C. C. Peters and W. R. Van Voorhis, *Statistical Procedures and Their Mathematical Bases* (McGraw-Hill, New York, 1941), pp. 279–286.

1. A normal distribution is bell-shaped, that is, it is high in the center and low at both ends. Its two halves are symmetrical.

2. Measurements obtained from a group of persons usually approximate this type of distribution.

Measures of Central Tendency

While the frequency polygon is helpful in giving an immediate graphic description of a set of data, that is, indicating general trends, it is often desirable to present certain quantitative figures that supplement the graphic picture. One of the most useful of such numerical values is a measure of the central tendency of the data. A measure of central tendency may be defined as a single figure or value which is representative of the entire set of data. Three such measures that are in common use are the arithmetic mean, the median, and the mode.

The arithmetic mean

The arithmetic mean, sometimes simply called the mean, may be defined as the sum of the measures divided by the number of measures.[2] Or it may be thought of as a point of balance which could be found if all values in the distribution were assigned the same weight and then arranged along a horizontal beam. The physicist might define it as that point in the distribution around which the moments are equal.

In the case of the 60 values previously discussed from which a frequency polygon was constructed, the mean is obtained by finding the total of the 60 measures and dividing this total by 60, thus:

$$\text{Arithmetic Mean } (A.M.) = \frac{\text{Sum of measures}}{N} = \frac{2016}{60} = 33.6$$

This is the procedure followed in computing the exact value of the arithmetic mean of any set of values. In practice a shorter method of computation utilizing the data as tabulated in a frequency distribution and yielding an approximation (rather than the exact value) of the mean is often used. This shorter method assumes that each score as tabulated in a frequency distribution has the same value as the midpoint of the c.i. in which it falls. For further convenience in calculation, the mean is first computed in c.i. units from an arbitrary base selected near the center of the distribution at the midpoint of one of the c.i.'s. The base selected is entirely arbitrary—it may be taken as any point in the distribution. We have chosen one near the center of the distribution to simplify computation.

If this method is applied to the frequency distribution in Table XLII the arrangement shown in Table XLIV is obtained.

In the above tabulation the d column represents the number of c.i. units each c.i. is located above or below the c.i. arbitrarily chosen as the base for calculations. In the c.i. 51–53 there are 2 scores. This c.i. is 6 c.i. units above the arbitrary base. Thus, in computing the

[2] H. E. Garrett, *Statistics in Psychology and Education* (Longmans, Green and Company, 1937), p. 18.

TABLE XLIV

COMPUTATION OF THE ARITHMETIC MEAN FROM A FREQUENCY DISTRIBUTION

c.i.	f.	d.	fd.
51–53	2	6	12
48–50	2	5	10
45–47	3	4	12
42–44	4	3	12
39–41	6	2	12
36–38	9	1	9
33–35	9	0	0
30–32	7	−1	−7
27–29	5	−2	−10
24–26	4	−3	−12
21–23	4	−4	−16
18–20	2	−5	−10
15–17	2	−6	−12
12–14	1	−7	−7
	60		$\Sigma fd = -7$

Formula for Computing $A.M.$

$$A.M. = M° + c.i. \cdot \frac{\Sigma fd}{N}$$

$M°$ = assumed mean
$c.i.$ = size of $c.i.$
$\frac{\Sigma fd}{N}$ = summation of deviations from assumed mean divided by N

$$A.M. = 34 + 3\left(\frac{-7}{60}\right)$$
$$= 34 - .35 = 33.65$$

A.M. in c.i. units from the arbitrary base, these two scores would each have a value of 6, resulting in the number 12 which appears in the fourth, or fd, column. In like manner, there are 2 scores in the c.i. 48–50, and these two scores are each 5 c.i. units above the arbitrary base, resulting in the number 10 which appears in the fd column. All scores tabulated in c.i.'s below the arbitrary base are represented by negative values in the fd column. The algebraic sum of this column (Σfd) divided by the number of cases indicates how far the computed mean will deviate from the assumed mean (base) in terms of c.i. units. From the tabulation, this deviation in c.i. units from the arbitrary base (assumed mean) is defined as:

$$\text{Deviation in c.i. units from base} = \frac{\Sigma fd}{N}$$

Carrying through this computation for the data under consideration shows that:

$$\text{Deviation in c.i. units from base} = \frac{\Sigma fd}{N} = \frac{-7}{60} = -.117$$

This is interpreted to mean that the $A.M.$ is .117 of a class interval below the midpoint of the arbitrary base (see formula in illustrative problem). In order to transmute this deviation ($-.117$) into raw score units we would multiply it by 3 (the size of the class interval). Thus, in terms of raw score units, the deviation is $-.35$. The mean, as computed by this method, is therefore .35 raw score units below the midpoint of the 33–35 c.i. As the midpoint of this is 34, the mean is $34 - .35 = 33.65$. This approximation does not agree exactly with the exact method in which all raw data are added and the sum is divided by the number of cases; but the approximation is sufficiently close to justify its use in many cases. The student may note, however, that essentially the same procedures are used in both solutions. The procedure in using the "exact method" may be thought of as involving the computation of a mean by assuming the mean to be zero, computing the deviations from zero in raw score units, and dividing their sum by N as in the short method.

The median

The median is a measure of central tendency defined as that score (or value) which exceeds, and is exceeded by, half the measures, that is, it is that point in the distribution above and below which 50 per cent of the values lie. A logical (though laborious) method to determine the median consists in arranging all the raw data in rank order from lowest to highest and counting off the bottom half of the measures. The value at this point is the median. If this method is followed for the data in Table XL, the following arrangement of the scores is obtained.

TABLE XLV

ARRANGEMENT OF DATA FOR THE COMPUTATION OF THE MEDIAN DIRECTLY FROM RAW DATA

53	45	41	38	36	34	32	29	26	21
51	44	40	38	36	34	31	29	25	20
49	43	39	37	35	33	31	28	24	19
48	42	39	37	35	33	30	28	23	16
47	42	39	37	35	33	30	27	22	15
46	41	38	36	34	32	30	26	21	13

Counting from the lowest score up, we find that the 30th from the low end is 34, and the 31st from the low end is also 34. The median score would therefore be 34. If there had been a difference between the 30th and 31st scores, the median would be the value halfway between these scores. If an odd number of cases were included in the original set of scores (as 61 instead of 60) the median would be the value of the middle score.

In practice, the median as well as the mean may be conveniently approximated from a tabulated frequency distribution. To illustrate this process we may use the same frequency distribution previously discussed.

TABLE XLVI

COMPUTATION OF THE MEDIAN FROM A FREQUENCY DISTRIBUTION

Class Intervals	f	Cumulative f	Formula for Median
51–53	2	60	
48–50	2	58	$Md. = l + c.i. \dfrac{\left(\dfrac{N}{2} - F\right)}{f_m}$
45–47	3	56	
42–44	4	53	
39–41	6	49	l = lower limit of c.i. upon which median lies.
36–38	9	43	
33–35	9	34	$c.i.$ = class interval
30–32	7	25	$\dfrac{N}{2} = \dfrac{1}{2}$ of the scores
27–29	5	18	
24–26	4	13	F = no. of scores in all c.i.'s below l
21–23	4	9	f_m = no. of scores in c.i. in which median falls.
18–20	2	5	
15–17	2	3	
12–14	1	1	$Md. = 32.5 + 3\dfrac{(μ - 25)}{9}$
Total	60		$= 32.5 + 1.7 = 34.2$

Knowing that 60 cases are included in the distribution, it is necessary to find the score which separates the lower 30 from the upper 30. The value of this score is the median. Counting up from the lower part of the distribution, we first fill the column *cumulative f*, which indicates for each c.i. the number of cases *in and below that c.i.*

It will be noted that 25 cases are included in or below the 30–32 c.i., and that 34 cases are included in or below the 33–35 c.i. The median, or point midway between the 30th and 31st case, must therefore be with the 33–35 c.i. Now if we assume that the 9 cases in the 33–35 c.i. are distributed evenly throughout this interval, we must go up into this c.i. far enough to cover the lowest 5 of these 9 cases in order to reach the median. This may be illustrated graphically as follows:

It will be noted that the "real limits" of the 33–35 c.i. are considered 32.5 and 35.5, that is that the c.i. extends one-half a score unit above and one-half a score unit below the tabulated values. This is necessary because otherwise there would be a whole unit between each pair of adjacent c.i.'s that does not logically fall in either c.i.

In this case, the median would be $\frac{5}{9}$ of the size of the c.i., added to the lower limit of the c.i., or Median $= \frac{5}{9} (3) + 32.5 = 34.2$. This value, 34.2, differs slightly from the value computed by arranging the scores in rank order, but the approximation is sufficiently close to justify its use in most instances. Exactly the same procedure can be followed in defining other points in the distribution, for example, the 25th percentile—the point in the distribution below which 25 per cent of the scores lie and above which 75 per cent lie.

The mode

A third measure of central tendency is the mode, which is defined as the measure appearing most frequently. This value, as well as the mean and the median, may be determined directly from the raw data (if one value appears more often then any other) or may be approximated from a frequency distribution of the data.

In computing the mode directly from the raw data, the values are inspected to determine which one appears most frequently. Sometimes, as in the case of the values shown in Table XL, several of the measures appear an equal number of times. In this case, the figures 30, 33, 34, 35, 36, 37, 38, 39 each appear three times. It is incorrect, therefore, to say that any one of these is the mode. Furthermore, there is reason to believe that if a larger sample than 60 inspectors had been included in the distribution, and if the c.i. used in forming the distribution were smaller than 3, the frequency polygon obtained would be more even in curvature and only one single high point would be found. Under such circumstances, this high point would be the mode. An approximation of this value may be obtained from a frequency distribution by means of the following empirical formula:

$$\text{Mode} = 3 \text{ Median} - 2 \text{ Mean}$$

In the case of the data we have been discussing, this formula gives the following value for the mode:

$$\text{Mode} = 3(34.2) - 2(33.65) = 35.30.$$

When to use the mean, median, and mode

Why is it necessary to have three different measures to indicate the central tendency of a set of data? The answer is that each is best adapted to certain uses, that is, in some cases one may be most representative of a set of data, while in other cases, another measure may be most suitable. The mean is ordinarily used if the distribution is approximately normal. (If the distribution is perfectly normal, the three measures of central tendency have the same value.) If, on the other hand, there is a preponderance of extreme cases at either end of the distribution, the mean may give an incorrect impression of the central tendency of the data. Under these circumstances, the median or mode is more suitable. Consider, for example, the following yearly incomes of five persons:

$800 $900 $850 $750 $5000

The mean for these five incomes is

$$\frac{\$800 + \$900 + \$850 + \$750 + \$5000}{5} = \$1660.$$

This figure, though an accurate statement of the mean, is not typical of the group as a whole because it is so markedly affected by the one income of $5000 which is considerably larger than the other four. The median income is $850, and this value is more typical for the group as a whole than is the mean income of $1660. If a great deal of data were available for computation, it would also be enlightening to know the mode, or most common income. Certain other principles also help determine which measure of central tendency is most appropriate in any specific case. We may generalize the above illustration by saying that if a distribution is very much *skewed* (that is, contains more cases at one extreme than at the other), the median or mode is more likely to give a representative picture of the typical score than is the mean.

Measures of Variability

In addition to a measure or value to represent the central tendency of a set of data, there is also quite frequently a need for some measure of the spread, or variability, of the data. The need for a measurement of this type may be seen by comparing the data shown in Table XL and tabulated in Table XLIV (the mean of which, computed from the frequency distribution, was found to be 33.65) with another set of data which, for purposes of illustration, we might assume to consist of 21 scores of 33 and 39 scores of 34, making 60 scores in all. The mean of 60 such scores may readily be found to be 33.65.

$$\frac{(21)(33) + (39)(34)}{60} = 33.65.$$

While both distributions have the same mean, they differ markedly in variability or spread. The former distribution is made up of scores varying from 13 to 53, while the latter consists entirely of scores of 33 and 34. A quantitative measure of variability is therefore of considerable value. Statistical procedures have been designed which yield a single value descriptive of this variability; as in the cases of means and medians, these measures tell us something about the group as a whole. Two measures of variability of a set of scores or other data are the Mean (or Average) Deviation and the Standard Deviation.

The mean or average deviation

This measure of variability is defined as the average deviation of the scores from the central tendency, usually the arithmetic mean, but sometimes the median or mode. If the arithmetic mean is used as the central point from which the mean deviation is computed, the computation involved for the 60 scores tabulated in Table XLIV would be as follows:

In Table XLVII columns 1–4 are identical with the corresponding columns in Table XLIV. Column 5 gives for each c.i. the deviation between the midpoint of the interval and the arithmetic mean of the distribution. For the c.i. 51–53 this deviation is 52–33.65 = 18.35, which appears as the first value in the fifth column. Since there were two scores in this c.i., and since each deviates by 18.35 from the mean of the distribution, the fD column contains 2(18.35) = 36.70 as the first entry. In like manner, the amounts of deviation of all scores in the remaining c.i.'s has been computed and entered in the fD column. The sum of this column is the total of the deviations of all 60 scores, and this total divided by 60 gives the Mean Deviation of the distribution.

Had the 60 scores been bunched around the mean to a greater extent, the Mean Deviation would necessarily have been smaller.

TABLE XLVII

COMPUTATION OF THE AVERAGE DEVIATION (A.D.) FROM A FREQUENCY DISTRIBUTION

c.i.	f	d	fd	D* Raw Score Deviation from Mean	fD
51–53	2	6	12	18.35	36.70
48–50	2	5	10	15.35	30.70
45–47	3	4	12	12.35	37.05
42–44	4	3	12	9.35	37.40
39–41	6	2	12	6.35	38.10
36–38	9	1	9	3.35	30.15
33–35	9	0	0	.35	3.15
30–32	7	−1	−7	2.65	18.55
27–29	5	−2	−10	5.65	28.25
24–26	4	−3	−12	8.65	34.60
21–23	4	−4	−16	11.65	46.60
18–20	3	−5	−10	14.65	43.95
15–17	2	−6	−12	17.65	35.30
12–14	1	−7	−7	20.65	20.65

$$\Sigma fd = -7 \qquad\qquad \overline{441.15}$$

$$\text{Mean} = 34 - (\tfrac{7}{60})3 = 33.65$$

$$\text{Mean dev.} = \frac{441.15}{60} = 7.35$$

* Note that all deviations, whether above or below the mean, are taken as positive.

If, for example, all 60 scores had been exactly *at* the mean, the deviation between the mean and each of the scores would have been zero, the sum of the 60 deviations would be zero, and the Mean Deviation would be zero. In the illustrative case previously referred to consisting of 60 scores made up of 21 scores at 33 and 39 scores at 34, the mean deviation, though not zero, would be very small. In this case, the Mean Deviation may be computed in the following fashion: the 21 scores at 33 contribute 21(.65) = 13.65 units of deviation, while the 39 scores at 34 contribute 39(.35) = 13.65 units. The sum of these values divided by 60 gives the mean deviation.

$$\text{Mean Deviation} = \frac{13.65 + 13.65}{60} = \frac{27.3}{60} = .46$$

This figure, .46, indicates quantitatively the variability in this set of 60 scores. When compared with a set of data such as shown in Table XLVII, the mean deviation of which was found to be 7.35, the difference in spread is seen to be reflected in the size of the mean deviation figures. In interpreting the mean deviation, it will be helpful to think of it as defining two points on either side of the mean which enclose a large proportion of the scores (values). In a normal distribution, the mean deviation, when measured off on the scale above and below the mean, will mark the limits of the middle 57 per cent of the scores.

The Standard Deviation

The Standard Deviation is the most widely used measure of

variability. It is defined as the square root of the mean square deviation. Defined by formula:

$$\text{Standard Deviation} = S.D. = \sigma = \sqrt{\frac{\Sigma D^2}{N}}$$

where ΣD^2 is read "the sum of the squared deviations of the scores from their mean" and N is the number of cases. S.D. and σ are abbreviations for the Standard Deviation. They are used interchangeably.

Although the Standard Deviation may be computed directly from a set of raw data by means of the formula $S.D. = \sqrt{\frac{\Sigma D^2}{N}}$, this process is laborious. For example, in the case of the set of data we have been using for illustrative purposes (tabulated in Table XL), we would proceed by determining the difference between each raw score and the mean of the 60 scores, squaring these differences, summing the 60 squared differences, dividing by 60, and extracting the square root of the quotient. The first score tabulated is 15. The difference between this value and the mean of the 60 scores (as computed directly from the raw data) is $D = 33.6 - 15.0 = 18.6$. D^2 would therefore be $(18.6)^2 = 345.96$. This must be repeated for every one of the 60 scores before the sum of the squared deviations can be obtained.

Because of the excessive labor in computing the S.D. directly from the raw data, a simple process which approximates the true value of the S.D. has been developed. This is used in the computations shown in Table XLVIII, in which is computed the Standard Deviation of the data shown previously in Table XLIV.

TABLE XLVIII

COMPUTATION OF THE STANDARD DEVIATION FROM A FREQUENCY DISTRIBUTION[1]

c.i.	f	d	fd	fd²	
51–53	2	6	12	72	
48–50	2	5	10	50	$\text{Mean} = M^\circ + \text{c.i.} \left(\frac{\Sigma fd}{N}\right)$
45–47	3	4	12	48	
42–44	4	3	12	36	
39–41	6	2	12	24	$\text{Mean} = 34 + 3\left(\frac{-7}{60}\right) = 33.65$
36–38	9	1	9	9	
33–35	9	0	0	0	$S.D. = \sqrt{\frac{\Sigma D^2}{N}} = \text{c.i.} \sqrt{\frac{\Sigma fd^2}{N} - \left(\frac{\Sigma fd}{N}\right)^2}$
30–32	7	−1	−7	7	
27–29	5	−2	−10	20	$= 3\sqrt{\frac{537}{60} - (.117)^2}$
24–26	4	−3	−12	36	$= 3\sqrt{8.950 - .014}$
21–23	4	−4	−16	64	$= 3\sqrt{8.936}$
18–20	2	−5	−10	50	$= 3(2.99)$
15–17	2	−6	−12	72	$S.D. = 8.97$
12–14	1	−7	−7	49	
			$\Sigma fd = -7$	$\Sigma fd^2 = 537$	

[1] The derivation of the formula for computing the standard deviation by the method used in Table XLVIII is given below. Working in c.i. units rather than raw score units, let

$D_1, D_2 \cdots D_n$ = deviations of the scores in c.i. units from their mean.

c = difference in c.i. units between the mean of the scores and the midpoint of the zero c.i., i.e. the arbitrary base.

The standard deviation is the most commonly used measure of variability. Usually when the mean value of a set of data is given, the S.D. is also given to indicate the variability of the data.

$d_1, d_2, \cdots d_n$ = deviations of the scores in c.i. units from the arbitrary base. Then

$$D_1 = d_1 - c$$
$$D_2 = d_2 - c$$
$$\cdots\cdots\cdots\cdots$$
$$D_n = d_n - c$$

If the above equations are squared on both sides, we have

$$D_1{}^2 = (d_1 - c)^2 = d_1{}^2 - 2d_1c + c^2$$
$$D_2{}^2 = (d_2 - c)^2 = d_2{}^2 - 2d_1c + c^2$$
$$\cdots\cdots\cdots\cdots\cdots$$
$$D_n{}^2 = (d_n - c)^2 = d_n{}^2 - 2d_nc + c^2$$

Summating the above to determine the sum of the squared differences, we have

$$D_1{}^2 + D_2{}^2 + \cdots D_n{}^2 = (d_1{}^2 + d_2{}^2 + \cdots d_n{}^2)$$
$$+ (2d_1c + 2d_2c + \cdots 2d_nc) + Nc^2$$

The above, written with summation signs, becomes:

$$\Sigma D^2 = \Sigma d^2 - 2c\Sigma d + Nc^2 \qquad (1)$$

Now it will be remembered from page 339 that c, which is the difference in c.i. units between the mean of the data and the arbitrary base (i.e. the mean in c.i. units away from the arbitrary base) was determined by adding the d values of the scores and dividing this sum by the number of scores. Since there are f_1 scores at d_1 deviation; f_2 scores at d_2 deviation; etc.; this summation is given by $f_1d_1 + f_2d_2 + \cdots f_nd_n = \Sigma fd$, which, divided by N gives $\dfrac{\Sigma fd}{N}$.

We may therefore substitute in (1) $\dfrac{\Sigma fd}{N}$ for c, giving

$$\Sigma D^2 = \Sigma d^2 - 2\frac{\Sigma fd}{N}\Sigma d + N\left(\frac{\Sigma fd}{N}\right)^2$$

But the Σd and Σfd are the same, since Σfd is only a simpler method of determining the Σd that involves grouping together all scores of the same d, and multiplying this d by f, the number of such scores. For the same reason, Σd^2 is the same as Σfd^2. The above equation therefore may be written:

$$\Sigma D^2 = \Sigma fd^2 - 2\frac{\Sigma fd\Sigma fd}{N} + N\left(\frac{\Sigma fd}{N}\right)^2$$
$$\Sigma D^2 = \Sigma fd^2 - 2\frac{(\Sigma fd)^2}{N} + \frac{(\Sigma fd)^2}{N}$$

If both sides of the above equation are divided by N, we have

$$\frac{\Sigma D^2}{N} = \frac{\Sigma fd^2}{N} - 2\left(\frac{\Sigma fd}{N}\right)^2 + \left(\frac{\Sigma fd}{N}\right)^2$$
$$\frac{\Sigma D^2}{N} = \frac{\Sigma fd^2}{N} - \left(\frac{\Sigma fd}{N}\right)^2$$

Extracting the square root of both sides

$$S.D. = \sqrt{\frac{\Sigma D^2}{N}} = \sqrt{\frac{\Sigma fd^2}{N} - \left(\frac{\Sigma fd}{N}\right)^2}$$

which is the equation used in the computations accompanying Table XLVIII to determine the standard deviation of the distribution in c.i. units. The value yielded by this expression is then multiplied by the size of the c.i. to give the S.D. in raw score units.

Comparable scores

The S.D. performs another useful function—it can be used in the comparison of individual scores from different distributions. For example, suppose that two inspectors from departments A and B, who are working at different inspection jobs, detect respectively 45 and 89 defects during a week of work. How can we compare the efficiency of these two employees? It will be seen immediately that a direct comparison of the figures 45 and 89 is not valid, because the two inspection jobs may be very different. It will also be seen that we can say little concerning the position of these inspectors in their respective groups except that they fall above or below the mean of their group in inspection work. To make a comparison, then, we must first compute the mean number of defects spotted by all inspectors in Department A, and the mean number spotted by all inspectors in Department B. Suppose that those means are respectively 38 and 95. We thus see that the inspector from Department A is $45 - 38$ = 7 pieces *above* the mean for that department, and that the inspector from Department B is $89 - 95 = -6$, or 6 pieces *below* the mean of inspectors from that department. We can thus say, at this point, that the inspector from Department A is above average in ability on the job and that the inspector from Department B is below average. But how about their relative distance from the average? To answer this question we must compute the S.D.'s of the two distributions and determine how many S.D.'s each inspector is above or below average.

Suppose we find the S.D. of the operators in Department A to be 5.5 pieces. Our first inspector is therefore $\frac{45 - 38}{5.5} = 1.27$ S.D.'s above average. If the S.D. of the inspectors in Department B is 9.5, the inspector from the group who detected 89 pieces is $\frac{89 - 95}{9.5}$ $= -.63$ or .63 S.D.'s below average. *The deviation of a score from the mean of the distribution expressed in S.D. units results in a measurement which is comparable with similarly determined measurements from other distributions.* Thus, we may say that our first inspector is about *twice* as far above average, in terms of comparable scale units, as the second operator is below average. Scores computed in this manner are known as Z-scores. The formula for a Z-score is as follows:

$$\text{Z-score} = \frac{\text{Raw Score} - \text{Mean of Raw Scores}}{\text{S.D. of Raw Scores}}$$

The Z-score is helpful not only when comparing scores from one distribution to another, but also when, for any reason, it is desired to combine scores with the same or differential weighting. A typical example of an industrial situation that requires this technique is in the combination of items used in a merit-rating blank. Suppose that each employee has been rated by his supervisor on a chart containing items such as the following:

Industrious-ness	0	10	20	30	40	50
	Always loafs if not watched	Often loafs when not watched	Sometimes loafs and sometimes works when not watched	Usually is hard at work	Always is hard at work	

Knowledge of Job	0	10	20	30	40	50
	Knows little about the job	Knows routine only	Is fairly well informed on his work	Well informed on details relative to his work	Thorough knowledge of present job and related work	

We may suppose, for purposes of illustration, that it is now desired to combine these two traits into an overall merit rating. (If more than two traits are included in the chart, as is usually the case, the procedure is identical.) Suppose that an employee, Mr. A, has received 40 points on industriousness and 30 points on knowledge of job, making a total of 70 points if the ratings are added directly. Suppose that another employee, Mr. B, has received 30 points on industriousness and 40 points on knowledge of job, which also results in a total of 70 points if added directly. It is clear that such direct and immediate combination of ratings would result in identical overall ratings for these two employees. The question which we may raise is whether such a statement of equal ratings is justified. The answer is that it is not. If the mean rating of all employees on industriousness was 33 with a S.D. of 3, then A's rating would be $\frac{40 - 33}{3} = 2.33$ or 2.33 S.D.'s above the mean and B's would be $\frac{30 - 33}{3} = -1.00$, or 1.00 S.D. below the mean on this trait. If the mean rating for all employees on knowledge of job were 25, with a S.D. of 6, A would be $\frac{30 - 25}{6} = +.83$, or .83 S.D.'s above average in knowledge of job while B would be $\frac{40 - 25}{6} = 2.50$, or 2.50 S.D.'s above average in this respect. Now, the proper combination of the two traits, if we wish to weight them equally, would be:

Employee	Rating in Industrious-ness	Rating in Knowledge of Job	Z-Score in Indus-triousness	Z-Score in Knowledge of Job	Sum of Scores for Both Units
A	40	30	+2.33	.83	3.16
B	30	40	−1.00	2.50	1.50

This transfer of ratings into Z-scores and the adding of the Z-scores shows that the two employees A and B are not equal in rating (as we would infer if the raw ratings were added), but rather that A is definitely higher than B. The procedure described has assumed that the two trait ratings, being combined, should be given equal weight, and the procedure shows how they can be combined with equal weight into a composite score. One might think that conversion of raw scores to Z-scores is not necessary if the raw scores are to be given equal weight in the combination score. Actually, if we do not give the raw scores equal weight in converting them into Z-scores, the scores will weight themselves according to the size of their respective standard deviations. In other words, if combined directly, the raw scores will be weighted too much or too little, depending upon their position relative to the means of their respective distributions and upon the variability of the distribution of which they are a part. When scores are combined, they are *always* weighted in some manner, whether we deliberately weight them or not. It is highly important, therefore, to weight them deliberately (either with equal weight or otherwise) by converting them into Z-scores and then combining them.

It does not follow from the above discussion that combined scores should always be weighted equally. Indeed, it is often desirable to weight various scores according to some plan that has been decided upon before the scores are combined. When this is desired, such weighting can be accomplished very easily by multiplying each Z-score by the appropriate weight before they are combined. In our illustrative case, suppose that we have decided that *industriousness* should be given twice as much weight as *knowledge of job* in determining the total rating. This would be accomplished as follows:

Employee	Z-Score in Industriousness	Z-Score in Knowledge of Job	Weighted Z-Score in Industriousness	Weighted Z-Score in Knowledge of Job	Combined Weighted Z-Scores
A	+2.33	+.83	+4.66	+.83	5.49
B	−1.00	+2.50	−2.00	+2.50	+.50

The combined ratings so obtained show a still greater difference between employees A and B than was obtained when the scores were equally weighted. If, on the other hand, it was desired to give the rating in knowledge of job twice as much weight as the rating on industriousness, the following computations would be made:

Employee	Z-Score in Industriousness	Z-Score in Knowledge of Job	Weighted Z-Score in Industriousness	Weighted Z-Score in Knowledge of Job	Combined Weighted Z-Scores
A	+2.333	+.833	+2.333	+1.666	4.0
B	−1.000	+2.500	−1.000	+5.000	4.0

This last procedure results in giving identical total scores to employees A and B, which, it will be remembered, also occurred when the raw scores were added directly (30 + 40 = 70). Now, if we remember that the assumed standard deviation for the knowledge of job ratings was 6, which is twice as great as the standard deviation of 3 assumed for the industriousness ratings, we can see why a direct combination of raw scores gives the equality that is obtained when the respective Z-scores are weighted in the ratio 2:1. In this instance the original ratings whose Standard Deviation is 6 are automatically given twice as much weight (when raw scores are combined directly) as the original ratings whose standard deviation is only 3. Thus, we obtain the same final result (equality) by direct combination that is obtained when the *knowledge-of-job* ratings are deliberately given a weight twice as great as the industriousness ratings.

Many other problems arise in which it is necessary to weight scores to achieve a particular result. For example, an industry faced with the problem of selecting a number of electrical apprentices desires to give this training to those boys who have the greatest aptitude for the job and who are therefore most likely to succeed. Careful consideration and discussion of the problem by management and supervision resulted in the decision that four factors should determine whether an employee should be given this training. These four factors were general intelligence, present knowledge of electricity, previous merit rating, and seniority with the company. It was further decided in conference that, although all of these four factors should be considered, they are not of equal importance. It was decided that a fair weighting of their relative importance was as follows:

General intelligence...................................... 40%
Knowledge of electricity................................. 30%
Merit rating... 20%
Seniority or service with the company.................... 10%

To score the applicants according to this plan, each was given a general intelligence test and a test covering technical phases of electricity. Merit ratings and seniority were obtained from the company records. Each of the four scores was converted into a Z-score and the four resulting Z-scores were respectively multiplied by 40, 30, 20, and 10. For each employee the sum of the weighted Z-scores was used in indicating whether or not he was given the apprenticeship training.

Correlation

In numerous experimental situations, two variable quantities are so related that they vary, or tend to vary, with each other. A common problem in industrial psychology is to reduce to a simple and meaningful statement the facts that have been discovered concerning such a functional relationship. Suppose that a number of punch-press operators during a given period of time have each punched a certain number of pieces and have each mispunched, or otherwise wasted, a certain number of pounds of stock material. In such a situation, it might be of considerable importance for management to know whether any relationship exists (and, if so, how much) between quantity of work done and amount of material wasted. Indeed, the company's policy with respect to speed of work recommended as well as the quality control in the form of penalty or bonus might well be formulated correctly only in the light of specific knowledge of the relationship between speed and accuracy.

Consider a department employing eight operators for whom the following figures for production and waste in pounds are available:

Operator	Production	Waste
1......	95	3.0
2......	103	4.5
3......	88	3.5
4......	98	4.0
5......	93	3.0
6......	107	4.5
7......	114	4.0
8......	106	5.0

It is difficult, if not impossible, to determine from a gross inspection of these two columns of figures whether any relationship exists between speed and accuracy. It is necessary to employ some type of graphic or computational procedure to determine the amount of relationship

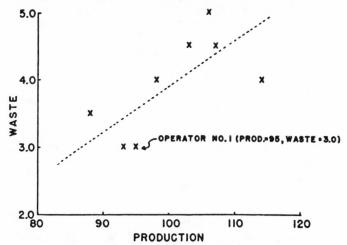

Fig. 93—A plot of the production and waste records for the eight punch-press operators shown above.

which may exist between these two sets of data. One simple and sometimes satisfactory method consists of a simple plotting of the values on co-ordinate axes and rough inspection of the results. If we let production be represented on the X or horizontal axis, and waste on the Y or vertical axis, then the production and waste of each operator will locate him on a chart, giving the result shown in Figure 93.

A plot such as is shown in Figure 93 gives a much better indication of the presence or absence of a relationship between the data than can be obtained from the columns of raw data from which the chart was prepared. The chart shows that some relationship does exist, and it is even possible to draw in by inspection a line or curve that represents this relationship in an approximate form.

Although this simple method of studying the relationship between two variables is sometimes adequate for very simple problems or for those that involve only a small amount of data, it is not adequate for an exact study because it does not result in a quantitative statement of the degree of relationship. The slope of the dotted line cannot be considered such a quantitative statement because: (1) this line is drawn in by inspection and, (2) its slope depends upon the units of measurement on both the X and Y axes.

Two commonly used quantitative methods for measuring the degree of relationship between two paired sets of data are rank-order correlation and product-moment correlation.

Rank-order correlation

The use of this method may be described by applying it to the data for the eight punch press operators.

TABLE XLIX

COMPUTATION OF RANK-ORDER CORRELATION RANK

Operator	Production	Waste	Rank in Production	Rank in Waste	Difference in Rank (D)	(D)²
1......	95	3.0	6	7.5	1.5	2.25
2......	103	4.5	4	2.5	1.5	2.25
3......	88	3.5	8	6	2	4.00
4......	98	4.0	5	4.5	.5	.25
5......	93	3.0	7	7.5	.5	.25
6......	107	4.5	2	2.5	.5	.25
7......	114	4.0	1	4.5	3.5	12.25
8......	106	5.0	3	1.0	2.0	1.00
						22.50

$$R = 1 - \frac{6 \Sigma D^2}{N(N^2 - 1)} = 1 - \frac{135}{504} = .73$$

In Table XLIX the two columns headed *Rank* give, respectively, the rank of the operators on the two measures (production and waste). The highest producing operator (in this case the seventh in the list) is given a rank of 1, the second highest a rank of 2, and so on. In like manner, the rank of each operator in wastage is placed in the waste-rank column. In case two or more operators are tied for a given rank (as in the case of the second and sixth operators who are tied at 4.5 pounds of waste each), the tied scores are all given the same rank, which is the average of the ranks that would have been assigned to the tied scores if they had not been tied. The values in the D^2 column are obtained by squaring each D value. The sum of the D^2 column is then determined and the correlation computed by means of the formula:

$$R = 1 - \frac{6\Sigma D^2}{N(N^2 - 1)}$$

N is the number of cases entering into the computation.

This formula for the rank-order correlation is an empirical formula. It yields a value of $+1.00$ if the data are in exactly the same rank order. (The reason for this may be seen from the fact that if all ranks are the same, all D's are zero, all D^2 values are zero, ΣD^2 is zero, and the formula becomes $1 - 0 = 1$.) If the data are in exactly reverse order (that is, if the individual who ranks highest on one series is lowest on the other, and so on) the formula will yield a value of -1.00, but if no relationship exists between the two sets of data, a correlation of zero will be found.

The use of this formula is ordinarily more satisfactory than a simple plotting of one variable against the other because it yields a quantitative statement of the degree of relationship and not simply a graphic representation that cannot be reduced to a numerical statement.

However, if an appreciable number of cases is involved, the rank-order method of computing the degree of relationship is extremely laborious. For this reason—and for other reasons of a mathematical nature—it is ordinarily used only when the data are limited to a very few cases (less than 30).

The product-moment coefficient

This is the most widely used measure of relationship. Like the rank-order correlation, it may vary from $+1.00$ (indicating perfect positive relationship) through zero (indicating no relationship) to -1.00 (indicating perfect negative relationship). The product-moment correlation, represented by the symbol r, may be defined in several ways. One of the simplest definitions is that *r is the slope of the straight line which best fits the data after the data have been plotted as z-scores on co-ordinate axes;* that is, it is the tangent of the angle made by this line with the base line.

Several terms in this definition require further definition. By *slope* is meant steepness with which the line rises. The slope of a straight line drawn in any manner across co-ordinate paper is defined as the distance, y, from any given point on the line to the x intercept, minus the distance, a, from the origin to the y intercept, divided by the distance, x, from the point on the line to y intercept. Thus the slope, which we will call b, is defined in Figure 94 as follows:

$$b = \frac{y - a}{x}$$

It should be remembered that, on co-ordinate axes, distances above and to the right of the origin are positive, while distances measured below and/or to the left of the origin are negative. The slope of any line which *rises* as it goes from left to right will therefore be positive (the greater the rise in a given distance to the right the larger the positive value of the slope) and the slope of any line which *falls* as it goes

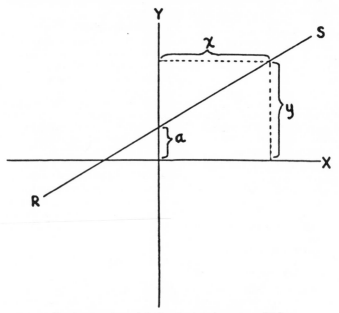

FIG. 94—The slope of the line R S is defined as $b = \dfrac{y - a}{x}$.

from left to right will be negative (the greater the fall in a given distance to the right, the greater the negative value of the slope).

By line of *best fit* in the definition is meant a line so drawn that the sum of the squared deviations in a vertical direction from the original points to the line is less than the sum would be for any other straight line that might be drawn.

A rough approximation of the value of r may be obtained by plotting the z-scores of the two variables, fitting a straight line to these points by inspection, and graphically measuring the slope of this straight line. Although this method is never used in practical computation (because it is both inaccurate and laborious), the application of it to a set of representative data may serve to clarify the meaning of the correlation coefficient, r. Returning to the data for which we have previously computed the rank-order correlation (see Table XLIX on page 352), we first compute the z-scores for each measure:

TABLE L

PRODUCTION AND WASTE FOR EIGHT PUNCH PRESS OPERATORS, WITH
CORRESPONDING Z-SCORES OF THE PRODUCTION AND WASTE FIGURES

Operator	Production	Waste	Z-Score in Production	Z-Score in Waste
1.	95	3.0	$-.69$	-1.38
2.	103	4.5	$+.31$	$+.82$
3.	88	3.5	-1.56	$-.65$
4.	98	4.0	$-.31$	$+.09$
5.	93	3.0	$-.94$	-1.38
6.	107	4.5	$+.81$	$+.82$
7.	114	4.0	$+1.69$	$+.09$
8.	106	5.0	$+.69$	$+1.56$
Mean.	100.5	3.94		
S.D.	8.0	.68		

These pairs of z-scores are used as the x and y values for eight
points which are plotted on co-ordinate axes as in Figure 95. The
straight line that seems best to fit these points is then determined (as
with a stretched string which is moved about until the desired location

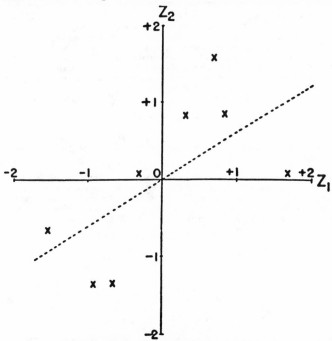

FIG. 95—A plot of the z-scores for production and waste records of the eight
punch-press operators shown above.

is obtained) and drawn on the graph. The correlation, r, as determined by this crude method, is obtained by measuring the slope of this line. The procedure applied to Figure 95 gives a value of $r = .61$, but it should be emphasized that this value is affected by:

1. The accuracy with which the straight line has been located, and
2. The accuracy with which the slope of the line has been measured after it has been drawn.

Both points (1) and (2) operate to eliminate the possibility of complete accuracy in this method of determining a correlation coefficient. Therefore, a mathematical method has been devised to make the computation, so that no plotting of points or graphic measurements are required. This method involves determining the equation of the straight line which, if plotted, would best fit the points and computing the slope of this straight line of best fit from the equation.

It may be proved mathematically that the slope of the straight line of best fit is given by the following equation:[4] Slope $= r = \dfrac{\Sigma Z_x Z_y}{N}$,

---

[4] The proof of this formula is as follows:

$Z_{x1}, Z_{x2}, Z_{x3}, \ldots Z_{xn}$ are the z-scores for the x variable
$Z_{y1}, Z_{y2}, Z_{y3}, \ldots Z_{yn}$ are the z-scores for the y variable

The equation of any straight line is: $y = a + bx$. The problem is to find the values of the constants a and b in this equation which will give the straight line that "best fits" the data according to the criterion of best fit stated on page 354, that is, the straight line which will give a minimum value to the sum of the squared deviations between the line and the original points.

The first point (whose co-ordinate points are Z_{x1} and Z_{y1}) will deviate from the line by an amount:

$$d_1 = Z_{y1} - a - bZ_{x1}$$

this deviation squared will be

$$d_1{}^2 = (Z_{y1} - a - bZ_{x1})^2$$

If the sum of all such squared deviations of the points from the line be represented by u, then

$$u = \Sigma d^2 = \Sigma(Z_y - a - bZ_x)^2$$

For the values of a and b which result in u being a minimum, the derivatives of u with respect to a and b, respectively, must be zero. To find the correlation coefficient it is therefore only necessary to differentiate the equation with respect to a and to b, to set the resulting derivatives equal to zero, and to solve for b (which is the slope of the straight line of best fit). This is done as follows:

$$\frac{\partial u}{\partial a} = 0 = 2\Sigma(Z_y - a - bZ_x)(-1) \tag{1}$$

$$\frac{\partial u}{\partial b} = 0 = 2\Sigma(Z_y - a - bZ_x)(-Z_x) \tag{2}$$

(1) above becomes:

$$0 = -\Sigma Z_y + Na + b\Sigma Z_x$$
$$\Sigma Z_y = Na + b\Sigma Z_x \tag{3}$$

(2) above becomes:

$$0 = -\Sigma Z_x Z_y + a\Sigma Z_x + b\Sigma Z_x{}^2$$
$$\Sigma Z_x Z_y = a\Sigma Z_x + b\Sigma Z_x{}^2 \tag{4}$$

It will be remembered that a z-score is obtained as follows (see page 347):

$$Z_x = \frac{X - M_x}{\sigma x}$$

where $\Sigma Z_x Z_y$ is read "the sum of the products of the z-scores for the pairs of points or values."

Where X is a given raw score, M_x is the mean raw score, and σ_x the standard deviation of the raw scores.

The sum of all z-scores is therefore:

$$\Sigma Z_x = \frac{\Sigma(X - M_x)}{\sigma_x}$$

$$= \frac{\Sigma X}{\sigma_x} - \frac{N M_x}{\sigma_x}$$

$$= \frac{\Sigma X}{\sigma_x} - \frac{N \frac{\Sigma X}{N}}{\sigma_x}$$

$$= \frac{\Sigma X}{\sigma_x} - \frac{\Sigma X}{\sigma_x}$$

$$= 0$$

In a similar way it can be shown that

$$\Sigma Z_y = 0$$

By substituting 0 for ΣZ_x and ΣZ_y in (3) we find immediately that a in the equation of the straight line of best fit is zero.

Working with (4), we find the value of b (which is the slope or the correlation coefficient) as follows:

$$\Sigma Z_x Z_y = a \Sigma Z_x + b \Sigma Z_x{}^2$$

since $\Sigma Z_x = 0$, this becomes:

$$\Sigma Z_x Z_y = b \Sigma Z_x{}^2$$

$$b = \frac{\Sigma Z_x Z_y}{\Sigma Z_x{}^2} \qquad (5)$$

It may be shown as follows that $\Sigma Z_x{}^2 = N$

$$Z_x = \frac{X - M_x}{\sigma_x}$$

$$Z_x{}^2 = \frac{(X - M_x)^2}{\sigma_x{}^2}$$

$$\Sigma Z_x{}^2 = \frac{\Sigma(X - M_x)^2}{\sigma_x{}^2}$$

$$\Sigma Z_x{}^2 = \frac{\Sigma(X^2 - 2XM_x + M_x{}^2)}{\sigma_x{}^2}$$

$$\Sigma Z_x{}^2 = \frac{\Sigma X^2 - 2M_x \Sigma X + N M_x{}^2}{\sigma_x{}^2}$$

$$\Sigma Z_x{}^2 = \frac{\Sigma X^2 - 2 \frac{\Sigma X}{N} \Sigma X + N \left(\frac{\Sigma X}{N}\right)^2}{\sigma_x{}^2}$$

$$\Sigma Z_x{}^2 = \frac{\dfrac{N \Sigma X^2 - 2(\Sigma X)^2 + (\Sigma X)^2}{N}}{\dfrac{\Sigma X^2}{N} - \left(\dfrac{\Sigma X}{N}\right)^2}$$

$$\Sigma Z_x{}^2 = \frac{\dfrac{N \Sigma X^2 - (\Sigma X)^2}{N}}{\dfrac{N \Sigma X^2 - (\Sigma X)^2}{N^2}}$$

Applying the formula to the data in Table XLIX, we may compute the correlation as in Table LI.

TABLE LI

COMPUTATION OF r BY Z-SCORE METHOD BETWEEN PRODUCTION AND WASTE FIGURES

Operator	Production	Waste	Z-Score in Production	Z-Score in Waste	(Z_1Z_2)
1......	95	3.0	$-.69$	-1.38	$+.95$
2......	103	4.5	$+.31$	$+.82$	$+.25$
3......	88	3.5	-1.56	$-.65$	$+1.01$
4......	98	4.0	$-.31$	$+.09$	$-.03$
5......	93	3.0	$-.94$	-1.38	$+1.30$
6......	107	4.5	$+.81$	$+.82$	$+.66$
7......	114	4.0	$+1.69$	$+.09$	$+.15$
8......	106	5.0	$+.69$	$+1.56$	$+1.08$
					$+5.38$

$$r = \frac{Z_xZ_y}{N} = \frac{+5.38}{8} = .67$$

The value of r thus obtained by computation, .67, differs from the value of .61 obtained by plotting and inspection. The plotting and inspection method yielded a value which was somewhat in error for the data in question.

While the z-score method of computing a correlation coefficient illustrated in Table LI may be used with any number of cases and will yield the correct mathematical value of r, the use of this method when many pairs of data are to be correlated is very laborious. It is therefore recommended, under such circumstances, that a modification of the fundamental formula $r = \dfrac{\Sigma Z_xZ_y}{N}$ which makes it possible to compute r from raw score values rather than z-score values be used. One convenient formula[1] for determining the coefficient of correlation

$$\Sigma Z_x{}^2 = \frac{N^2(\Sigma X^2) - N(\Sigma X)^2}{N \Sigma X^2 - (\Sigma X)^2}$$

$$\Sigma Z_x{}^2 = \frac{N[N \Sigma X^2 - (\Sigma X)^2]}{(N \Sigma X^2 - (\Sigma X)^2}$$

$$\Sigma Z_x{}^2 = N \qquad\qquad (6)$$

Substituting the value of $\Sigma(Z_x)^2$ given in (6) in equation (5), we have the slope or

$$r = b = \frac{\Sigma Z_xZ_y}{N}$$

[1] The proof of this formula is as follows:

$$r = \frac{\Sigma Z_xZ_y}{N}$$

$$= \frac{1}{N} \Sigma \frac{(X - M_x)}{\sigma_x} \frac{(Y - M_y)}{\sigma_y}$$

$$= \frac{1}{N} \Sigma \frac{(XY - XM_y - YM_x + M_xM_y)}{\sigma_x\ \sigma_y}$$

directly from the raw data is:

$$r = \frac{N\Sigma XY - \Sigma X \Sigma Y}{\sqrt{N\Sigma X^2 - (\Sigma X)^2} \sqrt{N\Sigma Y^2 - (\Sigma Y)^2}}$$

When we apply this formula, for illustrative purposes, to the data tabulated in Table LI, the computations shown in Table LII result:

TABLE LII

COMPUTATION OF r DIRECTLY FROM RAW DATA

Operator	Production (x)	Waste (y)	X^2	Y^2	XY
1.....	95	3.0	9025	9.00	285.0
2.....	103	4.5	10609	20.25	463.5
3.....	88	3.5	7744	12.25	308.0
4.....	98	4.0	9604	16.00	392.0
5.....	93	3.0	8649	9.00	279.0
6.....	107	4.5	11449	20.25	481.5
7.....	114	4.0	12996	16.00	456.0
8.....	106	5.0	11236	25.00	530.0

$\Sigma X = 804 \quad \Sigma Y = 31.5 \quad \Sigma X^2 = 81312 \quad \Sigma Y^2 = 127.75 \quad \Sigma XY = 3195.0$

$$r = \frac{N\Sigma XY - \Sigma X \Sigma Y}{\sqrt{N\Sigma X^2 - (\Sigma X)^2} \sqrt{N\Sigma Y^2 - (\Sigma Y)^2}}$$

$$r = \frac{8(3195) - (804)(31.5)}{\sqrt{8(81312) - (804)^2} \sqrt{8(127.75) - (31.5)^2}}$$

$$r = .67$$

When a considerable number of pairs of data are to be correlated, the use of a chart will still further simplify the computations. Several forms of such a chart have been prepared. One convenient form is shown in Figure 96. This chart shows the computation of the cor-

$$\frac{\frac{1}{N}\Sigma\left(XY - \frac{X\Sigma Y}{N} - Y\frac{\Sigma X}{N} + \frac{\Sigma X\Sigma Y}{N^2}\right)}{\sigma_x \sigma_y}$$

$$= \frac{1}{N}\frac{\Sigma XY - \frac{\Sigma X\Sigma Y}{N} - \frac{\Sigma Y\Sigma X}{N} + \frac{N\Sigma X\Sigma Y}{N^2}}{\sqrt{\frac{\Sigma X^2}{N} - \left(\frac{\Sigma X}{N}\right)^2}\sqrt{\frac{\Sigma Y^2}{N} - \left(\frac{\Sigma Y}{N}\right)^2}}$$

$$= \frac{1}{N}\frac{\frac{N\Sigma XY - \Sigma X\Sigma Y}{N}}{\sqrt{\frac{N\Sigma X^2 - (\Sigma X)^2}{N^2}}\sqrt{\frac{N\Sigma Y^2 - (\Sigma Y)^2}{N^2}}}$$

$$= \frac{1}{N}\frac{\frac{N\Sigma XY - \Sigma X\Sigma Y}{N}}{\frac{\sqrt{N\Sigma X^2 - (\Sigma X)^2}}{N}\frac{\sqrt{N\Sigma Y^2 - (\Sigma Y)^2}}{N}}$$

$$= \frac{1}{N}\frac{N^2(N\Sigma XY - \Sigma X\Sigma Y)}{N\sqrt{N\Sigma X^2 - (\Sigma X)^2}\sqrt{N\Sigma Y^2 - (\Sigma Y)^2}}$$

$$= \frac{N\Sigma XY - \Sigma X\Sigma Y}{\sqrt{N\Sigma X^2 - (\Sigma X)^2}\sqrt{N\Sigma Y^2 - (\Sigma Y)^2}}$$

relation between time used in inspecting 300 pieces of material and the number of defective pieces detected. In using this chart the following steps should be followed:

1. Decide upon appropriate class intervals for one of the variables

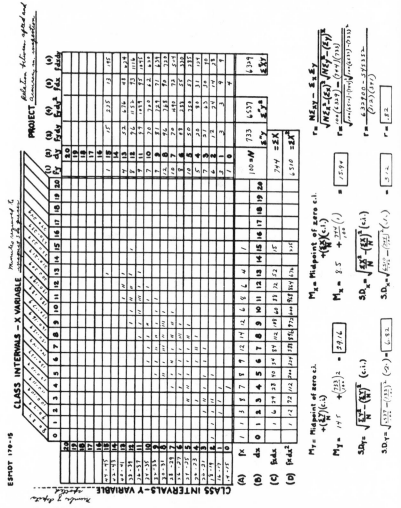

Fig. 96—A chart used in the computation of a product moment coefficient of correlation.

(using the rules given on page 334) and write these in on either the x or the y axis.

2. Decide upon appropriate class intervals for the other variables and write these in on the axis not used in (1) above.

3. Place one tally mark on the scattergram for each pair of values being correlated. For example, if an inspector spotted 33 defects in 16.5 minutes, the tally mark would go in the pigeonhole that is found at the intersection of the *row* containing 33 defects and the *column* containing 16.5 minutes.

4. After all tally marks have been placed on the chart, the rows should be added horizontally and the sum of the tally marks in each row written opposite this row in the f_y column (Column *1*).

5. The tally marks in each column should be added and the sum written at the bottom of each column in the row (A), the f_x row.

6. The f_y column should be added and the sum written opposite N at the bottom of this column. *The value of N thus obtained may be checked by adding the values in the f_x row. The sum of these values should also give the value of N.*

7. Each value of f_y in the column so headed should be multiplied by the value of d_y opposite it, and the resultant product written in Column *3*, headed $f_y d_y$. *The sum of Column 3 is the value of ΣY, which is used in the formula.*

8. Each value in Column *3*, the $f_y d_y$ column, should be multiplied by the corresponding value in Column *2*, the d_y column, resulting in the values for Column *4*, or the $f_y d_y{}^2$ column. *The sum of Column 4 is the value of ΣY^2 which is used in the formula.*

9. The values going into Column *5*, the $f d_x$ column, are determined by finding, for each row, the sum of the products of the number of cases in each cell times the x value of that cell. For example, in the first row in which a tally mark appears, there is only a single case, which appears in the cell under an x value of 13. The value to go into the blank in Column *5* is therefore $(1)(13) = 13$. In the next row no tally marks appear; therefore this row is blank. In the next row, one tally mark appears in the cell under an x value of 11, two in the cell with an x value of 12, and one in the cell with an x value of 13. The value to go into the third cell in Column *5* is therefore $(1)(11) + (2)(12) + (1)(13) = 48$. The remaining cells in Column *5* are filled in a similar manner.

10. The cells in Column *6*, the $f d_x d_y$ column, are filled with values obtained by multiplying each value in Column *2*, the d_y column, by the value in that same row appearing in Column *5*, the $f d_x$ column. The value in the first cell in Column *6* is therefore $(15)(13) = 195$. *The sum of Column 6 is the value of ΣXY which is used in the formula.*

11. The values in row (C) are obtained by multiplying each value in row (A), the f_x row, by the value directly below it in row (B), the d_x row. The values appearing in row A have already been obtained (see Step *5* above). The resultant values are entered in row (C),

the $f_x d_x$ row. *The sum of the values appearing in row C is the value of ΣX which is used in the formula.*

12. Each value in row (B), the d_x row, should be multiplied by the value directly below in row (C), the $f_x d_x$ row. The resultant values should be entered in row (D), the $f_x d_x^2$ row. *The sum of the values in row (D) is the value of ΣX^2 which is used in the formula.*

13. The values for N (see Step 6), ΣY (see Step 7), ΣY^2 (see Step 8), ΣXY (see Step 10), ΣX (see Step 11), and ΣX^2 (see Step 12) are now entered in the formula. The indicated arithmetic computations are then performed, yielding the value of r.

The use of this method assumes that each measure has the value of the midpoint of the class interval in which it falls. The computations indicated on the chart result in obtaining not only the value for r but also the mean and the standard deviation of both the X and Y arrays. It will be noted that these are the same formulas previously considered on pages 339 and 345.

Appendix B
Taylor-Russell Tables [1]

Tables of the Proportion Who Will Be Satisfactory Among Those Selected, for Given Values of the Proportion of Present Employees Considered Satisfactory, the Selection Ratio, and r

Proportion of Employees Considered Satisfactory = .05
Selection Ratio

r	.05	.10	.20	.30	.40	.50	.60	.70	.80	.90	.95
.00	.05	.05	.05	.05	.05	.05	.05	.05	.05	.05	.05
.05	.06	.06	.06	.06	.06	.05	.05	.05	.05	.05	.05
.10	.07	.07	.07	.06	.06	.06	.06	.05	.05	.05	.05
.15	.09	.08	.07	.07	.07	.06	.06	.06	.05	.05	.05
.20	.11	.09	.08	.08	.07	.07	.06	.06	.06	.05	.05
.25	.12	.11	.09	.08	.08	.07	.07	.06	.06	.05	.05
.30	.14	.12	.10	.09	.08	.07	.07	.06	.06	.05	.05
.35	.17	.14	.11	.10	.09	.08	.07	.06	.06	.05	.05
.40	.19	.16	.12	.10	.09	.08	.07	.07	.06	.05	.05
.45	.22	.17	.13	.11	.10	.08	.08	.07	.06	.06	.05
.50	.24	.19	.15	.12	.10	.09	.08	.07	.06	.06	.05
.55	.28	.22	.16	.13	.11	.09	.08	.07	.06	.06	.05
.60	.31	.24	.17	.13	.11	.09	.08	.07	.06	.06	.05
.65	.35	.26	.18	.14	.11	.10	.08	.07	.06	.06	.05
.70	.39	.29	.20	.15	.12	.10	.08	.07	.06	.06	.05
.75	.44	.32	.21	.15	.12	.10	.08	.07	.06	.06	.05
.80	.50	.35	.22	.16	.12	.10	.08	.07	.06	.06	.05
.85	.56	.39	.23	.16	.12	.10	.08	.07	.06	.06	.05
.90	.64	.43	.24	.17	.13	.10	.08	.07	.06	.06	.05
.95	.73	.47	.25	.17	.13	.10	.08	.07	.06	.06	.05
1.00	1.00	.50	.25	.17	.13	.10	.08	.07	.06	.06	.05

Proportion of Employees Considered Satisfactory = .10
Selection Ratio

r	.05	.10	.20	.30	.40	.50	.60	.70	.80	.90	.95
.00	.10	.10	.10	.10	.10	.10	.10	.10	.10	.10	.10
.05	.12	.12	.11	.11	.11	.11	.11	.10	.10	.10	.10
.10	.14	.13	.13	.12	.12	.11	.11	.11	.11	.10	.10
.15	.16	.15	.14	.13	.13	.12	.12	.11	.11	.10	.10
.20	.19	.17	.15	.14	.14	.13	.12	.12	.11	.11	.10
.25	.22	.19	.17	.16	.14	.13	.13	.12	.11	.11	.10
.30	.25	.22	.19	.17	.15	.14	.13	.12	.12	.11	.10
.35	.28	.24	.20	.18	.16	.15	.14	.13	.12	.11	.10
.40	.31	.27	.22	.19	.17	.16	.14	.13	.12	.11	.10
.45	.35	.29	.24	.20	.18	.16	.15	.13	.12	.11	.10
.50	.39	.32	.26	.22	.19	.17	.15	.13	.12	.11	.11
.55	.43	.36	.28	.23	.20	.17	.15	.14	.12	.11	.11
.60	.48	.39	.30	.25	.21	.18	.16	.14	.12	.11	.11
.65	.53	.43	.32	.26	.22	.18	.16	.14	.12	.11	.11
.70	.58	.47	.35	.27	.22	.19	.16	.14	.12	.11	.11
.75	.64	.51	.37	.29	.23	.19	.16	.14	.12	.11	.11
.80	.71	.56	.40	.30	.24	.20	.17	.14	.12	.11	.11
.85	.78	.62	.43	.31	.25	.20	.17	.14	.12	.11	.11
.90	.86	.69	.46	.33	.25	.20	.17	.14	.12	.11	.11
.95	.95	.78	.49	.33	.25	.20	.17	.14	.12	.11	.11
1.00	1.00	1.00	.50	.33	.25	.20	.17	.14	.13	.11	.11

[1] These tables are reproduced by permission from H. C. Taylor and J. T. Russell, "The Relationship of Validity Coefficients to the Practical Effectiveness of Tests in Selection: Discussion and Tables," *Journal of Applied Psychology*, XXIII (1939), pp. 565–578.

Proportion of Employees Considered Satisfactory = .20
Selection Ratio

r	.05	.10	.20	.30	.40	.50	.60	.70	.80	.90	.95
.00	.20	.20	.20	.20	.20	.20	.20	.20	.20	.20	.20
.05	.23	.23	.22	.22	.21	.21	.21	.21	.20	.20	.20
.10	.26	.25	.24	.23	.23	.22	.22	.21	.21	.21	.20
.15	.30	.28	.26	.25	.24	.23	.23	.22	.21	.21	.20
.20	.33	.31	.28	.27	.26	.25	.24	.23	.22	.21	.21
.25	.37	.34	.31	.29	.27	.26	.24	.23	.22	.21	.21
.30	.41	.37	.33	.30	.28	.27	.25	.24	.23	.21	.21
.35	.45	.41	.36	.32	.30	.28	.26	.24	.23	.22	.21
.40	.49	.44	.38	.34	.31	.29	.27	.25	.23	.22	.21
.45	.54	.48	.41	.36	.33	.30	.28	.26	.24	.22	.21
.50	.59	.52	.44	.38	.35	.31	.29	.26	.24	.22	.21
.55	.63	.56	.47	.41	.36	.32	.29	.27	.24	.22	.21
.60	.68	.60	.50	.43	.38	.34	.30	.27	.24	.22	.21
.65	.73	.64	.53	.45	.39	.35	.31	.27	.25	.22	.21
.70	.79	.69	.56	.48	.41	.36	.31	.28	.25	.22	.21
.75	.84	.74	.60	.50	.43	.37	.32	.28	.25	.22	.21
.80	.89	.79	.64	.53	.45	.38	.33	.28	.25	.22	.21
.85	.94	.85	.69	.56	.47	.39	.33	.28	.25	.22	.21
.90	.98	.91	.75	.60	.48	.40	.33	.29	.25	.22	.21
.95	1.00	.97	.82	.64	.50	.40	.33	.29	.25	.22	.21
1.00	1.00	1.00	1.00	.67	.50	.40	.33	.29	.25	.22	.21

Proportion of Employees Considered Satisfactory = .30
Selection Ratio

r	.05	.10	.20	.30	.40	.50	.60	.70	.80	.90	.95
.00	.30	.30	.30	.30	.30	.30	.30	.30	.30	.30	.30
.05	.34	.33	.33	.32	.32	.31	.31	.31	.31	.30	.30
.10	.38	.36	.35	.34	.33	.33	.32	.32	.31	.31	.30
.15	.42	.40	.38	.36	.35	.34	.33	.33	.32	.31	.31
.20	.46	.43	.40	.38	.37	.36	.34	.33	.32	.31	.31
.25	.50	.47	.43	.41	.39	.37	.36	.34	.33	.32	.31
.30	.54	.50	.46	.43	.40	.38	.37	.35	.33	.32	.31
.35	.58	.54	.49	.45	.42	.40	.38	.36	.34	.32	.31
.40	.63	.58	.5!	.47	.44	.41	.39	.37	.34	.32	.31
.45	.67	.61	.55	.50	.46	.43	.40	.37	.35	.32	.31
.50	.72	.65	.58	.52	.48	.44	.41	.38	.35	.33	.31
.55	.76	.69	.61	.55	.50	.46	.42	.39	.36	.33	.31
.60	.81	.74	.64	.58	.52	.47	.43	.40	.36	.33	.31
.65	.85	.78	.68	.60	.54	.49	.44	.40	.37	.33	.32
.70	.89	.82	.72	.63	.57	.51	.46	.41	.37	.33	.32
.75	.93	.86	.76	.67	.59	.52	.47	.42	.37	.33	.32
.80	.96	.90	.80	.70	.62	.54	.48	.42	.37	.33	.32
.85	.99	.94	.85	.74	.65	.56	.49	.43	.37	.33	.32
.90	1.00	.98	.90	.79	.68	.58	.49	.43	.37	.33	.32
.95	1.00	1.00	.96	.85	.72	.60	.50	.43	.37	.33	.32
1.00	1.00	1.00	1.00	1.00	.75	.60	.50	.43	.38	.33	.32

Proportion of Employees Considered Satisfactory = .40
Selection Ratio

r	.05	.10	.20	.30	.40	.50	.60	.70	.80	.90	.95
00	.40	.40	.40	.40	.40	.40	.40	.40	.40	.40	.40
05	.44	.43	.43	.42	.42	.42	.41	.41	.41	.40	.40
10	.48	.47	.46	.45	.44	.43	.42	.42	.41	.41	.40
15	.52	.50	.48	.47	.46	.45	.44	.43	.42	.41	.41
20	.57	.54	.51	.49	.48	.46	.45	.44	.43	.41	.41
25	.61	.58	.54	.51	.49	.48	.46	.45	.43	.42	.41
30	.65	.61	.57	.54	.51	.49	.47	.46	.44	.42	.41
35	.69	.65	.60	.56	.53	.51	.49	.47	.45	.42	.41
40	.73	.69	.63	.59	.56	.53	.50	.48	.45	.43	.41
45	.77	.72	.66	.61	.58	.54	.51	.49	.46	.43	.42
50	.81	.76	.69	.64	.60	.56	.53	.49	.46	.43	.42
55	.85	.79	.72	.67	.62	.58	.54	.50	.47	.44	.42
60	.89	.83	.75	.69	.64	.60	.55	.51	.48	.44	.42
65	.92	.87	.79	.72	.67	.62	.57	.52	.48	.44	.42
70	.95	.90	.82	.76	.69	.64	.58	.53	.49	.44	.42
75	.97	.93	.86	.79	.72	.66	.60	.54	.49	.44	.42
80	.99	.96	.89	.82	.75	.68	.61	.55	.49	.44	.42
85	1.00	.98	.93	.86	.79	.71	.63	.56	.50	.44	.42
90	1.00	1.00	.97	.91	.82	.74	.65	.57	.50	.44	.42
95	1.00	1.00	.99	.96	.87	.77	.66	.57	.50	.44	.42
1 00	1.00	1.00	1.00	1.00	1.00	.80	.67	.57	.50	.44	.42

Proportion of Employees Considered Satisfactory = .50
Selection Ratio

r	.05	.10	.20	.30	.40	.50	.60	.70	.80	.90	.95
00	.50	.50	.50	.50	.50	.50	.50	.50	.50	.50	.50
05	.54	.54	.53	.52	.52	.52	.51	.51	.51	.50	.50
10	.58	.57	.56	.55	.54	.53	.53	.52	.51	.51	.50
15	.63	.61	.58	.57	.56	.55	.54	.53	.52	.51	.51
20	.67	.64	.61	.59	.58	.56	.55	.54	.53	.52	.51
25	.70	.67	.64	.62	.60	.58	.56	.55	.54	.52	.51
30	.74	.71	.67	.64	.62	.60	.58	.56	.54	.52	.51
35	.78	.74	.70	.66	.64	.61	.59	.57	.55	.53	.51
40	.82	.78	.73	.69	.66	.63	.61	.58	.56	.53	.52
45	.85	.81	.75	.71	.68	.65	.62	.59	.56	.53	.52
50	.88	.84	.78	.74	.70	.67	.63	.60	.57	.54	.52
55	.91	.87	.81	.76	.72	.69	.65	.61	.58	.54	.52
60	.94	.90	.84	.79	.75	.70	.66	.62	.59	.54	.52
65	.96	.92	.87	.82	.77	.73	.68	.64	.59	.55	.52
70	.98	.95	.90	.85	.80	.75	.70	.65	.60	.55	.53
75	.99	.97	.92	.87	.82	.77	.72	.66	.61	.55	.53
80	1.00	.99	.95	.90	.85	.80	.73	.67	.61	.55	.53
85	1.00	.99	.97	.94	.88	.82	76	.69	.62	.55	.53
90	1.00	1.00	.99	.97	.92	.86	.78	.70	.62	.56	.53
95	1.00	1.00	1.00	.99	.96	.90	.81	.71	.63	.56	.53
1 00	1.00	1.00	1.00	1.00	1.00	1.00	.83	.71	.63	.56	.53

Proportion of Employees Considered Satisfactory = .60

Selection Ratio

r	.05	.10	.20	.30	.40	.50	.60	.70	.80	.90	.95
.00	.60	.60	.60	.60	.60	.60	.60	.60	.60	.60	
.05	.64	.63	.63	.62	.62	.62	.61	.61	.61	.60	.60
.10	.68	.67	.65	.64	.64	.63	.63	.62	.61	.60	.60
.15	.71	.70	.68	.67	.66	.65	.64	.63	.62	.61	.60
.20	.75	.73	.71	.69	.67	.66	.65	.64	.63	.61	.61
.25	.78	.76	.73	.71	.69	.68	.66	.65	.63	.62	.61
.30	.82	.79	.76	.73	.71	.69	.68	.66	.64	.62	.61
.35	.85	.82	.78	.75	.73	.71	.69	.67	.65	.63	.62
.40	.88	.85	.81	.78	.75	.73	.70	.68	.66	.63	.62
.45	.90	.87	.83	.80	.77	.74	.72	.69	.66	.64	.62
.50	.93	.90	.86	.82	.79	.76	.73	.70	.67	.64	.62
.55	.95	.92	.88	.84	.81	.78	.75	.71	.68	.64	.62
.60	.96	.94	.90	.87	.83	.80	.76	.73	.69	.65	.63
.65	.98	.96	.92	.89	.85	.82	.78	.74	.70	.65	.63
.70	.99	.97	.94	.91	.87	.84	.80	.75	.71	.66	.63
.75	.99	.99	.96	.93	.90	.86	.81	.77	.71	.66	.63
.80	1.00	.99	.98	.95	.92	.88	.83	.78	.72	.66	.63
.85	1.00	1.00	.99	.97	.95	.91	.86	.80	.73	.66	.63
.90	1.00	1.00	1.00	.99	.97	.94	.88	.82	.74	.66	.63
.95	1.00	1.00	1.00	1.00	.99	.97	.92	.84	.75	.67	.63
1.00	1.00	1.00	1.00	1.00	1.00	1.00	1.00	.86	.75	.67	.63

Proportion of Employees Considered Satisfactory = .70

Selection Ratio

r	.05	.10	.20	.30	.40	.50	.60	.70	.80	.90	.95
.00	.70	.70	.70	.70	.70	.70	.70	.70	.70	.70	
.05	.73	.73	.72	.72	.72	.71	.71	.71	.71	.70	.70
.10	.77	.76	.75	.74	.73	.73	.72	.72	.71	.70	.70
.15	.80	.79	.77	.76	.75	.74	.73	.73	.72	.71	.70
.20	.83	.81	.79	.78	.77	.76	.75	.74	.73	.71	.71
.25	.86	.84	.81	.80	.78	.77	.76	.75	.73	.72	.71
.30	.88	.86	.84	.82	.80	.78	.77	.75	.74	.72	.71
.35	.91	.89	.86	.83	.82	.80	.78	.76	.75	.73	.71
.40	.93	.91	.88	.85	.83	.81	.79	.77	.75	.73	.71
.45	.94	.93	.90	.87	.85	.83	.81	.78	.76	.73	.72
.50	.96	.94	.91	.89	.87	.84	.82	.80	.77	.74	.72
.55	.97	.96	.93	.91	.88	.86	.83	.81	.78	.74	.72
.60	.98	.97	.95	.92	.90	.87	.85	.82	.79	.75	.73
.65	.99	.98	.96	.94	.92	.89	.86	.83	.80	.75	.73
.70	1.00	.99	.97	.96	.93	.91	.88	.84	.80	.76	.73
.75	1.00	1.00	.98	.97	.95	.92	.89	.86	.81	.76	.73
.80	1.00	1.00	.99	.98	.97	.94	.91	.87	.82	.77	.73
.85	1.00	1.00	1.00	.99	.98	.96	.93	.89	.84	.77	.74
.90	1.00	1.00	1.00	1.00	.99	.98	.95	.91	.85	.78	.74
.95	1.00	1.00	1.00	1.00	1.00	.99	.98	.94	.86	.78	.74
1.00	1.00	1.00	1.00	1.00	1.00	1.00	1.00	1.00	.88	.78	.74

Proportion of Employees Considered Satisfactory = .80
Selection Ratio

r	.05	.10	.20	.30	.40	.50	.60	.70	.80	.90	.95
.00	.80	.80	.80	.80	.80	.80	.80	.80	.80	.80	.80
.05	.83	.82	.82	.82	.81	.81	.81	.81	.81	.80	.80
.10	.85	.85	.84	.83	.83	.82	.82	.81	.82	.81	.81
.15	.88	.87	.86	.85	.84	.83	.83	.82	.82	.81	.81
.20	.90	.89	.87	.86	.85	.84	.84	.83	.82	.81	.81
.25	.92	.91	.89	.88	.87	.86	.85	.84	.83	.82	.81
.30	.94	.92	.90	.89	.88	.87	.86	.84	.83	.82	.81
.35	.95	.94	.92	.90	.89	.89	.87	.85	.84	.82	.82
.40	.96	.95	.93	.92	.90	.89	.88	.86	.85	.83	.82
.45	.97	.96	.95	.93	.92	.90	.89	.87	.85	.83	.82
.50	.98	.97	.96	.94	.93	.91	.90	.88	.86	.84	.82
.55	.99	.98	.97	.95	.94	.92	.91	.89	.87	.84	.82
.60	.99	.99	.98	.96	.95	.94	.92	.90	.87	.84	.83
.65	1.00	.99	.98	.97	.96	.95	.93	.91	.88	.85	.83
.70	1.00	1.00	.99	.98	.97	.96	.94	.92	.89	.85	.83
.75	1.00	1.00	1.00	.99	.98	.97	.95	.93	.90	.86	.83
.80	1.00	1.00	1.00	1.00	.99	.98	.96	.94	.91	.87	.84
.85	1.00	1.00	1.00	1.00	1.00	.99	.98	.96	.92	.87	.84
.90	1.00	1.00	1.00	1.00	1.00	1.00	.99	.97	.94	.88	.84
.95	1.00	1.00	1.00	1.00	1.00	1.00	1.00	.99	.96	.89	.84
1.00	1.00	1.00	1.00	1.00	1.00	1.00	1.00	1.00	1.00	.89	.84

Proportion of Employees Considered Satisfactory = .90
Selection Ratio

r	.05	.10	.20	.30	.40	.50	.60	.70	.80	.90	.95
.00	.90	.90	.90	.90	.90	.90	.90	.90	.90	.90	.90
.05	.92	.91	.91	.91	.91	.91	.91	.90	.91	.90	.90
.10	.93	.93	.92	.92	.92	.92	.92	.91	.91	.91	.90
.15	.95	.94	.93	.93	.92	.92	.92	.92	.91	.91	.90
.20	.96	.95	.94	.94	.93	.93	.92	.92	.91	.91	.90
.25	.97	.96	.95	.95	.94	.93	.93	.92	.92	.91	.91
.30	.98	.97	.96	.95	.95	.94	.94	.93	.92	.91	.91
.35	.98	.98	.97	.96	.95	.95	.94	.93	.93	.92	.91
.40	.99	.98	.98	.97	.96	.95	.95	.94	.93	.92	.91
.45	.99	.99	.98	.98	.97	.96	.95	.94	.93	.92	.91
.50	1.00	.99	.99	.98	.97	.97	.96	.95	.94	.92	.92
.55	1.00	1.00	.99	.99	.98	.97	.97	.96	.94	.93	.92
.60	1.00	1.00	.99	.99	.99	.98	.97	.96	.95	.94	.92
.65	1.00	1.00	1.00	.99	.99	.98	.98	.97	.96	.94	.93
.70	1.00	1.00	1.00	1.00	.99	.99	.98	.97	.96	.94	.93
.75	1.00	1.00	1.00	1.00	1.00	.99	.99	.98	.97	.95	.93
.80	1.00	1.00	1.00	1.00	1.00	1.00	.99	.99	.97	.95	.93
.85	1.00	1.00	1.00	1.00	1.00	1.00	1.00	.99	.98	.96	.94
.90	1.00	1.00	1.00	1.00	1.00	1.00	1.00	1.00	.99	.97	.94
.95	1.00	1.00	1.00	1.00	1.00	1.00	1.00	1.00	1.00	.98	.94
1.00	1.00	1.00	1.00	1.00	1.00	1.00	1.00	1.00	1.00	1.00	.95

Appendix C
Publishers of Tests

1. This summary is reproduced in part from *Experience with Employment Tests*, Studies in Personnel Policy, No. 32, National Industrial Conference Board, Inc., 247 Park Avenue, New York, N. Y.

I. Intelligence Tests

Title	*Publisher*
Army Alpha, Bregman's Revision	Psychological Corporation, 522 Fifth Avenue, New York City
Army Alpha, Forms 5 and 7	Psychological Corporation
Army Alpha, Form 6	Psychological Corporation
Army Alpha, Nebraska Revision	Sheridan Supply Company, P. O. Box 837, Beverly Hills, Cal.
Army Alpha, Schrammel-Brannan	Bureau of Education Measurements, Kansas State Teachers College, Emporia, Kansas
Benge Test of General Knowledge	Management Service Company, 3136 N. 24th Street, Philadelphia, Pa.
Bureau Test VI	Psychological Corporation
Detroit General Aptitudes Examination	Public School Publishing Company, Bloomington, Ill.
Henmon-Nelson Tests of Mental Ability	Psychological Corporation
O'Rourke General Classification Test	The Psychological Institute, 3506 Patterson St., N. W., Washington, D. C.
Otis S-A Test of Mental Ability	World Book Company, Yonkers, N. Y.
Pressey Senior Classification Test	Public School Publishing Company
Pressey Senior Verifying Test	Public School Publishing Company
Purdue Industrial Training Classification Test, Forms A and B	Science Research Associates, 1700 Prairie Ave., Chicago, Ill.
Roback Mentality Tests	C. H. Stoelting, 424 N. Homan Avenue, Chicago, Ill.
Scott Company Mental Alertness Test	C. H. Stoelting
Stanford Scientific Aptitude Test, D. L. Zyve	Stanford University Press, Stanford University, Cal.
Terman Group Test of Mental Ability	Psychological Corporation
Vocational Aptitude Examination (Cleeton & Mason)	Psychological Corporation
Wonderlic Personnel Test	E. F. Wonderlic, 919 N. Michigan Ave., Chicago, Ill.

369

2. Clerical Tests

Title	*Publisher*
Benge Clerical Test D	Management Service Company
Benge's Stenogauge	Psychological Corporation
Bennett's StenographicTest	Psychological Corporation
Blackstone Typewriting Test	Psychological Corporation
Clapp-Young Arithmetic Test	Psychological Corporation
Clem Senior Typewriting Test	Public School Publishing Company
Cole Guidance Examinations in the Fundamental Vocabulary	Public School Publishing Company
Detroit Clerical Aptitudes Examination	Public School Publishing Company
Link's Context Test	C. H. Stoelting
Markham English Vocabulary Tests	Public School Publishing Company
Michigan Vocabulary Profile Test Form BM	World Book Company
N.U.I.P. Clerical Test	Psychological Corporation
Minnesota Test for Clerical Workers	Psychological Corporation
O'Connor's English Vocabulary, Worksample 95, Form EA	Stevens Institute of Technology, Hoboken, New Jersey
O'Rourke Clerical Aptitude Test, Junior Grade	Psychological Institute
Otis Arithmetic Test	World Book Company
Pressey Diagnostic Test in Eng. Comp	Public School Publishing Company
Rogers' Stenographic and Typing Tests	C. H. Stoelting
Schorling—Clark Potter Arithmetic Test	Psychological Corporation
Scott Company File Clerk Test	C. H. Stoelting
Shellow's Intelligence Test for Stenographers and Typists	C. H. Stoelting
Thurstone Examination in Clerical Work, Form A	World Book Company
Thurstone Examination in Typing, Form A	Psychological Corporation
Tressler Minimum Essentials Test (English)	Public School Publishing Company

3. Mechanical Tests

Bennett's Test of Mechanical Comprehension, Forms A and AA	Psychological Corporation
Detroit Manual Ability	C. H. Stoelting
Detroit Mechanical Aptitudes Examination, Form A	Public School Publishing Company
Kent-Shakow Industrial Form Boards	C. H. Stoelting
MacQuarrie Test for Mechanical Ability	California Test Bureau, 3636 Beverly Boulevard, Los Angeles, California
Minnesota Mechanical Assembly Test	Psychological Corporation
Minnesota Paper Form Board, Series B, Revised Series AA	Science Research Associates
Minnesota Rate of Manipulation Test	Psychological Corporation
Minnesota Spatial Relations Test	Psychological Corporation
O'Connor Finger Dexterity Test	C. H. Stoelting
O'Connor Tweezer Dexterity Test	C. H. Stoelting
O'Connor Wiggly Block	Stevens Institute
O'Rourke Mechanical Aptitude Test, Junior Grade	Psychological Corporation
Purdue Pegboard	Science Research Associates
Stenquist Mechanical Aptitude	Psychological Corporation

4. Personality Tests

Title	Publisher
Allport Scale of Values Test	Houghton Mifflin Company, 2 Park Street, Boston, Mass.
A-S Reaction (Beckman's Revision)	Psychological Corporation
Bell's Adjustment Inventory	Stanford University Press
Benge Interest Test	Management Service Co.
Bernreuter Personality Inventory	Psychological Corporation
California Test of Personality, Secondary Form A	California Test Bureau
Humm-Wadsworth Temperament Scale	D. G. Humm Personnel Service, Los Angeles, California
Inventory of Factors S T D C R	Sheridan Supply Company
Keeler Polygraph	Associated Research Inc., 431 South Dearborn St., Chicago, Illinois
Kuder's Perference Record	Science Research Associates, 1700 Prairie Avenue, Chicago, Illinois
Laird's I-E Test	Psychological Corporation
Psycho-Somatic Inventory	Psychological Corporation
Root's New I-E Test	Psychological Corporation
Thurstone Personality Schedule	University of Chicago

5. Interest Tests

Brainard-Stewart Specific Interest Inventories	Psychological Corporation
Cleeton Vocational Interest Inventory	Psychological Corporation
Le Suer Occupational Interest Blank	Psychological Corporation
Link's Personality Quotient Test	Psychological Corporation
Manson Occupational Interest Blank for Women	Psychological Corporation
Minnesota Interest Analysis	Psychological Corporation
Strong Vocational Interest Blank for Men	Stanford University Press
Thurstone Vocational Interest Schedule	Psychological Corporation

6. Trade Tests

Purdue Vocational Tests
1. Machine Shop and Machine Operation (Total score for general machinist and sub-scores for operators of lathe, shaper and planer, milling machine, and bench workers) — Science Research Associates
2. Electricity — Science Research Associates
3. Industrial Mathematics — Science Research Associates

7. Industrial Vision Tests

Bausch and Lomb Visual Classification and Placement Tests	Bausch and Lomb Optical Company, Rochester, New York
Keystone Visual Safety Tests	Keystone View Company, Meadville, Pennsylvania

INDEX

TITLES IN THIS SERIES

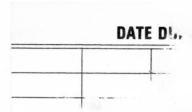

DATE DUE